ABOUT THE COVER

The painting on the cover is an original oil painting by William David, internationally known lecturer, reader of the Akashic Records, and author of the best-selling book, *The Harmonics of Sound, Color and Vibration.*

The painting depicts three faces of the essence of Jesus Christ. The face in the center-front is the essence which was sent from God. It is warm, radiant and loving. It is a picture of the essence of the Most Radiant One. The face in the back left is the essence as established by the Western Church. It is an essence of faith, albeit a faith which takes a subdued, second place to the Church as Rome follows the Augustinian directive that *"He can no longer have the God for his Father who has not the church for his Mother."* The face in the back right is the essence as established by the Eastern Church. It is the essence of a presence which has been placed on the Throne as Constantinople followed the decree that its Emperors were to be considered *sacred* as the *"living image of Christ on Earth."*

One of the major reasons for writing this book is the author's belief that those who love and follow Christ are to return to the essence of Christ which was sent by God. This is a warm, loving essence which presents no dogmas other than that of radiant, unconditional love. It is the Christ whose essence is presented in the front, center.

Cover design

What Previewers Have Said About This Book

* Excellent work! The theological scholarship is outstanding!

* You have done a thorough job, beginning with the excellent treatment of how the biblical canon came to be promulgated. Far too often the laity of the church are left with the misconception that the King James Version of the Bible in its red letter edition dropped out of the sky onto the collective heads of the 20th century church.

* As you have so aptly described, those who made up the hierarchy of the early Church were both autocratic and authoritarian and thus unfailingly established doctrines which invested their office and themselves with absolute power over the baptized both in this life and the life to come. It continues today!

* This book will not be read by the fundamentalists of the Far Right who would rather burn it than read it. It will not be read by the members of the Christian hierarchy who already know it but do not want their congregations to know it. It will not be read by the Christian scholars who already know it, but want only to talk with other scholars. But this book *should be read by every Christian who wants to think and to understand*!

Father John W. Groff, Jr., Episcopal priest

* One of the strong themes in this monumental and much needed work is the nagging question of why Jesus Christ, the most tolerant man who ever lived, spawned a religion that is noted for its intolerance.

* A very provocative book which suggests that those who cannot subscribe to the rigidity of many Christian sects should seek their personal relationship with Christ, or their "Christianess," by returning to the original intentions of a Jesus unaltered by men.

Jack Clarke, reviewer for *Conscious Business Network*

* This book simply <u>must</u> be published. I have a substantial list of people who are eagerly waiting to read it!

Sabra Stein, Reviewer for *The Aquarius*

* There is a lot of truly wonderful and incredible information presented in this book. It is knowledge which must be made available to everyone.

* This book contains a well described history of how ideas are put together for a philosophical development in life.

William David, author of *The Harmonics of Sound,*
Color and Vibration

* This is a much needed work which could lead to the Second Reformation of the Church. This work is desparately needed, and so is the Second Reformation. The present Church is simply not doing what has to be done.

Ordained Presbyterian Minister who
requested to remain anonymous

DEDICATION

Most books are dedicated by the author to a person or to persons who have helped along the way. As an example, I dedicated the first book of this series to all the members of the families to which I have belonged: to the family of blood; to the family of religion; and to the family of mankind.

This dedication will be significantly different, for it will be directed to a silent family whose names are unknown to me.

This book is dedicated to the family which consists of those who love, believe in and follow Jesus Christ, but who have left the Church which bears his name for reasons of conscience. There may have been times when the members of this family did not know why they felt they had to leave the sectarian Church with its doctrines and dogmas; but they did so because staying just did not seem right to them. Possibly through the pages of this book, they will start to understand why they felt they had to leave; and possibly through the lessons of this book, they will find comfort in the hard and lonely decision which they made.

And finally, just as the first book was dedicated to the man who provided the quotation below, so is this one; for it is in that quotation that the understanding of the major lesson of this book can be found.

"I never told my own religion nor scrutinized that of another. I never attempted to make a convert, nor wished to change another's creed. I am satisfied that yours must be an excellent religion to have produced a life of such exemplary virtue and correctness. For it is in our lives, and not from our words, that our religion must be judged."
Thomas Jefferson, 1816

THE

CHRISTIAN

CONSPIRACY

HOW THE TEACHINGS OF CHRIST

HAVE BEEN ALTERED BY CHRISTIANS

DR. L. DAVID MOORE

PENDULUM
PLUS

PENDULUM PLUS PRESS
ATLANTA, GA

The author acknowledges the tremendous help and encouragement given by his wife Jan, his daughter Sherry, and those who gave their honest appraisals in the preview of this work: *viz.* Father John W. Groff, Jr., Jack Clarke, Sabra Stein, William David, and Erik Myrmo. The author also acknowledges that he recieved a lot of help and guidance from his higher self and those "unseen ones" who are in his heart, unseen or not.

First Edition, 1994

ISBN 0-9635665-2-0

Library of Congress Catalog Card Number 94-066236

Published by

PENDULUM PLUS PRESS
141 INDIAN TRAIL
JASPER, GA 30143-2829

Printed in the United States of America
10 9 8 7 6 5 4 3 2 1

TABLE OF CONTENTS

Notes from the Author

Winston Churchill is thought to have said that Capitalism is the worst system with the possible exception of all the others. In the same vein, it could be said that in finding God, the systematic approach as defined by the sectarian Christian Churches[1] represents the worst system, with the possible exception of all the other systematic approaches. What this really says is that the path back to God is an individual one to which a systematic or sectarian approach may not be possible, even though such an approach may be better than no approach at all.

This book is a look at how an approach to God was proposed by Jesus Christ, and how that approach has been changed by the sectarian Christian Churches. It will use historical information to present how the concepts of Christ were altered by man, who did it and why it was done. It will thoroughly examine the Apostolic Tradition, and will take a serious look at the theological theories of the fourth and fifth centuries CE.[2] It will suggest that a Christian can expand his belief system; for the restrictive teachings of the Church[3] have been developed by man rather than by God.

There may be those who would question how I can refer to "the Church" when there is so much diversity within the sectarian churches of Christianity. Because of this diversity, there may be a tendency on the part of some to think that I am not referring to their church when I say that their leaders have altered the teachings of Christ. There may be some justification in this thought, for as many Christians will readily declare, there is a great difference between the practices of a Roman Catholic and a Methodist; between the practices of an Eastern Orthodox and a Presbyterian; or between the practices of an Anglican and a "born again" Baptist. I would agree that the practices are certainly different. But I would submit that the *beliefs* are the same. Those *beliefs* are presented in creeds or statements which say that Jesus Christ is divine in a way that no other human could ever be divine while also being totally human; that his divinity allows him, and *only* him, to generate our reconciliation with God; and that he is indeed God incarnate, the *only* God incarnate who has ever been on this Earth. These dogmatic *beliefs* are uniform, even though the practice of them may differ greatly. Because of the uniformity of these *beliefs*, I feel fully justified in referring to "the Church" as I address the issue of *How the Teachings of Christ have been Altered by Christians.*

There may be some interest in understanding why a lifelong Christian would write such a book. It is true that I am a lifelong Christian and have been a dedicated teacher of Christian subjects. On many occasions, I have stood before an adult Sunday School class and made the following statement: "My name is Dave Moore and I am a Christian Pilgrim. By 'Christian' I mean that I believe in Jesus Christ and Him crucified. By 'Pilgrim' I mean that I am on a journey back to God. It is a journey which will take an eternity, and Jesus Christ is a vital part of that journey." That statement is still true. However, there has recently been a change in venue, for I no longer belong to the Christianity of the organized Church in which there would be adult Sunday School classes. Instead of belonging to the Christ of the Church, I have chosen to belong to the spiritual and compassionate Christ of the individual Christianess.

If the term "Christianess" is confusing, I would recommend that you read an excellent essay by Raimundo Panikkar, entitled *The Jordan, the Tiber and the Ganges* in which he contrasts "Christendom" [the civilization] with "Christianity" [the organized Church] and "Christianess" [a personal religiousness].[4] He states that Christianess is a personal relationship with the Christ. He further states that an individual does not need to belong to all three or even to any two of the three but can, instead, belong to only one. In other words, he believes that one can have a personal relationship with Christ without either belonging to the Church or the Nation which sponsors Him; and further, that one can participate in the Christian Church or the Nation without personally knowing Christ. This essay makes good points. It is short, but powerful.

Within the concept of Panikkar's definitions, I have never been a part of Christendom and am no longer a part of Christianity. In this book, it is my intent to present an in-depth justification of the position that an individual can be a follower of Christ without being a follower of his Church; and can have Christianess without being a part of either Christianity or Christendom. A recent book entitled *Jesus Before Christianity* by Albert Nolan, a Catholic priest, was a great aid in helping me believe that this is possible. [5]

I did not leave the established Church of Jesus Christ with its dedicated community service and loving members and go out into the loneliness of the Christian without a congregation in a lighthearted manner; nor did I do it with any sense of anger in my heart. Instead, it was done with a great sense of sadness and loss. It is not presently my intent to see the Church closed down in any way, for it does serve the community in a manner which is rarely duplicated; and it does serve a very vital function when it introduces an individual to Christ. However, I believe that the Church is losing its ability to touch humanity's soul and to support an individual who wants to work on his intensely personal process to <u>become</u> Christ. This is the greatest sadness of all. In its attempt to be so exclusive in its faith and to shut out all who do not believe exactly as it does, the Church has accomplished two things: [1] it has forced many to follow the conscience of their soul by leaving the Church in order to find their own personal way; and [2] it has forced many who stay to do so because of their fear about leaving rather than their love for what is there. The major purpose for writing this book is to give the sincere follower of Christ enough knowledge about how the Christian Church developed, so that he can decide for himself whether it is still necessary to follow the teachings of the Church in order to be a follower of Christ.

I think I should now explain what is meant by the title of this book, *The Christian Conspiracy*. The word "conspiracy" has recently taken on its legal meaning for most of its uses. In legal terms, a criminal conspiracy is "an agreement of two or more persons to do an illegal act by unlawful means." That is not the sense in which the title of this book was developed. Instead, I have gone back to the original meaning of the word. Conspiracy means "to conspire." The word "conspire" comes from the Latin word *conspirare* which literally means "to breath together." From that it came to mean "to unite in a purpose, or to plot mischief together secretly."[6] And that is exactly what happened within the Christian Church. During the time of the early Church Fathers, a period called the "patristic period," the men of the Church established many of the doctrines and the dogmas of Christianity. A doctrine is that which is taught; and a dogma is a series of doctrines which have been proclaimed as being the truth. The acts which created these doctrines and dogmas were certainly not illegal, and these thoughts were probably generated with a deep sense of honesty, dedication, sincerity and belief. However, when the Church Fathers *required* that these thoughts be subscribed to in order to follow Christ, then they certainly created a whole lot of mischief! In that sense, these men were a part of a conspiracy. They constituted *The Christian Conspiracy* as they altered the teachings of Christ.

The patristic period covered the first twenty five percent [about five hundred years] of the Church's existence. During this time, the early Church Fathers did "breath together" to protect and defend their definitions of the concepts of Christ; and anyone who did not "breath with them" was discarded along the way. In this manner, the Church Fathers defined the concept of Christ in a way that was significantly changed from the Christ who had lived in Judea.

I have a problem with the <u>fact</u> that the Church has altered the definition of Christ from that presented in the Scriptures and that presented by the Apostles who had known him. But most of all, I have a problem with the Church saying who is a Christian [i.e. a follower of Christ] and who is not when the definitions used by the Church were established by man rather than by God. In a recent book, *Basic Christian Doctrine*, [7] John Leith states that his particular statement of faith uses the four classical statements of Christian theology as its foundation. They are: scriptures, the theology of the ancient catholic church, Protestant theology and Reformed theology. Although the Reformation of the sixteenth century did change many abusive practices of the Church and Vatican II also helped, the basic ancient concept of *extra ecclesiam nulla salus* [no salvation outside of the Church] remains extant. This and other concepts are the "theology of the ancient catholic church" which most sectarian churches use as a part of their present foundation. This foundation causes problems, such as the fact that while belief in Christ and in God is at an all-time high in the United States, membership in sectarian Christian Churches continues to decline, particularly within those of the mainstream. And as Christians continue to become a smaller and smaller percentage of the world's population, two questions have to be asked in relation to the exclusion formula of *extra ecclesiam nulla salus* developed as theology by the ancient catholic church. They are:

[1] is the belief in the superiority of the Western Church similar to the feeling we used to have about the superiority of Western technology? In other words, is the feeling that *"Only* the Church can save" similar to *"Only* Detroit can build good cars?"* If so, are both of these thoughts doomed for the same fate?; and

[2] is the belief in the superiority of Christianity as the *only* religion which is final, the *only* religion which is true, or the *only* religion which can grant salvation a form of idolatry which will doom Christianity just as all idolatry does? In other words, how many persons will decide to abandon the idol represented by the exclusiveness of Christianity because they find Christianity's intolerance to be intolerable?

I decided to leave Christianity for Christianess for several reasons, not the least of which was the intolerance represented by the Church. Intolerance has dictated that I could never be a part of Christendom, whether it was the Christendom of the Crusades [in which a Crusader considered himself unworthy of redeeming the Holy Land from the Moslems until he first killed a Jew][8]; or the Christendom of the Conquistadors [who committed the greatest genocide the world has ever known when fifty million Maya were killed in the name of the benevolent Christ][9]; or the Christendom of today's Religious Right [who talk about the love of Jesus while rejecting those of their own faith who are sexually different than they]. But it is more than just that kind of intolerance, for there is also an intolerance in today's sectarian Christianity even when it is not associated with the Religious Right. It is an intolerance which states that the debates held 1600 years ago are binding on us today and that any rejection of them cannot be tolerated. It is an intolerance which uses the results of those debates, many of which were politically inspired at the time, to categorically reject belief systems such as reincarnation, karma, the God within, dimensionality and the like, even though there is more justification in the Scriptures for those concepts than there is for orthodox concepts such as the Trinity, or the "two natures of Christ," or the condemnation of anyone who believes that the soul existed before the physical body, or other such concepts designed by man.

Having decided to leave the Christianity of the organized Church, I then felt the need to write this book. The purpose of this book is to examine the first 500 years of the Church's existence in order to see how the teachings of Christ were altered by man and how the Church came to its present position, a position which makes many people of the Christian faith feel the need for a Second Reformation. In this examination, some basic premises of Christianity's faith will be challenged, not in an attempt to dissuade a Christian from this belief, but in an attempt to gain acceptance for the belief that Christianess can exist outside of the Christianity of the Church. As a few examples of the issues to be discussed, it is factual that according to the Scriptures, Jesus Christ never said that he was divine; but some 300 years after the Crucifixion, the men of the Church did. Is this important? It is also factual that in the language in which the New Testament was originally written, the Scriptures do not say that Jesus Christ was the only son of God; but some 400 years after the Crucifixion, the men of the Church did. Is this important? It is also factual that Jesus asked his followers to love their enemies; but the men of the Church directed a Crusade which killed the Christian Cathars simply because they had left the Church. Is this important? It is also a scriptural fact that Jesus rejected the temptation of Satan who offered to have the world bow down to him; but Boniface VIII required that "for salvation, every creature must be subject to the Roman Pontiff."[10] Is this important? And as a final question, must a Christian be involved in Christianity in order to have his Christianess become evident? In other words, is there salvation outside the Church or does the Church still insist that *extra ecclesiam nulla salus* reigns supreme. Is this important?

In an attempt to answer these and other questions, I took a journey. That journey was to immerse myself in the people, the controversies and the events of the Christian Church during the first twenty five percent of its existence. This journey generated much understanding about the Christian experience on Earth. This journey also generated many personal feelings. As an example of those, I found myself liking Origen, Arius, Pelagius and Nestorius; but not particularly liking Jerome, Augustine, Hippolytus, and Cyril of Alexandria. This is just the opposite of the Church's reaction, but it was my experience. I also had the experience of rejecting most of what Justinian stood for, even though history considers him to be a great man and a respected builder of churches. Nevertheless, my personal experience with him was not a pleasant one. This book will try to share that and other personal experiences with you as together we try to address *How the Teachings of Christ have been Altered by Christians.*

Those who have spent time with my first book on religion know that I have become associated with what is commonly called the New Age, a term which is so broad as to be almost meaningless. I consider myself to be a New Age Christian, or a Christian of the New Age.[11] Because of the change from sectarian Christianity, there is a question which has often been asked of me. That question is, "When you have been raised in a Christian environment, why did you start to study the New Age?" It is true that I was raised in a Christian environment. I have always been active in local churches, and during high school and early college, I participated in a gospel quartet which visited small rural churches in Appalachia. When I graduated from West Virginia University, I was accepted at the Princeton Theological Seminary, but the United States Army got to me first. It is also true that I tried to practice Christianity throughout my business career, that I have taught adult Sunday School classes for over 20 years in mainstream Christian Churches, and that I consider myself to be a Christian today. And finally, it is true that I consider my involvement in the New Age as an activity which has strengthened and broadened the meaning of Christ to me.

But the question asked is why did I <u>start</u> to be interested in the New Age; and why do I believe that the New Age offers much toward the development of Christianess. My answer is that I started such thinking when I accepted the modern concept of Time and Space; and when I started to understand what those subjects implied for all of the established religions.

In respect to Time, if God were only just a little older than Judeo-Christianity, there would be no need for me to investigate the basics of the New Age religion; for all that He did would be represented to me by my study of the Judeo-Christian heritage. But God is much older than that; for God was in existence even before there was a material universe. Otherwise, He could not have created it. Although it is not certain, it is thought that the material universe was created at least 18 billion years ago. It is also thought that Earth is only about 4 billion years old, which means that some portions of the material universe have been in existence for almost five times as long as the Earth.

Judeo-Christianity is considered to start with Abraham, a man who is thought to have lived about 4,000 years ago. If the age of the Earth were to represent one year, then those "ancient days" of the beginning of Judeo-Christianity would constitute only the last 32 seconds of this Earth year. Or if we were to set the age of the universe so that it would be represented by one year, then those "ancient days" which started Judaism would constitute merely the last 7 seconds of that Universal year; and Christ would have appeared in only its last 3-4 seconds. The point that I am making is that in relation to the time that God has been in existence and has been interested in those "created in His image," the length of the Judeo-Christian existence does not even make a ripple. It is but a minor part of the Time of God.

The question then becomes, *"What was God doing during all of that time which existed before Judeo-Christianity even began? Was He doing only that which has been reported by the Judeo-Christian heritage?"* A God who would do so little for all of that time is not the kind of God I believe in. And since God seemed to want companionship by creating "man" [or "male and female"] in His own image [Genesis 1:26-27], then I have to believe that the living consciousness represented by the Biblical word "man" was also around for a long time before the Judeo-Christian period began.

Let us leave Time and think for a moment about Space. We

tend to think that the moon is a great distance away from the Earth, but at about 230,000 miles, it is only about ¼ of 1% as far away as the Sun. We therefore tend to think that the Sun is a great distance away, and at 93 million miles, it is a big step. If we were to be able to cover the distance from the Earth to the Sun in one step, then it would take a mere 657 million of those steps to walk across our Galaxy, the Milky Way. But our galaxy is not a very big galaxy as galaxies go, and it is only one of billions of such galaxies. In addition, there is more distance between the galaxies than there is within them. And God is present in all of this Space. The point that I am making is that the Earth, the speck of dust upon which we live, is similar to being only one grain of sand within the entire Sahara desert. Although important to us and therefore to God, Earth certainly does not represent the "everything" that the Church Fathers visualized when they established their doctrines and dogmas.

This consideration of Time and Space then leads to a question posed by many people, including many Christians. It is: *Why does the Eternal God of the Universe allow those whom He created in His image only one existence of a mere 80 years on one small speck of dust, when He has all of this vastness of Eternal Time and almost eternal Space under His control; and when He possibly could use the help of those created in His own image to bring other parts of His creation along toward oneness with Him? Why does He?*

The consideration of Time and Space also leads to another logical question which is: *With all of this time and space available to God, why does the recently developed religion of Christianity demand that it be so exclusive and be the only representative of God; and furthermore, why does Christianity as it has been developed by man believe that it is the final religion and that it is not possible for anything more representative of the ineffable God ever to come along? Why does it?*

There may be one other question which needs to be asked, and that is: *Who cares about Time and Space when it is only this Earth and only the ministry of Jesus Christ on this earth which means anything to me?* If that is true, then possibly this book is not for you, especially if your mind is made up. The early Church Fathers who decided that Jesus Christ was the only Son of God have handled your case very well, for they <u>assumed</u> as a *truth* that this small speck of universal dust which we call Earth was the only place inhabited by those who were created in God's image. This, therefore, would be the only place to which God would send his unique Son. But in all the vastness of God's Time and Space which is now known to us but which was unknown to the early Church Fathers, can such an assumption *still* be accepted? That is the real question which needs to be asked.

With these questions firmly in mind, it is now time to leave these "Notes from the Author" and get on with our journey to examine the first twenty-five percent of the existence of the Christian Church. We will try to see how the Church got to be like it presently is and how the Christian was changed by these activities of the Church. In addition, we will try to see if Christians have to accept everything which the Church presently teaches and reject everything which the Church does not teach in order to be allowed to be a part of the Christian way. It could be an interesting journey, for it could become a reason to open the doors of Christianity to all people; or it could become an additional reason for Christianity to withdraw further behind its protective shield of the doctrines and dogmas of exclusiveness. Although I would personally prefer the former, I would tend to bet on the latter. In either case, let us start on this journey together. I wish you well, and **God speed!**

PREFACE

This book is the second of a proposed trilogy involving religious beliefs. The first book was entitled *Christianity and the New Age Religion*. It was published in 1993 and is an introduction to the basic tenets or thoughts of Christianity and of the New Age. It made an attempt to establish a bridge of mutual understanding which could connect the two. Christianity and the New Age do not understand each other; and there is much misinformation which has been presented by each in opposition to the other. This is unfortunate, for if any two groups should generate an understanding of and tolerance for each other, it is Christianity and the New Age. In fact, there are many who consider themselves to be Christian New Agers, i.e. those who follow Christ and do not believe that their New Age thoughts deny him in any way. But the majority of those in either camp tend to reject the other in the belief that theirs is the only "true" understanding and that the other has nothing to offer. The first book of this series tried to introduce each to the other.

Before making comments on what this second book attempts to do, I feel the need to describe what this book is not. This book is not intended to be scholarly; or to be a hunt for the Christ without his Church; or to be a condemnation of the Church which man has put together to represent Jesus the Christ.

First, this book is not a presentation of the history of the Christian Church on an intellectual level, although some may feel that it tends to go in that direction. However, that job has already been done in a manner far beyond my abilities to duplicate. If the reader is interested in such a presentation, I would recommend *A History of the Christian Church* by Williston Walker. This classic work is interesting, informative, and highly readable. I recommend it as a history which can hardly be surpassed. It was consulted often in the preparation of this book.

Secondly, this book is not an attempt to define the life, the teachings and the divinity of Jesus the Christ before the existence of the Church. That job would require many lifetimes trying to follow the threads of "Christ before man interpreted him" backward through the webs of thought which separate us from the unadulterated Christ. And besides, that job has been attempted many times, some of which have been successful. If the reader is interested in such a presentation, I again would recommend *Jesus Before Christianity* by Albert Nolan. This modern classic is in its third edition since 1976. I may have a particular fondness for this book because unlike St. Augustine, Nolan states that each individual has the free will choice to make about Christ; and he asks the individual to make his choice without using any dictates which the present Church attempts to make. I like that approach.

Third, this book is not a condemnation of the Christian Church and what it has tried to do for the world. There have been books which have tried to do that, but I hope that this is not considered to be one of them. As a personal and spiritual experience, I have enjoyed the time I spent within the Christian Church; and I am not writing these books in an attempt to "straighten it out." In fact, I recommend that everyone spend a significant period of time in the organized church of his or her choice before moving on. I feel that this would be a positive experience.

Instead of those approaches, I am writing the three books of this series in an attempt to suggest that the frontiers of religious belief may have been static for too long, and that someone has to propose a "much needed bridge between traditional belief systems and the new paradigm of thinking and perceiving in our world." This quote was offered me by an ordained Presbyterian minister who is quietly running a center at which those who need a new beginning can find it.

The first book of this series tried to introduce the Christian to the New Ager and vice versa. This particular book, the second book of the series, is an attempt to introduce the Christian to himself by taking a look at what the Christian Church did in its early existence and how what happened then makes Christianity and the Church what it is today. As stated much more thoroughly in the Introduction which follows, during the early part of its life, the character of a person gets substantially developed and hardened. Although it continues to modify itself in the following years, when "push comes to shove," the character of that individual will tend to revert to that which was developed earlier. The same is true with an institution such as the Church.

It has been fascinating to examine the first 500 years of the Christian Church, and then to try to analyze the character of the Church as it developed in that time period. I found that there are many similarities between the beliefs of the early Christians and some New Agers of today. However, I found that these similarities were greatly modified by the early Church Fathers. I believe that few Christians today understand how the belief system presented by the Church was developed. I found myself wondering if Jesus Christ himself would recognize what came about based on the debates of the first five Ecumenical Councils when much of what we affirm as Christians today came into being.

The third book of this series, tentatively titled *The Essence of Christ in the New Age* will address the issue of what direction the spiritual needs of this world will take in the future. There are already many signs of what that might be. Some of those indications are presented in *Book Three* of this volume.

As a final part of the Preface to this book, I feel I should repeat three statements made in the first book, and then add three new statements peculiar to this book. Those statements are:

1. The term "New Age" is objected to by many in the movement. However, it is a name which communicates, and will be used until something more appropriate or descriptive is developed.

2. In this book, I have used the words he, him, himself and the like. I mean them to designate a human; I do not mean them to designate a particular sex. I know that some are offended by these terms because they consider them to be sexist. I will admit that I tried writing this book with other terms, but just as Albert Nolan admits in his revised edition of *Jesus Before Christianity*, it is a difficult way to write. For those to whom it is important, I apologize. The use of the masculine pronouns to stand for either sex was the way I was taught to write. I do not intend it to be sexist, and I do not in any way intend it to imply superiority; for that is about as far from my true belief as it is possible to get.

3. As a concerned author, I feel that I have to emphasize that this is not an escape novel or a book to be read in any sort of light-hearted manner. Instead, it is a book which was written to transmit understanding. I have tried to make it as readable as possible, but the material is, at times, weighty stuff.

4. I started to make a footnote which told where I found every single piece of intellectual material presented in this book. By the time I had 500 footnotes, I found that they had seriously jeopardized the readability of the work. Consequently I have eliminated footnotes when the material represents historical consensus or non-controversial points. If this book were intended to be a truly scholarly work, such an activity would detract from its merit. But minimizing footnotes did make the book more readable and seemed to be a prudent compromise. The major books which I used in developing this work are presented in the Bibliography; and an important concept, a major controversial point or a piece of quoted material is generally given a footnote.

5. Because some of the historical people, the controversies and the terms used in this book may be unknown to many people, I have included Appendix A which is an Expanded Glossary covering the people and the controversies. In addition, there is a conventional Glossary which presents the terms. Finally, much of the major reference material has been moved from the text to an appropriate Appendix in an attempt to enhance the readability of the text. There are three major Appendixes at the end of this book.

6. Finally, this book contains seven maps. In my opinion, most maps contained in history books contain so much information that they lose their effectiveness in presenting their major concept. Consequently, the maps in this book are simple outline maps which make a single point. The effect may not be pretty, but I feel that it is effective. The use of simple, single point maps was a deliberate one on my part. With that final note, this author sends you love and the hope that you enjoy and gain something from this attempt to transmit understanding.   **GOD BLESS!**

INTRODUCTION

Most Christian scholars date the beginning of the Christian Church from the Day of Pentecost, fifty days after the crucifixion of Jesus Christ, when the Holy Spirit came upon the assembled ones during a sermon by Peter. However, if one purpose of the Church is to broadcast the message of the Risen Christ, then a more logical starting point may be some forty-eight days earlier when the two Marys, Mary Magdalene and Mary the mother of James and Salome, came to the tomb and found that it was empty. They were told by an angel that Jesus Christ had risen. The two Marys immediately went out and told others about the Risen Christ [Matthew, Chapter 28], and in one sense, started the Church. However, the primacy of women as the Apostolic witness has often been overlooked by the Christian Church, possibly because Paul did not mention these women as a source of Apostolic authority in 1 Cor. 15:5-8. This omission has angered women for years.

But the neglect of women is not the only thing which has changed within Christianity since its leader was crucified. There are many reasons for the changes which were made; and many individual people, both "saints" and "sinners," have participated in the events which caused these changes. It would be fascinating to interview the Christ who sits on the right hand of God to see how he feels about these events, and whether or not he would agree with all that had been done to grow his Church from the two Marys in a small corner of the globe to a worldwide assemblage of almost 1.8 billion people. Unfortunately, short of a miracle which would be accepted by only a few, or a mystical experience which would be accepted by even fewer, or a meeting in heaven from which very few reports have ever issued, such an interview is not possible.

In its stead, our only recourse seems to be an evaluation of some of the key steps in this 2,000 year journey, particularly the steps of the first 500 years or twenty-five per cent of the journey. The reason for emphasizing the first part of the life of the Christian Church is because that is when the character of the Church was developed. Psychiatrists state that in human terms, the very early period of the life is the most important. In a life span of some eighty years, most of what a person will become is established by the time he is twelve years old; and by the time he is twenty, the basic character of that human can rarely be modified by subsequent activities. This does not mean that a human can not reform in the later years of his life; and in fact, many alcoholics have abstained for the rest of their life as a part of something which may have happened well after the age of twenty. However, given a releasing of the reins and a completely free chance to do what he wants to do, even a well-reformed alcoholic may well revert to the character which was established during the first twenty-five percent of his life.

The 2,000 year life of the Christian Church is analogous to the human life described above. During the first twenty-five percent of its existence, the Christian Church had the major part of its character developed and refined. Although the Church was reformed from its almost drunken bout with absolute authority during the Great Reformation in the sixteenth century, given a chance, the Church seems to want to resort to its original character. That character is based on the firm conviction that the Church not only has the authority to tell people what to believe, it also has the right to promise them punishment if they do not accept what is presented to them

Therefore, the question to be examined is that of trying to understand how the Church of Jesus Christ came to develop this character. How did a Church, established by the compassionate and forgiving power of the Holy Spirit, become such that it wanted the dictatorial and unforgiving power to decide under what terms it would accept those who wished to follow Christ? What happened during the first twenty-five percent of the Church's life which caused this tremendous change in character? How did the Church use the weight of history to establish such a restrictive set of doctrines and dogmas?

The first part of this volume, *Book One*, is just such an examination. It will examine what events happened, who made those events happen, why those events were brought about and what those events subsequently generated. It will cover roughly the first twenty-five percent of the Church's life by describing the activities which occurred during a period covering "from late Christ to late Justinian" or from about 33 CE to the Fifth Ecumenical Council in 553, a period of slightly more than 500 years.

During the first 300 years of this period, the Church became interested in social and economic activities; became firmly established in North Africa and Asia Minor; established a foothold in Rome; fought Gnosticism, Monarchianism, Montanism, Modalism and other movements which it declared heretical; established the western tradition of liberal arts education at the catechetical school in Alexandria under Clement and Origen; and progressed from a Roman declaration of being a *religio illicita* or "unauthorized religion," to being recognized as a *religio licita* or "accepted religion" by the Edict of Milan in 313. Consequently, a Church which at the beginning of the period had addressed itself solely to man's relationship with God, had become vastly broadened in its scope, even to the point of being accepted by the greatest Empire on Earth. What caused this change? Who caused it? How did the character of the Church become established as it did? What alternatives were discarded and why? Such questions are not easy to answer, but an examination of this history may generate an understanding of where the Church is today and how it came to be there.

During the next 200 years of this period, the Church underwent considerable additional change. No longer were the large cities in North Africa or the small cities of Asia Minor the centers of debate and theological definition, for they had been replaced by the metropolitan cities of Rome and Constantinople. During this very active period, Jesus became defined in a way that he may never have expected; numerous heresies were fought and breakoff sects were punished; the Pope and the Patriarch assumed tremendous religious and secular power which often was shared with the Emperor; and the Church attempted to enter into and possibly control every aspect of individual life. Again the questions presented before need to be asked in order to understand why the agency which represents Christ's mission on Earth developed its character in this manner. Again, how did the Church use the weight of history to establish such a restrictive list of teachings and beliefs?

The remaining seventy-five percent of the Church's life will be examined only in highlight terms in a separate Chapter at the end of *Book One*. The review of this 1500 year period will be brief because the major purpose of this book is to examine the decisions made by the early Church Fathers and to understand how they affected the entire history of the Church; for the Church really did not change its character much after 553 CE–it just got bigger. Although it continued to extend its absolute power to that of life and death over those who disagreed with its theology during the 1,000 years which followed the Fifth Ecumenical Council, this extension of power was based on the character which the Church had developed early on. As a consequence of this addiction to absolute power, the Church had to be reformed. And just like an addicted human who "takes the pledge," the Church was changed during the Reformation and the Age of Enlightenment which followed. However, the Church of today often acts as if it has the same character it had when it first had to be reformed. It seems to be reaching for power over people and their lives. It seems to be imposing itself on the political agenda of the United States just as it did in Rome; and it seems to be requiring that certain "litmus tests" be applied and passed before people can be accepted as followers of the Risen Christ. In all of this, it seems to be reverting to the character which was established early in its growth period. Again, it seems to be the first twenty-five percent of the Church's history which is truly important to understand. As a consequence, the more recent history will be addressed in a relatively short chapter.

Book Two contains an analysis of the changes which occurred during the first 500 years of the Church's existence; and also examines the thought that many of the beliefs which invigorated the people of the very early Christian Church have been rejected by the Church of today. In doing this, *Book Two* will compare the thoughts of a Christian in 55 CE with the thoughts of a Christian 500 years later. The change in thinking is striking. This presentation may be the most meaningful of all, for in understanding what those who first believed in the divinity of Jesus Christ were thinking, we might be able to understand where the thoughts of those who now accept the divinity of Jesus Christ will take them in the future, especially if those thoughts do not require conformity to the doctrines established by man rather than by Spirit or by Scripture.

Some possibilities for this future direction are presented in *Book Three*; but most will be reserved for the third book of this series. There are many dedicated people who are struggling with the desire to find a better approach for the future. There is an ordained Presbyterian minister in the mountains of northern Georgia, and an ordained Anglican priest in the northern region of Alabama, each of whom has established a spiritual retreat center in which their flock can find a new beginning, unencumbered by the dogmatic restrictions of the Church which each once served. Each of these men of Christ longs for a Second Reformation of the Church. And there are the many individuals who are examining the freedom generated by the New Age as one way to remove the restrictions placed on the followers of Christ by the theological definitions of the fourth through the seventh centuries. In this way they are trying to moderate the weight of history which restricts what they can believe. It is hoped that this book can generate an understanding of why and how the weight of history generated by the Church placed those restrictions; for only by understanding how the Church became as it is, can the restrictions be removed for an unfettered approach to God in the future.

As a concerned author and also a compassionate one, I feel the need to give some advice on how this book might be read. *Book One* presents a historical narrative on the important events of the period being examined. However, the actual biographies of the people involved, the in-depth descriptions of the controversies, and the presentation of the creeds which the early Church developed as its statements against heresy, have all been moved to the Appendix section because much of it is truly weighty stuff. Each personal portrait, each controversy and each creed should be understood in an in-depth manner in order to put some perspective on what happened. However, such vignettes can be absorbed only in relatively small doses; for the concentrated and consecutive reading of each story, charming and interesting though each one may be in small doses will, if done for too long, lead to boredom. Consequently, if the reader wants to understand more about a specific person, controversy or creed mentioned in the narrative, this arrangement will require that he jumps from *Book One* to the appropriate Appendix and then back again thus tying the people, the controversies and the events together in some depth. This may be preferable to reading the total section on the people, then the controversies, and then the events.

History books have been written in many different styles. Many are written as a chronological narrative, interlacing an in-depth presentation of the events, the people and the conflicts in one presentation. Occasionally this works, but many times it does not because the material becomes so weighty that the reader gets turned off. The arrangement of this book allows the reader to get only a general picture, or one which has more depth if the serious student is willing to do some jumping. In essence, this arrangement lets the reader design the historical narrative in any depth which he might want.

In presenting these thoughts, this author is not, in any way, trying to tell the reader how to read a book which has become his. However, the design of the historical narrative in a variety of depths to satisfy each different reader could be an interesting experience. I hope you enjoy it.

BOOK ONE
FROM CHRIST TO JUSTINIAN:
THE CRUCIFIXION [33 CE]
TO THE FIFTH ECUMENICAL COUNCIL [553 CE]

CHAPTER ONE
BACKGROUND INFORMATION

According to the Bible, Jesus was born in Bethlehem, a small town less than fifteen miles south of Jerusalem. Although the time of his birth is not known, it most certainly was not in 0 CE, a time which was erroneously established in 525 by Dionysius Exiguus, a Scythian canonist who was trying to settle a long dispute over how the time for Easter was to be calculated. He decided that Jesus had been born exactly 753 years after the establishment of Rome. Most scholars believe that he made an error and that in his system, 5 BCE is a reasonable guess as to the date of Jesus' birth. Because he was born at that time and place, the beginning of the Christian era occurred when Rome reigned supreme.

The Roman world at the beginning of the Christian era extended from Hadrian's Wall in the north of Britain, to a point south of the city of Jerusalem. It included all the land areas which bordered on the Mediterranean Sea. In addition, it included all Gaul [France] all Iberia [Spain and Portugal] and all the Hellenistic monarchies in the East which had succeeded the empire of Alexander the Great. A simple presentation of the extent of the Roman Empire at the time of the birth of Jesus is presented in Map 1 on page 89.

Rome ruled this vast territory for three reasons: [1] they had the armies; [2] they had the roads over which the armies could rapidly travel; and [3] they had the local administration which the Roman Legions would support. Rome had the only effective armies in the entire territory. These armies were held together by strong discipline and by loyalty to the Emperor or to the Roman Senate, whichever was in power. The core of the army was small, but it could get to any part of the Empire rapidly by way of the excellent roads built by the engineers who accompanied the army wherever it went. And the government administrations, often manned by local people who were loyal to Rome and were backed by the army, were effective in collecting the taxes demanded by Rome and in carrying out the directives supplied by Rome. No other state in the Mediterranean area could effectively compete with Rome. At the beginning of the Christian era in the Mediterranean part of the world, Rome reigned supreme.

Although this Empire contained diverse ethnic and cultural groups, the Empire was held together by three things: [1] shared political allegiance to Rome; [2] shared commercial interdependence; and [3] shared higher culture, that of the "Hellenistic" culture which grew in the wake of the conquests by Alexander. All the inhabitants of the Empire had a common political dependence on Rome for their laws which generated internal order, for their armies which generated protection from the outside, and for their system of justice. As one aspect of this system of justice, many people within the Empire were crucified by Rome for a number of transgressions; for crucifixion was a very common method for keeping discipline within the Roman political system. In respect to shared commercial interdependence, all the major cities of the Empire were commercially interactive. As one example, Alexandria shipped Egyptian-produced grains throughout the Empire in trade for grapes from Rome and olives from Asia Minor. This commercial interdependence was a powerful force for keeping the Empire intact. But possibly the strongest stabilizing force of all was the Greek language and culture. Greek became the language of the intellectual and the learned. Although the local languages such as Latin, Aramaic, Punic and the like did not disappear, they were the languages of the uneducated and of the non-city people. More and more, Greek was the language and the culture of the cities. It also became the language of politics, of law and of commerce.

Although there were many cities within the Empire, there were three cities in this Roman world which were important to the establishment of Christianity during the early period. They were Jerusalem, Alexandria and Carthage [near present-day Tunis]. Jerusalem was important for Christians because without the background of Judaism, Christianity might not have survived in its early stages; and the home city for Judaism was Jerusalem. Alexandria was important for two reasons. First, it had become the intellectual center of Hellenistic culture and contained the greatest library the world had ever known. Secondly, it held the largest population of Diaspora, those Jews who lived outside Judea. Because of its Hellenistic culture and its large Jewish population, Alexandria became the focus of the Eastern branch of the Christian Church during its first 300 years. Carthage is important because of its location. It was distant enough from Rome to be relatively safe from religious persecution by those in the capital of the Roman Empire, but close enough to influence the Christians who remained in Rome. Consequently, Carthage was the focus of the western branch of the Christian Church until that function was taken over by Rome after the time of Constantine [ca. 313 CE].

There were three religious practices which were prevalent at the beginning of the Christian era. They were: [1] the traditional religion of the home and community gods prevalent in the Hellenistic system; [2] the secretive religion of the mystery cults; and [3] the intellectual religion of Knowledge or Wisdom, often based on philosophical concepts. The traditional religion was one of civic duty and social status. It was steadfast and unchanging in its beliefs. The secretive religion was almost always based on Oriental systems of voluntary brotherhood which offered their adherents salvation from the worldly problems of Fate and Fortune. Quite often these secretive religions proposed significant changes, a few of which might be the abolition of slavery, the participation of women, and even the radical religious thought that there was only one God. The intellectual religion was very prevalent in the Hellenistic culture, first proposed by the thoughts of Plato in the fourth century BCE; countered by the Stoicism of Zeno in the third century BCE; re-countered by the Middle Platonism of the last century BCE; and finally presented by the Neo-Platonism of the third century CE which had such an effect on the development of Christian thought. Greek philosophy was a developing and almost constantly changing religion during its almost 1,000 years of existence.

Finally, at the beginning of the Christian era, there was a profound change in thinking on the part of mankind. This change was bound to affect the way that people thought about their religion. No longer was the world thought of as a flat plain with a heaven that arched over it. Such a picture had been the one which had been presented in the early writings of Judaism and other religions of that time. Within this picture, both Gods and man would preside on this flat plain together. By the beginning of the Christian era, people were thinking of the Earth as a sphere suspended motionless in the center of all things and around which the sun and the planets rotated while certain of the stars remained fixed in their position. They further started to think of mankind as being on Earth and the Gods as being in the Heavens, with the Heavens not being mechanical, but being a lively site which held the power of the Gods. In such a picture, man on Earth would be far removed from the power of the Gods.

With all of this in place, we have a picture of the Mediterranean world at the time when Jesus the Christ entered the world. Outside of Judea, the world did not change much during the relatively short lifetime of Jesus Christ. Therefore, this is also the picture of the Mediterranean world at the time of the Crucifixion of Jesus Christ, a time estimated to have been about 29-35 CE.

Shortly after the Crucifixion, the Christian Church became established and started to develop. In the establishment and development of any institution of great importance, there are <u>three stages</u> which that institution will normally go through. The first is the <u>exploratory</u> stage during which the institution is examined in an attempt to understand the scope of activities which the institution could cover. The second is the <u>definitive</u> stage during which the institution is defined in such a way that those who wish to participate can understand where their devotions are going. This then leads to the third, which is the <u>developmental growth</u> stage during which the institution attracts those people who accept the definitions developed in the second stage.

To understand how these three stages might be applied to a particular institution, let us apply these three stages to a short analysis of the nation now known as the United States of America.

From 1492 until about 1700, our part of the world was in its <u>exploratory</u> period. During that time, the people had only a minor interest in governing, in establishing citizenry, in establishing repetitive commerce and trade and in establishing schools, major cities, transportation facilities and the like. Instead, their time and energy were primarily devoted to understanding what they had found, how extensive the New World was and whether or not it contained riches which were readily available instead of having to be developed. It was a typical exploratory stage in the overall development of what later became a great nation. It was necessary because great things have to be explored before they can be defined.

From the early 1700s until about 1870, this nation defined itself. The first part of this <u>definition</u> stage was to decide, with the help of its parent, that it would be English rather than French. The second part was then to define itself as a free and independent nation rather than as a colony of a foreign power. At the same time, it defined itself as a nation which would have separation of church and state, which would not be governed by a king, which would be composed of separate and independent states with representation in the central government, which would have freedom of worship and freedom of speech, which believed that it had the manifest destiny to extend as a nation from sea to sea, which would be composed of free white men, which would be composed of free men without regard to color after the armed conflict of 1861-1865, etc. The point is that after the exploratory stage, the United States became defined. The definition stage happens to all great institutions.

Following those two stages is the third stage. It is a <u>developmental growth</u> stage during which the defined entity is developed and grown to the fullest extent possible. This stage has been occupying the attention of the United States of America for the past 130 years. It will continue to occupy our attention until the human potential of the United States is fully realized, developed and utilized.

In a similar manner, the Christian Church had an <u>exploratory</u> stage during which it tried to determine what had been found. It tried to determine how extensive the new religion could be and whether this new religion had immediate riches of the spirit or only the kind which had to be developed. For the Christian Church, this period covered the time from which it was discovered as a new religion by the resurrection of Jesus the Christ, until it became recognized as a religion accepted by the known world of its day. This exploratory period covered the time from about 33 CE until 313 when the Edict of Milan freed it to define itself.

Again, after the exploratory stage comes the stage in which the discoverers of the new world have to define what they have discovered. They have to do this before they can develop it; for of what use is it to try to grow something if you can't define exactly what it is that you are trying to grow? In addition, the definitive stage is necessary in order to attract those whom the institution hopes to incorporate into its growth cycle.

The <u>definition</u> stage for the Christian Church covered the period of 240 years from about 313 CE until at least 553 at the end of the Fifth Ecumenical Council or possibly for a period of about 367 years until about 680 at the end of the Sixth Ecumenical Council. However, since the Sixth Council really made only a minor addition to the definitions given in the previous five Councils, and had its major merit in confirming that the definitions generated in the previous five Councils were applicable to all the Church, then this presentation of the Church's definition stage will include only the 240 years which ended at about the year 553.

The <u>development growth</u> phase of the Christian Church started in the seventh or the eighth centuries. It continues today.

The major emphasis in *Book One* will be applied to the exploratory [what do we have?] and the definitive [this is what we have] stages of the Church's development.

CHAPTER TWO
THE IMPORTANT EVENTS

It is impossible to cover all of the events which happened in even a very small section of the world during a time period of five centuries. Consequently, this Chapter will address only those events which had a significant impact on the development of the Christian Church and its doctrines. Most events will be presented in the chronological order of their beginning. However, since the sections overlap, the reader will have to restart his thinking with each section as if it were a new event in history. The sections of this Chapter consist of:

1. The Resurrection of Jesus Christ;
2. Writings which were later made canon [i.e. ended up in the Bible] and therefore are a source of Christian doctrine;
3. Other writings or philosophies which established important points of Christian doctrine;
4. The missionary journeys which spread Christianity and Christian doctrine throughout the Mediterranean World by use of the Apostolic Tradition;
5. The proposals which were not accepted as Christian doctrine and which were therefore designated as heresies;
6. The Edict of Milan;
7. The first five Ecumenical Councils including the historical, ecclesiastical and political conflicts which caused each to be called, and what happened during each;
8. Other conflicts which created schisms within the Church;
9. The final establishment of the canon of today's Bible;

10. Books previously considered sacred which were left out of the canon; and

11. Summary and conclusion.

In this Chapter, terms which are not in common use today are presented in the Glossary. In addition, biographies of the people who are mentioned in the text and many of the controversies which caused the creation of various Christian doctrines or dogmas are presented in Appendix A; creeds which resulted from those controversies are presented in Appendix B; and a detailed examination of the controversial Fifth Ecumenical Council is presented in Appendix C.

1. THE RESURRECTION OF JESUS CHRIST

The major event which opens this Chapter is the same major event which opened the world to Christianity. That was the Crucifixion and the Resurrection of Jesus Christ, an event which is reported to have taken place during the administration of the procurator, Pontius Pilate [26-36 CE], possibly about the year 33 although some well-known scholars have proposed dates as early as 29 or as late as 35.

When a practicing Christian recites the Apostles' Creed, he states that he believes that Jesus Christ *"...was crucified, dead, and buried; the third day He rose again from the dead; he ascended into heaven, and sitteth on the right hand of God the Father Almighty; from thence He shall come to judge the quick and the dead..."* Although all the words of The Apostles' Creed are important to the Christian, possibly the most important are the words *rose again*; for without that having happened, nothing else would have mattered. The most important central issue to the faith of a Christian is his belief in the Resurrection of Jesus Christ. Good Friday is the day during which the Christian remembers the Crucifixion; and Easter is a day during which the Christian celebrates the Resurrection of Jesus Christ. Easter is the Christian's most important day. Without Easter there would be no Christmas, for there would be no need. Without Easter, there would be no Christians, for the movement would simply have folded up and disappeared. Easter is the single event which established the Christian Church.

The Crucifixion happened. It is recorded in historical records other than the Bible. In both the history of the Jews as written by

Josephus[1] and in Roman historical records[2], it is recorded that during the procuratorship of Pontius Pilate in Jerusalem, the man known as the "Christ" had been crucified by the Romans. Since there were thousands of crucifixions performed in Palestine during the rule of the Romans, if the crucifixion of Jesus Christ had not been recorded, then Christians could not have assumed that it did not occur; but since it is recorded, then Christians must assume that it not only happened, it made such an impression on both the Romans and the Jews that each recorded it in their separate histories of the time. By all logical arguments, the Crucifixion is a fact of history.

The Resurrection of Jesus Christ falls more into the area of Christian belief than into the area of historical fact as substantiated by non-Christian records. Nevertheless, the Christian bases his belief on three rather striking facts:

1. Those who were there were convinced that it did happen;
2. The Resurrection did not have to occur to fulfill Old Testament prophecies;
3. The Resurrection is accepted as fact by all believing Christians.

Any doubt that those who were there were convinced that it happened can be dispelled by merely reading the fifteenth Chapter of 1 Corinthians. This Letter from Paul to the church at Corinth is one of the earlier writings of the New Testament. It was written in about 52 CE, some 10-25 years before the Gospels were written [see Section 2]. Paul did not write this part of the Letter to convince anyone; he merely wrote it to remind everyone of that which they know to be true. It starts out with, "Now I would remind you..." and then goes on to state in unequivocal terms that Christ was raised from the dead and that the Risen Christ had been seen by more than five hundred disciples, many of whom were still alive when Paul wrote this Letter and thus could either confirm Paul's belief or challenge it [1 Cor. 15:6]. Those who were there at the time never doubted the Resurrection. They accepted it as a fact.

But possibly even more remarkable is that a band of disciples, who should have been depressed and disillusioned by their Master's Crucifixion, were transformed into a strong band of Apostles who courageously witnessed that Christ was alive and active. They had no hesitation in attributing the change in themselves to the Resurrection; for it was not something that they merely talked about, it was something that they were willing to die for. People are not generally willing to die for something unless they believe it to be true. In addition, in order to be an Apostolic preacher in the early days, you had to have seen the Risen Christ. That was also a requirement when the disciples searched for a replacement for Judas. From all of this, it is obvious that those early Christians who were there were convinced that the Resurrection actually happened.[3]

In addition, since the Old Testament expresses a somewhat negative attitude about the possibility of resurrection, then it did not have to happen in order to fulfill Old Testament prophecies. None of the prophecies about the Messiah refer to his resurrection in any way. Instead, the Resurrection is a watershed from Old Testament to New Testament philosophy. The Resurrection became an integral part of the new life of every early Christian. It was required as a belief by all of them. Paul, the earliest recorded writer in the New Testament of the Bible, presents that requirement without ever mentioning the Virgin Birth. To Paul, "Easter" was everything, and "Christmas" was of no import.

It is the critical importance of the Resurrection to the Christian which leads to its being the opening statement of not only this Chapter, but of the entire experience of Christianity.

2. BIBLICAL WRITINGS[4]
New Testament

It is generally believed that the Gospels of Mark, Luke, Matthew and John were written between 65 and 95 CE. Augustine thought that Matthew was written first, that Mark was written as a summary of Matthew, that Luke then used both Matthew and Mark as source material, and that John was independently written somewhat later. These beliefs were accepted until the twentieth century when modern scholarship presented the belief that Mark was written first in about 65 CE, followed by Matthew and Luke about 10 years later, and followed by John another 20-25 years after that.

It is generally believed that the Letters of Paul were written between 50 and 64 CE; that the other Letters of the New Testament were written between 55 and 95 CE; and that the Revelation to John was written about 95 CE.

All of these dates are guesses and none is known with certainty. In addition, the authors of the four Gospels are not known with certainty, although Luke does have some substantive evidence for his identity.

For purposes of this narrative, it is not important that the exact dates of writing or the exact authors are known with certainty. Instead, it is important to understand the following:

1. That the books or letters which presently make up the New Testament were written over a period of about 40 years;

2. That the book of the present New Testament which was written first was a letter such as Paul's first letter to the Thessalonians or his first letter to the Corinthians, each of which has been dated fairly accurately as having been written in 50-2 CE, some twenty years after the resurrection; and

3. That the letters of Peter also were early letters, that the early letters were written before the first gospel was written and that all of the books and letters which were proposed as the generally accepted final canon of the New Testament in 367 CE were finished before the end of the first century.

The timing to any finer degree is really not relevant for our purposes, and probably is not possible anyway. These events establish that the scripture upon which much of the Christian doctrines are based was written 20-70 years after the resurrection of Jesus the Christ; and that nothing else of a canonical nature was written after the year 100 which is the beginning of the second century CE.

Old Testament

In about 240 CE, Origen finished work on the "Hexapla." This work is one of the most astounding intellectual achievements in the history of the world. In addition, it was used to tie-in New Testament activities with Old Testament prophecy thus granting increased stature to the New Testament writings. Consequently, it deserves special attention.

By the beginning of the 3rd century, the most frequently used Greek translation of the Old Testament was known as the Septuagint, so named because it allegedly was translated from Hebrew to Greek by the work of 72 translators over a period of 100 years. The translation into Greek was done because most of the early converts to Christianity were readers of Greek.

This was not the only version of the Old Testament in Greek which was available at that time. One version was the Aquila version which had been translated in about 130 CE by Aquila, a convert from Judaism to Christianity. Another version was the one presented by Theodotion. It was a smoothed-up version of an earlier Greek translation. Finally, the Greek translator, Symmachus, and many other translators had presented their versions. These versions varied widely.

In the period 230-240 CE, Origen took six versions and laid them side by side in six parallel, vertical columns. They were:

1. The Hebrew text written in Hebrew which Origen had to learn in order to generate the "Hexapla";
2. The same text done in Greek letters without being translated but created by merely substituting Greek letters for the corresponding Hebrew ones; and
3. The Greek versions of Aquila, Symmachus, the Septuagint, and Theodotion in that order.

Origen then compared the columns laid out side-by-side in order to get a consistent translation into Greek. He had to spend most of his effort editing the Septuagint which had so many different translators and different translation styles that it was extremely difficult to follow. This is an important point which is developed further in the next paragraph.

This total effort, know as the "Hexapla," was a work of such magnitude that it was never reproduced *in toto*. However, Origen did publish an abbreviated version, the "Tetrapla," which contained only the last four columns. Fragments of that work still exist today. This monumental work led to a version of the Old Testament which was generally accepted at the time and which was used by most early Christian writers and thinkers. This version, along with the Septuagint, was used 150 years later by Jerome in his development of the Vulgate Bible [in about 400 CE]. In turn, a later version of the Vulgate Bible became the major reference work used in generating the King James Version of the Bible in English. Consequently, those who have used the King James Version of the Bible for the study of their faith owe much to the pioneering work of Origen. However, because many translators were used to put together the Septuagint, modern scholars believe that some errors have been introduced into the Vulgate and subsequently into the King James Version. An example is the use of the word "virgin" in the King James Version of Isaiah 7:14.[5]

Although it is not in proper chronological order, it is worth examining the history of the Vulgate Bible. <u>Vulgar Latin</u> was the Latin used for speech by the middle class in Rome and in the provinces. <u>Classical Latin</u> was used for written work when Greek was not used, but the middle class could no more read classical Latin than they could read <u>Ecclesiastical Latin</u>, the form invented by Tertullian. In 382 CE, Pope Damasus commissioned Jerome, the leading biblical scholar of his day, to produce an acceptable version of the Bible from among the various interpretations then in use. Jerome chose to produce this Bible in a written version of Vulgar Latin. To do so, Jerome had to "invent" a new written language. It was written Vulgar Latin, and the Bible written in this new language became known as the "Vulgate Bible" or simply the "Vulgate." The Vulgate went through many revisions during the succeeding centuries, finally being produced as the Paris edition in the thirteenth century. The earliest printed version of the Vulgate was based on the Paris edition. In 1546, the Council of Trent decreed that the Vulgate was to be the exclusive Latin authority for the Bible, but also decreed that it should be produced with as few errors as possible. In 1592, Pope Clement VIII issued the Clementine Vulgate which became the definitive Latin Bible until replaced by the Confraternity Version in 1941. The Clementine Vulgate was the version used to generate the King James Version of the Bible in English.

And so in one relatively short paragraph, we have followed a definite trail of translation which proceeds from the Hexapla of Origen through Jerome and Clement VIII to the King James Version, the Bible which most of the English-speaking world used until the twentieth century, and which some of that world still chooses to use.

How the Old and the New Testaments Came Into Existence

Although it may be somewhat difficult for some to believe,

the Bible in its present form did not always exist. In fact, there is a lot of historical evidence which states that the Old Testament, in its present form, did not exist until some 60 years after the death of Christ; and the New Testament in its present form did not exist until almost 300 years after that. Each happened with the establishment of the canon [from the Greek *kanon*, literally meaning "cane used as a measuring rod" or loosely translated as a "rule" or a "standard"].

The Hebrew canon, known to the Christian community as the **Old Testament**, was officially established by a synod of rabbis held at Yavneh, Palestine, in about 90 CE. In establishing this canon, the rabbis left out several semi-sacred books which were later called the Apocrypha [Greek for "hidden away"] by the Christians. One of the major reasons the Jewish canon was officially established was because of the fall of Jerusalem and the Diaspora [i.e. the dispersal of the Jewish people to parts of the world outside of Palestine]. Because of this, it was felt that the faithful needed an officially accepted reference text to take with them. Another and even more pertinent reason was because the Christians had been using their version of the Old Testament as the reference work for that which had preceded the coming of their Christ, and had been doing so to their advantage. As one example of this activity, the Christians translated the Hebrew word *alma* ["young woman"] in Isaiah 7:14 into the Greek word *parthenos* ["virgin"], thus implying that there had been Judaic prophesy that the people would recognize their savior because he would be born of a virgin. The Judaic Old Testament had said nothing of the sort.

The established Hebrew canon consists of 24 books referring to the 24 scrolls on which these works had been recorded in ancient times. The canon is divided into three parts: the *Torah* [or Pentateuch] meaning "Instructions" or "Law"; the *Neviim*, meaning "Prophets"; and the Ketuvim, meaning "Writings." The early Christian Churches [as, for example, in the works of Origen] seem to have used a 22-book canon; and the English Bible today contains 39 books because of the practice of making two books out of Samuel, Kings and Chronicles; and of presenting Ezra, Nehemiah and the 12 Minor Prophets as separate books.

The major point to be understood is that the Old Testament

upon which so much of early Christianity depended in order to have a historical basis and to become legitimized, did not officially exist until well after Christianity had been established and even after much of what later became the New Testament had been written. In addition, one major reason for establishing the Old Testament as canon was because during the first century CE, Christianity was distorting the historical record in order to enhance their own new religion.

The **New Testament** presently contains 27 books. These are the survivors out of many books and writings generated by the followers of Christ during the first four centuries after the Resurrection. As previously described, the authors of most of these works are unknown, and even some of the Letters attributed to Paul are in dispute. However, this was no problem, for it was widely accepted that most of the church writings during the first 200 years or so were either anonymous [i.e. the author is unknown] or pseudonymous [i.e. the work was given the name of an important or apostolic person even though written by another]. In the early days, this did not bother the Church, for the true author was always considered to be the Holy Spirit. [Contrast this with how the canon was actually selected as presented on page 81.]

The need for an established canon in Christianity was identical to that in Judaism: *viz.* if authenticity were not established by presenting certain writings as the "standard" and leaving others out, then some might start to use the Holy writings to their own advantage. One example was Gnosticism which presented a book entitled *Gospel of Truth*. Another was Montanism which presented writings stating that the post-Christ revelations by Montanus were authentic. But possibly the greatest impetus for establishing a Christian canon was because of the work of Marcion who established a canon of his own [see Section 5]. Because of the publication of Marcion's canon, the Church got busy and started to debate about what should be included in its own canon. During this debate, some writings which were accepted by many Christians as being Scripture were excluded from the accepted canon. A more detailed description of the selection debate is presented in Section 9 of this Chapter; and some of the excluded writings are described in Section 10.

Even though 367 CE is often mentioned as the date for

establishing the Christian canon, there is no true date short of 1546. The 367 date is often presented because in the fourth century, Athanasius, Bishop of Alexandria and a significant theologian, wrote an Easter letter to the churches of his See which proposed a canon of 27 books. Athanasius hoped that his proposal would limit the number of books in the New Testament and would settle a long dispute between the East and the West branches of the church. As a part of the compromise, he proposed that Revelations and Hebrews be included, the latter because it was believed at that time to be a part of the writings of Paul, a conjecture which has been rejected by almost all modern biblical scholars. The resulting 27 books, and only they, were generally accepted as being canonical. The Greek Church continued to reject the inclusion of Revelation; but the Latin Church, under the influence of Jerome, accepted fully the decision of Athanasius. However, many published Bibles continued to include other books without stating that they were non-canonical. In the fourth-century *Codex Sinaiticus*, the *Letter of Barnabas* and the *Shepherd of Hermas* are included without any accompanying notation; and in the fifth-century *Codex Alexandrinus, Clement I* and *II* [the two letters of Pope Clement I] are included. In addition, the Syriac canon consisted of only 22 books until well into the seventh century. Finally, the Reformation caused quite a stir over which books really belonged in the Bible. Consequently, during the Counter-Reformation Council of Trent [1545-63], the canon of the entire Bible was set as being that of the Vulgate, based on Jerome's Latin version. Martin Luther considered that only books which would drive directly toward Christ should be included. By this test he wanted to reject Hebrews, James, Jude and Revelation; but he bowed to tradition and kept these books in his version of the New Testament.

And thus, after much controversy which lasted for almost 1600 years, the books of the New Testament of the Bible were accepted as they are today. But while living with that acceptance, the interested Christian should understand that the final result was not one which was always unanimously accepted even by those whom the Church venerates.

3. OTHER WRITINGS OR PHILOSOPHIES[4]

Two philosophies were of extreme importance to the development of Christian doctrines and beliefs. They are Judaistic philosophy and Greek philosophy. Although there is an overlap between them, they will be examined separately.

Judaistic Philosophies

Judaism was the cradle in which Christianity was nurtured; and Judaistic philosophy left a deep imprint on the liturgy, identity and teaching of the Christian Church.

Judaistic philosophy came in two versions, and each had a great impact on Christianity. The first version came from Palestinian Judaism and impacted the early Christian teaching, particularly that presented by the Apostolic Fathers. The second version came from Hellenized Judaism which was prevalent in Alexandria at the beginning of the Christian era. It strongly influenced all Christian teaching by the end of the second century, and even started to displace Palestinian Judaistic philosophy as the Hellenistic ideas began to come to the fore. This explains why the teaching of the Apostolic Fathers often strikes a strange note when judged by later standards of orthodoxy. In other words, the teachings of the Apostolic Fathers [i.e. those who had known Jesus] seem a little strange to Christians whose Christianity has been influenced by those who came into the Church during the second and subsequent centuries and were strongly influenced by the Greek philosophers who had <u>not</u> known Jesus.

The two features of Palestinian Judaism which may seem strange to modern Christians are its attitude toward divine *"hypostases"* and its heightened interest in angels, each of which helped to create the Christian conception of God as three-personal. Students of the Old Testament are familiar with the Judaic tendency to personify Wisdom and to assign creative functions to it; and New Testament writers such as Paul availed themselves of a similar idea in order to explain the status of Christ [see Section 4, footnote 6]. In later Judaism, there are a number of allegorical figures such as "Wisdom," and God's "Glory" or "Presence," and His "Word" and His "Spirit" and many others. In one text it was "Wisdom" to whom

God said, "Let us make man in our image." Another text has God's "Spirit" as His agent in creation. Because they may have been considered substitute phrases for God Himself, Judaism never made them separate "Persons" as Christianity did. However, it is virtually certain that this late Judaistic tendency to hypostasize [i.e. to symbolize a concept in a concrete form] had a great influence on the development of the Christian teaching of the three "Persons" of God.

At the same time, there was an enormous Judaistic expansion in the belief in angels, and in the belief that these angels were the ministers of God. It is possible that this belief in angels was a Judaic assumption of earlier God-forms from various surrounding cultures; but for whatever reason Judaism started accepting angels, the expansion of that acceptance was dramatic. Some of these angels were given personal names; and there were seven archangels who executed God's will in His world as His deputies. These archangels were first mentioned in the noncanonical *First Book of Enoch* and were named as: *Uriel* [leader of the heavenly hosts and guardian of *sheol*, the underworld]; *Raphael* [guardian of human spirits]; *Raguel* [avenger of God against the world of lights]; *Michael* [guardian of Israel]; *Sariel* [avenger of the spirits "who sin in the spirit"]; *Gabriel* [ruler of paradise, the seraphim and the cherubim]; and *Remiel*, also called *Jeremial* [guardian of the souls in *sheol*]. There was even an angel, *Ureic*, appointed to regulate the movement of the stars. The canonical Old Testament mentions that in the heavenly court, two angelic powers, sometimes identified as *Michael* and *Gabriel*, stand before God's throne interceding for men, somewhat similar to the job which the Christians later assigned to Christ. Additional thoughts on angels are presented in *Book Two*.

In addition to the philosophy presented by Palestinian Judaism, there was a special brand of Judaism which flourished at Alexandria. It produced the Septuagint version of the Old Testament, and in the Christian period it provided a highly sympathetic channel for introducing Hellenistic culture into the early Christian Church. Greek ideas had always attracted the Jews of Alexandria, and it was here that the most learned attempt was made to interpret Jewish theology in terms of Hellenistic philosophy. This effort was made by Philo [30 BCE to 45 CE], who was not only a scholar, but also was a person of social and political influence in the Jewish community. Although faithful to the practice of Judaism, he was drawn to the Greek philosophers, especially Plato. Philo believed that Plato's ideas had been anticipated in the Jewish Scriptures. The scrolls of the Pentateuch [or Torah] were his favorite study; and he regarded the Bible as fully inspired in the sense that God used its authors as passive instruments for communicating His will.

Two aspects of his thought are of special interest to students of Christian doctrine. The first was his method of allegorizing Scripture to show that the truths set forth by revealed religion were identical with those of the philosophers. Allegorical exegesis [i.e. critical exploration or analysis] was often used in Greek philosophy to find hidden meanings in the poems of Homer and to read modern messages into the ancient myths. Philo borrowed from this practice and used allegory very effectively to show that the Scriptures hold a deeper meaning than they might appear to have on the surface. In this manner, he explained the story of Adam and Eve as a myth symbolizing the creation of the human soul, the seduction of human intelligence by pleasure and material things, and the ways by which humans could return to their original state, thus merging the Bible version of creation with Greek philosophy. This is merely one of many examples which he used to show that Scripture was a divinely authorized veil covering a whole complex of Greek philosophical ideas. Because of this background, it was rather easy for the philosophy of the day to accept a new religion coming out of the East which would present yet another Oriental allegory of the concept of salvation. That religion was Christianity. Because of the acceptance of this allegorical treatment, many Christian Church Fathers used similar methodology in the following years to establish doctrine by Tradition rather than by Scripture as in the *Epistle of Barnabas*, a treatise written in Alexandria in 130 CE which uses allegorical methods to explain the "true" [i.e. Christian] interpretation of Jewish law.

The second aspect of Philo's thought which impacted on Christian doctrine was his concept of the *Logos*, or "Word." Guided by the Middle Platonists he so much admired, Philo taught that God is utterly transcendent in that He is above even virtue, knowledge and absolute goodness, the eternal Forms which Plato had postulated.

Philo taught that God is pure "being," which can be described as "without quality" or unlike finite beings. The question thus arose of His relation to the world, which contemporary Platonism solved by interposing a hierarchy of divine beings between God and the material order. This hierarchy created and ruled the material world. Philo could not accept this since to him, nothing must interfere with the uniqueness of the God revealed in Scripture. Instead he conceived of intermediary powers which were not distinct "beings," but were God's way of operating apart from Himself. Among these intermediaries, the supreme and most important was the *Logos*, which he called "the eldest and most akin to God of all the things which have come into existence." From this, the early Christian scholars quickly identified the *Logos* with Jesus who was the Christ and the agent of God in the creation of the world.

Philo's teaching about the *Logos* may be somewhat confusing, but its main elements are clear. As intermediary between God and the universe, the *Logos* has a double role: it is God's agent in creation, and it is also the means by which the human mind understands God. In this approach, Philo was guided by his Bible in which God created the world by His <u>Word</u>, and by His <u>Word</u> He revealed Himself to the prophets. Philo may not have regarded the *Logos* as a personal being as the Christians did later; but since he did believe that the world had to be created, then he needed the divine *Logos* to create and to govern the real and rational world as a part of the real and rational universe. His *Logos* was both immanent [i.e. "exists within"] in the world as well as transcendent [i.e. "surpasses all others"] in the divine Mind. It therefore was "the captain and steersman of the universe." Philo also believed that by contemplating the *Logos*, men could come to the knowledge of God.

All of this philosophy was not only accepted and adopted by the early Christian scholars, it was also emphasized by the later Church Fathers as they tried to explain the nature of the Christ or the *Logos* during the first five Ecumenical Councils.

Greek/ Roman Philosophies
Although Judaistic philosophy was important, it is virtually impossible to exaggerate the importance of Greek/Roman philosophy

on the development of Christian doctrine; for the more one examines the debates of the first five or six Ecumenical Councils, the more one hears the debates which had previously generated the various forms of Greek philosophy, especially Neo-Platonism. Because of this importance, this section will try to do a concise review of the major Greek philosophies, which were later adopted by the Romans and even later adopted by Christianity. In doing this, it should be emphasized that the Greek/Roman philosophy had little if any influence on Scripture; but it had a deep and significant effect on Tradition, especially the interpretation of Apostolic Tradition.

Within the Greco-Roman culture at the beginning of the Christian era, philosophy was the deepest religion of most thinking people. In other words, the intelligentsia accepted the religious depth of philosophy more than they accepted the worship of the various "society" gods. Because of this, philosophy and its concepts provided Christians and non-Christians alike with an intellectual framework for expressing their ideas.

The two major Greek philosophies were <u>Platonism</u> and <u>Stoicism</u>. <u>Platonism</u>, founded by Plato in about 400 BCE, was primarily based on knowledge as generated by the intellect rather than by the senses. Thus the intellect could generate a Form or Idea which had no sensual basis. Plato considered that all of these Forms or Ideas were headed by the most universal Form of all, the Form of Good which he later called the One. The One was, of course, transcendent [i.e. "above and beyond the material worlds" or in other words, "not of the world of senses"].

<u>Stoicism</u> presents an entirely different picture. Founded by Zeno in about 300 BCE, it was a closely knit system of logic, metaphysics and ethics, all of a very high moral character. It focused strongly on the brotherhood of man and considered the things developed by the senses to be preeminent. It considered that God [or *Logos*] was a very fine type of matter which permeated the universe. As matter, it could be detected by the senses. Stoicism also believed that since the soul of man was an emanation [i.e. that which flows forth] from the divine fire [or *Logos*], then it also could be detected by the senses. This material soul would exist after the material body was gone; and would continue to exist until consumed in a world conflagration.

Stoicism also considered that since the things developed by the senses were preeminent, then they were developed by God rather than by man. Therefore, a Stoic will deny pain, joy, and sadness because those passions of the senses do not exist in things developed by God.

By the time of Christianity, both Platonism and Stoicism had changed greatly from their founding form. Platonism had rebelled from the changes of Aristotle and had returned to its roots with Middle Platonism which was later followed by Neo-Platonism. In the meantime, Stoicism had borrowed from Platonism to a significant degree. In the Christian debates which came in the fourth through the sixth centuries, the debaters often borrowed from each Greek philosophy in order to make their points and to defend their definition of the Christ. The ultimate definition was based strongly on Neo-Platonism.

In Neo-Platonism, the tendency to make God transcendent was carried as far as it could go. It flourished for about 300 years, starting in the middle of the third century CE. It is best exemplified by Plotinus [205-270 CE], the Greek-speaking Egyptian who was its founder and also one of the greatest thinkers of the ancient world. Plotinus was a monist, or one who sees reality as a unified whole. He conceived reality as being a vast hierarchical structure with grades descending from what is beyond "being" to what falls below "being." His highest principle, or *hypostasis*, is God, more properly designated as the One. The One is the source from which "being" derives and the goal to which "being" ever strives to return. The One is beyond "being," and even beyond mind which earlier forms of Platonism had equated with God. The process by which the One creates "being" is described as emanation, but it leaves the One undiminished and unchanged. Ineffably simple, the One cannot be the subject of any attributes. For example, although we can call *It* good, *It* is not good in the sense that *It* possesses goodness as a quality, but that *It is goodness*.

Immediately below the One in the hierarchy of Plotinus comes the second *hypostasis*, Mind or Thought; and immediately below that comes the third *hypostasis*, Soul. Soul issues directly from Mind, while Mind contemplates its effort to return to the One. Soul is divided into two: the higher soul, which transcends the material order; and the lower soul, or Nature, which is the World-Soul. All individual souls are emanations from the World-Soul; and like it, they have a higher element which is related to Mind, and a lower element which is directly connected with the body. Matter which is unilluminated by form, is darkness or non-being, and as such is Evil.

Two features of Neo-Platonism deserve to be stressed. First, it represents an optimistic attitude to the universe; for although the universe is Material, it was created and ordered by the higher soul and thus it is good. The Christians later used this argument to declare that Gnosticism [which believed that anything material was evil] was heretical. Secondly, the religious attitude of Neo-Platonism is based on an "overflow" of the One and an ardent longing for ultimate union with the One Itself. The Christians later used this argument to emphasize their desire to return to God.

Other Writings of this Period

All of the philosophical impact on Christianity mentioned above initially influenced only the Eastern branch of the Christian Church. The Western branch was quite different. For historical reasons, Rome and the churches immediately associated with her (Gaul, Spain, North Africa, etc.) tended to ignore the intellect during their development, although a few Western writers, particularly Tertullian, did accept the concept of the *Logos*. As a consequence of this tendency, the early creeds, liturgies and doctrines of the Western Church were primarily based on faith; whereas the Eastern creeds and doctrines were based on definitions generated from intellectual debate.

Because they were somewhat hostile to philosophy, the West applauded the simple believers who were content with the rule of faith. On the other hand, the early teachers of the East such as Origen and Clement of Alexandria went so far as to distinguish two types of Christianity, with two grades of Christians corresponding to them. The first and lower type was based on "faith," i.e. the literal acceptance of the truths declared in Scripture and in the Church's teaching; while the second and higher type was described as *"gnosis,"* i.e. an esoteric form of knowledge which started with the Bible, but then went on to unravel a deeper meaning and to explore the more profound mysteries of God, His universe and His scheme of salvation.

Since the background which the East used in their debates

about the nature of Christ has been adequately covered by the philosophies presented above, this section will concentrate solely on the West and in particular on the writings of several Western Church Fathers whose biographies are presented in Appendix A.

Clement I wrote several epistles. Among these, the greatest honor has been given to *Clement I*, a letter written from the Roman church to the Christians at Corinth in about 95 CE. For almost 200 years this letter was considered by most Christians to be Scripture. It dealt with the problems of trying to develop order in a church which faced a rebellion of the congregation against the discipline instituted by the church elders. It is important because it pictures a church which did not always obey the presumed discipline required in the worship of Christ, and because it states the recommendations which the central Church would make in order to resist any such rebellion. The second letter of Clement, *Clement II*, listed the Apostolic Fathers whose words were to be respected as a part of the Apostolic Tradition for presenting Church doctrine. The Letters of Clement are also discussed in Section 10. The Apostolic Tradition will be discussed further in the next section.

Irenaeus of Lyons wrote many works which criticized the religious activities of the Gnostics. He also wrote that the four Gospels of Scripture were really speaking as a unified and single statement of witness. However, his two best known works were his *Demonstration of Apostolic Preaching* and his *Against Heresies*. In the former, he taught that the teaching-tradition of the Church started with the Apostles and then preceded though the ordained bishops, thus presenting a true teaching of authentic Christian faith. In the latter, he argued that *gnosis* or knowledge developed outside of the Apostolic Tradition was false teaching. In both presentations, he wrote heatedly that those who were appointed by the Church to develop true Church doctrines had the ability and the guidance to do so.

Tertullian wrote often against the Gnostics. In particular, he defended the doctrines of creation, of the fleshly incarnation of the *Logos*, and of the resurrection of the flesh. In addition, his *On Baptism* was possibly the first description of how solemn and serious this sacrament was to the life and the consciousness of the Church. Although these were important works, his most important writing was arguably the tract *Against Praxeas* in which he attacked a "Monarchian" teacher who had denied the reality of the *Logos* as being distinct from the Father. In this tract he presented the first definitive doctrine of the Trinity, arguing that there is one divine substance which administered into three distinct but continuous "persons": Father, Logos/Son, and Spirit. This *"una substantia—tres personae"* became the formulation for the Trinity which, after much debate, was accepted by the Church as a "Revealed Truth" some 500 years later. In this tract, Tertullian also presented the argument that the single "person" of Christ existed in two distinct, unconfused "substances," one divine and one human. This insight provided much of the debate which was conducted at the first six Ecumenical Councils. Tertullian, therefore, wrote much which was made into doctrine by the Church some 100-500 years later.

Hippolytus wrote often in condemnation of Monarchianism and its subsequent sects, Adoptionism and Sabellianism. In this writing, particularly *Refutation of All Heresies,* he supported the view that the *Logos* was a "person" distinct from the Father but created by God for the express purpose of carrying out His will. Possibly the most important of his writing was that contained in *The Apostolic Tradition* in which he not only emphasizes the importance of Communion and other liturgical "offices" which were to be carried out each day, but also proposes such activities as being part of the Church doctrines, not because they were Scriptural, but because they were a Tradition of the Church which had been handed down by the Apostles.

Cyprian wrote several epistles in which he supported the supremacy of the Church. In one he wrote that "There is no salvation outside the Church"; and in another, aptly titled *On the Unity of the Church,* he made the oft-repeated statement that "He can no longer have the God for his Father who has not the church for his Mother," a statement which was later accredited to Augustine.

It is rather obvious that these writings of the Western Church Fathers are important to the development of Christian doctrines for three reasons: [1] they emphasize faith rather than reason as a basis for the teaching of the Church; [2] they establish tradition, particularly the Apostolic Tradition, as a source of teaching equivalent to Scripture; and [3] they establish that the Church is the sole mechanism for finding God. In this manner, in its very early stages Western Christianity took a major step in establishing that Faith/Tradition/Church were more important than Understanding/Scripture/Individual Path in finding God. This belief system was epitomized about 1,000 years later when the Church forbid the reading of the Bible by laymen [see Footnote 11 on page 149].

4. MISSIONARY JOURNEYS
AND THE APOSTOLIC TRADITION[4]

The great missionary journeys of the early Church occurred before either of the two prior sections had much effect. This section is presented now because only now could it be appreciated just how important the establishment of the Apostolic Tradition became to the later establishment of the Church doctrines and dogmas. As just mentioned, the Western Church considered Tradition to be equal to Scripture as a basis for doctrine

The initial missionary journeys were instituted by the Great Commission as presented in Matthew 28:18-20 which says, *"And Jesus came and said to them, 'All authority in heaven and on earth has been given to me. Go therefore and make disciples of all nations, baptizing them in the name of the Father and of the Son and of the Holy Spirit, teaching them to observe all that I have commanded you; and lo, I am with you always, to the close of the age.' "* This admonition was augmented by the Holy Spirit who came to the Apostles on the day of Pentecost and among other things prompted Peter to say to the assembled crowd, *"For the promise is to you and to your children and to all that are far off, every one who the Lord our God calls to him."* [Acts 2:39]

Following this, the Pharisee Saul who had been persecuting those who belonged to the Way [i.e. those later called "Christians," a name which was not used by the Church before the second century], is reported to have participated in the stoning of Stephen, the one who had been chosen Apostle to replace Judas Iscariot. The death of Stephen, the first Christian martyr recorded in the Scriptures, was a part of the general persecution of Christians in Jerusalem. The persecution became so great that many Christians dispersed into the cities of the Jewish Diaspora [i.e. those Jews who lived outside of Judea] and took the good news of Jesus with them wherever they went. As one result of this dispersing, Antioch, the capital of the province of Syria, became a second focal point of Christian life and many other centers were also established, including one in Damascus.

Saul continued to be ardent in his persecution of the Christians, so much so that he requested permission to seek out "those belonging to the Way" in Damascus, to capture and to bind them, and to bring them back to Jerusalem for further persecution. Saul was granted this right, but as he approached Damascus, a blinding light came from heaven with a voice which cried out, "Saul, Saul, why do you persecute me?" The voice was identified as that of Jesus; and as a result, Saul, the persecutor of Christians, was converted. He became Paul, who, after meetings with Peter in Antioch, became the major Christian missionary to the gentiles. All of this is recorded in the Scriptures in Acts, particularly in Chapters 8-11.

In this way, "those belonging to the Way" started reaching out from the Jewish communities to the various cities of Asia Minor. This reaching out was primarily accomplished by missionary journeys, including the four well-known missionary journeys of Paul as well as the other missionary journeys of the Apostles such as those of Peter, John and Philip. These are the only missionary journeys of the Apostles recorded in the Scriptures and the only ones which have, so far, been accepted by history. In other literature, primarily that of the New Age, it is recorded that Thomas made missionary journeys to India and to other parts of the East. In addition, the possibility of Thomas making a missionary trip to Egypt is mentioned in at least one book. Since these missionary journeys are not recognized by the orthodox Christians who place so much emphasis on the Apostolic Tradition, they do not address the major purpose of this section and will not be addressed here.

The first mission of Paul occurred in about 46-48 CE and was instigated by and guided by the Holy Spirit. Paul was accompanied by Barnabas and John Mark as they went from Antioch of Syria to Cyprus. From there, Paul and Barnabas proceeded to visit the cities of Antioch, Iconium, Lystra and Derbe, all in Prisidia, a region of Asia Minor in Galatia, presently known as Central Turkey. They subsequently returned to Antioch of Syria through Perga, a city on the southern coast of present-day Turkey. The first Missionary Journey of Paul is depicted in outline form in Map 2 on page 90. The total Journey was about 1300 miles. The distance from the first to the fourth of the four cities visited in Asia Minor was about 160 miles. At the extreme end of the Journey, Paul was less than 170 miles from his starting point.

The second mission of Paul occurred in about 49-52 CE. It included Silas and later added Timothy. This mission started in Antioch of Syria. From there, it took the shorter overland route into southern Galatia to visit the cities previously visited; then went further to Ephesus, to Philippi, to Thessalonica, to Corinth [with a side trip to Athens]; and then returned from Corinth by sea to Ephesus, to Rhodes and to Caesarea; then overland to Jerusalem followed by the overland return to Antioch. The second Missionary Journey of Paul is depicted in outline form in Map 3 on page 90. The total Journey was almost 2600 miles.

The first two Missionary Journeys had established several churches in Asia Minor, a major center at Corinth, and the beginnings of a major center at Ephesus. To consolidate the latter, Paul started his third mission by traveling overland from Antioch to Ephesus where he remained for about three years while establishing churches nearby. When he heard of troubles at Corinth, he proceeded there, then returned to Ephesus from which he went into Macedonia to the churches at Philippi and Thessalonica. From there he again went to Corinth; and then by a labored route, returned to Jerusalem where he had been called by Peter and James to participate in disputes arising from his Letter to the Romans. That Letter was an attempt to spread the message of Christ to the far West, at least to Rome and possibly even to Spain. The dispute in Jerusalem was about whether or not the message was getting too far away from "God's chosen people, the Jews"; and also whether or not Paul was changing the message of Christ from that which had been heard by those who had known him. Paul was doing this, of course, just as the Church Fathers did later.[6]

During the layovers on the extended trip which became known as Paul's third Missionary Journey, Paul wrote many of his most important letters, including the one to the Romans and several to the major church at Corinth, only two of which have survived, the second of which may be a compendium of several other letters. The major parts of the extensive and complex third Missionary Journey of Paul are presented in Map 4 on page 91. The total Journey was in excess of 2700 miles. It occurred in about 53-57 CE.

The fourth trip, called a mission by some biblical scholars but merely a trip by others, began with Paul's arrest in Jerusalem and his transfer to imprisonment at the Roman headquarters in Caesarea. After two years there, the new governor, Festus, wanted to return Paul to Jerusalem for trial. However, Paul insisted that as a Roman citizen, he had the right to make a direct appeal to Caesar. Consequently, the trip [or mission] to Rome began. The sea voyage had several stops: in Myra, in Crete, in Malta [where a shipwreck delayed the travelers for three months], in Syracuse, in Rhegium and finally in Puteoli. This was followed by a short land journey to Rome where Paul was arrested and held for trial. At this point, the Scriptures end; but it is believed that Paul was convicted and executed. This final trip of Paul is depicted in Map 5 on page 91. It occurred in about 59-62 CE. The straight line distance between Jerusalem and Rome is about 1800 miles.

These three or four mission trips of Paul are the major missionary journeys recorded in the Acts of the Apostles. The only other missionary journeys recorded in the Scriptures are considered by some biblical scholars not even to be journeys at all. They include the trip of Philip to Samaria and the preaching he did there, followed by the similar trips of Peter and John. Samaria was very much hated by the Jews in Judea, and the fact that these three Apostles did go there and did convert people there certainly represents an extension of Judean Christianity. However, the fact that the city of Samaria was only about 30 miles north of Jerusalem and only about halfway between Jerusalem and the Sea of Galilee, would present the argument that if these were missionary journeys, they were not of the kind which would spread the word of Jesus for any great distance.

This section would not be complete without some additional words about the work of Peter. After the crucifixion, Peter spent most of his life in and around Jerusalem. He was imprisoned there by King Agrippa, and barely escaped execution. The Scriptures have very little to say about the latter part of Peter's life, although it is thought that he spent some time in Asia Minor and possibly visited the church in Corinth. He ultimately settled in Rome where he described himself as "fellow elder" which means that although he was one of the leaders of the church in Rome, he was not the sole leader. Peter is believed to have been martyred in Rome during Nero's persecution of the Christians in about 64 CE. Most present-day scholars believe that Peter spent 3-4 years in Rome at the most. As a consequence, he can hardly be given credit for establishing the church in Rome, although Rome later used his martyrdom there to lay claim to being the chief Church. As to whether or not the visits by Peter to Corinth and to Rome would constitute missionary journeys would depend entirely on definitions; but they are included here to make the record complete. It should also be mentioned that the apocryphal *Gospel of Peter* was initially attributed to Peter. However, it was later declared to be the work of an unknown heretical author by the Church and was never made a part of the canonical Bible.

The names of the twelve disciples of Christ, or Apostles as they were later called, are presented in Mark 3:13-19 as follows: *"Simon whom he surnamed Peter; James the son of Zebedee and John the brother of James, whom he surnamed Boanerges, that is, sons of thunder; Andrew, and Philip, and Bartholomew, and Matthew, and Thomas, and James the son of Alphaeus, and Thaddaeus, and Simon the Cananaean, and Judas Iscariot, who betrayed him."* After the crucifixion, Stephen was chosen to replace Judas. Paul is considered an Apostle for two reasons: first and possibly foremost, his writings were accepted as equivalent to the Gospels in their impact on Christianity and people would often refer to them as containing the words of "the Apostle"; and secondly, Paul always insisted that his teachings came directly from Jesus the Christ and therefore he was as much a disciple [or Apostle] as any one who had actually worked with Jesus in the flesh. Peter seemed to concur, and so Paul has been known throughout the centuries as "the Apostle Paul."

The major point to be made about the recorded Apostolic missionary journeys is that they were to relatively minor cities in Asia Minor, Macedonia or Greece. There is no record of any Apostle visiting Alexandria or Carthage, the two most important centers of Christian thought during the first hundred years following the death of the last Apostle. In fact, in his marvelous book *A History of the Christian Church*, Walker states that by 130 there was a large Christian community in Alexandria, but nobody knows how it got there.[7] In addition, there is no record of any Apostle reaching the city of Byzantium, a city which later became known as "New Rome" and still later as Constantinople. Although it could be argued that Paul's second and third Missionary Journeys came within 250 miles of Byzantium, this occurred about 300 years before that city became an important Christian site. To think that the Apostle had a great effect on that city would be like saying that General Montcalm's visit to Ticonderoga in 1758 has a great effect on New York City today. Any effect would be tenuous and indirect at best, and would hardly be the material from which an Apostolic Tradition could be made. Finally, there is no great record of teaching in Rome, for Peter and Paul, the only two Apostles known to have reached Rome, were kept well under wraps during their time there. Peter is thought to have died early in the Christian movement, only some thirty years after the Crucifixion with at least half of that time having been spent in Jerusalem; and Paul was virtually under arrest for his entire stay in Rome. The Scriptures do say that during a two year period, Paul welcomed all who came to visit him and he taught them unhindered. However, he never established the Apostolic Tradition by speaking to great throngs in Rome.

In addition to this major point, a minor point should be made. That point relates to the seven churches which make such an impact in the second and third chapters of The Revelation to John in the New Testament. Those seven churches were: Ephesus, Smyrna, Pergamum, Thyatira, Sardis, Philadelphia, and Laodicea. The location of each of these seven churches is presented in Map 6 on page 92. As can be seen, these seven churches are closely bunched in a small corner of southwestern Asia Minor. There is less than 140 miles which separate the first from the last of these churches. There is no scriptural reference to any of these churches having been visited by an Apostle other than the previously mentioned visits of Paul to Ephesus. It therefore becomes somewhat difficult to tie this scriptural effort into any sort of Apostolic Tradition, especially since recognized biblical scholars are virtually unanimous in their opinion that the John to whom the Revelation was made was not an Apostle.

And yet, despite the lack of any record stating that any Apostle had ever visited any of the centers which provided most of the inspiration for the Apostolic Tradition, and despite the difficulty of tying the last book of the New Testament to any Apostolic visitation or Tradition, in the 200 years which followed the death of the last Apostle, great volumes were written which presented Church doctrines justified not by Scripture, but by the traditions of those who had known the Christ. In other words, those doctrines were justified by the Apostolic Tradition.

As a consequence of all of this, much of the dogma generated by the Church was generated by men who had never known Jesus the Christ; nor had they ever met one who had known Jesus the Christ. And yet, they established the teachings of the Church, much of which is at variance with Scripture. They did this based on Apostolic Tradition with which they were not directly familiar, but which they had only heard by oral tradition over a period of several hundreds of years.

I think we must conclude that at best there is a tenuous thread which ties the Apostolic Tradition to the teachings of the Christ. This particular conclusion will become more evident in the words of *Book Two*, particularly in the Section starting on page 146.

5. PROPOSALS NOT ACCEPTED AS CHRISTIAN DOCTRINE[4]

During the first 300 years of the Church's existence, a number of proposals and statements were made which presented a cornucopia of fresh ideas. By the sixth and seventh centuries, the generation of fresh ideas had burned itself out and had been replaced by a reign of conformity. As a consequence, after the finish of the first six Ecumenical Councils there was a doctrinal homogeneity which differed from the range of theology proposed during the formative early centuries.

Because of the variety of opinions in the early time, even on issues of prime importance such as the mystery of the Atonement, certain fathers of the early period were later adjudged heretics, even though they had been considered very orthodox during their lifetimes. Origen is a classic example of such an occurrence. This did not happen because the early Church was indifferent to making a distinction between orthodox and heretical views; but it happened because eventually an organization will demand conformity to such an extent that the spark of creativity is destroyed. This phenomena applies to all human activities and not just to religion. One need think only of what happened to creativity at several major U. S. corporations during the 1980s in order to have a pertinent clue as to what happened to the Church as it increasingly demanded conformity. This particular section will present a short overview on the specific viewpoints of a few people whose creative thoughts were rejected in an attempt to generate doctrinaire conformity.

First, all of the controversies which were mentioned in Appendix A could readily be included; but it is not the purpose of this section to repeat what was immediately declared as heresy other than in the following general statements:

1. Judaism considered everything which God created as being good and they gave thanks for it. This included everything: wheat, trees, knee joints, sex organs, giraffes, monkeys, mountains—everything. Therefore, all dualistic religions which proposed the evilness of material things could not fit within the Judeo-Christian movement of the early centuries. As a consequence, the basic premises of Gnosticism and Manichaeism could not be made a part of Christian doctrine. They were therefore declared to be heretical.

2. Although Monarchianism and its siblings Adoptionism, Modalism and Sabellianism were fought by the early Church, the Christian doctrines which rejected them were not officially accepted by the Church until after the debates which were held at the Ecumenical Councils. Thus, they will be discussed in Section 7.

3. This leaves Marcionism, Montanism and Origenism to be discussed here, each for a specific reason.

Marcionism was established by Marcion who was a wealthy Christian ship owner born in Asia Minor. He moved to Rome in 139 CE and joined the Christian Church there with a substantial donation for charitable work. He then started to preach his version of the

Gospel which was primarily based on the writings of Paul and a form of the Gospel of Luke. Marcion's teaching was based on his belief that the God which Jesus talked of was not the God of Judaism and had nothing to do with the Scriptures of Judaism. He believed this because the God of Jesus was a God of love and mercy; whereas the God of the Old Testament was a God of judgment and harsh justice.

His preaching was so powerful that his followers left the mainstream Christian Church and established a competitive church of their own. This church was based on the Christian principles of law and grace as espoused by Paul and rejected anything which had to do with the Old Testament as a background for Christianity. It accepted the thought that the God and Father of Jesus Christ did not exist until He had been disclosed by the Christ; and therefore the previous God of the Old Testament must have been some sort of an inferior God. Later, this church adopted some of the thoughts of the Gnostics, particularly the belief that anything not of the God of Jesus was material and thus was evil. In this way, Marcion accepted duality.

The movement was well organized, a trait which Christianity could not claim at the time. It became well established, particularly in Syria. It not only made the mainstream churches of Christianity face some viable competition, it made them face the question of the disorganized status of their own Church. It also made them address the issue of the continuity of Christianity with its Judaistic heritage. Furthermore, it forced the mainstream Church to defer the full acceptance of Paul's writings as being Christian truth until they became championed by Augustine somewhat later. But most importantly, it forced mainstream Christianity to develop and gradually accept its own New Testament canon, a task which was not completed in any way until the compromise of 367 CE [see page 35], and which was not really completed until almost 1200 years after that. Finally, it forced mainstream Christianity to accept the Old Testament of Judaism as a part of the total Christian Bible. It forced thoughts about a canonical Bible because Marcion had a well developed "Bible" of its own which had been accepted as canon by his church. Thus, the presence of Marcion made Christianity start to define its own organization and its own doctrines, including the belief that Judaism had been a historical precedent for Christianity.

And so the point about Marcion is not so much that Christian doctrine rejected his beliefs, but instead that he gave them a reason to establish their own system of organization and of doctrinal beliefs. However, since Marcion rejected the Judaism of history and later accepted duality, he was declared a heretic by the Church.

Montanism generated two beliefs which were not accepted by mainstream Christianity. The first of these beliefs concerned the revelations given under trance by Montanus. These revelations or prophecies were rejected by the Church because no one could attribute them either to Christ, or to one of the Apostles. Consequently, they were considered false prophecy and were declared heresy by the Church. In this matter, we can see that the Church was developing a closed mind about anything not generated by the established Apostolic Tradition.

The second rejected belief of Montanism had to do with the strong moral attitudes which they required. This moral attitude so appealed to Tertullian that he left Christianity in favor of Montanism. However, Tertullian was one of the few who took such a step. Despite verbal statements supporting the vows of chastity and poverty, there are strong reports that the early men of the Church acted otherwise. These reports include Tertullian calling the pope a "shepherd of adulterers" and of people being threatened with excommunication for speaking out against the luxury in which the priests lived. Thus, even at this early stage the Church was starting to reject some of the Apostolic teachings related to worldly possessions and moral character. *Book Two* presents more on this subject.

There is much to consider in **Origenism**. Most of this will be presented later or in Appendix A. In this short preview we will examine only two of the teachings of this school.

Clement of Alexandria and his student, Origen, were the early Christian thinkers who were most exposed to the influence of Gnosticism as a competitive force. This is because of their location in Alexandria which also was the major site of Gnosticism. In an attempt to merge some of the better parts of each religion, Clement and Origen proposed a system of knowledge or *gnosis* which would establish two classes of Christians: a lower class which would be based totally on faith; and a higher class based on the accumulation of certain esoteric knowledge, with "esoteric" meaning "intended to be understood by only a few." They felt justified in doing this, for several times Jesus had said that he was teaching esoteric knowledge. He did this when justifying his use of the parables, a prime example of which is presented in Matthew 13:10-17. But the thought that some Christians could be advanced by *gnosis* was not a thought which was accepted as mainstream Christian doctrine.

Origen also presented the thought that the soul was eternal and had existed before the physical body had been created. This "pre-existence of the soul" was believed in by many Christians, but was later made to be anathema [i.e. one who accepted such a belief was to be cursed and excommunicated] by Emperor Justinian in 543. Although it has never been officially rejected by the Church, the mainstream Church has never supported it either. Further detail on this subject is presented in Appendix C.

Other thoughts were proposed by the early Fathers of the Church, and were rejected for inclusion in Christian doctrines. Some were rejected immediately, but most were rejected only much later after the Church had organized itself into a set pattern of beliefs. The purpose of presenting a few of them in this section is merely to give feeling as to how the Church stifled creativity while striving for doctrinaire conformity.

6. THE EDICT OF MILAN [313 CE]

The "Edict" of Milan was one of the most important steps in making the Christian Church what it is today. The word "Edict" is put in quotation marks, because is was not really an officially issued edict of the Roman empire. However, it was proposed by Constantine, the new Emperor in the West, and grudgingly accepted by Licinius, the Emperor in the East. Its origin was in an edict of toleration for Christians issued by Emperor Galerius from his death-bed in 311. The support by both of the new Emperors made the general public accept the Edict; for when a new Emperor made his wishes known in the Roman Empire of that day, those wishes were followed whether they were an official act or not.

The Edict of Milan proposed religious toleration for both pagans and Christians. In essence, it stopped the persecution of Christians. Consequently, it allowed the Church to grow without the fears which previously had forced it underground. As a result, the Church stopped being the persecuted and, to a certain extent, became the persecutor. The understanding of this event is important to the understanding of the basic message being presented in this entire work. To understand the reason for this importance, some understanding of Constantine and his effect on the Christian Church is required.

The Church of Christ became a worldwide religion because it was accepted as the state religion of Rome by Theodosius and Gratian in 380 CE. From there it grew to all corners of the Earth. The beginnings of Rome's acceptance of Christianity occurred in 305. In that year, Rome became so badly split that Diocletian abdicated as emperor. After several years of internal conflict, the two most likely successors for the throne in the West were Constantine who was in the field, and Maxentius who was in Rome. As often happened in those days, the two contestants rounded up their loyal followers and prepared to come to battle. When Constantine approached Rome for the decisive battle, he found that he was greatly outnumbered by Maxentius. In addition, Maxentius had a strong defensive position and was supported by the Praetorian Guard who had always picked the winning side.

According to later testimony, on the 27th of October in 312, Constantine had a dream. He was shown a sign which was the combination of the Greek letters *Chi* and *Rho*. These are the first two letters of the name "Christ" in Greek and had been adapted in monogram form by the persecuted Christians in Greece. In Constantine's dream, the Latin words, "*Hoc signo victoreris*" appeared beneath the Greek monogram. These words mean, "By this sign you shall be victor." At dawn, Constantine ordered the sign to be painted on every soldier's shield, and the soldiers were challenged with, "By this sign, you will be victorious." Against overwhelming odds and against a very strong defensive position, on the 28th of October the soldiers of Constantine were victorious at a battle which was later to change the world, the Battle of Milvian Bridge.

After the battle, Constantine accepted Christ, and gave Christ credit for all of his triumphs. In just this manner, the alliance between the Throne and the Altar was forged. Although this alliance was rather startling at the time, within only a few years it was considered to be very standard Christianity. But this standard Christianity was not won without a price. As Williston Walker commented, "In winning freedom from its enemies, it [the Christian Church] had come largely under the control of the occupant of the Roman imperial throne. A fateful union with the state had begun."[8]

As will be seen in the discussions of the Ecumenical Councils, Constantine did exert considerable control over the Alter; and so did those who occupied the Throne after him. In modern-day terms, Constantine could hardly be considered as much of a Christian. As an example, he never relinquished his title *Pontifex Maximus.* This was the title given to him as the head of the state pagan cult, which was either Mithraism or Sol Invictus, two distinct but similar religions. In addition, the coinage of his reign continued to depict the Sun God [Sol Invictus]. Finally, it is reported that he personally murdered one of his own sons, had his second wife drowned, had his nephew and brother-in-law killed after he had guaranteed safe passage, etc. However, during all of this he sponsored Christianity because it had been useful to him in winning a decisive battle.[9]

In his initial activities as Emperor, Constantine had to proceed slowly in convincing his followers to follow him into Christianity, for most of them were still pagan, particularly the army and the nobility from which he drew his officials. He helped ease in to the acceptance of Christianity in two ways. First, he allowed many Mithraic [or Sol Invictus] practices to be adopted by Christianity. In so doing, he gave Christianity some of its most cherished traditions such as worshipping on Sunday, celebrating Christmas on December 25, and the European tradition of representing the Nativity scene in a cave [see Mithraism in Appendix A]. Secondly, in the Edict of Milan, he proclaimed tolerance for Christian subjects; and used this proclamation of tolerance to close certain pagan temples which were particularly offensive to Christians, such as those which were dedicated to ritual prostitution. Through this proclamation, he also frowned upon public sacrifice.

As a consequence of Constantine's pronouncement of religious freedom for all, Christians stopped meeting in secret like the mystery religion which they had been, and started to hold public worship and to build buildings dedicated to public Christian worship, an act which would have been impossible prior to Constantine. Christianity thus entered into the period of its greatest percentage growth. It was changed from a system of disparate beliefs followed by a number of individuals who believed in Jesus the Christ, to become a religion intended for use by all of the known world. As such, it had to "get its act together" by stating in no uncertain terms what it believed and by getting rid of those who did not believe likewise. To do this, it had to establish doctrines and dogma and to be tough with those who did not adhere to this defined system of beliefs. In other words, the tolerance presented to Christianity by the Edict of Milan gave way to a significant amount of intolerance which was practiced by the resulting Church and the Throne to which it had become attached. Within less than two hundred years of Christianity's being accepted as a state religion, Justinian passed a law which required baptism into Christianity as requisite for citizenship in the Empire.

And so, the Edict of Milan closed the door on the exploratory stage of Christianity and opened the door on its definition or definitive stage.

7. THE FIRST FIVE ECUMENICAL COUNCILS[4]

Christianity, and the Church within which it resides, was founded by the resurrection of Jesus Christ; but it was defined by the debates which occurred during its synods or council meetings, particularly those which have been recognized as Ecumenical Councils.

To date, the Christian Church has had twenty-one Councils which have been designated as Ecumenical [or Worldwide] Councils. It should be noted that these Councils discussed issues of varied importance and that some of them were hardly "worldwide." As a few examples, the Eleventh in 1179 CE and the Twelfth [1215] had the condemnation of the Jews for killing Jesus as one of their major goals; the Thirteenth [1245], the Fourteenth [1274] and the Fifteenth [1311] Councils all addressed mostly local political issues, many of them French; and the Seventeenth [1438] through the Nineteenth [1545] Councils accomplished little, if anything, of a "worldwide" nature. However, the Twenty-first Ecumenical Council which lasted from 1962 to 1965 and is often called Vatican II, has had such

far-reaching effects that the dust still has not settled. As a matter of
opinion, Vatican II has changed the Roman Catholic Church to such an
extent that it will never again be uniform in its worldwide practices.

In addition to a sometime lack of worldwide issues, not all of
these Councils had a worldwide attendance. As an example, the first
eight Councils were almost totally manned by Eastern representatives. The book *The Throne of Peter* [by Friedrich Gontard] states
that over 2800 bishops attended the first eight Councils, only five of
whom were from the Western Church, all of whom attended the First
Ecumenical Council only. At the second through the eighth Councils,
there were no Western bishops. Instead, there was a total of fifteen
legates from the pope, generally two or three legates at each Council
except the fifth which had no Western representation [although Peter
De Rosa in *Vicars of Christ* states that 25 Western bishops attended
the fifth Council out of a total compliment of 165 bishops]. Whether
Western bishops were present or not, it is a matter of historical record
that the pope was refused admittance to the Fifth Ecumenical
Council even though he was in Constantinople at the time. As a
consequence of all of this, it would seem that there were 100-500
times as many Eastern as Western representatives at each of the first
eight Councils. However, the West soon caught up, for there has been
no voting representation from the East at any Council held after the
eighth Council; and of course, although Protestants have had worldwide council meetings of their own, no Protestant has ever voted at
any of the twenty-one Ecumenical Councils of the Church.

If people are interested in how the Christian Church became
what it is today, they must understand what happened at the first five
Ecumenical Councils; for despite the Eastern influence, these Councils
changed the entire Church in a way that will be permanent unless
changed back by those who want to see the Church become what it
once and forever could be, possibly by a Second Reformation.

For this reason, this section will examine the first five
Ecumenical Councils using a general outline which will consist of:
[1] the historical, political and/or ecclesiastical reasons for which
the Council was called; [2] who had the real authority at the Council;
[3] what was decided at the Council; and [4] what lasting effect those
decisions have had on the Church of today.

The First Ecumenical Council [325 CE]

The Roman Empire was one which had always had the love or adoration of the Emperor as one of its reasons for coherent strength. Unlike the governments of the United States or the United Kingdom, there was rarely an organized "loyal opposition" in the Roman Empire. Consequently, when a new Emperor would assume the throne, all who wanted to be a part of the "ins" would try to be as much like him as possible. The emperor would change the fashions, the desire for certain kinds of food, and even the religion. Therefore, when the Christian, Constantine, assumed the Throne, all who wanted to be among the "ins" also became Christian, even though Christianity did not become the preferred state religion for another seventy years. In their following of Constantine, people started to accept both the monogram "Chi-Rho" and the cross as things to wear for identification.

There were many at that time who felt that the decision for Christianity on the part of so many previously pagan worshippers changed the Church in a way that was not positive, for it allowed one to become a Christian because it was "the thing to do" and not because it was a "true belief." That argument continues today. As to whether or not it had such an effect then, it is a matter of historical fact that the artists who had been making pictures of Greek Gods such as Apollo, merely changed the name under the picture to that of Christ. Paintings are still in existence in which only the symbol "Chi-Rho" identifies the portrait as that of Jesus. Otherwise it is clearly that of Apollo, or of some other handsome Greek youth. In addition, ceramic mosaics still exist which show Jesus as the Sun God riding in his chariot. In this and in many other similar ways, Jesus of Nazareth started to lose some of his Jewish humanity and started to become a more nearly idealized picture of the type of a God who would appeal to the Romans.[9]

As the "ins of Rome" started to follow Christ, they became confused about just who this Christ was. It was because of this confusion that the poetic work of Arius entitled *Thalia* [see Appendix A] received such an acceptance. The concept which Arius proposed could be readily grasped by the Romans as well as the Greeks, especially since this concept was so similar to the hierarchy of Gods with which each was familiar. Because of its simplicity and familiarity, the teachings of Arius became widely accepted as the true definition of Christianity, not only by the people, but also by many of the leaders of the Church. It was accepted so well that a virtual war of debate broke out between those who accepted Arianism and those who did not [see Appendix A]. The resulting confusion approached anarchy.

Constantine, who was now Emperor in the East as well as the West, was dismayed to find that his Empire was being torn apart by religious confusion and a theological debate. He tried to overcome the confusion caused by Arianism by sending his advisor, the Spanish bishop Hosius [or Ossius], to Alexandria asking that the debates over such a minor detail be stopped. This conciliation attempt did not work. On his journey back to Rome, Hosius attended a bishop's conference in Antioch at which he was handed a confession of faith written by Eustathius. This confession stated that the Christ was "begotten not from nonexistence but from the Father, not as made but properly an offspring" and that he lasts forever, immutable and unchanging. These words were familiar to words previously used in Eastern orthodoxy. Constantine had previously handled the Donatism issue [see Appendix A] by calling a council of bishops at which his wishes were given the weight of Church authority. He decided to try the same thing on Arianism. And so, he called a Council of the bishops of the Roman Empire to meet in 325 CE at Nicaea, a small city in Asia Minor near Nicomedia, east and slightly south of Constantinople.[10]

The Council was opened by Constantine although it is thought that Hosius presided over most of the working sessions. There were 220 bishops in attendance, only five of whom were from the Western Sees. It almost goes without saying that these bishops, all of whom previously had been persecuted by Rome, were delighted to find that they could not only travel at the expense of the Imperial court, but that they were also under Imperial protection when at the Council. Pope Silvester I did not attend, but was represented by two presbyters. The Council was held under Imperial aegis, meaning that it not only had Imperial protection, it also had Imperial sponsorship.

At this Council several decisions or declarations were made among which were: [1] the Church and the State were to be aligned with each other; [2] the teachings of Arius were to be condemned; [3] the priests of the Church were forbidden to marry after ordination although those already married could continue in wedlock and unwed priests could live with their mother, sister or aunt; [4] the date of Easter was to be universally fixed; and [5] after rejecting a creed of faith presented by the Arians, the Creed of Nicaea was declared. This Creed is similar in intent, but is not identical to the Nicene Creed which was proposed at the Second Ecumenical Council in 381 and which was finally affirmed as the belief of all assembled bishops and representatives at the Fourth Council at Chalcedon in 451. Each Creed is presented in Appendix B.

Some histories have stated that only two bishops refused to subscribe to the Creed of Nicaea; but since so little is known about the First Council except from much later reports, most historians believe that this statement is based on the later actions of these bishops rather than knowledge of their actual voting activity at the Council. In a somewhat different approach, De Rosa presents the interesting thought that the majority of the bishops present were Arians who voted for the Creed only because, in their opinion, that was the only way that they could continue to keep their position as bishop.

Constantine rejoiced at what he believed was a God-given reconciliation which would create harmony throughout his Empire, but later events showed that the accord was deceptive at best. This will be described in the section describing the Second Council.

The First Ecumenical Council did two things. First it gathered a large number of diverse people together to talk about a common problem. Some historians have reported that attendance at the First Council ranged from a country bishop driving a herd of sheep before him, to the most learned and sophisticated city bishop. Secondly, it set precedent in that the Church defined Jesus Christ as being equal to God in all ways and vowed to excommunicate anyone who did not agree that Jesus was fully divine.

The Second Ecumenical Council [381 CE]

Constantine sincerely hoped that the decisions of the Council at Nicaea would settle the theological debates within the Empire thus unifying both the Church and the Empire. Unfortunately for him, this did not happen. However, his handling of this situation after Nicaea deserves much of the blame for continuing the split and subsequently requiring the calling of the Second Ecumenical Council.

Although the Creed of Nicaea [some times referred to as the "Faith of Nicaea"] was resoundingly accepted at the first Council, many bishops later expressed doubt about it. This doubt was primarily caused by the Greek word *homoousios*, the word which is translated as "of one substance" or "consubstantial" in the English version presented in Appendix B. The meaning of this word is rather vague, for it is a non-technical term which could range all the way from meaning "exactly like" to meaning "similar to." Consequently, some leaders of the Church continued to be confused, as were the people. One Church leader who had substantial doubts about the usefulness of the Creed was Eusebius of Caesarea [see Appendix A].

But Constantine also sowed seeds of doubt in the way he handled those who were admitted Arians. One striking example is how Constantine handled Eusebius of Nicomedia. First, Constantine exiled him as an Arian, then later recalled him and proclaimed him bishop of the Imperial capital and ecclesiastical advisor to the Emperor. This is the same Eusebius who brought charges against Athanasius and against Eustathius, both of whom were avid anti-Arianists. It is also the same Eusebius who baptized Constantine on his death bed in 337.

As a consequence of all of this, although the anti-Arians had won at Nicaea, many of their strong spokesmen were silenced in the subsequent twelve years and Arianism continued to split the Empire. The debate continued to rage around the concept of "was the Son identical to Father." Depending on which of Constantine's three sons was in the most power at the time, bishops were exiled or forgiven depending on their position in the debate. Specific examples of Church leaders who were exiled at one time and praised at another were Athanasius, Marcellus of Ancrya and Eusebius of Vercelli [see Appendix A]. In the meantime, the politically competent Arianist, Eusebius of Nicomedia, was made bishop of Constantinople in 339 and thus was, in effect, the leader of the Eastern bishops, most of whom had voted as anti-Arianists in the First Council.

Each of the three sons of Constantine tried at various times to find a middle road to the schism, but no one could readily come up with a formula which would combine the Eastern need for three *hypostases* [technically three substances] with the Creed's statement of one substance [the non-technical Greek term *ousia*].

After the death of Constantine's final son, his cousin, Julian, became sole ruler. Julian was dedicated to the revival of the pagan religions in Rome. As a consequence, he forgave all bishops, whatever their belief about the nature of Christ, in the hope that as they continued their debate, there would never be a united Christianity to oppose the return of paganism in Rome. However, Julian's reign was short as was the reign of Jovian who followed him. In the meantime, a new generation of anti-Arian Church leaders had been developed. These leaders, later designated the "Cappadocian Fathers," were Basil the Great of Caesarea, Gregory of Nazianzus, and Basil's younger brother, Gregory of Nyssa. These leaders continued to fight the battle against Arianism which also had a new wrinkle; for among the former Arians who now admitted the divinity of the Son, there were several [called the "Spirit-fighters" or the "Macedonians"] who denied the divinity of the Holy Spirit.

The work of the Cappadocian Fathers finally bore fruit when Theodosius, a Spanish soldier and administrator, became Emperor in the East in 379 AD, the year of Basil's death. Theodosius I [also called "the Great"] was really the first Emperor who actively fought the Arians. As Jerome later said about this period, "The whole world groaned in astonishment at finding itself Arian."

Theodosius summoned a council of Eastern bishops to meet in Constantinople in 381 CE. This council, now generally recognized as the Second Ecumenical Council, was attended by 150 bishops from the Eastern Sees. Pope Damasus was not in attendance, and no other bishops, legates or other representatives from the West were present. This Council, like all of the early Councils, was held under Imperial protection and sponsorship.

Along with a number of local political and church administrative matters which were decided, the second Council made three important decisions or declarations as follows: [1] the Deity of the Holy Spirit was affirmed against the Macedonians; [2] the bishop of Constantinople was affirmed as having the "primacy of honor" after the Bishop of Rome primarily because Constantinople was known as the "new Rome"; and [3] the Nicene Creed was proposed. Although the Nicene Creed was not officially affirmed for the entire Church until the Fourth Ecumenical Council, it was used informally and frequently during the subsequent 70 years as a mechanism to fight Arianism and other heretical movements. Its use showed that the Second Ecumenical Council was a triumph of Nicene orthodoxy over all other movements. The Nicene Creed became the basis for many of the ultimate doctrines and dogmas of the Christian Church. It is a part of today's Church. The complete Nicene Creed is presented in Appendix B.

Although the second Council could be called a success in that it defined the Christ and started a definition of what is now called the Trinity, it also caused a tremendous political problem for the Church with its definition of the standing of the bishop of Constantinople. This definition flew in the face of Rome and Alexandria being the "senior" churches. It also angered the Romans who believed that the "honor" of a church or a See depended on the closeness of that church to Peter rather than on the political clout of the city in which it was located. And finally, it angered the Christians in Alexandria because the patriarch of the Eastern Church would now be in Constantinople rather than in Alexandria. In retrospect, it was a politically motivated, unilateral decision. In this way it was like many of the decisions of the first five Ecumenical Councils.

The Third Ecumenical Council [431 CE]

In 378 CE, slightly before the Second Ecumenical Council was held, the battle of Adrianople marked the beginning of the end of the Roman Empire. Theodosius delayed the inevitable with bribes, but after his death in 395, the Empire continued into its decline. During the next fifty years, the power of Rome was destroyed in Britain, Gaul, Spain and North Africa. Even in Italy the power of the Emperor was made subservient to the power of the generals. At the same time, the power of the papacy continued to grow.

However, both in the East and in the West the Emperors held on to the ability to call Imperial councils to settle theological disputes. In fact, the first general council called by a pope was the Ninth

Ecumenical Council in 1123. Prior to that, all councils were called by the Emperor. It is very interesting to note that although the Emperor of the Roman Empire had lost political and governmental powers, he retained tremendous power over the activities of the Church. It is almost as if he had substituted the Altar for the Throne.

By the early part of the fifth century, the dispute between Nestorius and Cyril had assumed such proportions that Emperors Valentinian III in the West and Theodosius II in the East summoned a council to meet at Ephesus, a city in Asia Minor near the southwest coast of present-day Turkey. This council has become known as the Third Ecumenical Council. It was conducted under the aegis of Theodosius II and was attended by 190 bishops, all Eastern. Pope Celestine I was represented by three legates. Augustine was invited, but died prior to the Council's opening. The politics of this Council make it one of the most interesting of the early Councils.

Cyril and his followers arrived in time for the opening date as did Nestorius. However, the followers of Nestorius were delayed. Cyril insisted that the Council be opened. It was, although Nestorius refused to attend. In a one day meeting, Nestorianism was condemned, Nestorius was deposed and the Creed of Nicaea as interpreted by Cyril was affirmed.

However, a few days later, the supporters of Nestorius arrived, met in assembly and condemned Cyril and his followers.

Finally, the delegates of Pope Celestine arrived, sided with the supporters of Cyril, and further deposed John of Antioch and condemned Pelagianism. All of this so confused Theodosius II that he interned leaders of both sides until he could sort things out. Since the aggressive diplomacy of Cyril coincided with his own sympathies, the final result was that Nestorius and his followers were condemned and Mary was proclaimed as the Mother of God. In return for the condemnation of Nestorius, Cyril was requested to assent to a modification in the words used to confess the nature of Jesus Christ.

There were three major results from the Third Council which impact on the Church today. The first is the definite understanding that the results of this Council were due to a compromise of extreme viewpoints, and that diplomacy and political acumen were more important in winning the debate than theological purity. Although this can be seen between the lines of all the Councils, it is most readily apparent in this one. The second result led to the veneration of Mary as the Mother of God, a result which has had tremendous influence in the direction taken by several parts of the Christian Church. The third major point was that the definition of the nature of Christ established in this Council did not last. One major result of the Third Ecumenical Council, therefore, was that it led directly to the Fourth Ecumenical Council.

The Fourth Ecumenical Council [451 CE]

In 433 CE, two years after the ending of the Third Ecumenical Council, John of Antioch presented a document entitled *Formula for Reunion* which proposed a "reunion of all" by accepting the term *theotokos* [God-bearer] for Mary and explaining that Christ is "complete God and complete human being" but also that a complete "union of two natures has occurred as a consequence of which we confess...one Son." This proposal completely doomed the Nestorians. Cyril enthusiastically accepted this proposal, even though it seemed to contradict some of his earlier thoughts, many of which had been clearly Monophysitic [see Appendix A]. It seemed as if the *Formula for Reunion* might bring lasting peace. However, this peace was short-lived. Within ten years, everyone was declaring that the other side had reneged on the deal and was reverting to their old stands. The controversy with Eutyches [see Appendix A] became a part of this dispute. In addition, Pope Leo I caused the new debate to grow when he presented his *Tome*, which some interpreted as being little better than sheer Nestorianism.

Because of all of this, Leo petitioned the Emperor to call a new council to be held in Italy. While this was being considered, Emperor Theodosius died accidentally, and the throne passed to his sister, Pulcheria, and her husband, Marcion. These new sovereigns denied Leo's request, but then called a council of their own to be held in Chalcedon, a city near Constantinople. This council is now known as the Fourth Ecumenical Council.

The Council was attended by 350-600 bishops, all Eastern. Pope Leo was represented by five legates. The Council granted peace to all who accepted the *Formula of Reason*, "canonized" both the

Second Letter of Cyril to Nestorius and the Letter of Cyril which had accepted the *Formula of Reason* [although as described in the next section, neither Letter was ever officially placed in the Bible], accepted Leo's T*ome* as defining the faith against Eutyches, and, at the insistence of the Imperial court, presented and affirmed as a Church declaration the "Definition" of the Council of Chalcedon [see "Monophysitism" in Appendix A for a review of the "Definition" and Appendix B for the complete "Definition"].

The Fourth Council is a vitally important one for the subsequent Christian Church for two major reasons. First, it "defined" Jesus the Christ in a way which has been accepted as orthodox belief ever since. Secondly, since it now became normal practice for the Council's decrees to become Imperial law, the "Definition" of Chalcedon became the law of the land. This law offended many Eastern Churches which simply could not accept the two natures of Christ which the "Definition" demanded. As a consequence of this offense, many Eastern Churches, particularly those in the Mid-East and Egypt, declared themselves to be Monophysitic [i.e. "one-nature"] Churches; and the orthodox [i.e. "two-nature"] Eastern Church became concentrated primarily in Greece [and later Russia] rather than in Asia Minor as it had been since the missionary work of the Apostle Paul.

With the closing of the Fourth Council and its "Definition," the Christological Controversies left the center stage. Although arguments about the definition of the Trinity continued for almost another 200 years [see *Christianity and the New Age Religion*], and although Monothelitism, the belief that Jesus Christ had only one will, had a brief introduction in the seventh century, the definition of Jesus the Christ which was accepted as being orthodox has not changed. This "Definition" made many people into Saints and many others into heretics. All had originally been devout in their beliefs. The "Definition" remains with us today, as does rejection by the sectarian Christian Churches for those who choose not to accept it. Indeed, the results of the Fourth Council, even those results dictated by the Imperial court, are still with us today. Additional information on the ancillary activities of the Fourth Ecumenical Council is presented in Appendix A under the heading "Monophysitism."

The Fifth Ecumenical Council [553 CE]

Although the Fourth Ecumenical Council was a very political Council, the Fifth Ecumenical Council was probably the most political of any of the early Councils. It was called by Emperor Justinian and no western bishops or legates attended. Pope Vigilius did not attend even though he was in Constantinople at the time.

The political struggles leading up to the Fifth Ecumenical Council were instigated by the controversies generated by the "Definition of Chalcedon" from the Fourth Council. The politician who wanted to settle the controversy was Emperor Justinian. The conflicts which preceded the calling of the Council and the role played by Justinian in trying to settle these conflicts are outlined as follows:

1. As mentioned in Appendix A, Justinian's political ambitions were always driven by a desire of unity within the Empire. One very strong political ambition was to reunite the Roman Empire by re-conquering the West. He partially succeeded in this goal, but bankrupted the Byzantine Empire in so doing. As a part of this grand plan, he wanted a single unified confession of faith for the five great Christian patriarchates of the Eastern and the Western branches at that time: Rome, Constantinople, Alexandria, Antioch and Jerusalem. The division of the Church into its Eastern and Western branches at this time is presented in Map 7 on page 92.

Justinian intended that the previous four Ecumenical Councils be the basis for his unifying confession. In particular, he wanted the Definition of Chalcedon, as interpreted by Cyril of Alexandria, to be the mechanism for bringing all into the fold. To accomplish this, he created comprises with the Monophysites. Some of these compromises included one which outlawed paganism and another which required that all the citizens in his kingdom be baptized as Christians in order to retain their citizenship.

2. In further attempts at unity, Justinian continued to make additional compromises with the Monophysites. As examples, he pardoned exiled leaders of that faith and tried to persuade them that "One of the Trinity suffered in the flesh" did not in any way reduce the divinity of Jesus the Christ. Such an appeasement to the Monophysites angered Pope Agapetus I who protested to Justinian.

When the Monophysites still refused to accept the Definition of Chalcedon, Justinian published a definition of his own which declared that Christ is the divine Word who assumed human nature and endured suffering in that nature.

3. When this definition of Justinian's did not create unity but in fact exacerbated the schism between the Chalcedonians [i.e. those who accepted the Definition of Chalcedon] and the Monophysites, Justinian recanted his definition and went back to pushing the concept of "accepting the decisions of the first four Ecumenical Councils." In order to placate the Chalcedonians who felt that Justinian had deserted them in his attempts to placate the Monophysites, in 543 CE Justinian followed their desires and established numerous anathemas which condemned the writings of Origen [see Appendix C]. This happened some 300 years after the death of Origen.

4. Then, in 544 CE in an attempt to woo back the Monophysites, Justinian condemned the "Three Chapters" [see Appendix A] by inferring that these Chalcedonian writers were really Nestorians in disguise. Since two of the writers of the "Three Chapters" had been declared orthodox at the Fourth Ecumenical Council, this stand was a perilous one for it could have meant that Justinian was questioning the decisions of the Fourth Council. However, with his usual political skill, Justinian pulled it off.

5. Despite these political skills, Justinian did not win back the Monophysites. In fact, this ploy backfired on him by alienating the Western leaders against his "neo-Chalcedonian" policies such as his selection of the interpretation placed on the "Definition" by Cyril of Alexandria. This placed Justinian at odds with Pope Vigilius.

6. Therefore, Justinian's attempts to foster unity only created greater disunity. In response, Justinian did what every good Emperor would do in a similar situation. He called a Council. This Council met in Constantinople in 553. It is now known as the Fifth Ecumenical Council. Because it is a Council which has been greatly misunderstood, the details of this Council are presented in Appendix C.

As a summary, the Fifth Ecumenical Council made three decisions. Its first decision was to reject Nestorianism by defining the unity of Christ in two distinct natures. By so doing, it not only rejected Nestorianism, it rejected all Monophysitism. The Monophysites reacted by forming their own separate churches in Syria, Egypt, Armenia, Ethiopia and Persia. Later, this movement spread throughout the far East. The second decision was to condemn the "Three Chapters" thus excommunicating three writers who had previously been considered as very devout and orthodox Christian teachers in Antioch. The final decision was to reiterate the condemnation of Origenism which had been having a revival in Palestine, the original home of Christianity. In so doing, the Council justified some of the action taken by Justinian who had condemned the writings of Origen nine years earlier. However, at the Council, only the Christological writings of Origen and the Origenistic monks were condemned [see Appendix C]. Nothing relating to Origen's writings about the soul and its preexistence was officially condemned by the Council.[11]

The "Three Chapters" controversy has not had a lasting effect on the mainstream Christian Church, although the conscience of any spiritually oriented organization should be offended by such a blatantly political move. In truth, neither of the other results has had much of a lasting effect either, although misunderstandings about what was done at the Council regarding Origen's thoughts on the preexistence of the soul have had quite an effect. Again, as documented in Appendix C it would seem that the Fifth Ecumenical Council did nothing regarding Origen's thoughts on the soul; and therefore, it would seem that the Church has never taken any such action on an official basis.

Summary

These five Ecumenical Councils represent major steps which occurred during the "definition" stage of the Church's development. Their activities need to be understood, for it was these Councils that defined many of the doctrines and the dogmas taught by the Christian Church of today. Many of these doctrines are concerned with Christology [or "who was Jesus Christ"]. By the time of the Fourth Ecumenical Council, the Council at Chalcedon in 451, it had been decided that Jesus was: [1] divine in the sense that he was equal in all ways to the divinity of God; [2] human in his incarnation in the sense that he was not unlike us in any way; [3] different than God by more than just name; [4] in possession of two natures, not just one and not with one nature merely being an extension of the other; [5] in possession of only one person, not two even though that one person had two natures; [6] and on and on. With this to work on, and with the insistence on the part of the Imperial court that the Council at Chalcedon define Christ once and for all, the Council adopted a formula usually referred to as the "Definition" of the Council of Chalcedon. To satisfy Cyril's desires on the unity of the Christ, this Definition affirmed that Christ was "one and the same Son...complete in his deity and complete...in his humanity"; but to satisfy those who had been winning the recent debates, he was also said to exist in two natures which are at once unconfused and unaltered [against Eutyches] and on the other hand are undivided and inseparable [against Nestorius]. As another way of saying some of this, the decree said that " Christ was acknowledged in two natures without being mixed, transmitted, divided or separated." With this "Definition," the great Christology debates became history, although there was an additional flare-up concerning the "will" of Christ which had to be settled at the Sixth Ecumenical Council. In that Council it was decided that Jesus Christ had two wills.

Although it is important to examine the historical records to understand what was decided at these Councils, it is also important to examine the records to understand what was not decided as an official action even though some may have thought that it was. Origen's thoughts about the soul at the Fifth Ecumenical Council are such a case, for the official historical records say nothing about this. But it is of possibly even greater importance to understand what is missing from those historical records; for with the exception of what the Councils were against as outlined above, today there is no way to know what other doctrines or dogmas might have been proposed, how close they might have come to being accepted, and how much closer they might have been to the original teachings of Jesus Christ than those which were actually voted upon. That is something for the thoughtful Christian to ponder.

And with this summary of the first five Ecumenical Councils, we will leave them to examine some other conflicts within the Church. An analysis of the effect which these Councils had on the practicing Christians of that time will be presented in *Book Two*.

8. CONFLICTS WHICH CREATED SCHISMS
WITHIN THE CHURCH[4]

A lthough the conflicts between Christianity and the heretical movements presented in Appendix A were intense, the internecine conflicts which occurred within the Church were equally intense. The petty jealousies, the fighting for position, the intolerance for another's viewpoint and the acrimony created between geographical branches of the same faith are almost too much to comprehend. It is almost as if the meaning of Christ was lost in the fight to show who loved him the most and defined him the best. The final schism which occurred between the Eastern and Western branches of this Church supposedly based on love, was the great schism of 1054 during which the Pope excommunicated the Patriarch and the Patriarch retaliated by excommunicating the Pope. These excommunications were not lifted until 1965, over 900 years later.

But the great schism of 1054 was not an isolated case. It was merely the culmination of a series of smaller separations which had torn the Church apart during the preceding 1,000 years. This short section will outline a few of those conflicts.

In 251 CE, the Noviatian schism at Rome was caused by jurisdictional matters such as who could properly forgive apostates. This schism festered for over 50 years until it finally came to a head in the fight against Donatism. This fight created a great schism between the Church in Rome and the North African Churches as described in the section on Donatism in Appendix A. Partially as a result of this schism, North Africa was an easy target for Islam some 400 years later.

In the early fifth century, a schism developed within the Western Church which involved the question of whether faith is caused by divine grace or by human freedom. This issue considered whether the free will of man had any place in generating faith. Pelagius believed that it did; Augustine believed that it did not. The fight against Pelagianism is described in Appendix A. The determination as to whether or not man can use his own free will to diagram the destiny of his life still creates a separation within the Church of today.

The schisms within the Church caused by the "big three"

controversies of Gnosticism, Arianism, and Nestorianism have been adequately described in Appendix A. This Chapter will merely reiterate that these controversies not only created conflicts with that which was defined as heretical, they also created conflicts within orthodoxy, often related to what particular person or specific argument or geographical area would have its orthodox approach accepted as the resolution to the conflict. In other words, ego rather than spirit often led the way.

The major schism of 1054 was based primarily on jurisdictional and territorial prerogatives rather than doctrinaire issues such as those covered by the controversies mentioned above. It all started considerably earlier with the move of the seat of the Roman Empire from Rome to "New Rome" which later became known as Constantinople. During the early part of the fourth century, the Church had three bishops whose power was roughly equal based on the political influence of the cities in which they ruled: Alexandria, Antioch and Rome. At the Second Ecumenical Council in 381, the bishop of Constantinople was declared as second only to the bishop of Rome. Later, the influx of Islam to Alexandria and Antioch reduced those Christian Sees to the minor category. In the meantime, the calmness of theological debates in the West versus the intensity of the fights in the East strengthened the position of the popes who made increasingly stronger claims to preeminence, a direction which was never accepted in the East. Consequently, any time the East had theological troubles and the pope tried to abdicate or adjudicate the differences, the interference was resented by the East. Conversely, any time that a pope would try to condescend to the Patriarch or the Emperor in the East, it would anger the West. An example of this would be when the conciliatory gestures of Pope Vigilius toward Justinian created jealousies in the West that raged on until about 700 CE, some 150 years after the death of Vigilius.

An additional reason for the conflicts between the East and the West was the theological base upon which each rested. The Eastern theology had its roots in Greek philosophy; whereas the Western theology had its roots in Roman law. Because of this differing basis, the East believed that the Holy Spirit came from the Father; whereas the West stated that the Holy Spirit proceeded from the Father and the Son, and declared this as a theological fact without ever having consulted with the East. The importance of the Eastern viewpoint is presented in *Book Two*, for that viewpoint makes the Holy Spirit available to everyone whether they believe Jesus is as fully divine as the Father or not.

A further reason for conflict was the Eastern resentment of the Roman enforcement of clerical celibacy and the use of unleavened bread in the Eucharist. Finally, there were the political needs of the East which were never acknowledged by the West. For almost 300 years the patriarchs and the Emperors of the East tried to bring the Monophysites back into the fold of the mainstream Church for if they did not, then the Eastern territories of Syria and Egypt would be lost to the Church. The West never accepted the East's need to do this. They constantly admonished the East to excommunicate anyone who did not accept the Definition of Chalcedon. Attempts by the East to interpret the Definition in a politically acceptable manner such as those of Cyril of Alexandria, were constantly rejected by the West. One such rejection led to the "Acacian" schism which lasted until Emperor Justin restored the Definition of Chalcedon in the East in 519 CE. But this did not stop the East from trying to win back the Monophysites.

The final attempt by the East to win back the Monophysites was a formula proposed by the Chalcedonians under the influence of Emperor Heraclius in the middle seventh century. This formula, called Monothelitism, proposed that Christ had two natures but only one will. This proposal not only did not win back any Monophysites, it was immediately declared heretical by the West. The attempt to change the West's mind about Monothelitism lead to a martyr pope, Martin, who was imprisoned and tortured by the Byzantines because he refused to follow the theological directives laid down by Emperor Heraclius. Martin later died in exile in the Crimea. This obviously did not make the West love the Eastern Church. But in defense of the East, it should be noted that this happened at the same time that the Eastern Church was fighting for its life, first against Persia and later against the Islamic campaigns to subjugate unbelievers by conquest.

Later, Pope Honorius supported Monothelitism. However, when Monothelitism was condemned at the Sixth Ecumenical

Council at Constantinople in 680 CE attended solely by Eastern bishops, the Council also condemned Pope Honorius. This, of course, alienated the West which felt that such a condemnation was an attempt to limit papal prerogatives. Partially as a result of this "insult," the West refused to grant Ecumenical status to a Council held at Constantinople in 692. This decision by the West alienated the Greek Church which had won some major points at that particular Council.

In the eighth century, the East got involved in the iconoclastic struggle. This struggle was based on the Emperor's decision that icons and other sacred images were to be destroyed. The West objected to this, for they considered the holy pictures to be devotional aids. At the Seventh Ecumenical Council in 787, icons were declared to be all right. However, because this struggle had been based on an Emperor's decision and the Emperor was in the East, the West started to look for Imperial protection of its own. This search led to the Franks [i.e. the Germans along the Rhine] who agreed to look after the interests of the Western Church. This, in turn, led to the papal coronation of Charlemagne as the Holy Roman Emperor at Rome on Christmas Day, 800 CE. The Holy Roman Empire lasted until 1806. During that millennium, the Western Church could declare to the Eastern Church, "We have an Emperor of our own!"

After the iconoclastic struggle was fully settled in about 843, the complicated Photian schism brought another break. At the same time, Rome expressed resentment that the Greeks were carrying Eastern practices into the Balkans which Rome considered to be its territory. The real issue in all of this controversy was that of whether or not Rome could call the shots for jurisdiction over all of the Church [believed by both Pope Nicholas and Adrien], or whether Rome was merely the senior of five semi-independent patriarchs [believed by Photius and the Greeks] and thus had no right to interfere in the internal affairs of another patriarch.

Although the Photian schism settled down, it generated seeds of distrust which exploded 200 years later when Rome forced Latin religious customs on the Greek communities in southern Italy. The Patriarch retaliated to this "insult" by closing down the Latin Churches in Constantinople. The Pope retaliated to this 'insult" by sending a Cardinal to Constantinople who laid a bull of excommunication on

the altar of the great church, Hagia Sophia. This bull excommunicated the Patriarch and not only condemned the Greek doctrine of
the Holy Spirit [i.e. from the Father and not from the Father and the
Son], but also condemned the Greek practices of having married
priests and of using leavened bread for the Eucharist. Following this
"insult," the Patriarch issued a bull excommunicating the Pope.
Although the excommunications were nullified in 1965, the breach
between the two great branches of the Christian Church has never
been healed.

And thus, a Church which was supposedly founded on love,
found itself making war and not love. It is indeed sad to realize that
internecine intolerance has run rampant within the Church whose
belief system supposedly was based on the most tolerant entity ever
to walk the face of this Earth—on the person of Jesus the Christ.

9. THE ESTABLISHMENT OF A CANONICAL BIBLE[4]

The major steps in establishing the canonical Bible [i.e. the standard book by which Christianity would be measured] were
presented in Section 2. Those steps will not be repeated here. Instead
a summary of that section will be presented and then the chronological
steps and debates which finally led to the establishment of the New
Testament will be presented in somewhat greater detail.

The summary of the information presented earlier would state
that the canon of the Old Testament was officially established by
Judaism for two reasons: [1] because the Jewish people had been
forced out of Jerusalem as a result of the Jewish Rebellion of 66-70
CE and the dispersed people needed a reference to their faith to take
with them; and [2] because Christianity had been misquoting
Judaism to the advantage of the followers of Christ by mistranslating
certain Hebraic or Aramaic words. In respect to the canon of the
New Testament, the information presented earlier would say that it
took almost 1600 years before the New Testament was fully and
officially accepted by the Christian Church.

This particular section will not cover the full time span
previously presented. Instead, it will cover only the debates and
controversy over the New Testament canon which occurred between
about 170 CE [our earliest original document which presents a canonical

list] and 367 CE when the traditional canon was unofficially accepted by the majority of the Church. In this way it will be rather easy to see what kind of controversy there was in establishing what the present Church likes to call "God's inspired word."

The New Testament presently consists of 27 books. These are the residue from many writings of the first and second centuries which the people of the Church have at various times considered sacred. Some of the omitted writings will be described in Section 10.

There would have been no canon established unless the Church undertook the task of establishing it. To establish the canon, the Church used certain selection criteria which were: [1] that the list of the books which would be accepted as canon by the Church would be limited; [2] that the canon had to be in writing because the oral tradition was becoming distorted after about two generations; [3] that the books had to be written by or at least sponsored by an Apostle; [4] and that the book had to be recognizably orthodox in its content and publicly used by a prominent church or a majority of churches. This latter point was stressed by both Origen and Jerome who believed that it would be impudent to base theological affirmations on books having less than universal recognition or sponsorship.

In the early 1700s, an Italian publisher named Lodovica Antonio Muratori discovered a list of writings now known as the Muratorian Canon. It was a crude 8th century manuscript which had been copied from a Greek list written in Rome in about 170 CE. The canonical books presented on this list include the four gospels, thirteen letters of Paul, Acts, two letters of John, Jude, the Revelation of John, the Wisdom of Solomon and the Revelation of Peter. The Letter to the Hebrews was not included. This is the first known listing of canonical books.

In the late second century, Irenaeus insisted that there be only four gospels. By this insistence, the well-known *Gospel of Thomas* and *Gospel of Peter* were excluded, as were the lesser known *Gospel of the Hebrews, Gospel of the Egyptians, Gospel of James, Gospel of Mattheus, Gospel of Truth* and *Gospel of Mary* [see Section 10]. In addition, Irenaeus did not acknowledge the authority of 2 John, 3 John, James or 2 Peter, all of which were later accepted as canon.

By the early third century, the list was further refined. The

Wisdom of Solomon and the *Revelation of Peter* were excluded as was the *Secret Book of James* and the *Dialogue of the Savior*, each of which was probably of Gnostic origin. At this time, the Letter to the Hebrews was loved in the East but rejected by the West; whereas the Revelation of John was rejected by the East but desired by the West.

By the beginning of the fourth century, Eusebius of Caesarea summed up the situation by stating that the only books still in dispute were James, 2 Peter, 3 John and Jude since these were "spoken against" by some but supported by many. However, Hebrews was still rejected by the West because of the doubts about authorship; and the Revelation of John still confused many in the East, especially Eusebius.

Based on a proposal and erudite arguments by Athanasius in an Easter letter delivered within his See in 367 CE, the Eastern Church finally reached a consensus by accepting as canon the 27 books which presently comprise the New Testament. They also recommended that new converts read the *Didache,* the *Shepherd of Hermas, 1 Clement* and *The Letter of Barnabas.* These were books which up until then had been highly regarded, and believed by many to be Scripture. Later, the Eastern Church rejected the Revelation of John and demoted the general letters, but restored all of them to the canon by the end of the seventh century although the Greek bishops continued to grumble about the Revelation of John.

In the meantime, the West, also following the proposal presented by Athanasius, had accepted Hebrews based on its attractive contents and the belief that it had been written by Paul [since disproved]. Consequently, although not officially accepted until the sixteenth century, the canon of the present New Testament was fairly well established by 367 CE. This canon is the one which had been proposed by Athanasius and which Jerome used for his translation into the Vulgate Bible.

The interesting part of this short history on the establishment of the New Testament canon is that many books which had been considered for many years as being sacred Scripture by many people were not included. Some examples of this would be the two *Letters of Clement*, the *Didache*, the *Shepherd of Hermas* and the *Letter of Barnabas*, all of which had been considered sacred Scripture for over

250 years. In addition, the Letters of Cyril which were later canonized by an official Church body at the Fourth Ecumenical Council at Chalcedon in 431 CE were never admitted into the New Testament canon. *All of these were rejected because they were not written by or sponsored by an Apostle.* This fact becomes even more interesting when modern scholarship has concluded that *none of the Gospels or The Acts of the Apostles was written by or sponsored by an Apostle; and neither were the Letters of John, the Revelation of John, or The Letter to the Hebrews.* And although Paul considered himself to be an Apostle, he was not one in the sense of having been with the Christ and spoken with the Christ when the Christ was in flesh. Consequently, in the strict sense of the word, only James and the Letters of Peter would today pass muster as Apostle-related books of the canon. However, the early Church used the "Apostle-related" criteria because they felt that since the Church had been established based upon the *preaching* of the ones they considered to be Apostles, then it should be grown based solely on the *writings* of those same Apostles.

As an additional point of interest, the *Gospel of Thomas* was rejected even though modern scholarship [i.e. the Jesus Seminar] attributes as many authentic sayings of Jesus to this Gospel as to any of the four Gospels which were chosen as canon.[12] Thomas was an Apostle, and although no one knows whether he actually wrote the Gospel or merely had it attributed to him, that should not detract from its comparative validity; for again, no one knows for certain who really wrote the four chosen Gospels anyway.

Finally, although it is Protestant orthodoxy that the authority of the Bible is generated by the inspiration of the Holy Spirit, the early Church declared that none of the canon was selected based on "inspiration." Instead, the canon was chosen based on supplying the needs of the Church. In other words, although inspiration was thought to affect the writings of many sacred works, and these sacred works justified the need for the existence of a Church, the Church did not utilize the inspiration of the Holy Spirit to choose its canon.

It is therefore a fact of history that over a 1600 year period, the Church decided that what was canon was based solely on what the Church said was canon. That is a fact of history, whether Christians like to hear it or not.

10. BOOKS WHICH WERE
OMITTED FROM THE CANON[4]

Several books and other writings which had been considered as sacred Scripture for many hundreds of years were not included in the canon of the Bible. Although the specific reasons for exclusion have been lost in the dustbins of history, it is believed that some otherwise worthy works were eliminated solely because they were admired by sects which had been declared heretical. Based on modern critical scholarship, some of these writings are now considered to present the thoughts and teachings of Jesus Christ in a manner which is at least equivalent to those books which were chosen.

This Chapter will try to address, in a very concise manner, what a few of those works said. The list which follows is in no way a complete one, but these works may give a feeling as to the selection process which the early Church Fathers went through when they selected a final canon.

1 Clement was originally titled *Letter to the Church at Corinth*. It was written by Clement I, Bishop of Rome, in about 96 CE and, along with *2 Clement,* was considered to be Scripture for over 300 years. This Letter was concerned with a dispute in which the younger members of the church had deposed older men from the ministry. Clement proposed that the orders of the ministry were established by the Apostles and thus were the word of God which could not be overturned by man. The Letter established the orders of the ministry [bishops, priests, deacons] and supported the Apostolic succession in which the bishops would represent a direct, unbroken line of succession from the Apostles.

2 Clement was a sermon rather than a letter. It emphasized the high teaching of Christ and suggested that the seal of Baptism would be best preserved by maintaining the purity of the flesh in anticipation of the bodily resurrection. It also listed the Apostolic Fathers whose works fit in to the Apostolic Tradition.

Didache [Teaching of the Lord to the Nations by the Twelve Apostles] is probably one of the first of the Christian Church orders. The *Didache* [a word which means "teaching" in Greek] was probably written in the early second century in Egypt or Syria. In sixteen short chapters it deals with morals, ethics, church practice [Baptism, fasting, prayer, the Eucharist and the like] and the hope for the Second Coming of Christ. It is not a coherent or unified work, but instead is a series of regulations which had become almost law by use in many scattered churches. It was assembled by an unknown author and was considered canonical by many of the early Church Fathers.

Shepherd of Hermas was considered to be one of the most sacred books of the second through the fourth centuries, particularly in the Eastern Church. The author, Hermas, was thought to be a Christian slave who was given his freedom, became wealthy, lost his property and did penance for his past sins. He was also thought to have been a brother of Pope Pius I [died in 155 CE]. The book records five visions experienced by Hermas, including that of the angel of repentance who was the fifth vision and appeared as a shepherd, thus giving the book its title. The work also contains twelve moral commandments and ten parables. The basic theme is that post-baptismal sin can be forgiven at least once and that a day of repentance is coming after which sins cannot be forgiven. The work was regarded as Scripture by Irenaeus, Clement of Alexandria, Origen and Tertullian; but Jerome stated that it was little known in the Western Church during his time. It was denied participation in the canon, possibly because its author was known not to have been an Apostle.

Gospel of Thomas is a collection of sayings purported to be the words of the risen Christ, the living Lord. A complete copy was discovered in 1945 at Nag Hammadi. It was originally thought to have first appeared in a Gnostic manuscript covering the teachings of Valentinus, a Gnostic teacher in Alexandria of the early second century. It also appeared in Greek manuscripts of the middle second century. The Church Fathers in the second to the fourth centuries warned that it was heretical. Recent evidence has presented the thought that it was a much earlier document, dating from the last quarter of the first century or about the time of the Gospels of Matthew and Luke. It has been voted by modern scholars as containing a truly amazing collection of the sayings of Jesus Christ.[12] In addition, it presents the thought that the Apostle Thomas [a name which means "twin"] was really Judas, the brother of Jesus, who assumed the name Thomas because of the bad connotations associated with the name

Judas. In *The Secret Book of James*, a book also discovered in 1945 at Nag Hammadi, it is stated that James was the other major brother of Jesus. All of this became ignored when Jerome wrote his treatise *The Perpetual Virginity of the Blessed Mary* in which he used a complex argument to state that all the "brothers" of Jesus were really just cousins and that Mary had no children other than Jesus.[13]

Wisdom of Solomon was an Old Testament book accepted in the Roman version of the Old Testament because it identified "Wisdom" as a feminine personification of an attribute of God. She is "a breath of the power of God, and a clear effluence of the glory of the Almighty." This gave the Church Fathers a concept of the *Logos* by which they could explain the relationship of Jesus Christ to God. The book was written by a Jew in Alexandria in the first century BCE to defend Judaism by applying Hellenistic philosophical concepts to the Jewish concept of God. The book was never accepted in the Jewish canon of the Old Testament. However, copies of it were found in the Essene community at Qumran, and its inclusion in the Roman version of the Old Testament did give the early Church Fathers an historical justification for developing their concept of Christ.

Letter of Barnabas was the work of a Greek Christian writer of the middle second century who ascribed the authorship to St. Barnabas the Apostle. The actual author is unknown but refers to himself in the letter as a teacher. The Letter was a treatise on the use of the Old Testament by Christians. It claimed that the Jews could not understand the Old Testament since it could be understood only by those who could read it while looking for types or prefigurations of Jesus. It was considered scriptural in Egypt and was praised by Clement of Alexandria, but it was not thought of as highly elsewhere, and few Christians continued to read it.

Infancy Gospel of Thomas is an apocryphal gospel which may be an entirely lighthearted spoof of the infant Jesus. Nevertheless, it was written very early and could give some insight to the power of Jesus by describing a boy who had the skills to make clay pigeons and then cause them to fly; and who could merely use a word in order to slay a playmate. These miracles are no more unbelievable than the miracles which were presented in the canon.[14]

Gospel of Peter has a legendary account of the resurrection, including the statement that Jesus was seen by the guards posted outside his tomb on Easter morning bearing his cross and with his head arching high above the clouds. Because it presented the thought that the risen Christ had only the appearance of reality, it was believed by the Church Fathers to have been written by a member of the Docetist sect [see Gnosticism in Appendix A]. Later scholarship believes it to be of second century Gnostic origin which, in an attempt to convince all of the reality of the Resurrection, claimed that Roman soldiers and Jewish officials witnessed the event.[14]

Revelation [Apocalypse] of Peter is a work by an unknown author which dates from the first half of the second century CE. The author, who claimed to be Peter the Apostle, constructed a conversation between himself and Jesus regarding events at the end of the world. It tells of eternal rewards and torments. The torments, some of which get to be quite gruesome, are given credit for introducing the horrors of hell into Christian literature. This work was recognized as scripture by Clement of Alexandria. An almost complete copy of this work was discovered in 1910.

Gospel According to the Hebrews was well read and acclaimed by many. However, when Eusebius examined it in the fourth century, he judged it to be "spurious and disputed." He thus refused to accept it as canon and gave the same evaluation [and dismissal] to the *Acts of Paul* and the *Apocalypse of Peter*.

Gospel of Truth is another gospel which is probably Gnostic in origin since Irenaeus said that such a book was used by the followers of Valentinus in the second century. It presents a mystical picture of ways in which the Jewish-Christian individual can attain oneness with God.

Gospel of Mary is possibly one of the more interesting books omitted from the canon. It was the only Gospel attributed to a woman. The Mary in this case was Mary Magdalene, and her Gospel presents the teachings of a thoroughly Gnostic belief system with its ordered heavenly hierarchy [see Appendix A for the description of a typical hierarchy taught by Gnosticism]. In addition, this Gospel discloses a heated debate in early Christianity regarding the role of women in the Church, for it advocates the strong spiritual leadership of women. However, the Church, despite the openness of Jesus to women, moved decidedly to follow the dictates of society and to subordinate women, including their exclusion from leadership roles in the Church. The Gnostic belief system presented in this Gospel does not detract from the historical fact that the debate about women did occur and that the Church subsequently denied full participation to women. Although the non-Apostolic status of Mary and the Gnostic bent are the general reasons given for omitting this gospel from the canon, the desire to deny the right of women to have full participation in the Church could possibly be another reason that the power brokers of Christianity rejected the *Gospel of Mary*. The subject of women's denial by the church is covered in great detail in the outstanding book, *Eunuchs for the Kingdom of Heaven*, by Uta Ranke-Heinemann.

Gospel of Philip is considered to be a product of Valentian Gnostic teaching and consequently had no chance ever to be considered for the canon.

Gospel of Nicodemus is also considered to be a Gnostic treatise. However, it presents the rather delightful picture of Jesus battering down the gates of Hell, binding Satan in irons, and leading Adam and the patriarchs out of captivity and into heaven. This is hardly the picture that the Church Fathers were trying to paint, for they were trying to get their followers to become submissive to Christ's will and thus they had to make Christ seem to be submissive to God's will rather than being an angelic superstar.

Although there were other works which were considered to be Scripture during the formative years of the Church, these can give a feeling as to what writings interested the early Christians.

11. SUMMARY AND CONCLUSION

This Chapter has presented a summary of the activities which helped to explore and define the new religion of Christianity during the first five hundred years of its existence. The people who participated in these activities were as diverse as any group of people could be; and so were the controversies which they created. In an earlier draft of this Chapter, the biographies of the people and the descriptions of the controversies were placed in the text. This made it very difficult to focus on the continuity of the events and made the text virtually unreadable. Consequently, the people and the controversies, important as they were to the events which occurred, had to be relegated to the Appendixes. They are there for anyone who wishes to dig deeper, for their lives and conflicts do tend to add drama to the bare-boned events which have been recorded here.

The first five hundred years of the existence of the Christian Church was a period during which the Church was changed forever. It was a time when each new Pope or Patriarch tried to be more autocratic or authoritarian than his predecessor; and in becoming so generated more rules and regulations than the Emperor. It was a time when the seven deadly [or cardinal] sins were defined by Pope Gregory I as being pride, lust, envy, anger, covetousness, gluttony, and sloth; and all who were accused of one by a Church official were cut off from God's Grace. It was a time when the commission of a cardinal sin could be overcome only by performing the greatest of penances or by paying off the greatest of indulgences; and thus became a time when the sale of indulgences gladdened the heart of every Church official, for "As soon as the coin into the coffer doth ring, another soul from purgatory doth spring!" It was a time when excommunication [or "eternal damnation"] was applied for the merest of unorthodox opinions; and only rarely could such an "eternal damnation" be reversed. It was a time during which the Church was explored and defined. It was a time when *The Teachings of Christ Were Altered by Some Christians Who Followed Him.*

The activities of this period made the Church what it is today. By the end of the fifth century of the Church's existence, people were excommunicated if they were not orthodox as defined by the powers of the Church. On a more subtle basis, that is still true; and intolerance for anything not traditional or orthodox remains a pertinent part of the Church. However, I think this Chapter [plus the material in the Expanded Glossary] has given a flavor for the fact that the definition of what is orthodox was in no way a unanimous decision. The great range of what the very early Christians were allowed to believe was changed over a period of time. It is the belief of this author that this narrowing of acceptable beliefs was instituted by man and not by God. Anything instituted by man can be changed by man. That was one message from the Great Reformation, and could be a message for the Second Reformation as well.

The next Chapter will take a short digression as some of the events of the next eleven hundred years will be reported. These events happened because of the character the Church established during its first five hundred years. After that digression, we will proceed to *Book Two* which will return to the Church of the first five hundred years and show how the Church changed during that time and how the range of options for the early Christian was narrowed by orthodoxy. In essence, *Book One* has recorded the events or activities. *Book Two* will generate an understanding of the effect which these events have had on the Christian in his Church, an effect which continues today.

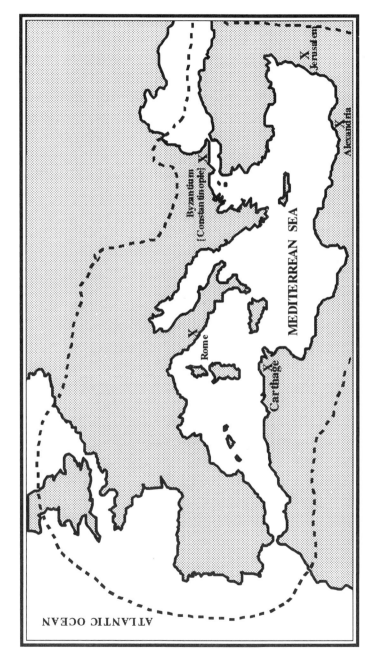

Map 1 presents the Roman Empire during the second century CE. The approximate extent of the Empire is shown by the dotted line. This map also shows the location of the five major cities which were of extreme importance to the Christian Church during the first five hundred years of its existence.

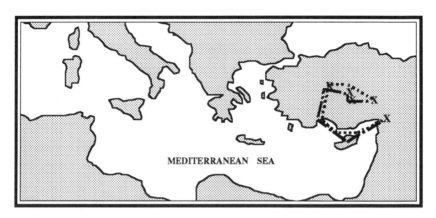

Map 2 presents the first Missionary Journey of Paul. The city from which he journeyed and to which he returned [Antioch of Syria] and the four cities he visited [Antioch, Iconium, Lystra and Derbe in Prisidia] are marked with an "X". The outbound journey is marked in —.—.—.—.—.—.— The return journey is marked in ---------------------------.

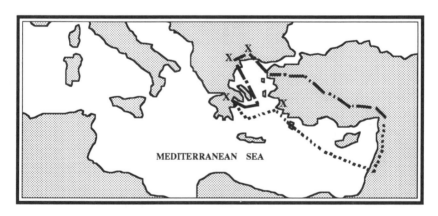

Map 3 presents the second Missionary Journey of Paul. This Journey started in Antioch of Syria and returned there by way of Jerusalem. It included the four cities in Asia Minor previously visited plus the cities of Ephesus in Asia Minor and Phillipi, Thessalonica and Corinth in Macedonia and Greece. The new cities are marked with an "X". The outbound and return portions of the Journey are depicted as described in **Map 2**.

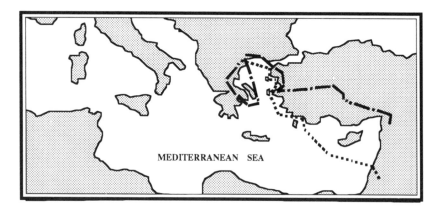

Map 4 presents the third Missionary Journey of Paul. This Journey started in Antioch of Syria and ended in Jerusalem. As described in the text, the Journey was more complex than shown here. Nevertheless, this Map conveys the essence of the Journey. The outbound and return portions of the Journey are depicted as described in **Map 2.**

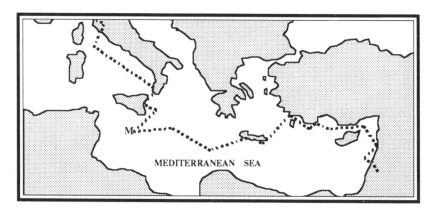

Map 5 presents the final journey of Paul. Some historians call this a Missionary Journey; others merely call it a trip since Paul was under arrest the entire time. The Island of Malta where Paul was shipwrecked for three months is too small to be presented on a map of this scale. Consequently, its location is shown by the letter "**M**". This one-way trip started in Jerusalem and ended in Rome.

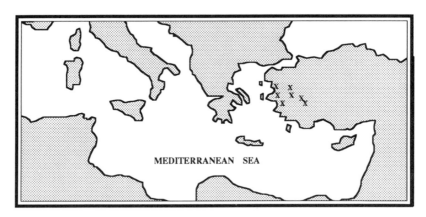

Map 6 presents the location of each of the seven churches which are mentioned so prominently in the opening part of The Revelation to John [The Apocalypse].

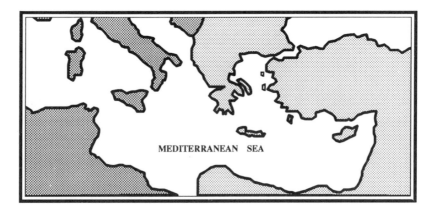

Map 7 presents the "Mediterrean Christian World" as it was split between the Eastern and the Western Churches at about the time of the Fifth Ecumenical Council [553 CE]. The Eastern [generally Eastern Orthodox] portion is shown in light gray; the Western [generally Roman Catholic] portion is in darker gray.

CHAPTER THREE
IMPORTANT EVENTS:
553 CE TO THE PRESENT[1]

In order to cover the important events of almost seventeen hundred years, comment on the miscellaneous events selected will be concise, and will be presented as general periods of history.

Western Europe Christianization
and Monastic Movement [410-1095]

During the fifth century, Rome started to be overrun by a number of invaders including the Visigoths [410], the Vandals [455], and the Germans [493]. During this same period, the Franks [Germans along the Rhine] became Christians primarily because their dynastic leader, Clovis, converted to Christianity in 496. As a result, most of Roman Gaul and Germany became Christian prior to the beginning of the sixth century. This was followed by England's conversion under Pope Gregory I the Great [see Appendix A]. None of the dates for these conversions is meant to imply that there was no Christian activity in the lands prior to that time, for there were many small missions which had been sent to each part of Europe. However, it does mean that Christianity was not the state religion prior to these dates. Thus, the fall of Rome as a source of government in Europe was countered by a corresponding rise of Rome as a source of religion. Roman Christianity had expanded into Western Europe.

As the Roman Empire started into its decline, what is commonly called the Dark Ages descended over Europe. This period is generally considered to have started in about 566 and to have continued until about 1095. During this time, the glory and learning that was Greece and the grandeur that was Rome disappeared from the stage of Western Europe. Arts such as education, literature, painting, music and the like also disappeared. People merely survived. It was during this period that the Church performed a superb service for civilization. This happened in the monastic movement. During the Dark Age, almost all learning and saving of the arts in Western Europe was done within the monasteries. The Western Monastic movement was instigated by Benedict of Nursia [see Appendix A]. When European civilization was ready to leave the Dark Ages, it was in the monasteries that they found the records of what civilization had been like.

Heaven and Hell [1095-1307][2]

Heaven and Hell have always been a part of the Judeo-Christian heritage. The Old Testament often mentions heaven; but in Hebrew, the word *samayim* is plural though in English it is often translated in the singular. Thus Judaism tended to think of "the heavens" more than it thought of "Heaven." The Old Testament also had the concept of Hell. The Hebrew word *Sheol* is used 65 times in the Judaic Old Testament. Sheol was thought to house the dead and the infernal deities. It therefore was a place rather similar to the Greek *Hades* or the English *Hell*. The English word "Hell" is derived from a German verb meaning "to cover" thus inferring that one who is in Hell is hidden from God.

In the New Testament, possibly the most poignant description of Heaven and Hell is given in the parable of Dives [a rich man] and Lazarus [a poor man] in Luke 16:19-31. This parable teaches that the rich who die ungodly will have a wretched afterlife; whereas the poor, after an Earthly life of woe, will enter into everlasting joy. In this parable, Heaven is for the poor and Hell is for the rich. This parable even presents a request on the part of Dives to Father Abraham that he "send me Lazarus to dip the end of his finger in water and cool my tongue; for I am in anguish with this flame." Abraham refuses and Dives continues in his misery. In the New Testament, there is another reference to the "eternal punishment" of Hell. It is in Matthew 25:46 which is the only time the word "eternal" is used in connection with punishment or damnation.

However, despite its presence in the teachings of the Church, Heaven and Hell were not particularly emphasized during the first one thousand years of the Christian Church. This is not to say that the concepts were not discussed, for they certainly were. As one example, in about 230 CE, Origen presented the thought that Hell was not an eternal situation. Instead, he proposed that it was merely a temporary expedient which would be superseded by the restoration of all to God at which time only Heaven would exist. Origen was considered unorthodox in this thought, for the orthodox view of Hell was that it was a place of eternal punishment for the wicked in which the punishment was punitive rather than redemptive. This orthodox view was presented by Pope Gregory I in *Magna moralia* when he said, "Hell is no mere phase; it is a dark and bottomless subterranean abyss created from the beginning of the world; it is inextinguishable fire, corporeal and yet able to sear soul as well as flesh; it is eternal, and yet it never destroys the damned, or lessens their sensitivity to pain. And to each moment of pain is added the terror of expected pain, the horror of witnessing the tortures of loved ones also damned, the despair of ever being released or allowed the blessing of annihilation."[3] In addition to this and other graphic representations of Hell, there were descriptions of Heaven. Augustine presents a truly beautiful picture of Heaven in his magnificent book, *The City of God.*

But again, although the concepts of Heaven and Hell were present during the first millennium, they were not emphasized. This is understandable, for the Church had spent its first 600 years defining the nature and person of Jesus Christ. The Church was kept busy defending that definition, becoming comfortable as the state religion of the greatest Empire in the known world, and fighting, with the help of that Empire, those who did not agree with the orthodox definitions. Then the Dark Ages descended on the territory occupied by the Church. During this time, civilization and intellectual thinking tended to stand still. Instead of Christianity being presented to the public from the pulpits of the church, it tended to remain within the cloistered monasteries of the ascetics. And when the message was preached to the faithful, it tended to be the message of the Second Coming of Christ, particularly as the year 1000 approached; for all thought that Jesus Christ surely would reappear in the year 1000.

As the year 1000 approached, the message which was emphasized throughout Christianity was that the end of the world was coming and that the Second Coming of Christ was eminent. Because of this approaching event, all were advised to repent and to be ready for the end of times. The end of times did not happen. Its absence was a great disappointment, for it had been the expectation of over forty generations of Christians. When the Second Coming did not happen, the Church had to change its message. By the "official" end of the Dark Ages in 1095, the message which the Church emphasized had been changed from that of the end of the world to that of the Last Judgment in which the individual would be damned to an eternal Hell or would be saved for eternal bliss by the Church. The Church would generate this salvation by using her sacraments to administer the divine grace earned by the Redeemer's death.

To emphasize that the Last Judgment had replaced the Second Coming as the pivotal point of the Christian religion, no longer was Jesus pictured as the loving Jesus, meek and mild. Instead, he was depicted as the stern avenger of every mortal sin. Nearly all churches displayed some representation of Jesus as the stern Judge; and many had pictures of the Last Judgment with the tortures of the damned being much more prominently displayed than the bliss of the saved. As a consequence, men started to hope for Heaven, but they truly dreaded Hell. This happened because the Church preached salvation with its concurrent pictures of Heaven and Hell as it never had been preached before.

In a very general sense, the primary purpose of any religion is to provide salvation for its adherents, with salvation meaning the deliverance from conditions such as suffering, evil, finitude [i.e. the quality of being finite] or death. However few religions have ever presented the concept of salvation as the primary purpose of the religion to the extent that Christianity did in the early days of the second millennium. The Christian was told often and firmly: **[1] that man deserved to be damned by God for the original sin which he inherited from Adam as well as for his own sins; [2] that Christ had saved man from eternal damnation by the crucifixion which was a sacrifice paid for all mankind; and [3] that if you believed this and submitted to the sacraments of the Church, then you**

were saved for Heaven; but if you did not believe this and did not accept the Church, then you were condemned to the eternal flames of Hell. In other words, the concept of salvation which was preached at this time proposed that the adherent be granted a reward if he submitted; but that he be granted a terrible punishment if he refused to do what he was asked to do. In the religious emphasis of the first five hundred years of the second millennium, the reward was Heaven and the punishment was Hell.

Possibly the greatest description of the rewards of Heaven or the punishments of Hell was presented in 1307 when the great Italian poet Dante Alighieri first transcribed his epic work *The Divine Comedy*. In this story, Dante is lost in a dark and frightening forest where strange beasts block his way. As he bemoans his fate, the poet Virgil approaches and offers to conduct Dante through Hell, Purgatory and the blissful Paradise. The scenes of terrible punishment in Hell are truly terrifying, for these were the souls who had committed one of the seven deadly sins of pride, lust, envy, anger, covetousness, gluttony or sloth. These cardinal or mortal sins committed the sinner to an eternity of anguish. In comparison, the scenes in Purgatory are rather pleasant, as those souls who had committed merely a common or venial sin were instructed in the ways to be redeemed from their easily pardonable sins. Then the two poets are transported on the road to Paradise where Virgil leaves and Beatrice takes over to lead Dante through the ascending levels of Heaven. Dante ascends through the nine levels of Heaven until he finally receives the grace to contemplate the glory of God circled by nine orders of angels, and to glimpse for a moment the greatest of mysteries, the Trinity and man's union with the divine.

Dante did not establish the punishments of Hell or the rewards of Heaven, for they had been presented from the pulpit and in the work of other writers and artists for over 200 years before Dante's work was transcribed. In addition the Fourteenth Ecumenical Council at Lyons in 1274 and the Seventeenth at Florence in 1439 presented the doctrinal belief that at death, souls would go immediately to Hell, Purgatory or Heaven. However, to many who have read Dante, his work put the final icing on the cake. He did record these activities in a way that has survived. In reading the words of Dante, we can gain a picture of the sermons which Christian parishioners were receiving from their priests. Those sermons must have been truly frightening to them.

There has never been a period in the history of the Christian Church when Heaven and Hell were presented with such emphasis. Today, there is little reference to either site in most Christian sermons other than those of the "Hell, Fire and Brimstone" evangelists of the far right. As a result, people are much less frightened about the afterlife. In a national survey conducted by *Newsweek* for their edition of March 27, 1989, it was found that 77% of the people believe in Heaven and almost all of them believe that they have a good chance of getting there; whereas 58% believe in Hell and only 6% believe that they will go there. A similar survey conducted in 1320 would probably have generated vastly different results.

And so, the rewards of Heaven and the punishments of Hell were preached by the Church. The emphasis continued for several hundred years. Although this emphasis may have caused many repercussions, possibly the most tragic result was the belief that it was a Christian's duty to save an individual from eternal damnation even if it cost that individual his life. This particular belief will be addressed in the next section.

Conversion by the Sword [1022-Present]

Once the concepts of Heaven and Hell had become firmly entrenched as a part of Christian psyche, devout Christians started to think that they had the need to save the soul of another, even if doing so required coercion or the taking of a life. This "become a Christian or else" philosophy has become known as "Conversion by the Sword". This section will present four examples of this phenomena covering almost 1,000 years of Church history. Many other examples could have been chosen such as examples from the British experience in India, examples from the missionary experience throughout Africa, and examples from the American experience with slavery; but these four should suffice to make the point that all conversions to the acceptance of Christ were not voluntary. The four examples chosen are: the Crusades; the Cathars [in which the Inquisition is introduced]; Witchcraft; and the Conquistadors.

The Crusades [1096-1291][4]

The Crusades are among the most remarkable events of the Middle Ages. They spanned the time period of 1096 to 1291 and have presented us with some of the most enchanting and romantic myths ever developed. They also have presented us with some of the most frightening tales of hardship and despair ever created.

The Crusades represent attempts to convert by love as well as by the sword. Historians have presented many thoughts as to why there was ever a Crusade in the first place. Most have justified the Crusades on economic principles, noting that as the trade routes from the East were closed by the growing power of the Muslims, merchants in western Europe demanded that the armed might of Europe reopen these routes. Others have emphasized the population growth of Western Europe and have suggested that the population expansion of Europe and the territorial expansion of the Muslim Empires were bound to clash in a war such as the Crusades. Still others have emphasized the tremendous evangelical awakening among the Christians of Western Europe during this time, and the desire of those pious Christians to visit the Holy Land, a desire which was forbidden by the Seljuk Turks who controlled Jerusalem after 1079.

But despite these various reasons for justifying the Crusades, it is a fact of history that they would not have commenced if the popes, initially Pope Urban II, had not blessed them. In addition, the manpower would not be available if the popes had not promised those who participated that they would receive the Crusade "indulgence" in which all of their previous sins would be wiped away and each participant would be restored to a state of spiritual innocence.

The first Crusade was the so-called Peoples Crusade of 1096. As a military activity, it was an absolute disaster. However, it did demonstrate that successful military activities require trained armies rather than a mob of people, no matter how ardent their religious belief. Consequently, four sizable armies were raised by the feudal nobility of Western Europe to conduct what history calls the First Crusade. It lasted from 1096 to 1099. It was highly successful and captured the Holy Land. As a result of this Crusade, Christians held Jerusalem for almost 100 years, until 1187.

Because some of the territory outside Jerusalem had been captured in 1144, Pope Eugenius proclaimed the Second Crusade [1147-49]. It accomplished little. When Jerusalem was taken by the Muslims in 1187, Pope Gregory VIII proclaimed the Third Crusade [1189-92] which again had little success, for Jerusalem remained in the hands of the Muslims.

In 1199, Pope Innocent III proclaimed the Fourth Crusade [1202-04] which developed as one of the strangest events in the history of Christianity. It was a small crusade in number, but a major crusade in terms of its political and religious results. The major result was one which was not anticipated or even desired at the time by Pope Innocent III; but it is one which he later used for the benefit of the papacy's goals. This result happened because although the Fourth Crusade did not have much success in fighting the Muslims, it had tremendous success in fighting its fellow Christians. Along its way to the Holy Land, the armies of the Fourth Crusade conquered the Eastern Christian Church for Pope Innocent and replaced the Eastern Patriarch with a Latin one. This activity so weakened the Eastern Church that its members were an easy prey to the subsequent religious approaches of Islam. In addition, this activity of the Fourth Crusade created a lasting animosity between the Greek and the Latin Churches.

During the same time period as the Fourth Crusade, there occurred one of the saddest episodes in all Christian history. Stirred by the fervor of recovering the Holy Land for Christ, a large number of children left northern Europe in an attempt to reach the Holy Land and to conquer it with love. Most of the members of this "Children's Crusade" perished from exposure and starvation as they tried to walk over the Alps. Sadly, none reached the Holy Land, or at least the Holy Land of this Earth.

The Fifth Crusade [1217-1221] had some initial success against Egypt, but it also ended in failure to conquer the Holy Land. This led to the Sixth Crusade [1228-9] which is the most curious of all. It was more of a state visit than a war; but by negotiation, Jerusalem was handed over to the Christians who stayed there until 1244 when Jerusalem was permanently lost to the Muslims. In 1291, the Crusaders lost their stronghold in Acre and the Crusades were effectively over, even though talk about possible new crusades continued for almost 200 years.

The major purpose of the Crusades was to conquer territory. In doing so, the Crusader did not necessarily try to convert his Muslim foe in order to save his soul. Instead, he tried to kill him to take his land. In addition, along the way to the Holy Land the dedicated Crusader killed as many Jews as he could find, not in an attempt to convert them or to save their souls but as an extreme expression of anti-Semitism. Consequently, it could be argued that a description of the Crusades does not belong in a section which is devoted to describing how the Church used the Sword to convert individuals to Christianity. However, that argument would miss the major lasting "benefit" which the Crusades gave to western Christianity. That benefit was not the restoration of the Holy Lands; for as we have already seen, they were permanently lost in 1244. Instead, the lasting "benefit" was to establish the authority and prestige of the medieval papacy as the defender of Christendom, as the protector of Christian ideals against the infidels and the heretics of the world, and as the organizer of the military might of Western Europe. In other words, the Crusades generated the concept of using military power against the heretical and even the political foes of the papacy. As we will see in the next sections, the activities of the Fourth Crusade against fellow Christians developed a concept which was used by many popes, particularly Pope Innocent III, to overcome problems of the Church, whether those problems were generated by Christians within the Church or by Christians from outside of the Church.

Conversion by the Sword started with the Crusades. The concept may never have been generated if it had not been for the Crusades. It is a relevant starting point for some of the darkest episodes in the history of Christianity. The religious fervor which the Church used in some of its later activities can only be understood by recognizing the zealous religious dedication generated by the Crusades.

The Cathars, the Waldenses and the Inquisition [1184-1966]

During the twelfth century as the Dark Ages disappeared, a tremendous number of evangelical awakenings occurred within the European society. Two of these awakenings combine to present one of the blackest chapters in the history of the Christian Church. These awakenings are known as the "Cathars" and the "Waldenses." Their evangelical awakening led to the establishment of the Inquisition by the Church

The Cathars were also known as the Albigenses from the town of Albi which was one of their main seats in southern France. The term "Cathar" is of Greek origin and means "Pure Ones." The Cathars [or Cathari] believed in baptism by the laying on of hands rather than by water. This was their first heresy. They, like the Gnostics, also believed in duality, i.e. the evil material world and the good spiritual one. In this sense, the Church was again fighting Manichaeism [see Appendix A] which already had been declared heretical. The Cathars also promised to remain celibate, to avoid oaths, to avoid war and the possession of property, and never to eat meat, milk, cheese or eggs since all of these had been produced by the sin of reproduction. After all of these vows and the reading of the first seventeen verses of the Gospel of John, the Cathar initiate became termed a "good Christian," implying that other Christians were not as good. Even though this kind of intolerant belief was exactly what Rome did, the Church declared such an activity to be heretical. Like the Gnostics, the Cathars believed that redemption came through knowledge, again a heretical viewpoint in the mind of the Church. But despite all of these heretical viewpoints, in reality the Cathars were some of the most pious and morally rigorous believers in Christ that the world has ever seen. Their main desire was to be left alone to practice their faith. However, they did leave the Church, and they did teach a belief in reincarnation; and as a consequence, the Church considered them to be hostile to her interests. As described later, the Church did not leave them alone.

The Waldenses originated with no conscious hostility to the Church. If they had been treated diplomatically, they may never have left the Church. In about 1175, their founder, Valdes, asked a master theologian how to find God. He was told to "sell what you had and give the proceeds to the poor and follow Christ." Valdes, like Francis of a generation later, did exactly that. After providing for his wife and daughters, he gave the rest of his wealth to the poor and subsisted as a preacher, living solely on what he was given. He thus lived a life of voluntary poverty, just as the Apostles had done. Soon, a band of followers joined him. This aroused the anger of the local bishop who not only was losing parishioners, he was hearing that someone who was not of the clergy was preaching. Lay preaching was forbidden by canon law. Consequently, the Waldenses had committed their first offense against the Church.

In 1184, the Waldenses and the Cathars were declared heretical by Pope Lucius III and were excommunicated by the Church. Later a similar group, the Humiliati of northern Italy, was also excommunicated, primarily because this group held religious meetings in their homes rather than attending church.

After leaving the Church, the Waldenses felt that the Bible, especially the New Testament, was the sole rule of belief and life, but that Scripture must be followed completely and faithfully. Their preachers went out two-by-two as admonished in the Bible. They preached the redemption of sins, heard confessions, rejected oaths, and rejected the shedding of blood. They even allowed women to preach, an advancement in Christian thinking which some churches have still not accepted.

By the beginning of the thirteenth century, the Cathars and the Waldenses were much more popular in southern France, northern Italy and northern Spain than the Roman Catholic Church was. Several missions to these non-mainstream organizations were tried without success. Consequently, in 1209, Pope Innocent III proclaimed a Crusade against the "heretics " in these regions, offering the same rewards as would be won in a crusade to the Holy Lands. The resulting army was composed of nobles from northern France under the leadership of Simon de Montfort. For the next twenty years, warfare waged with great destruction. During this time, it is estimated that hundreds of thousands of people were killed, including more than 20,000 Christians in one day and including one huge funeral pyre in which 400 Cathars were burned at one time because they would not renounce their faith.[5] The Crusade was not declared over until 1243 when the Cathar bastion at Montsegur was finally captured after a long and costly siege. This effectively ended the existence of the Cathars, but some of the Waldenses continued to exist by fleeing to the Alpine mountains and going underground. At the Reformation, most of the Waldenses accepted the principles of Protestantism. They thus became the only medieval sect to survive the Crusade against them and to continue into modern times, albeit with a significant modification of their original principles.[6] During this Crusade, more than ten Christians were killed for each Muslim who had been killed in the Crusades of the East. But that was not the end, for in reality the Crusade against those who did not obey the papal system was just beginning.[5]

This new beginning was instigated by the question as to how to investigate and punish these, or other heretics. This was solved by Pope Gregory IX in 1233 by the establishment of a permanent institution for the suppression of heresy. This was the papal Inquisition or Holy Office. In the beginning, it was generally manned by Dominicans. Later, the Jesuits became involved. The Inquisition became a formidable and fearsome organ whose proceedings were secret. In addition, it would withhold the names of the accusers from the accused.

In 1252, Pope Innocent IV issued a bull which permitted the Inquisition to use torture in order to get a confession of heresy. The punishment for heresy, whether confessed or not, was generally a burning at the stake. This was done because heresy, or treason against God, was considered to be a more heinous crime than treason against the King, itself punishable by a more gentle death such as hanging or beheading. In addition to personal punishment, those considered guilty of heresy would have all of their property confiscated and divided among the lay and ecclesiastical authorities. As a consequence, heresy was a profitable endeavor, both for the accuser and for the Church.

The Inquisition really hit its stride in the sixteenth century against the Moors and Jews in Spain. In Spain, the Inquisition reported directly to King Ferdinand and Queen Isabella under a bull issued in 1478 by Pope Sixtus IV. Within a few years of being granted the administration of the Inquisition, the King and Queen enthusiastically passed a law that all Moors and Jews had to become Christian. The penalty for refusal was death or exile. Since the Church could not be absolutely certain that these confessed Christians were truly Christian, it had to find out even if it killed those Christians during the discovery process. And of course, when they had been killed by the Inquisition, their property was divided between the Church and the Crown. These activities were about as far away from the love which had been taught by Jesus Christ as it is possible to get.

More than just Spain was enthusiastic about the activities of the Inquisition. Gian Pietro Caraffa, bishop of Chieti who became Pope Paul IV in 1555, was inspector-general of the Inquisition prior to becoming pope. In a zealous pursuit of his job, he equipped his own home as a torture chamber at his own expense and stated that, "If my own father were a heretic, I would personally gather the wood to burn him." Paul IV is even better known by history as the one who established the Index of Forbidden Books upon which every book considered to be pernicious was to be placed and forbidden to be read by any Christian. The Index was kept for more than four centuries until discontinued by Pope Paul VI in 1966.[7]

Robert Richard Madden, a devout English Catholic in the mid-nineteenth century, reviewed the torture chambers actually used in the Inquisition and read official records of what it had done. This activity led him to state, "This must be a true religion, for if it had not a divine and vital principle in it, it never could have survived the crimes that have been committed in its name." However, another devout Catholic has been quoted as saying, "It would be better to be an atheist than to believe in the God of the Inquisition"; and another said, "Jesus himself would have suffered and died at the hands of the pope's inquisitors, for he talked with heretics and sinners and he dined with publicans and prostitutes."[8]

All of these activities of the Inquisition got their start with a Crusade against the Cathars and the Waldenses. These gentle people were conquered by an army sent out by the pope, were tortured until they died if they did not confess to heresy, or were burned at the stake if they did confess to heresy. And all that they had wanted to do was to be left alone and to follow Christ in their own way.

Sorcery or Witchcraft [1200-1700][9]

The major attempts by Christianity to exterminate witchcraft by subjecting witches to "Conversion by the Sword" were concentrated in Western Europe during the period of 1200 to 1700. However, witchcraft itself is much older and much more widespread than that, starting with simple sorcery which has been found in practically every time period and every culture of the world since the beginning of recorded time.

The practice of simple sorcery is almost always an attempt to gain magical aid from the spirits, gods or goddesses. In general, there might be a recitation of magical incantations or a mechanical act of some sort in order to summon spirits and compel them to perform a desired activity. One example of a mechanical act in simple sorcery would be to perform sexual intercourse in a sown field as a magical invocation to the god that there would be a good harvest. Examples of representative incantations are difficult to come by; and it is some-times difficult to understand the difference between the use of a magical invocation in simple sorcery and the use of prayer in a religion such as Christianity. Possibly the only difference is that the purpose of the invocation is to compel aid from the god; whereas the purpose of prayer is to implore such aid or cooperation.

In any case, the early Church argued that God was in control of the Universe as its absolute Lord and Master and that His domin-ion was total. Therefore, the early Church had seen no need to develop rituals against the practice of simple sorcery other than to instruct the faithful that it was an un-Christian superstition to think that a sorcerer had superhuman powers which could influence humans. Church instructions of this type went back to the Council of Arles in 314 CE if not earlier. Despite this instruction, ordinary people were often entranced with the practices of simple sorcery; and often felt that there was great power in activities such as using astrology to cast a horoscope, or using other incantational activities in an attempt to understand what the gods had in store for an individual or for society.

By medieval times, things had started to change, particularly in Western Europe. This change was led by the Christian concept of Satan as a force which had to be fought and the belief that the simple sorcerer was no longer simple, but instead was a witch who was a subject of Satan. The word "witch" was developed specifically for this purpose. It comes from the Old English noun *wicca* which means "a sorcerer" and the verb *wiccian* which means "to cast a spell." It was believed in medieval times that anyone who could cast a spell [i.e. was a witch] could do so only because she was an agent of Satan. In this manner, the age of diabolical witchcraft [i.e. sorcery associated with Satan] descended on Europe.

The first formal trial for witchcraft was held in Orleans [France] in 1022. It was a trial which was conducted by the Church and which offered only ecclesiastical punishment for the offenders. The defendants were accused of holding orgies underground at night, calling up evil spirits, killing and cremating children conceived at previous orgies, using the ashes of these children to perform a blasphemous parody of the Eucharist, renouncing Christ, desecrating the Crucifix and praising the Devil. The non-Christian portions of these charges were similar to charges which the Syrians had made against the Jews in about 200 BCE; which the Romans had made against the Christians in about 100 CE; and which the Christians had made against the Gnostics in about 250 CE. They were merely updated as an accusation of the Christians against the witches. The Christians felt justified in bringing these accusations because of their belief that Christians had to fight against Satan, and that Satan had enrolled the witches on his side.

In the late twelfth century, things really started to get serious. The seriousness began in 1198 when Pope Innocent II ordered the execution of those who persisted in heresy after having been convicted and excommunicated. It continued in 1233 when Pope Gregory IX declared that the Waldenses were worshippers of Satan and therefore were heretics. In 1252, Pope Innocent IV authorized the use of torture by the Inquisition and in 1255 Pope Alexander IV gave the Inquisition jurisdiction over all cases of sorcery. In this manner, all witches were declared to be practicing heretics and were considered to be fair game for the Inquisition. This led to what some modern historians have called the "witch Craze"; and what others who specialize in the history of witchcraft have called "the Burning Time."

Returning to 1233, Pope Gregory IX, the instigator of the Inquisition, declared that the Waldenses were supporters of Satan because he was getting reports from his inquisitors that witchcraft was threatening the survival of the world. Consequently, Gregory felt justified in ordering the Church to go after the Waldenses and associated witchcraft with a vengeance. The effort against the witches was headed by a priest named Conrad whose principal belief was that pain was the best route to salvation for practicing heretics. Conrad is reported to have developed the infliction of pain into an art form. Within a few years, many people confessed to being practicing witches in an attempt to stop the infliction of pain. As a consequence of these confessions, many others were accused of witchcraft, and all witches were declared to be practicing heretics. The heretical practices they conducted were defined as having the following eight major elements: [1] a pact with the Devil; [2] a formal repudiation of Christ; [3] holding secret nocturnal meetings; [4] riding by night; [5] desecrating the Eucharist and the Crucifix; [6] holding orgies; [7] performing sacrificial infanticide; and [8] practicing cannibalism.

In 1484, Pope Innocent IV issued a bull confirming papal support for inquisitional proceedings against witches. This bull was included as a preface to the book *Malleus maleficarum* [The Hammer of Witches], a book by two Dominican inquisitors which was widely available because it had been printed on the recently developed printing press. In the Protestant and Catholic regions of Western Europe, this book outsold all books except the Bible. The book was filled with colorful descriptions of the diabolical, orgastic activities of witches. It also proposed court procedures for uncovering the practice of witchcraft. The major court proceedings were denunciation and torture. This notorious book was instrumental in convincing the public that Satan was actively leading a plot to overcome all Christian society.

As this book inflamed the Christians of Western Europe to exterminate witchcraft, the practice of inflicting pain as a route to salvation continued to develop as an art form which was used by many in the name of Christ. During the sixteenth and seventeenth centuries, particularly between 1560 and 1660, the popes who followed Pope Innocent VIII did their level best to wipe out witchcraft wherever they perceived it.[10] But there was absolutely no difference in the way Protestants and Catholics went after the witches. Luther and Calvin both advocated torture for producing confessions and recommended that the confessed witches be burned at the stake, just as the Catholics did. The American Protestants also participated in these activities as demonstrated by the Salem witch trials in 1692.

Some have claimed that based on historical records, nine million people were put to death for witchcraft in the three hundred years following 1484; and this estimate does not include the number who were sacrificed in the preceding centuries on the same accusation.[11] Others have doubted this number and have stated that between the beginning of the persecution of witches and 1450, the number of executions could be measured in the hundreds which increased to about a hundred thousand between 1450 and 1700. The truth is that the historical records do not exist which would give an accurate estimate of the number executed. However, almost every historical source states that during the "witch Craze" of 1450-1750, a period which has been described as one of the strangest mass delusions in history, millions were persecuted and more millions were intimidated by the threat of being named a witch, all in Western Europe and its colonies. History tells us that the final execution of a witch occurred in 1684 in England; in 1692 in America; in 1727 in Scotland; in 1745 in France; and in 1775 [barely 220 years ago!] in Germany.

But whether the number of executions was a hundred thousand or 140 times that number, there is truth in the statement that many innocent people were executed in the name of a religion which believed it had the right to kill the body in order to save the soul of a sinner. In order to practice this belief, they used the rack and other tortures, the sword, and the flame to gain conversions to Christ.

Jesus taught sinners. He also loved and granted a life of peace to them. He believed strongly in the value of human life. These teachings were altered by some who claimed to follow him.

The Conquistadors [1519-Present]

The Conquistadors [Spanish for "the conqueror"] is a term which refers to the leaders in the Spanish conquest of America, especially of Mexico and Peru in the sixteenth century. The Conquistador of Mexico is considered to be Hernan Cortes. In 1519, Cortes established a base camp at Veracruz with some 600 men. He marched inland with 400 men and conquered the Aztec capital of Tenochtitlan [now Mexico City]. By 1524, all of Latin America had been conquered by the Spanish. The Conquistador of Peru is considered to be Francisco Pizarro who departed Spain for Peru in 1531 with

180 men and 37 horses. After capturing the reigning Inca ruler, Atahualpa, Pizarro conquered the capital city of Cuzco in November, 1533. He established a new capital at Lima.

Both conquests were fast and relatively bloodless. Since the Conquistadors had more interest in the search for gold than they had for governance, they were quickly replaced by administers and settlers from Spain. Their conquering efforts have led them to being described as the bearer of "The Sword and the Cross" or as the first to use military prowess to convert souls to Christ in Latin and South America.

The Indian policy of the Spanish settlements is the major issue here. The Spanish explorers had as their motivation, "Gold, Glory and Gospel!" Consequently, one of their major goals was to convert the natives to Catholicism and to prohibit the introduction of Protestantism. This latter desire was based on the fact that Ferdinand and Isabella, "The Catholic Kings," and their immediate successors had been instrumental in fighting Protestantism during the European wars between Catholic and Protestant nations. The conversion efforts of the Spanish explorers seemed to be successful. In Mexico, in 1531, only seven years after the conquest was complete, the Franciscans reported that they had converted more than a million natives. With so few priests available, one wonders how this great a number could have been persuaded to convert unless there was more than just the teaching of Christ which was used as the "persuader."

But the Indian policy was more than just the Gospel. It also included Gold and enslavement. As early as the first landings of Columbus, the policy had been to demand daily tribute in gold dust and to require that the natives undergo forced labor to feed and support the Spanish settlers. In addition, the myth of El Dorado ["the Gilded Land"] fascinated the conquistadors and assured that many of them would come to America, for they "knew" that the fabled City of Gold had to be around someplace. It is reported that when they captured some Indians, they would choose a few to be torn apart by the dogs or to be burned alive to force the others to tell where the fabled City of Gold was. The Indians probably misled them often.[12]

After several years of enslavement, enforced labor and enforced conversion to Christianity, the New Laws were passed in

1542 which prohibited new enslavement and enforced service, but permitted the existing arrangements to continue, an arrangement which the King extended to the fifth generation. As a result, the existing arrangements became quite valuable, and the enforced labor became much more severe. In 1569, the Inquisition arrived in both Mexico and Peru. Less than 30 years later, there were regular complaints made in Spain about the vast amount of wealth which was being generated by the clergy in both Mexico and Peru, as well as the unusually large number of convents which they seemed to enjoy.

The exploitation and overwork of the natives generated a population decline which rapidly approached genocide. It is estimated that the Indian population in Mexico declined from about 25 million to less than 1 million in the 86 years between 1519 and 1605 [*Encyclopaedia Britannica*]; and further that in all of Latin America, fully 90% of the population, more than 50 million native Americans, lost their lives during the first century following the introduction of the "one true God." To these people, Christianity brought extortion, misery, disease and death [see footnote 9 of Notes from the Author]. Although European diseases are given much of the blame for the population loss, forced conversion to Christianity was also a factor; for in their conversion, the Indians were told that it was their Christian duty to work until death. The conditions in the silver mines of Mexico and in the silver and mercury mines of Peru were particularly onerous in promulgating a loss of the will to live. Associated with this was the Christian teaching that their reward was not on this Earth, but was to be received in heaven after death. This teaching often made the overworked slaves eager for death as a relief from their daily load of pain and misery.

The governmental policy toward the Indians was not universally accepted. Bartholome de Las Casas [1474-1566] was probably the greatest proponent of the humanity of Indians in Spanish America. This former conquistador took Holy Orders in 1512. Following a religious experience when he was preparing a sermon, he decided to spend the rest of his life [a long one] in defense of the Indian rights. He publicly returned his Indian serfs to the governor and devoted all of his efforts to the "justice of these Indian peoples and to condemn the robbery, evil and injustice committed against them."[13] In all of these efforts, Las Casas had to constantly fight against the greed of the Conquistadors and against the men of his own church. In essence, for every man such as Las Casas, there were at least ten opponents to Indian rights. Possibly the most influential of these was Dr. Juan Gines de Sepulveda [1490-1573] who argued that it was just to war against and enslave Indians, particularly since they had been conquered by "such an excellent, pious, and most just king as was Ferdinand the Catholic."[14] The two major adversaries [Las Casas and Sepulveda] conducted a full month's debate in front of the King's council in 1550. Although no written council decision has survived, from subsequent events it is evident that Sepulveda carried the day. The Conquistadors adored him, sent him presents and made his works their orthodox defense. His classic attack against the rights of the Indians was finally published in 1892.

And so, the men of a great nation went out as Conquistadors to a foreign land. They went there to find Gold and Glory. They found their Gold and gained their Glory at the expense of what has proved to be a highly intelligent, advanced native population. In justification for their actions against these people, the Conquistadors stood behind the Gospel of Jesus Christ of the Spanish Church. They used the Gospel to convert the natives to what today has become a very interesting blend of Roman Catholicism and ancient Mayan or Incan traditions. To introduce the Catholicism, the Conquistadors would not take "no" for an answer. That is why they are today known as the bearer of "The Sword and the Cross." They had very successfully used the one to introduce the other.

Francis and Clare of Assisi [1181-1253]

The record of the Church in the period immediately following the Dark Ages could not be told without telling the story of Francis of Assisi [1181-1226], for this indeed was a man of Christ. In addition, the story of Clare of Assisi is an important one.

Francis was born in Assisi, the son of Peter Bernadone, a wealthy Italian silk merchant. He was christened John by his mother during the absence of her husband. Upon his return, the father insisted that his son be re-christened Francis.

Francis was an extravagant youth, somewhat reminiscent of

the youth of Augustine [see Appendix A]. He went gaily to war and was taken prisoner in 1205. He experienced a vision of Christ at Spoleto followed by another on his return to Assisi. As a consequence, he changed his entire life-style. He went on a pilgrimage to Rome in 1206, and on his return devoted himself to a life of poverty and to the care of the sick and the poor. He was angrily denounced by his father as a madman and was disinherited in one of the most dramatic scenes in religious history during which Francis is reported to have said that henceforth he had no father but the Father in heaven.[15]

After repairing several churches in Assisi, he retired to a little chapel, the Portiuncula, and devoted himself completely to his life's work of poverty and preaching. He soon attracted numerous disciples, thus founding the Franciscans. In 1210, Pope Innocent III verbally approved the Order of Franciscans. Two years later, Francis was joined by Clare, who joined him over the violent objections of her family.

Clare [1194-1253] also was born in Assisi. She was the daughter of the noble Faverone Offreduccio and Ortolanadi Fiumi. She refused to marry in 1206 when she was twelve years old. In 1212, she was so impressed by a Lenten sermon of Francis that she ran away from home on Palm Sunday and received the habit from Francis at the Portiuncula. Since Francis did not, as yet, have a convent for women, he placed her in the Benedictine convent of St. Paul near Bastia. She resisted the forcible efforts by her family to remove her and bring her home. Later, she was joined by her younger sister, Agnes, who also received her habit from Francis. In 1215, Clare moved to a house adjoining the church of St. Damiano, was made superior by Francis and ruled the convent for 40 years.

In the meantime, Francis was obsessed with the desire to preach to the followers of Mohammed. In the fall of 1212, he set out for Syria but was shipwrecked along the way. A second attempt in 1213-14 also failed when he fell ill in Spain while on the way to Morocco. In 1216, he obtained the famous Portiuncula indulgence from Pope Innocent III. This indulgence previously had been announced by the pope at the Fourth Lateran Council [Twelfth Ecumenical Council] in 1215. It stated that the Franciscans were to be considered an existing order and therefore not subject to the Council's ban on new orders. In the following year [when he probably met

Dominic in Rome], Francis convened the first general chapter of his order at the Portiuncula to organize the huge number of followers he had attracted to his way of life.

In 1219, Francis sent his first missionaries to Tunis and Morocco. He went himself to Egypt to evangelize the followers of Mohammed in Palestine and Egypt; but although he met with Sultan Malek al Damil at Damietta Egypt, then under siege by Crusaders, and although he greatly impressed the Sultan with his faith, the Sultan did not convert to Christianity. He then hastened back to Italy to combat two separate movements in his Order to mitigate his original rule of simplicity, humility and poverty. His revised rules were later accepted by Pope Honorius III.

At Christmas 1223, Francis built a crèche [i.e. Nativity scene] at Grecchia, establishing a custom observed in the Christian world to the present day. On September 14, 1224 while praying in his cell on Mount Alverna, he received the stigmata, the climax of a series of supernatural events he had experienced throughout his lifetime. He died at Assisi on October 3, 1224. He was canonized in 1228.

Though never ordained, Francis has had a tremendous impact on religious life. Probably no Saint has affected so many in so many different ways as the gentle Saint of Assisi who, born to wealth, devoted his life to poverty and the concern for the poor and the sick. In addition, probably no Saint has been so delighted in God's works as revealed in nature. Among all those who have tried to live the life of Christ, Francis is noted as having had the most compassionate love for birds and animals. He did this in the imitation of Christ.

In the meantime, Clare had founded the Poor Clares at the convent near St. Damiano. Soon after, Clare was joined by her mother, another sister, three family members of the famous Ubaldini family of Florence, and others. The Poor Clares adopted a rigid rule and took a vow of strict poverty; and in 1253, two days before Clare's death, Pope Innocent IV granted her order the *priviligium paupertatis*, or the privilege of remaining poor, a privilege which was approved for all time.

During Clare's lifetime, her order flourished and spread to other parts of Italy and to France and Germany. Clare's influence became such that she was consulted by popes, cardinals and bishops.

She was credited with many miracles, and in 1241 her prayers were credited with saving Assisi from the besieging soldiers of Emperor Frederick II. She, next to St. Francis, was the most responsible for the growth and the spread of the Franciscans. She died at Assisi on August 11, 1253, and was canonized two years later.

Within the sectarian Christian Church, the Franciscans were the nearest to living in "apostolic poverty" and in literal fulfillment of the commands of Christ. Their only competition might have come from the Cathars and the Waldenses. The only difference is that the Franciscans were within the Church, whereas the Cathars and the Waldenses were outside of and therefore persecuted by the Church. Other than that difference, the Waldenses were really very similar to the Franciscans, and the Cathars somewhat so.

Thomas Aquinas [1225-1274]

Like Francis, Thomas Aquinas is a man whose story simply must be told. However, since his lifetime adds little to the events being covered in this Chapter, his story has been presented in the Expanded Glossary [under the letter "-T-"].

The Reformation [1517-Present]

It is probable that no event in the history of the Church was so needed as was the Reformation. Through the Inquisition, through the system of Indulgences, and through a series of debilitating church taxes, the fiscal house of the continually bankrupt Church had become corrupt. Through moral laxity such as clerical simony, nepotism, absenteeism and concubinage, the Church was becoming an open eyesore to the increasingly educated and literate laity. Through the use of the Bible which had become more readily available to all, thoughtful people were demanding a more biblical, purely apostolic church as pictured in the New Testament. Because of all of these influences, the Church simply had to be reformed.

There have been volumes upon volumes written about the Reformation and how on October 31, 1517 Martin Luther inadvertently started it by posting his memorable "Ninety-five Theses" on the door of the castle church in Wittenburg. There is no intent to duplicate those marvelous works in this book. Instead, it will have to suffice to say that without the Reformation, it is possible that there would have been no Protestant churches, there would have been no separation of Church and State, there would have been no freedom from ecclesiastical oppression, there would have been no Age of Reason or no Age of Enlightenment and there would have been no scientific revolution; for the existing Church would have resisted all of these, and probably would have won. In addition, it is quite possible that the one surviving Church, if indeed it would have survived, would have continued to hold sway over all potential thought and action. As one simple example, it is reasonable to think that if there had been no Reformation, we would still be teaching the "Revealed Truth" that the Sun revolves around the Earth instead of the other way around.

Without the Reformation, we would have had an overbearing Christian Church, or no Christian Church at all. But we did have the Reformation. And because of that, religious books such as you are presently reading can be printed whether they have the permission of the Church or not. In the absence of the Reformation, it is probable that books such as this would have been burned, if indeed they would ever have been printed in the first place.

Any further insight on this most important event will have to be obtained by the reader in books which specialize on the subject. As far as this book is concerned, the Reformation happened; and the author is indeed very happy that it did. As suggested by the information in *Book Two* and in *Book Three*, it is quite possible that the time has come for a Second Reformation of the Christian Church.

Vatican II [1962-Present]

Chapter 2 spent a considerable amount of time exploring what happened in each of the first five Ecumenical Councils, but possibly the most important Ecumenical Council for the future of the Christian Church is the Twenty-first Ecumenical Council. It is the second one which was held at the Vatican, and is therefore called "Vatican II." It was held between 1962 and 1965. The repercussions of this Council, including the new code of canon law signed by Pope John Paul II in 1983, are still being felt. Because of this Council, it is probable that the Roman Catholic Church will never again be totally uniform in its practices throughout the world. It is possible that because of Vatican II, the Roman Church will change again in the future in a way which cannot be defined at the present time. It was a momentous Council, not necessarily because of what happened during the Council, but because of what may happen in the future based on the spirit of the Council. What Vatican II actually did was curtailed by the untimely death of its guiding spirit, Pope John XXIII. What it may do in the future is guided by the bishops around the world as they continue to practice the lessons of their newly found freedom. It will be fascinating to watch.

But in addition to the hopes expressed above, there are two characteristics of Vatican II which are important enough to be mentioned here. The first is the mixed signals which were sent out as announcements; and the second is the daring of some of those announcements.

In respect to the mixed signals, although Vatican II in effect repealed *extra ecclesiam nulla salus* [no salvation outside of the Church] in one pronouncement, in another it effectively put it back by stating that *"All must be converted to Christ as He is made known by the Church's preaching."* In this way, Christianity has gone from intolerance to a benevolence, but still on the Christian Church's terms as it continues to call itself the only religion and to reject the fact that there have been worldwide saints in every major world religion.[16]

In respect to the daring of some of the pronouncements, it is highly probable that every document of Vatican II held in 1962 would have been declared heretical by Vatican I held less than 100 years earlier [1869-70]. Therefore, it is possible that something even as intransigent as the Christian Church may be able to accept that the orthodoxy of one age is not necessarily the orthodoxy of another.[17]

"The New Age" [The Present]

The New Age is a term which has confused many. Some believe that it is a closed society which involves Satan's kingdom on Earth and includes diabolical initiations and mind control; while others see it as the most open, tolerant, spiritual and holy path which one can follow. Some see it as another religion; while others see it as a "way of life." Some see it as a return to a static God; while others see it as an evolving process of growth. Some see it as a complete replacement of existing religions; while others see it as a logical extension to the path traveled so far. To all, the one common denominator of the New Age is that it covers a wide spectrum of beliefs and activities which is non-uniform in its practice. And based on the basic underlying principle of the New Age, that is as it should be.

This short section will in no way present all of the facets of this movement, possibly the fastest growing spiritual movement in the world or at least in the western world. Instead, it will present only a few underlying principles and suggest that Christianity in its early form and the New Age in its present form are similar. The rational for this statement is presented in *Book Two*.

The basic underlying principle of the New Age, and the reason that it is so diverse in its practice, is the belief that each individual is unique; and consequently as he or she walks the pathway, they do so in a unique manner. For this reason, there are no orthodox doctrines or dogmas within the New Age. In this sense it is correct to say that the New Age is not a religion; for the present connotation of the word ."religion" is that of an organized, dogmatic approach which has orthodox beliefs as its foundation. However, as each unique individual of the New Age walks the pathway, they do so in an attempt to bind themselves back to God. In this sense, the New Age is a religion; for the word "religion" comes from the Latin words *ligare* and *re*. *Ligare* means "to bind" and *re* means "back." Therefore, religion means to "bind back" or in other words to "return to God." In that sense, the New Age fits the definition of religion, for each individual on the pathway seems to be on a unique path which will return him or her to God, whatever that God means to the individual.

Although there are no universal beliefs in the New Age, three terms seem to be almost universally accepted by those who participate. Those terms are "reincarnation/karma," "dimensionality" and "unconditional love." These terms, and a few other terms which are almost as universal within the New Age, have been explained in-depth in *Christianity and the New Age Religion*. Consequently, they will not be explored further in this book.

Even though the New Age is based on the uniqueness of the

individual path and therefore should generate no controversies, there is one subject which evokes a great deal of discussion. That is the subject of **evolution**. Some within the New Age accept a "once-and-forever original belief system" which prohibits evolution. In the place of evolving growth, they feel that we are merely to awaken to what we once were and in reality have always been. These adherents justify this position by their belief that all were created in the very beginning with God; and that the reason for our existence in this physical form is to be awakened to what we once were in that original state. They accept the belief that God is immutable, meaning that He never changes. It is their desire to awaken to what we were with that immutable God at that time of the original creation. In this belief system, there is no such thing as evolution and an individual does not evolve. Instead, he awakens to return to his original position with God.

Those who accept an "evolution belief system" believe that all were with God at the creation and that God is immutable in that He never changes. Their difference with the "original belief system" is their belief that God is **ALL**, and through evolution and growth, the ALL can change. Therefore, whereas God does not change in the sense that He is always the ALL, He does grow to encompass the new ALL created by growth in those who were originally generated in His image. In this belief system, those who believe in God evolve and grow as they help Him to create the new ALL. If this happens, then those who do not evolve but merely return to where God was, will find that He is no longer there, for by encompassing the new ALL, He has evolved.

Those who believe in the evolution belief system feel that they evolve by gaining experience in a number of incarnations. The particular set of experiences for each incarnation is designed by their soul [or higher self] working in conjunction with spirit. This work occurs in the Monad, which is the first emanation of God. In the Monadic environment, soul [from the personality] and spirit [from God] evaluate the evolved progress of the personality and generate the particular set of experiences needed to create further evolution. The personality then incarnates to gain the experiences.

The New Age contains both those who accept the *original*

belief system and the *evolution belief system*. Even though there is this difference of opinion within the New Age, those of the New Age who are dedicated to the concept of unconditional love will accept the belief systems of each person without the expressing the intolerance practiced by the Christian Church. And to my knowledge, no one has ever been excommunicated from the New Age.

The New Age welcomes those who love, follow and become the Essence of Christ. They do this with three beliefs firmly in mind. Those beliefs are:

1. That one can love the Essence of Christ [i.e. be a Christian] without belonging to the congregation of an established church [i.e. without belonging to Christianity];

2. That one can expand his or her belief system, because the restrictions placed on the Christian's belief system have been placed there by the men of the Church and not by Christ and not by God; and

3. That the Christian New Ager is closer to the original teachings of Christ than the orthodox Christian of today, because the teachings of Christ have been altered by man.

CHAPTER FOUR
SUMMARY AND COMMENTS

The first three chapters of *Book One* plus the three associated Appendixes covered some of the people, many of the controversies, a few of the events, and several of the Creeds or Rules of Faith which were important to the development of the Christian Church during its first 2000 years. It covered this period in a historical manner with only a minor amount of analysis. A few analytical comments will be presented in this Chapter, but most will be reserved for *Book Two*. In essence, this Chapter is intended to summarize and present a finale of *Book One*. It is only a minor preview of the deeper analytical presentations of *Book Two*.

The first period examined covered the first 280 years of the Church's existence: from the Crucifixion in about 33 CE to the Edict of Milan in 313. Many events occurred during this exploratory stage. Sifting through all of the chaff to get to the wheat, one could say that there were two important characteristics of the Church which were developed during this period; that there were three important decisions which were made by the Church during this period; and that one vitally important event outside the Church happened during this period which changed the character of the Church forever. The following paragraphs present a concise picture of those six events.

The two important characteristics of the Church developed during this period were: [1] that the Church took an aggressive posture to defend what the Church felt was "true Christianity" by getting actively involved in a number of controversies; and [2] that the Church depended strongly on oral tradition in order to understand what the Apostles taught.

The three important decisions made by the Church during this period were: [1] that the teachings of the Church would be uniform; [2] that the uniform teachings of the Church would be based primarily on the Apostolic Tradition; and [3] that anyone not accepting the uniform teachings of the Church would be excluded from Church participation.

The vitally important outside event which changed the character of the Church forever was the fact that Constantine won the Battle of Milvian Bridge.

Although these six events might seem so simplistic that one would want to say, "Of course it happened that way," think for a moment what the Church might be like if these events had not happened. If Maxentius had become Emperor rather than Constantine, the only Christians the world might have known would be those who followed Jesus the Christ, not all the others who became Christian because it was the "thing to do" or because the state forced them to do it. In addition, the theological decisions made by several Emperors might not have happened. Finally, the most influential English Bible in history [the King James Version] might have been directly translated from Greek instead of being a forced translation from Latin with all the mistranslations which that caused [see *Christianity and the New Age Religion* for a few examples of this problem].

Going further, if the Church had not required the uniform teaching of material generated from non-scriptural sources such as the Apostolic Tradition, then instead of all the litanies, doctrines and dogmas which the Church requires its members to understand today, the only teaching of the Church would be to present the Bible and let each individual seek out what it means to him guided solely by the Holy Spirit working through his conscience and unencumbered by prior priestly presentations. What a difference! And if all the controversies had not been fought, then any Christian could believe what he might choose to believe so long as he accepted and followed Jesus the Christ and believed that Jesus Christ reflected God in the flesh. Again, what a difference!

The Church of today is what it is because these six events happened during the first 280 years of its existence. That is the only point which this review is trying to make. It is not the purpose of this work to propose that the Church should be different or that it would have been different if certain things had gone in another direction. But it is the purpose of this work to say that the Church is what it is because of what happened early in its existence. And these six events present a summary of what happened during the first 280 years of the existence of the Christian Church. They did effect the activities of the Church forever, for these six events are the basis upon which the Church started to define itself.

The definition stage of the Christian Church happened during the next 240 years, or until about the end of the Fifth Ecumenical Council in 553 CE. This Chapter will close *Book One* by giving only a brief synopsis of that definition stage; for the job of presenting an in-depth analysis and commentary on the definitions developed in this stage is the major purpose of *Book Two*.

During the first 520 years of the Christian Church, and particularly during the latter 240 years of that period, a lot of time and effort was spent trying to define who Jesus the Christ was. As a result of this effort, by the end of this period Jesus Christ was defined as being the "only begotten" Son of God who was born of a virgin and is both completely divine and completely human. In order to do this, Jesus Christ was defined as having two natures and two wills. However, he was not, in any way, two persons. Instead, he is "one and the same Son...complete in his deity and complete...in his humanity"; and although he is one "person" and one "substance," he exists in two natures which are at once unconfused and unaltered, and, on the other hand, undivided and inseparable. In this way, Jesus Christ was defined as being "God is with us," but as a complete and ordinary human being. Because of all the time and effort which had been put forth to develop this definition, those who did not agree completely with it were no longer considered to be a Christian.

In addition to this definition of Christ, those who followed the Christ were also defined. They were defined in at least three ways. First, they were defined as being a loyal subject of the supreme Church; for as Origen first said and Augustine and Cyprian later repeated when they supported the supremacy of the Church, *"extra ecclesiam nulla salus,"* or, "There is no salvation outside the Church." Secondly, they were defined as having a new Mother, for as Cyprian also said, "He can no longer have the God for his Father who has not the church for his Mother," a statement which was later repeated by Augustine. Finally they were defined as those who needed the Sacraments of the Church. According to the Bible, Jesus said, *"Whoever believes and is baptized will be saved; but he who does not believe will be condemned."* [Mark 16:16]; but during the definition stage of the Church, Augustine augmented this by saying that *"...those who do not receive the Sacrament [of Baptism] shall be condemned."* That statement is a major difference from what Christ is reported to have said.

As a consequence of these three definitions of an orthodox Christian, those who wished to follow Christ were defined as requiring the Church in order to do so. And they were not led to the Church because they chose to do so, but because they were required to do so. The orthodox Christian was defined as having no other choice.

In conclusion, Jesus Christ, his Church and his followers were defined during this period of 240 years. In presenting these definitions, the Church Fathers defined the Church [i.e. Christianity], the leader of the Church [i.e. Jesus Christ] and the followers of the Church [i.e. a Christian] in a way that was significantly different than any definition presented in the Scriptures or by any of the Apostles who had known Jesus. This point will be enlarged upon in *Book Two*.

BOOK TWO
HOW THE TEACHINGS OF CHRIST
HAVE BEEN ALTERED BY SOME
WHO FOLLOWED HIM

CHAPTER ONE
AN ANALYSIS OF THE CHANGES

This Chapter will use the information developed in *Book One* to answer four major questions which are:
1. What policies or teachings have been established by the Church which seem to have been altered from the concepts or the teachings of Jesus Christ;
2. How was the leader of the Church [i.e. Jesus Christ] defined;
3. How were the followers of Jesus Christ [i.e. Christians] defined? and
4. How was the "body of Christ" [i.e. his church] defined.

This Chapter will analyze several subject areas. The analysis of each will start by presenting the concept at the time of Jesus, and then describing how that concept was changed during the subsequent 2,000 years with emphasis on the first 500 years. That sub-section will be followed by a presentation on today's thinking, followed by a summary of what the changes have meant to a follower of Christ. It is believed that this series of analyses will show that the teachings of Christ have been altered by some who followed him.

Each of these subjects could take a full book, and each subject interacts with all the others. Consequently the following presentations will merely be an overview, albeit one presented in enough depth or detail to make the point. All indications or conclusions presented in each subject area have acceptable intellectual references which can be used for substantiation. Despite the "bare-bones" nature of this approach, it is believed that at the end of this Chapter, the interested reader will know more than he did at the beginning.

The following subject areas will be examined:
1. Christology [Definition of Jesus Christ]
2. Christian [Definition of a Follower of Christ]
3. Apostolic Tradition or Succession
4. Salvation
5. Soul
6. Intolerance
7. World Affairs
8. Reincarnation and Karma
9. Angels
10. Sex or Sexuality
11. Summary

1. CHRISTOLOGY[1]

Christology means "the definition of Jesus Christ based on studies of his person and qualities." By the end of the third century CE, it had become quite an art form. It is a subject which has made more Saints and more Sinners than any other subject in Christianity. The definition of who Jesus Christ was, is one of the four important questions to be addressed in this Chapter.

In the Scriptures, Christ was not defined in any clear-cut way which could be understood by all. In fact, it is quite evident that those who knew him best, his disciples, were somewhat confused by him, as were the common people. Because the Scriptures did not give an adequate definition, when the disciples [i.e. the Apostles] were no longer available for guidance, many people tried to define Christ in many different ways, some of which were immediately rejected as being heresy [i.e. untrue teaching] and others of which went through long periods of debate before they were accepted.

Obviously, Christology is a subject which could, and has, occupied many large volumes. This section will merely try to give an understanding of what the problem is.

Concepts at the time of Jesus.

1. In the gospels, there are 35 times when Jesus is called some phrase which could be interpreted as "Son of God." These references are presented in the Appendix of *Christianity and the New Age Religion* and will not be repeated here. In most of those references it is quite often God or the author of the gospel [especially in John] who gives him this name. Only rarely could any statement be interpreted as Jesus calling himself by that title.

It should be noted that during this time, the title "Son of God" was commonly used in the Near East to signify a special servant of God. It was often used for a king, a pharaoh, a great philosopher, a miracle worker, a holy man, or even a hero of the people.[2] In the Bible, David is told by God that He [God] will be his father and he [David] will be My son [2 Samuel 7:14]. Consequently, even David, who was considered to be a mighty king but never a God, was called the Son of God.

However, when the gospel went out from the Near East and into the Roman Empire, this title was taken literally as dogma. It signified that Christ was divine because he was the Son of God. This divine nature of Christ was officially accepted by the Church at the Council of Nicaea in 325 CE. It then required another 150 years and three more Ecumenical Councils before it was decided that Jesus had two natures: one human and the other divine. Many were excommunicated from the Church because they had a hard time accepting that belief. It is possible that Jesus himself would have had a hard time accepting that belief, because it was certainly far removed from his teachings or statements.

The concept of the Son of God being a hero to the people of the Near East is particularly important in trying to understand Mark 15:39 which has a centurion stating, *"Truly this man was the Son* [Note: or *a Son*] *of God"*; for either the centurion, a man not generally noted for having a great intellect, came to a conclusion which it took the Christian theologians over 400 years to resolve [i.e. that

Jesus was both man and God], or else he merely meant that this <u>man</u> was truly a hero.

The point being made here is that although Jesus may have been known as a Son of God, in his society that was a title which had been used for a number of people.

2. There are only three times in the gospels and four times in the entire New Testament in which Jesus Christ is called the *only* Son of God. All of these are presented by the author of the Gospel and Letters of John. The word "only" in English is a mistranslation of the Greek word *monogenes*. The background, in detail, of this mistranslation is presented in *Christianity and the New Age Religion* and will not be repeated here except to say that many biblical scholars agree with the conclusion that the Scriptures, in their original language, do *not* say that Jesus was the *only* Son of God; and that certainly, Jesus never made that claim. Consequently, in the time of Jesus, he was never considered to be the *only* Son of God.

3. In reading the New Testament, it is interesting to note how few times the Hebrew or Aramaic word "Messiah" or its Greek equivalent "Christ" [each which means "the anointed one"] is used. In Mark, probably the first gospel to be written, the word is used only seven times, one of which is in the title. Of the other six uses, only three [Mark 8:29; 9:14; and 14:61-2] refer to Jesus being the Christ or Messiah. Consequently, in the time of Jesus, he was only rarely said to be "the anointed one."

4. It is also interesting to note that in Mark 14:62, the only time which Jesus clearly admits to being the "Christ, the Son of the Blessed," he does so by saying *"I am; and you will see the Son of man seated at the right hand of Power, and coming with the clouds of heaven."* Thus, after admitting to being the Son of God for the only unequivocal time, he immediately calls himself something else, the "Son of man." This is the most commonly used title for Jesus in the gospels. It is used fourteen times in Mark's gospel, and thirty-one times in the longer gospel of Matthew in which the title "Son of God" is used only four times.

What Jesus meant by calling himself "Son of man" is still one of the most hotly debated subjects in New Testament study. It is a concept which has almost as many interpretations as there are theologians. These interpretations range all the way from being a substitute for "I," to being a supernatural representation of God who has come in a form which could serve mankind. The best understanding of the interpretation within the Jewish society of the time can probably be found in the Old Testament, where the term is used most often to represent a distinction between man and God. This use is presented in Numbers 23:19; Job 25:6; Psalms 8:4 and 146:3; and Isaiah 51:12. It was also used to state that a prophet was a man and not a God in Ezekiel 2:1 and Daniel 8:17. However, in Daniel 7:13-4 the term is used to present a supernatural representation of God. This is the only such use in the Old Testament. Consequently, when Jesus called himself "Son of man," to those of his society the weight of historical evidence would seem to indicate that he was saying, "I am a man, just like you, and I am distinct from God." However, to those who had knowledge of the writings of Daniel, he could have been saying, "a man can become a supernatural representation of God presented in a form which can serve you."

5. In John 7:12, we read "And there was much muttering about him among the people. While some said, 'He is a good man,' others said, 'No, he is leading the people astray.' " Thus it is obvious that the people were confused, but at best called him a good *man*.

6. In the 14th Chapter of John, after Jesus has said that those who have known him also know the Father, in verse 8 Philip says, "Lord, show us the Father and we will be satisfied." Jesus then takes over 20 verses to convince Philip and the other disciples that in seeing him, they have seen God. But it is rather obvious that the disciples did not see God in Jesus until after he had said, "Believe me that I am in the Father and the Father in me" [John 14:11]. Not only had the disciples failed to admit that Jesus was God, Jesus himself did likewise. In Mark 10:17-8 we read these words, *"Good Teacher, what must I do to inherit eternal life?" And Jesus said to him, "Why do you call me good? No one is good but God alone."* And in John 14:28, Jesus says, *"...for that the Father is greater than I."* Consequently, in at least these two cases, Jesus has said in no uncertain terms that he is <u>not</u> equal to God!

7. In Mark 8: 27-30, Jesus asks his disciples, *"Who do men say that I am?" And they told him, "John the Baptist; and others say*

Elijah; and others one of the prophets." And he asked them, "But who do you say that I am?" Peter answered him, "You are the Christ." And he charged them to tell no one about him. In this case, only Peter among the disciples recognized Jesus as "the anointed one." The others thought him to be one of the prophets, reincarnated in their time.

8. Although it was not a definition given at the time of Jesus, it is pertinent to note the words of Clement of Alexandria in the early second century. He called the Fourth Gospel a "spiritual gospel," because he felt that the Jesus of the first three gospels was certainly different than the more spiritual Jesus of the Fourth Gospel.[3] Consequently, there is a different interpretation of Jesus in the last of the four gospels chosen for the canon.

9. In the King James Version of the Bible, Jesus is called "Rabbi" thirteen times. In the Revised Standard Version, many of these have been changed to "Master" with a footnote saying, "or Rabbi"; but several have retained the Rabbi title, particularly in the Gospel of John such as in John 1:49 or 3:2. This is a very interesting title to give Jesus for two important reasons. The first is that Rabbi not only means "teacher," it also means one who is thought to be authoritative in their study, exposition and practice of Jewish law. Secondly, to be a Rabbi, you had to be married, for the Jewish Mishnaic Law is quite explicit on the subject that "An unmarried man may not be a teacher."[4] Consequently, it could logically be argued that at the time of Jesus, the people not only considered him to be a teacher who was well versed in the Jewish Law, they assumed [or knew] that he was married [see Section 10, pages 200-201].

10. In conclusion, the Scriptures give a very incomplete picture of who Jesus was as interpreted during his time, and even as seen by the early church theologians. The concepts range all the way from a human just like anyone else, to a prophet [probably the most prevalent concept], to a hero, to the Son of God who is the servant of God like many were, to the Son of God who is a one-of-a-kind [the correct translation of *monogenes*] Son, to a supernatural representation of God. To some of his disciples, he was the "anointed one" but they seemed to be confused as to whether he showed them God in any way other than the prophets had; and Jesus himself stated on more than one occasion that he was <u>not</u> identical with God.

But even though some may have considered him to be the "Christ" or the "anointed one," to no one was he the *only* anointed one of God; and although some may have become convinced that in seeing Jesus they had received a glimpse of God, or that in listening to the authority of the Sermon on the Mount they had received the words of God, no one including Jesus said that he *was* God. This is the best picture which the Scriptures present as to how the people of his time defined him, at least in the time before his Crucifixion and Resurrection.

Changes in Concepts

It is probable that the Apostles had no real problem defining Jesus Christ after his resurrection. Although there is little historical record of what they might have said, theirs was a simple faith of spirit. As they traveled the roads with full faith that they were on the Way, they probably said something like, "I have met a leader whom I follow. I follow him because I believe he lives. He was unjustly crucified, but he rose from the grave. My leader, Jesus Christ, has risen and he lives. I also believe that he is an anointed one from God who teaches great lessons of life and how to live it. Those who follow him, as I do, have no fears about this world and this life; and we know that by following him, we will be with God as he is." Incidentally, it is of interest to note that the early ones who followed him were not called "Christians." That term was not in common use within the Church until almost 100 years after the Crucifixion. Instead, the early followers were known as "belonging to the Way" [Acts 9:2].

But later, those who followed Christ had a big problem. It can be readily seen by a conflict between two principles which Origen espoused. The first principle is that the Savior must be *divine* in order to be able to save. The second principle is that the emanations from the Father down to the lowest levels are in degrees, and that the dividing lines are somewhat arbitrary. It was the latter point which caused some problems between the teachings of Origen and the Church, because the Church had decided that only Jesus was an emanation from God and that everything else was created, not emanated.

The conflict mentioned above not only was a problem to

Origen, it was a problem to the entire Church; for as the Church developed, the three central doctrines of [1] atonement, [2] incarnation, and [3] trinity had to come together as a complete package. To atone, Jesus had to be divine; but since he had been seen in the flesh, then he must be God incarnate. And since there is only one God or only one being, then there have to be at least two [later three with the Holy Spirit] persons in one being.

All of this, and all of the Christology arguments which were central to the Church's development during its first 500 years, are based on *one simple belief* which was accepted as a *truth* by the Church. That belief was that *only* God could generate atonement, with atonement meaning reconciliation with God. Since the Church believed it was an absolute truth that no man, no matter how talented or holy, could generate atonement, then if Jesus were to be the agent for atonement, he must be *divine*. And since there was *only* one God, then the divinity of Jesus could not cause a multiplicity of Gods, and Jesus must therefore *be one with God in all ways and equalities*.

If it ever could have been believed and accepted that God, who is all-powerful, was so powerful that he could have sent a message of redemption via a messenger whom He sent, and that with redemption there would be atonement, then none of the mind-boggling debates and rationalizations about the definition of Jesus Christ would have been necessary at all. Jesus would have been the one-of-a-kind [i.e. *monogenes*] anointed one who would lead those who follow him toward reconciliation with God. And possibly others sent by God could be a one-of-a-kind messenger who could also lead those who followed them toward reconciliation with God. Even within Christianity it is granted that God has sent more than one one-of-a-kind messenger. Isaac is called *monogenes* in Heb. 11:17-8. And John the Baptist is certainly called a messenger in John 1:6 which says, "There was a man sent from God, whose name was John."

But because the redeemer [i.e. one who sets others free] or savior [i.e. one who saves others] has to be *divine* in order to be the atoner [i.e. one who reconciles others to God], then he had to *be God* and not merely be a special messenger who brought God's powerful message for all to hear. Since there is only one God, then according to Christianity, Jesus had to be the *only* messenger who *was* God.

In a nutshell, that is why man had to define Jesus Christ, even though the Scriptures did not. The following paragraphs will outline some of the steps which were taken to generate this definition. The first paragraph will give a summary of the definition, presenting certain parts in bold print. Those parts will be elaborated upon in the subsequent paragraphs based on information about the councils of the Church presented in other parts of this book, and about the people and the controversies [presented in Appendix A] as well as the creeds [presented in Appendix B].

1. During the first 520 years of the Christian Church, a considerable amount of time and effort was spent trying to define who Jesus the Christ was. As a result of this effort, Jesus Christ was defined as being the **only begotten** Son of God who was born of a **virgin** and is both **completely divine** and **completely human**. In order to do this, he had **two natures** and **two wills**; but was not, in any way, two persons. Instead, as presented in the Definition of Chalcedon [Appendix B] he is "one and the same Son...complete in his deity and complete...in his humanity" and although he is one "person" and one "substance," he exists in two natures which are at once unconfused and unaltered as well as being undivided and inseparable. In this way, Jesus Christ was defined as being "God is with us," but as a complete and ordinary human being. Because of all the time and effort used to develop this definition, anyone who did not agree with it was no longer considered to be a Christian.

2. Only begotten means that God sired no other Son. The "only" part of this expression was first offered as a definition of Jesus Christ by Eusebius in the Creed of Caesarea in 325 CE, but was not officially accepted by the Church until included in the Nicene Creed and the Definition of Chalcedon, both of which were accepted at the Fourth Ecumenical Council in 451. The "begotten" portion was presented prior to that by the Creed of Nicaea which was officially accepted at the First Ecumenical Council in 325. Since the belief that he was the "only begotten" was not presented in the Scriptures and was not accepted by the Church until some 420 years after his resurrection and ascension, it may be interesting to examine some possible bases for this affirmation. Was it the ascension? As documented in *Christianity and the New Age Religion*, there are five cases of ascension recorded in the Scriptures, only one of which is Jesus Christ. Was it his uniqueness? There is no question that Jesus Christ was a *monogenes* [i.e. unique] Son of God; but Isaac was also a *monogenes* son of Abraham [Heb. 11:17]. However, Isaac's uniqueness did not make him the "only begotten" of Abraham, for the Scriptures show that Abraham had at least seven other sons. What was it that made Jesus the *only begotten* Son of God, a concept which seems to have little, if any, documentation in the Scriptures?

3. Virgin means that Jesus had no Earthly father. Again as documented in *Christianity and the New Age Religion*, there is no biblical justification for this concept. In fact, the scriptures in their original language neither predicted such a birth nor said that it happened. In addition, this definition, which was meant to make the birth of Jesus special, was never mentioned by Peter, the one who knew him the best, or by Paul, the one who reported on him the most. It was mentioned by Irenaeus in his Rules of Faith in 190 CE, but was not mentioned in the first great creed accepted by the Church, the Creed of Nicaea in 325. Instead, the first Church-wide Creed which used it was the Nicene Creed, accepted in 451 along with "conceived by the Holy Spirit" [see Appendix B].

4. Completely divine became a part of the definition of Jesus Christ in order to combat the first great conflict which arose in the Church after it became accepted as a legitimate religion by the State. That conflict was presented by Arius and was known as Arianism [Appendix A]. The Council of Nicaea in 325 defined Jesus Christ as being completely divine.

5. Completely human was never a question in the scriptures, for he is often described as a man and as one who said that other humans could do what he did as long as they believed in him [John 14:12]. But the concept of <u>completely human</u> confused a number of otherwise believing Christians who believed that his divinity overpowered his humanity. The **two natures** [i.e. completely divine and completely human] were not affirmed until the Fourth Ecumenical Council in 451. This then led some to think that although he had two natures, he had only one will. The **two wills** of Christ was not affirmed until the Sixth Ecumenical Council in 680 CE, about 650 years after the Crucifixion.

6. Many who disagreed with any part of the above definition were excommunicated from the Church. One very interesting case is that of Pope Honorius I [625-640] who was declared a heretic by the Sixth Ecumenical Council merely because he was working for peace and unity within the church and declared that whether or not Christ had two wills was simply not worth debating over. Because he took this stance, the Church kicked him out.[5]

7. The point of mentioning the heresy of Pope Honorius I is to present the point that much of the theology of the fourth and fifth centuries looks like futile quibbling about inconsequential details. Is the Son of God identical to the Father [*homoousios*], or merely similar to the Father [*homoiousios*]? Is the incarnate Lord to be recognized as one out of two natures or one in two natures? Is the Trinity represented by three times one equals one; and Christ's nature represented by two times one equals one? Why all of this convoluted thinking? Again, the Church needed this convoluted thinking because: [1] since Christ is the Savior and since *only* God can save, then Christ must *be God*; [2] since the only way that Christ can save is by touching us and our condition, then Christ must *be human*; and [3] these two aspects of Christ's identity must be kept distinct, but they must not compromise his unity with God since there is *only one God*.

8. These definitions were established by the Ecumenical Councils; but there were a few attempts at a definition of Jesus Christ even before the Councils started their efforts. One interesting definition happened very early. In the first century, Christians were taught that Christ had been God's agent in creation, meaning that Christ was the mechanism used by God to create all things.[6] This definition was startling and was not presented in exactly that way in the gospels, even though the gospel of John had emphasized that Jesus had been with God at the time of the creation. It also was not presented in exactly this way in Paul's first Letter to the Corinthians [see Footnote 6 on page 48]. However, this definition was not unique, for it previously had been used by the Jews with the personification of Wisdom in Proverbs [see Proverbs 1:20 as an example]; by the Egyptians with Isis; and by the Greeks with Athena. Thus, again the early Christians borrowed from Judaism and from other religions to get a definition of their leader, a borrowing which was later emphasized by the Church Fathers with their use of the *Logos* [see Chapter 2, *Book One*. Also, again see footnote 6 of that Chapter].

9. Looking at definitions which came much later than the Ecumenical Councils on Christology, in *The Quest of the Historical Jesus* [translated 1906], Albert Schweitzer, a world-noted theologian, says that, "The whole history of Christianity down to the present day...the real inner history of it, is based on the delay of the *parousia*, the non-occurrence of the *parousia,* the abandonment of *eschatology*, the progress and completion of the *deeschatologizing* of religion which has been connected therein." Once this conclusion is accepted, reasoned Schweitzer, contemporary theology will find that the historical Jesus "will be the Jesus who was Messiah and lived as such either on the ground of a literary fiction of the earliest evangelist, or on the ground of a purely eschatological messianic conception."[7]

Although this may seem to be rather difficult to understand, it is worth the effort. *Parousia* means "the Second Coming of Christ." *Eschatology* means "the theological study of the end of things such as death or the end of the world as we know it." Consequently, what Schweitzer is saying is that when Christ did not immediately appear and change the world, then his religion had to change. In that changing, Jesus Christ got redefined in an unusual way. If we look back to what Jesus Christ was before he got redefined, we will find that he was the anointed one who became such either because of a good press agent, or because of an end-of-the world concept which most of his followers no longer accept.

Despite presenting this definition, Schweitzer followed Jesus Christ, **as do I.**

Present-day Status

At the present time, Christology resides in two camps within the Christian Community. The first camp is represented by the Christians of the sectarian Churches. To them Jesus is the *only* Son of God, the *only* Savior of mankind, and the *only* source by which there is reconciliation with God. Since he can do all of these, then Jesus Christ must *be* God; not merely the Son of God, but God the Son. Because of this, there is no other way which God can be found. Because of this, all people should accept Christ as he has been defined by the Church because if they do not, they can never be with God.

The other camp is represented by the liberal, ecumenical Christians. To them, Jesus is the most viable way to God and the one which they have chosen, not because he is the only way but because he is the way of their choice. They are Christians of the spirit who have chosen Christ from love rather than from the fear that he is the only option available. Many of them are staying in the mainstream or sectarian churches because they feel that the Church represents an organization through which much good can be accomplished. However, more and more of them are leaving the sectarian churches as a matter of conscience as they note the intolerance of this religion toward the other religions of the world. It is the sense of ecumenical tolerance, without denying Christ, that motivates most of this camp

It must be very confusing to those of the sectarian churches as to how the other camp could consider themselves to be Christian; for they accept the possibility of routes to God other than that given by Jesus Christ when the Church states that Jesus is the *only* way. Also, the sectarian Christian must have a difficult time accepting the thought that Jesus was not the only emanation of God, but that all who were created in God's image came to that image as the result of an emanation and not as a creation out of nothing. Each of these goes against the teaching of the Church as developed by the "theology of the ancient catholic church," one of the foundations of the present sectarian churches.

But in reply, remember that this theology was developed by man. Although I feel certain that each man felt he was guided by the Holy Spirit when decisions were made which established such theology, every human being has the necessity to fight being led by his own ego rather than by Spirit. And although it is not any human's right to judge another [Matt. 7:1], it certainly seems as if many of the Church's decisions have been based on an individual's personal ego as much as on the guidance of Spirit.

The sectarian Christian might try to counter by saying that in the Scriptures, Jesus says, "I and the Father are one" [John 10:30]; and "no one comes to the Father but by me." [John 14:6]. In response to those quotations, in an essay entitled *"I" in the Words of Jesus*, Seiichi Yagi makes the rather interesting point that when the Jesus of the Fourth gospel [i.e. commonly called the gospel according to John] speaks, it is fundamentally the Father speaking through him.[8] Thus, in the "I and the Father are one" verse, Jesus is saying that "When the Father speaks through me, the Father which speaks through me and the Father are one"; and in the other verse, he is saying that "no one comes to the Father but through the Father [or God] in me." In this sense, it is the same as Paul meant when he said "Christ lives in me" [Gal 1:20] which he could do after Christ was revealed to him. Therefore, "Christ is revealed to me" equates to "Christ in me." The same is true when God revealed himself to Jesus and thus became "in him." This is what Professor Yagi believes the Fourth gospel refers to when Jesus uses the word "I" in the "I am" sayings. Thus, when Jesus said, "I am the bread of life" [John 6:35] he was saying "The Father in me is the bread of life." And when Jesus said that "no one comes to the Father but by me," he was saying that "no one finds God without finding the God which is within them."[8]

It is not my intent to convince anyone of this concept; merely to present it as a thought which differs from the teaching of the sectarian church. The essay in which this thought is presented has a background of Bible study and analysis which is as impressive as anything that the sectarian church has ever given me to read. I will also say that this essay makes a great deal of sense to me. As mentioned in the first section of this work, I have taught adult Sunday School in mainstream churches for a number of years. One of my favorite subjects was the Parables. I truly loved to teach those teachings of Christ. It bothered me that there were no parables in the Gospel of John. It was only after studying John Drane's magnificent book, *Introducing the New Testament*, that I came to realize that many of the "I am" sayings in John are really parables in disguise. In other words, they are meant to teach, rather than to represent a statement of fact. The essay by Yagi supports the concept that when Jesus of the Fourth Gospel uses the phrase "I am," he is teaching rather than describing. This makes a great deal of sense to me. It is my belief that it would make a great deal of sense to anyone who would approach it with a mind which is open and not encumbered by the theological theories developed by the early Church. Because of this belief, this essay is a good fit with the major theme of this Chapter.

And besides, it is a scriptural <u>fact</u>, that Jesus did <u>not</u> say, "*Only* I and the Father are one."

In conclusion, the present state of Christology presents two Christian camps: those who accept the theology of the first 500 years of the Church as a "Revealed Truth," and those who do not. It is a division almost as strong as that which led to the first Reformation of the Christian Church. There are some who hope that it can lead to a Second Reformation.

What do these changes mean to today's Christian?

Because of the two camps into which the Christian Community is dividing itself, the changes in the definition of Christ imposed by the first 500 years of the Church's history are forcing dedicated followers of Christ to decide whether they are following the Christ as they interpret him from the Scriptures, or as the Church has interpreted him from their debates. It is a conflict of conscience on the part of many Christians whose impact has not, as yet, been fully felt by the Church. It is a conflict which could lead to a complete schism, or could lead to a Second Reformation of the Church.

2. CHRISTIAN
[DEFINITION OF A FOLLOWER OF CHRIST][1]

Concepts at the time of Jesus.

There are many references in the Bible which describe the followers of Christ before the Church got organized. A few of these will be presented in paragraphs 1-7 which follow. Possibly the best description of the early followers of Christ is given in a letter, dating from the second century. It is presented in its entirety in paragraph 8.

1. In Matthew 4:19-20 we read, "And he said to them, 'Follow me, and I will make you fishers of men.' " The men whom Jesus addressed were Simon who is called Peter and Andrew, his brother. They were fishermen. Jesus made them his first followers and asked them to help him find some more followers. And so the very earliest followers of Jesus were people who believed in him enough that they wanted to tell others about him.

2. In Matthew 7:28, after the Sermon on the Mount, we read,

"And when Jesus finished these sayings, the crowds were astonished at his teaching, for he taught them as one who had authority, and not as their scribes." And so those who followed him were those who wanted to be taught, and to be taught with authority and not just as if the teacher were merely repeating what had previously been written.

3. In the eighth Chapter of Matthew, we read that those who followed him had to give up all of their worldly cares and possessions. Thus, those who followed him did so with no thought of worldly things.

4. In Matthew 9:10 we read, "And as he sat at table [or reclined] in the house, behold, many tax collectors and sinners came and sat down with Jesus and his disciples." Thus, his followers were not among the socially acceptable, but Jesus accepted them and they accepted him without consideration of social standing or propriety.

5. In Matthew 9:36 we read, "When he saw the crowds, he had compassion for them, because they were harassed and helpless, like sheep without a shepherd." Thus, his followers were the kind who wanted to be comforted and led.

6. There are many verses of Scripture which relate to the cures which Jesus made on those who were sick or lame. In most of these cases Jesus did not seek them out. Instead, a loved one brought them to Jesus. Therefore, the followers of Jesus were ones who believed that he could cure the earthly ills of their loved ones.

7. In Matthew 16:24-5, we read, "Then Jesus told his disciples, 'If any man would come after me, let him deny himself and take up his cross and follow me. For whoever would save his life will lose it, and whoever loses his life for my sake will find it.' " Thus, the followers of Christ were those who established a personal relationship with him in which they were willing to forsake everything, even their own lives.

8. These are just a few verses of Scripture which give a description of the followers of Christ. But all of these descriptions were written down by one who also was a follower of Christ. What did the Christians look like to those who were on the outside, those who were not necessarily followers of Christ? The following is from an anonymous Letter to Diognetus, possibly dating from the second century. It presents a picture of the followers of Christ prior to their definition by the Church.[9]

" *For Christians are not differentiated from other people by country, language or customs; you see, they do not live in cities of their own, or speak some strange dialect, or have some peculiar lifestyle.*

This teaching of theirs has not been contrived by the invention and speculation of inquisitive men; nor are they propagating mere human teaching as some people do. They live in both Greek and foreign cities, wherever chance has put them. They follow local customs in clothing, food and other aspects of life. But at the same time, they demonstrate to us the wonderful and certainly unusual form of their own citizenship.

They live in their own native lands, but as aliens; as citizens they share all things with others; but like aliens, suffer all things. Every foreign country is to them as their native country, and every native land as a foreign country.

They marry and have children just like every one else; but they do not kill unwanted babies. They offer a shared table, but not a shared bed. They are at present 'in the flesh' but they do not live 'according to the flesh.' They are passing their days on earth, but are citizens of heaven. They obey the appointed laws in their own lives.

They love every one, but are persecuted by all. They are unknown and condemned; they are put to death and gain life. They are poor and yet make many rich. They are short of everything and yet have plenty of all things. They are dishonoured and yet gain glory through dishonour.

Their names are blackened and yet they are cleared. They are mocked and bless in return. They are treated outrageously and behave respectfully to others. When they do good, they are punished as evildoers; when punished, they rejoice as if being given new life. They are attacked by Jews as aliens, and they are persecuted by Greeks; yet those who hate them cannot give any reason for their hostility.

To put it simply—the soul is to the body as Christians are to the world. The soul is spread through all parts of the body and Christians through all the cities of the world. The soul is in the body but is not of the body; Christians are in the world but not of the world."

9. And with that, we will conclude this definition of the followers of Christ during his time, and during the subsequent time until the Church got active in its definitions. In summary, the early follower of Christ was one who felt a personal relationship with him, unencumbered by rules and/or regulations. It was a relationship worth having, even if keeping it meant being persecuted or crucified.

Changes in Concepts

The major change in the definition of a follower of Christ has to do with placing the Church and its teachings between the follower and his Christ. Therefore, this topic will be the major subject of this sub-section. Before that, one other interesting difference between how Christ thought of his followers and how some of the Church Fathers did should be noted.

In the early third century, Hippolytus allowed himself to be elected antipope because he disagreed with Pope Callistus who had been elected in 217. Their disagreement had to do with whether or not those who had sinned should be allowed to enter the church. Callistus felt that they should, for only in that way could they be educated to follow Christ's teaching such as when he saved the woman from a stoning and said, "Neither do I condemn you; go, and do not sin again." [John 4:11]. Hippolytus, however, believed that the church was only for the redeemed and that it formed a society in which those who sinned could not be tolerated. In this way, although he differed from Origen who saw the church as a school for sinners, he agreed with the Pharisees who had shunned the sinners [Matt. 9:10-3]. He thus disagreed with Christ who loved the sinners and had a society with them. In this way, Hippolytus changed his concepts quite markedly from the concepts of Christ.

But again, the major difference in how the Christian got defined by man rather than by Christ is the fact that the Church placed itself squarely between the follower and his Christ. This thought has been presented so often in this work that it will merely be summarized in this section.

By the end of the first 500 years of the Church's existence, the Church had not only defined Christ, they had required his followers to accept those definitions. In addition, the Church defined the follower as being a loyal subject of the supreme Church. They did this in at least three important ways, all of which have previously been mentioned. First, they told the follower that he needed the Church; for as Origen said and Augustine and Cyprian later repeated when they supported the supremacy of the Church, *"extra ecclesiam nulla salus,"* or, "There is no salvation outside the Church." Secondly, they defined the Church as being as meaningful in the life of a Christian as God was, for as Cyprian said, "He can no longer have the God for his Father who has not the church for his Mother," a statement which was later repeated by Augustine. Finally the followers were defined as those who needed the Sacraments of the Church. Jesus said, "... he who does not believe will be condemned." [Mark 16:16]. Augustine brought the Church squarely into this by saying that "...those who do not receive the Sacrament [of Baptism] shall be condemned." In other words, a follower had to do more than just believe. He also had to submit to the sacraments of the Church or else he would be condemned. The statement by Augustine was quite a change from what Jesus had said. In fact, Jesus taught none of these three important requirements of the Church.

As a consequence of these activities on the part of the Church, those who wished to follow Christ were defined as requiring the Church in order to do so. And they were not led to the Church because they chose to do so, but because they were required to do so. The Christian was defined as having no other choice. In some countries, the <u>citizen</u> was defined as having no other choice.

It might be easy for some to say, "But that is ancient history. The Church was changed by the Reformation and so you are talking about something which no longer exists." Unfortunately, that is not true. As reported in Ramm's book [see bibliography], Karl Barth [1886-1968] said, "Liberal Christianity is not Christianity as historically understood and is therefore not Christianity." In justifying this statement, Ramm states that all the historical Christian concepts are either denied or changed by the liberal Christian. He specifically mentions such concepts as the Trinity, the deity of Christ, the incarnation, original sin and the vicarious atonement. As described in Section 1 and other parts of this book as well as in *Christianity and the New Age Religion*, most of these concepts have been developed by man, not by Scripture and not by Christ. Barth, a twentieth century theologian, is saying that if you do not accept them, then you are not a follower of Christ. Therefore, according to Ramm and Barth, liberal Christians who do not accept the alterations which the men of the Church have put on the teachings of Christ are not Christian.

In another part of Ramm's book, he makes the point that "whatever Christianity the theologians of liberal Christianity proposed, it is not the Christianity as understood from Justin Martyr of the second century to John Calvin of the 16th century." After reading about the intolerance of the Church developed by Justin Martyr and John Calvin [see Sections 6 and 11] and comparing those activities with the unconditional and compassionate love of Jesus Christ, I think I agree with him. It is one of my major reasons for leaving the Church by choosing Christianess over Christianity.

Present-day Status

The present status of the followers of Jesus Christ is somewhat similar to that presented in Section 1, in that the followers reside in two camps. One camp resides in the sectarian churches. That camp demands that to be a Christian, you must believe in the definition of Christ presented by the Church Fathers and must believe that the Scriptures are to be interpreted as literally as possible, with the definition of "literal interpretation" changing between the conservative to the liberal branches of the sectarian spectrum. But whatever degree of scriptural freedom is permitted within the Church, there is almost no degree of freedom permitted with the Christology definitions of the first six Ecumenical Councils. Those are accepted as "Revealed Truths" by the Church, particularly the definitions which have declared that Christ is the *only way*.

In the other camp are Christians who have chosen to follow Christ while accepting that there are other ways to return to God. They choose Christ as the most viable way for them, and are willing to stand up for that belief in any audience; but are not willing to reject out-of-hand all other possibilities, and are not willing to stand up for the decisions or the definitions made by the sectarian church.

These two camps will remain apart and probably never overcome their schism. But it is one fundamental viewpoint of this book that both camps contain Christians, and that the concepts of Christ as developed by man are not necessarily the only concepts of Christ which a Christian can accept.

What do these changes mean to today's Christian?

In the fourth and fifth centuries CE, Jesus Christ got defined in a way that was vastly different from the way he defined himself. He did not present himself as being God incarnate, nor did he present himself as the one who was going to establish a new religion; for a new religion was not needed if the kingdom of God were to come as soon as he taught. He was a teacher who showed the authority and the presence of God as he taught; and he did admit to being son of God which in his time and space meant that he was close to God, was in the spirit of God, and was a servant or instrument of God. The ancient Hebrew kings were often called a son of God when they lived as a servant or an instrument of God. It is relatively innocent language, and easily understood in the context of the ancient Near East. Even today when we want to identify those who are valued by God, we call them "children of God."

But the people of the Greco-Roman culture applied a different meaning to the term "son of God." They not only made a special title out of it and reserved that title for only one person, they also turned it around to make it "God the Son," one whose divine nature was identical in both quality and quantity to the Father, but whose human nature was identical in both quality and quantity to ours. Nothing which Christ said about himself relates to these concepts in any way. Instead, as described in Section 1, these definitions were needed by the Church in order to make atonement and salvation work, for man had already decided that he could not be saved by anything other than by a *total* God. Consequently, the fourth and fifth century definitions became a necessity on the part of the Church. They used them to teach that Jesus Christ was the *only* Son of God and therefore the *only* one who could save mankind. They also taught that the Sacraments were necessary in order to save mankind, and the Sacraments, of course, could *only* be given by the Church. They therefore concluded that the *only* follower of Christ was a man who obeyed the Church as his Mother, just as he obeyed God as his Father.

Despite all of this learned theology, I hold the belief that you can be a follower of Christ [i.e. a Christian] without subscribing to the theological definitions of the fourth and fifth centuries.

3. APOSTOLIC TRADITION or SUCCESSION[1]

Although an entire section of Chapter Two in *Book One* was used to discuss the Apostolic Tradition, the subject is so important in understanding how the teachings of Christ have been altered by man, that it will be discussed further in this section.

Concepts at the time of Jesus.

The Apostolic Tradition [or Succession, hereinafter referred to as "Tradition"] was instituted much later than the time of Jesus. Formally, the concept was introduced by Hippolytus in about 200 CE or so. However, the idea of Jesus teaching the Apostles [i.e. those who had known Jesus], and the Apostles teaching the Apostolic Fathers [i.e. those who had known an Apostle], and the Apostolic Fathers teaching the early Church Fathers, and the Church Fathers establishing doctrines which have taught the Church ever since, is a concept which predated Hippolytus. It was practiced at least as early as John the Evangelist who taught Polycarp who then taught Irenaeus who then wrote a basis upon which doctrines were established. A major part of this happened at least 100 years before the work of Hippolytus. In addition, the two early *Letters of Clement* describe how the teaching would proceed from the Apostles through the bishops to the Church. It is believed that these letters were written about 50-60 years after the Crucifixion [see page 82 and Appendix A], and therefore again preceded Hippolytus.

Despite the fact that the "Tradition" was instituted some time after the time of Christ, there are some clues about it in the Scriptures as presented in the following two paragraphs:

1. Jesus said, *"Truly, truly I say to you, he who believes in me will also do the works that I do; and greater works than these will he do, because I go to the Father."* [John 14:12]. In this, Jesus was telling his disciples [i.e. the Apostles] that they were to go out and repeat the works that he had shown them. The Apostles were therefore to follow in his tradition.

2. The major scriptural reference for the Apostolic Tradition is given in the Great Commission when Jesus said to the Apostles, *"All authority in heaven and on earth has been given to me. Go therefore and make disciples of all nations, baptizing them in the name of the Father and of the Son and of the Holy Spirit, teaching them to observe all that I have commanded you; and lo, I am with you always, to the end of the age."* [Matt. 28:18-20].

From this, the concept was given that the Apostles were to go out, and that from them, the world was to learn. This is the true concept of the Apostolic Tradition.

Changes in Concepts

The major changes in this concept happened because very few Apostles went out, and as was mentioned in Chapter Two of *Book One*, there is no record of any Apostle having reached the sites where the doctrines of the Church were first being established, *viz.* Alexandria and Carthage. Consequently, it is difficult to understand how the Tradition has given us many of the doctrines of the Church except possibly through an oral tradition in which the teachings of Christ were passed from mouth-to-mouth over great distances. Anyone who has played the old party game of "Telephone" knows how that will turn out. In that game, one person says something to one other person who then passes the saying on to one other person. By the time that the twelfth person is reached, the original message has become so garbled that it is completely unrecognizable. Although there is the possibility that persons specially trained to memorize large amounts of information could have traveled over these long distances to transmit the teachings, there is no evidence for them in any of the Church literature which I have been able to find. Moreover, we do have the statement that the canons had to be in writing, because after about two generations the oral tradition was becoming distorted [see page 79].

Consequently, the legitimacy of the doctrines established by the Apostolic Tradition seems open to question. Nevertheless, the Church believes that its doctrines, though often non-scriptural, have validity because the Apostles gave Christ's teachings to the Church Fathers who then established doctrines which the Church teaches to us today. This belief was given great impetus by Irenaeus in his fight against the Gnostics when he urged that Catholic teaching was validated because it had a continuous succession of teachers, beginning with the Apostles. This is the teaching portion of the Tradition.

Furthermore, the Tradition states that the pope who is Bishop of Rome, is a direct descendant of the Apostles because Peter, the one who was chosen by Jesus to be the foundation of his Church, came to Rome. Therefore, the papal throne is known as the "Throne of Peter" and becomes the "Succession" part of the Tradition.

Finally, it is through this Tradition that the "Revealed Truths" of the Church gain their validity, because through Tradition these "Revealed Truths" have an established history which goes straight back to the truth of God as revealed in the person of Jesus Christ. Therefore, "Revealed Truths" become valid through the Apostolic Succession part of the Tradition.

All of these beliefs represent a Tradition, but one which is difficult to accept in any way other than as a tradition. The problems with the Tradition, particularly in relation to the "Throne of Peter" and "Revealed Truths" parts, are outlined below.

1. As mentioned on page 50, it is doubtful that Peter spent more than 3-4 years in Rome, and certainly did not establish a major church or a "Throne" while there. However, because of a cult which spread up around Peter's name in Rome during the early third century, the popes have declared themselves to be the spiritual descendants of Peter. As a consequence, they believe themselves to be the spiritual leaders of the world, just as Peter was the spiritual leader of the twelve disciples. They therefore believe that they occupy the "Throne of Peter."

2. Despite this belief, it is astonishing to recognize that of the almost 100 heresies of the first six centuries, not one refers to becoming a heresy based on the authority of the Bishop of Rome, and not one was settled by him. And when the authority of the episcopacy or of any bishop was challenged during the first six centuries, no one went to the authority of the Bishop of Rome to settle the dispute because *no one had ever heard of such an authority.*[10]

3. By the time of Pope Gregory I the Great in 590 CE [see Appendix A], the papacy had grown to the point of starting to feel that it could dictate beliefs to the rest of the world. This continued through all the medieval popes with their Crusades and the like until finally, Clement XI in 1715 excommunicated all in the world who did not render obedience to the Holy Father and pay him their taxes when due. This is the same pope who in 1713 condemned all men who read the Bible or any form of Holy Scripture. He did all of this as a "Revealed Truth" in the spirit of the Apostolic Tradition.[11]

4. But the worst of all which was taught under the "Revealed Truths" justified by the Tradition was the "Revealed Truth" which decreed that the Sun orbited around the Earth thus denying the science of Galileo. In 1633, Galileo had to repent his astronomical findings under order by the Inquisition. He still has not been rehabilitated by the Church, although it is rumored that in the early 1980s, Pope John Paul II was heard to say something about "rehabilitating Galileo" some 350 years after the fact.[12] According to *Time* magazine, in 1992 John Paul did apologize for the irregularities of Galileo's trial, but excused the Church's agents as having acted within the scientific knowledge of the time. This is still no excuse for Pope Urban VIII having used the "Revealed Truth" theory for the original condemnation of Galileo.

5. In 1854 in *Ineffabilis Deus*, Pope Pius IX defined the Immaculate Conception of Mary. It is difficult to see how this could have resulted from the teaching portion of the Tradition because this declaration defied a lot of early church teaching. Until the twelfth century, Christians took for granted that Mary was conceived by original sin just like everybody else, for Pope Gregory I the Great had said, "Christ alone was conceived without sin." Ambrose and Augustine took the line that Mary had never done any actual sin; but Tertullian, Irenaeus, Chrysostom, Origen, Basil, Cyril of Alexandria and others accused Mary of many sins based on Scripture, for she was conceived in sin and committed actual sin. The New Testament said so. In fact, the early church argued that to remove all sin from Mary would dilute her grandeur and achievements which are those of a human like us in every way.[13]

However, in the middle of the twelfth century, the Tradition which had humanized Mary started to be changed, for there was a new feast in Lyons which was celebrated in honor of her conception.

This caused a lot of concern. Later Aquinas restated the Aristotelian concept that the fetus starts as a vegetable and then progresses through animal into human. Thus to have Mary conceived without sin would be like starting with a sinless radish. Dominicans agreed with their hero Aquinas, and originally the Franciscans also did. Later, Duns Scotus [a Franciscan] supported the belief that Mary was conceived without sin. The resulting conflict between the Dominicans and the Franciscans continued for centuries. In about 1480, Pope Sixtus IV ordered the Feast of the Conception to be kept in all churches. The Dominicans had a hard time accepting this *since Aquinas had said that the immaculate conception had not happened and Pope John XXII had said that to deny any teaching of Aquinas was heresy.*

In the 1854 declaration, it was affirmed that the Immaculate Conception was the law of the Church and instead of being an option as to whether or not a Catholic should accept it, it had become an act of excommunication if one did not accept it. Despite all the teachings of the early Church Fathers who had denied it, about 1870 years after Mary's conception it became heretical to deny that the conception was not immaculate. Thus, this concept went from blank papal denial to blank papal definition. In this way, the pope had fashioned a "Revealed Truth" which was an absolute, all justified in some way by the absolute power granted to the pope as a result of the Apostolic Succession which went from Apostle to Church Father to Pope.[13]

6. In 1864, Pope Pius IX published his Syllabus of Errors. This was based on the belief that the Roman Church had the fullest possible grasp on truth and therefore had the duty to be intolerant of the viewpoint of others. Among many others, some of the errors were: it is an error to believe that man can choose his own religion; it is an error to believe that the church can not use force to make people obey her; it is an error to believe that civil law has any effect on the church; it is an error to believe that the Catholic religion is not the only state religion to the exclusion of all others; and it is an error to believe that the Roman pontiff should come to terms with progress, liberal thinking or modern civilization. As one specific example, when the new Austrian constitution was published, the Vatican declared it to be null and void and forbade Catholics to obey it, particularly the part which allowed Protestants and Jews to have their own schools.[14]

7. The epitome of the Apostolic Tradition was reached at the Twentieth Ecumenical Council, known as Vatican I in 1869-70. At this council it was declared that the pope possesses "full and supreme jurisdiction of the Church in those matters which concern discipline and direction of the Church dispersed throughout the world." Consequently, the pope's power is supreme. The council declared that in doing this, they were following Scripture and also the dictates of the general councils of the Church. However, no early council and no Scripture supports this claim; and the Eastern Church which was responsible for most of the early doctrines of the church has never accepted it. Finally, the council declared that since the pope is supreme, then "when he speaks *ex cathedra*, that is when in exercise of his office as the pastor and teacher of all Christians" he is infallible, i.e. he can make no mistake.[15]

It is difficult to bring this kind of teaching into anything resembling the Apostolic Tradition; for Peter had made mistakes. An example of Peter's mistakes is given in Matt. 26:69-75 when three times he denies that he was with Jesus. Furthermore, *absolutely no council of the Church prior to 1870 had even <u>hinted</u> that the pope was infallible.* However, after 1870, there was no other choice for a Catholic to make. If the pope spoke *ex cathedra,* he was infallible and must be obeyed. This leads to a real problem, for any Church which has the ability to become infallible leaves itself in the position of not being able to admit to any mistake from the past. Consequently, despite the abundance of mistakes made by the Church in the name of Jesus Christ, admission to any of them is rare.

8. Finally, Pope John Paul's *Humanae Vitae* has become a foundation stone of Catholic orthodoxy even though it is a teaching which has no biblical background or Apostolic basis. It is a "Revealed Truth" without Apostolic foundation.[16]

Present-day Status

I was recently watching a television program which described the pope's visit to Denver. One charming sixteen year old was interviewed. Her statement was that since the pope represented Christ on Earth, then when he spoke, it was just as if Christ were speaking to her. Whether she realized it or not, she was stating that the Apostolic

Tradition is alive and well. It makes no difference that the unbroken stream of teaching from Christ to us today has been broken many times and has been desecrated with many acts which in no way resemble an act of Christ. To this young lady and to many others, the stream of teachings is believed to be that of Christ; for the Apostolic Tradition is alive and well in the hearts of many.

In addition, in many parts of the Christian Church, the Apostolic Succession is alive and well. It is presently held to be sacrosanct that each bishop consecrated in the Roman Catholic, the Eastern Orthodox and the Anglican [i.e. Episcopal in the U.S.] Church is able to trace his heritage back to an Apostle through a lineage of bishops which stretches unbroken for almost 2,000 years. It makes no difference that the actual "laying on of hands" may have been broken many times because of war, other civil disturbances or geography; today's catholic tradition is that the Apostolic Succession is alive and well and is therefore able to grant validity to the activities of each consecrated bishop.

What do these changes mean to today's Christian?

The changes in the teachings of Jesus Christ which have been developed by the Church over the years have to be a great concern to any thinking Christian. Just as the concept of Christ, and the concept of the follower of Christ, and the concept of compassion for others in face of Christian intolerance has changed drastically since the concepts were originally given us by Jesus Christ, so have the concepts which have been taught by the Church. Much of this change in teaching has been justified by the Apostolic Tradition, a justification which allows the Church to say that what it does is right because of the unbroken thread which ties it to the Risen Christ.

But look at the record and see if the present concept of the Apostolic Tradition is the same as its original concept. If you think that it is, then how is it that a Church which started in the non-worldly hearts of the Apostles could become so entangled in the affairs of the world [see Section 7]? How can any believer in the Tradition accept an institution which would excommunicate all who would deny that the pope is as infallible as God, and which thinks that it can invalidate State Constitutions, revoke great civil documents such as the

Magna Carta[17], and propose that the U.S. Constitution be used to support a protestant religious agenda?[49] Is this the teaching of the Christ?

I feel confident that many readers are now saying to themselves, "But it is other parts of the Christian Church which conduct these practices. The part I belong to has nothing to do with such activities." In practice, that may be right; and many examples have been presented in this section which relate solely to the Roman Catholic Church. That is because those practices have been the ones most frequently recorded by history. However, the justification for these practices is the same throughout Christianity. The feeling of being the *only* people in the world who are right generates an attitude of absolute power, and absolute power corrupts absolutely. One need only look at the practices of British Imperialism as they used their version of "God and King" to "civilize" the rest of the world to understand that it is the *belief of exclusiveness* which generates these practices; and that the *belief of exclusiveness* is a constant throughout the Christianity of the sectarian churches. It is a belief which has led to an intolerance against the beliefs of others. All of us who have followed Christ are guilty of this belief and its subsequent intolerance to the beliefs of others.

4. SALVATION[1]

S alvation is defined as "the deliverance of man or his soul from the power or penalty of sin; redemption." Redemption means the recovery of something which was pawned or mortgaged. Consequently, if the soul of man has been mortgaged by the power of sin, it is redeemed by salvation. The Christian has been taught that this can occur *only* through the sacrifice of Jesus Christ.

Concepts at the time of Jesus.

1. Salvation was a very important concept in Judaism. In the King James Version of the Old Testament, the word salvation is used 118 times, most often in Psalms with Isaiah being a respectable second. With all of this basis in Judaism, and with the prime importance that Christianity has placed upon it, it is somewhat strange to find that the word "salvation" is not used at all in the Gospels of Matthew or Mark, and is used only once in the Gospel of John. Luke uses the word five times. Three of these refer to what Jesus will do [e.g. in Luke 1:77] and one quotes the Old Testament prophet, Isaiah.

2. The fifth reference in Luke is the <u>only</u> one in all the Gospels which states how salvation *per se* will occur. It is a very enlightening statement which is found in Luke 19:1-10. In this story, Zacchaeus, a rich man and sinner, tells Jesus that he has given half of his goods to the poor, and will restore fourfold to anyone whom he has defrauded. In response to this, Jesus says, "Today, salvation has come to this house, since he also is a son of Abraham. For the Son of man came to seek and to save the lost." This is an answer similar to that which Jesus said to the man who asked how he should receive eternal life, and Jesus replied, "If you would be perfect, go, sell what you possess and give it to the poor, and you will have treasure in heaven; and come, follow me." [Matt. 19:21].

Consequently, during the life of Jesus, he teaches at least two times that salvation comes from giving what you have to the poor.

3. Never in the Gospels is Jesus led to say that salvation will come by believing in him, although he does say, "For whoever would save his life will lose it; and whoever loses his life for my sake and the gospel's will save it." He does this in Mark 8:35, Matt. 16:25, and Luke 9:24. In this way, Jesus is saying that he is a path to salvation. However, in each case he states that the man must first do something himself. In these cases, Jesus states that the man must give up or lose his present life, a statement similar to the one in which the man must give up his possessions to the poor in order to gain salvation or eternal life.

4. The first reference to the point that salvation is found in the name of Jesus Christ is presented in Acts 4:12 in which Peter says, "And there is salvation in no one else, for there is no other name under heaven given among men by which we must be saved." In this same sequence, Peter accuses the rulers, elders and scribes of having crucified the Christ and thus given him the name which leads to salvation.

5. As a consequence of all of this, at the time of Jesus, salvation was thought to be granted by accepting a total change in the life previously led, and by having that change lead to the doing of a good deed or to the following of the Christ. It was not until after the time of Christ that his disciples, being filled with the Holy Spirit, presented the thought that Jesus made a sacrifice which would lead to salvation for those who followed him.

Changes in Concepts

Any thought that good works would generate salvation was completely overturned, first by the statements of the disciples in Acts, and shortly thereafter by the theology of Paul. In the first chapter of the Letter to the Romans, an early Chapter in a very early Letter, Paul states that "He who through faith is righteous shall live." [Romans 1:17]. This led to the many concepts of salvation by faith which culminated in Martin Luther's breakthrough to the experience of being accepted in spite of being unacceptable. In Pauline terms, this is called "justification by grace through faith," a principle which does not appear before Luther's time.

The preceding paragraph has merely addressed concepts of salvation which are biblical, albeit not necessarily during the time of Jesus. However, the men of the Church continued to make many changes in the biblical concept of salvation. A representative few of these changes are presented in the following paragraphs.

1. Augustine said, "Outside of the Catholic Church, everything may be had except salvation."

2. The interpretation of St. Paul "In Adam all have sinned" [see Romans 5:12-4 for background on this] was taken by the Church to mean that all must be baptized by the Church or else they will not be saved and will roast in Hell. This was done by the Church in an attempt to prove their authority over all, a concept never presented in the Scriptures.

3. To understand why the Church would make such an interpretation, this paragraph will examine the term "salvation" in the *New Catholic Encyclopedia*.[18] According to this very orthodox presentation:

> Salvation is the generic term used to describe "the divine activation of restoring mankind to the state from which he had fallen by the sin of Adam." This is necessary, because although man was created in a state of right order toward

God and his fellow creatures, and was destined to the eternal enjoyment of union with God after a trial on Earth, this grace was lost by the disobedience of Adam. After Adam, man was born into a disordered universe. Deprived of grace, man could not attain heaven because the appetites of his own body and soul would entice him to sin.

The good news of Christianity showed how God, out of love and mercy, saved mankind by a several step process which finalized by having God the Son become man to save mankind by His teaching and His miracles, by example of His life, by His death, Resurrection and Ascension, and by establishing the Church and sending it the Holy Spirit. The core of Apostolic teaching is that Jesus alone saves. When man responds, the grace of Christ gradually frees him from the bonds of sin and for eventual reunion to the Father. However, God's call does not reach them through reason alone, but through definite manifestations of God in history, and through a positive sociological system which includes the Church outside of which there is no salvation. Therefore all people who want to be saved are required to have the Sacrament of Baptism.

Although this presentation does not appear in the teachings of the Christ or in Scripture, it is the orthodox teaching of the Church.

4. The need for the Church as a requirement for salvation was emphasized by the early Church Fathers as follows: [1] Irenaeus said that wherever there is the Church, there is the Holy Spirit; and wherever there is the Holy Spirit, there is also the Church and all grace; [2] Origen formulated the dogmatic axiom *Extra ecclesiam nulla salus* or "Outside the Church, no salvation"; [3] Cyprian wrote that "One cannot have God as one's Father unless one also has the Church as one's Mother," a statement later repeated by Jerome and Augustine. The necessity of the Church for salvation is explicitly defined by the Church as a "Revealed Truth." Boniface VIII asserts in *Unam Sanctam* [1302] that outside the Church of Christ, there can be neither salvation nor remission of sins; and Pius IX in *Singulari Quadam* [late nineteenth century] clearly states that this doctrine must be accepted as a matter of faith. The doctrine states that "just as there is no Salvation without Christ, there can be no salvation without the Church which is the Mystical Body of Christ." Although there have been many interpretations of this doctrine, the Church believes that this axiom is universally valid and can admit of no exception.

5. The doctrine of *extra ecclesiam nulla salus* was the basis for the assumption that Christianity was to spread throughout the world, replacing all non-Christian traditions. But this belief was not restricted only to the early days. As late as 1913, Julius Richter defined his subject of missionology as *"that branch of theology which in opposition to the non-Christian religions, shows the Christian religion to be the Way, the Truth, and the Life; which seeks to dispossess the non-Christian religions and to plant in their stead in the soil of heathen national life the evangelic faith and the Christian life."* This is the attitude which had given the industrialized Western nations their justification for colonizing and exploiting the rest of the world. It is also the attitude which has poisoned the relationship between the Christian minority and the non-Christian majority throughout the world.[19]

6. But to show that such an attitude can be modified, it is interesting to examine the effect that a few years of maturity had on Ernst Troeltlsch, a noted theologian of the "history of religions" school. In 1901, he wrote *The Absoluteness of Christianity*, in which he stated the premise that Christianity was "absolute," "unique," "final," "normative," "ultimate" and decidedly superior to all other religions as Christ was to all other Saviors. However, shortly prior to his death in 1923, Troeltlsch criticized his own earlier viewpoint and stated that Christianity was "absolute" for Christians, and that other world faiths were also "absolute" for their own adherents.[20]

7. No discussion of salvation would be complete without presenting some of the viewpoints of Meister Eckhart, a German Dominican mystic who died in 1327 and whose teaching was condemned by Pope John XXII in 1329. Eckhart said that the creature receives his being from God and has nothing when separated from God. The point in which the creature returns to God is the soul. The soul has within it a "spark" which is the very likeness of God and in which God dwells totally. In the concept of the "spark" [also called the "ground"], the Son is born into every soul. This universal event is more important than the particular birth of Jesus, and means that God can be born in the soul of everyone. When this happens, the creature loses himself and becomes one with God.[21]

In Eckhart's teaching, the process of salvation is that man gets rid of himself and of all things to become one with God. This is similar to the teachings of Jesus which were presented in the first part of this section, but quite different from the process of salvation taught by the Church. Despite this difference, the mysticism of Meister Eckhart was very influential in the Church for a long time. It is still influential in many people. Its enlightenment was a serious preparation for the Reformation. Possibly that can happen again.

Present-day Status

In 1965, Vatican II in effect repealed *extra ecclesiam nulla salus* in one pronouncement. However, in another it effectively put it back by stating that *"All must be converted to Christ as He is made known by the Church's preaching."* In this way, Christianity has gone from intolerance to a benevolence, but still only on the terms proposed by the Christian. If while recognizing other religions we continue to state as Paul Tillich did that the Christian revelation is "final and definitive," then we will be like the Hindus or the Buddhists who while recognizing other religions, believe that theirs is the only way through which the final reality can be known and understood. However, if the divine love [*Agape*] covers all, it is almost inconceivable that such a love could stop either at the boundary of the Christian Church or at the walls of the Hindu Temple.

All of this desire on the part of the Christian to convert the entire world to his way and to reject all other ways happened because Christianity was thought to be a universal religion which would gather all gentiles into Zion to worship the true God, a desirable goal which the Christian believed that the Jew had lost by not recognizing Christ. However, this thought happened only in the nations of the Greco-Roman culture. Nowhere has Christianity become the predominant form of religion among peoples who were not heirs of Greco-Roman culture. Thus Christianity has never been, and probably never will be, a universal religion.[22]

What do these changes mean to today's Christian?

Thankfully, today's Christian has progressed past the point of believing that salvation was so dependent on formal sacraments from the Church that if there were any fear of an embryo or a fetus dying before birth, then it must be baptized by placing holy water on the baby while it was still in the womb.[23] But is today's Christian really ready to accept that to the rest of the world, Christianity is seen as only one of the many streams of possible salvation? After all, there have been worldwide Saints in every major world religion, and although several Muslim countries were recently reported as guilty of using torture [e.g. Turkey, Iran, Iraq, etc.] so were many Christian nations [e.g. South Africa, Brazil, Spain, Argentina, Chile, etc.] as well as those which were Hindu [India], Buddhist [Sri Lanka] and Jewish [Israel]. In this way, many of the great religions of the world are fighting the birth of human rights almost as ardently as they once fought the birth of modern science.[24] Consequently, no one religion really has shown that it has earned the moral right to place itself above any other religion.

Is there a possibility of transforming sectarian religions into a religion which would put God at the center rather than putting those who have helped God at the center? Such a movement would contribute greatly to worldwide acceptance of one's fellow man. The New Testament presents a good case for a God-centered religion as do the Muslims; for at least in the beginning, Muslims believed their God to be the same God worshipped by the Jews and Christians, and later, a major part of Islam believed that their God was identical to the God of the Hindus. They thus have sponsored a God-centered ecumenicalism. Further, a major portion of Christian orthodoxy supports the possibility of a God-centered religion. The Eastern Orthodox belief that the Holy Spirit proceeds only from the Father and not from the Father and the Son has deep ecumenical significance, because it means that the Holy Spirit is available to those who accept God rather than *only* those who accept Jesus Christ. Finally, for Christians a God-centered religion would allow for the Mystery of God while permitting the uniqueness of Jesus Christ. It would allow for a commitment to God in the name of Jesus Christ without needing to reject those who commit to God via a different salvation or in the name of someone else. It could allow the continued quest for the meaning of Jesus Christ without at the same time rejecting the quest for the meaning of others.

In Mark 9:40 Jesus says, "For he that is not against us is for us." In that spirit, those religious paths which are not against Christianity, are for it. Each may be very different and each very unique, but each would be for each other; for if it is true that any viable religious belief in *Agape* must affirm that God will save all of his creatures, then how can there be one, and *only* one, religion which is the *sole* source of salvation?

5. SOUL[1,25]

In the early fourteenth century, Meister Eckhart [see page 157] proposed that the soul contained a "spark" or "ground" of God which was uncreated and existed with God before the creation. Prior to that, in the late fourth century, Augustine had said, "The life whereby we are joined unto the body is called the soul." Throughout Christian history, the soul has been an important, albeit confusing part of the Church's teaching. This differs from the Judaic teaching in which the soul had only a minor place.

Concepts at the time of Jesus.

1. In the Bible, the Old Testament uses the Hebrew word *nepes* [or *nefesh*] which comes from the verb "to breath" as their closest approach to the concept of the soul. This use is based on the belief that breath distinguishes life from death; and as a consequence, breath [or *nepes*] can mean life. However, *nepes* does not make a differentiation between "life" and "soul." Therefore, in Genesis 2:7 when God "breathed into his nostrils the breath of life," the Old Testament comes about as close as it can to saying that the soul [or life] of man comes from God. Because *nepes* was used interchangeably for both life and soul, any of the sayings of Jesus which have used the word "soul" in its English translation, may use the word "life" with equal justification. In the Hebrew thought which was prevalent at the time of Jesus, there was no immortal soul. It remained that way until the concept of the immortal soul was introduced into

Alexandrian Judaism by the Hellenistic influence during the first centuries of the Common Era.

2. In very early Greek thought, Empedocles [ca. 450 BCE] stated that the soul consists of all four intrinsic constituents [fire, earth, air and water], and both extrinsic principles [Love and Strife]. Plato [ca. 400 BCE] built his definitions of the soul on this beginning and continued by stating that "the soul is immortal and imperishable"; and "the soul is immortal, and is clothed successively in many bodies"; and "of all things which man has, next to the gods his soul is the most divine and most truly his own."

3. In a slightly different Greek thought, Aristotle [ca. 350 BCE] presented a progressive embryology which stated that the human embryo starts as a speck of vegetable. This non-human speck then becomes progressively animated as it makes its journey from a vegetable to an animal to a human while in the womb; and receives its immortal soul only when it reaches its human stage. This concept was retained by the Christian Church until the seventeenth century [see page 166].

4. It is in light of this Greek thought that the New Testament use of the word "soul" must be analyzed. In the New Testament, the Greek word used to correspond to *nepes* was *puce* which is generally translated into English as "psyche." It means the principle of life; and through Hellenistic influence it was opposed to the body and was considered to be immortal. Therefore, in those parts of the Bible which had Greek influence [e.g. all parts of the New Testament which are not the words of Jesus], the word "soul" can mean "psyche" which is different than either "life" or "body" and is immortal. However, it should be noted that the words "immortal" or "immortality" are rarely used in biblical thought, appearing only in the writing of Paul [Rom. 2:7; 1 Cor. 15:53-4; and three references in Timothy].

5. As a consequence, the concepts of the soul as presented by Jesus in his time must be considered solely from the Hebraic background without its Greek influence. That concept is that the soul and the body are together, that soul and life are interchangeable and that the soul is immortal only as "the breath of life from God" is immortal.

Changes in Concepts

1. While defending Christianity in *Discourse to the Greeks*, Tatian [ca. 160 CE] stated "The soul is not immortal, O Greeks, but mortal. Yet it is possible for it not to die." He did this in an attempt to establish the belief that the soul was not, by nature, an immortal entity, but was made so only as a gift of God through the resurrection of Jesus Christ. In doing this, he alienated many Greeks who believed that by its very nature, the soul was immortal.

2. Irenaeus tried to rationalize many contrasting viewpoints by stating that "the soul participates in life because God wills it to live; thus it will not even have such participation when God no longer wills it to live." In this way, he hoped to rationalize the Eastern viewpoints on immortality with the need for salvation as expressed in Christianity. But he went on to attack the Eastern notion of the pre-existence and the transmigration of souls, arguing that God confers on each individual body its proper soul to which it would be rejoined in the resurrection of the body. He used the parable presented in Luke 16:19-31 for this purpose. This is a long parable which will not be repeated here. It is the story of Dives, a rich man who died rich but without faith, and Lazarus, a poor man who died with faith. The parable tells what happened to each in the afterlife. Irenaeus used this story to show that since Dives recognized Lazarus, then the soul must retain the physical appearance of the body to which it had been enjoined on Earth.

3. By the very late second century, the issue of where the soul fit into Christianity was so confusing that Tertullian undertook in *De Anima* to review every human opinion on the soul. Like Irenaeus, he used the Lazarus example to state that the soul, though a spirit, is at the same time a body. This led him to state that "Adam's soul alone was created by God, while all others souls came into being by an act of generation." The latter was called "traducianism" and implied that the soul was a corporeal substance which was produced from two other souls just as a body is produced from two other bodies. Despite this belief, which was more Stoic than Christian, the *New Catholic Encyclopedia* states that most of Tertullian's opinions about the soul were decidedly "Christian."

4. In about 300 CE, another member of the Western Church,

Arnobius, in his *Adversus Nationes* ["Case against the Pagans"], attacked the immortality of the soul because that would make men into gods. He stated that men are merely beings not greatly different from the beasts, and for the most part do not act according to reason, a fickleness which shows that the soul was <u>not</u> created by God.

5. In the East, Origen had many thoughts on the soul. Some of these thoughts have been accepted as being orthodox; others have not. Among his more orthodox thoughts on the soul, Origen stated, "This is also clearly defined in the teaching of the Church, that every rational soul is possessed of freewill and volition; that it has to struggle to maintain with the devil and his angels, and opposing influences, because they strive to burden it with sins." Later, Origen described the soul as a spiritual substance identified with spirit or mind. He said, "Let those who think the mind and soul is a body tell me, if this were so, how it could receive and understand reasonings which are often difficult and subtle, and contemplate and know things invisible and incorporeal."

This kind of position marked a decided advance into the thought that the soul was independent of the body, a thought which was maintained by many of Origen's successors. One highly respected successor was Gregory of Nyssa, a theologian of great stature. He gave the first full definition of the soul which had been offered in Christianity when he saw it not only as a life-giving principle, but as identified with the mind. He said, "Soul is a produced, living, rational substance which imparts of itself to an organic body capable of sensation, the power of life and sensation, as long as the nature capable of such things exists." Thus, we are now seeing a completely accepted and orthodox Christian theologian describing body and soul as separate entities. This is quite a change from the Judaic concept.

6. Among his less orthodox thoughts, Origen stated that all rational creatures were created at once, in the beginning, pure, equal and alike. Since they were without body but were intelligible by nature, they could be called intelligences. But because they were creatures, they were equally capable of good and evil; and when God put them to the test, all fell except the soul of Christ. The result was the diversity and hierarchy of rational creatures: angels, souls and demons. The human soul was thus originally a *nous*, a purely spiritual

being which became soul [psyche] "because it waxed cold from the fervor of just things." This concept has been called the "pre-existence of souls." It has been challenged by many anti-Origenists, and even Gregory of Nyssa parted from his usual support of Origen by saying that to think that the soul was created before the body was a fantastic fable borrowed from Greek philosophy. He also said that to think that the soul is created after the body is contrary to manifest experience. He said, therefore, that both came into existence together. Gregory was at a loss to explain how this happened except to state that God would use his power to convert a sperm into a wondrous, fully living thing containing both body and soul.

7. Sometime later, Augustine became the first in the Western Church to agree totally with the Eastern concept of the soul as a spiritual substance which is separate but intimately united with the body. His thought became the teaching of the Church until about the twelfth century. He believed that God created man as a whole substance composed of body and soul. He then said, "The life whereby we are joined unto the body is called the soul." Augustine also said that how body and soul were united was beyond the comprehension of man, although he thought it to be a natural and positive union rather than one which was accidental or punitive such as the duality religions [e.g. Gnosticism] believed. Augustine felt that the soul was the active principle and the body the passive one, because the body receives form and life from the soul, while the soul is merged in such a way that it does not lose its identity. All of this is possible because the soul is an immaterial substance, close to the substance of God.

However, Augustine could not define the origin of the soul. He stated that Adam's soul was created by God, but as to the origin of all the others, he merely confessed an inability to choose between the opinions which others had offered. He did not like Tertullian's theory of traducianism, and considered it to be a perverse theory which would destroy the spiritual characteristics of the soul. He thought that the generation of the soul at the time of conception seemed possible, but he did not see how this could explain the transmission of original sin. Consequently, he wondered if all souls could have been created at once, then sent by God as needed to be infused into the conceived physical body. In conclusion, Augustine could only say that God created every soul, and that the soul was not an emanation from the divine substance, but was a creature made in the image of God.

8. Others of the early days seem to be as confused as Augustine, but each seemed to have an opinion. Pope Gregory I considered the question of the origin of the soul to be a difficult question which was beyond human comprehension. Pope Leo I denied "pre-existence" by stating that the Church teaches that the souls of men do not exist before they are breathed into their bodies, being placed there by God alone, who is the creator of souls and bodies. Jerome said that God daily fashions souls and does not cease to be the creator. Thomas Aquinas merely rejected every thought about the soul except the Aristotelian thought that the soul was a form which unites with the bodily form.

9. Seneca, a non-Christian Roman philosopher of the early first century had some opinions about the soul worth noting. He said, "The soul alone renders us noble"; and "The soul has this proof of its divinity: that divine things delight it"; and "The soul is our king"; and "Do you ask where the Supreme Good dwells? In the soul. And unless the soul be pure and holy, there is no room in it for God."

10. And there are two modern quotations of interest: "Man does not *have* a soul: he *is* one"; and "Man is not a human having a spiritual experience; he is a spirit having a human experience."

Present-day Status

1. Although the notion of the soul surviving after death is not readily discernible in the Bible, the doctrine that the human soul is immortal and will continue to exist after man's death and the dissolution of his body is one of the cornerstones of Christian philosophy and theology. For many centuries, the immortality of the human soul has been a truth that has been consistently asserted by professing Christians. It was taken for granted by both sides at the Reformation; and because of this agreement, neither the Catholic nor the Protestant Church has felt it necessary to make many official pronouncements about the soul. However, it is general orthodox thinking that each human soul begins to exist by a direct creative act of God at the moment of its union with matter to form the new human being. In other words, the soul is created by God at the time it is united with an embryo or a fetus to form a human. `

2. The exact time of this union is still a matter of great debate within the Christian community. The concept of infusion at the time of conception is accepted by most Catholics and by many other Christians as an article of faith, but the Church has never really spelled this out. On the Catholic side, Vatican II deliberately ducked the issue, and for good reason. Until the seventeenth century, the teachings of the Church followed the Aristotle progressive embryology previously described; and all Catholics, including the pope, took it for granted that the soul was <u>not</u> infused at conception, for they followed the teachings of Gratian. In 1140, Gratian presented *Decretum Gratiani* which was church law until 1917. In this writing, he stated that "He is not a murderer who brings about abortion before the soul is in the body." It was believed that the fetus took 40 days to become a male and 80 days to become a female and that prior to that time, it did not contain a soul.[26]

In 1621, the papal physician started to teach that there was no biological basis for the view of Aristotle and proposed that the soul infused immediately upon conception. This view was not accepted by the pope; and therefore, in 1869 when Pope Pius IX stated that any destruction of the fetus was an abortion which merited excommunication, he was going against several centuries of consistent Church teaching. This proclamation was followed in 1895 by one in which Leo XIII stated that the fetus could never be removed even if that were the only way to save the mother's life. This then was followed by the decision that if there were any fear of the baby dying, it must be baptized by placing the holy water on the baby while it is still in the womb in order to save its immortal soul.[26]

3. In the Protestant Church, there is a tremendous difference of opinion about the soul and its time of infusion. It is assumed from the Scriptures that human beings are soul and body, with the soul being that which contemplates the self, organizes all the energies and vitalities of life for freely chosen goals, and hears the word of God. Although some Protestants believe that man and his soul are separate, others stress the unity. There seems to be a trend toward the understanding that man is "flesh-animated-by-soul, the whole visualized as a psycho-physical unity"; but the timing of the soul's infusion remains a concept about which there is great debate.[27]

4. In the Eastern Orthodox Church, scholars present every thought from the complete dichotomy of body and soul to the unity of man as the likeness of God in the unified body and soul. Their doctrine concerning the separation of souls after death is considered by almost everyone within and outside of the Church to be an impenetrable and incomprehensible mystery.

5. A final comment on the Catholic belief seems worthy of note. This is presented in Vol. 13, page 471 of the *New Catholic Encyclopedia* and is quoted as follows:

"Origen, Priscillian and other Neoplatonists taught that the human soul existed separately before being united with matter. This opinion is considered heretical because it is believed that the human soul has as its proper role, the union with matter to form this man and no other. Hence, any existence previous to the man is contrary to the very meaning of soul as substantial form. The existence of soul after death does not contradict this, *since the soul retains previously acquired knowledge, a transcendental relation to matter, and even a certain exigency to be united with matter.* But before actual union with matter to form a body, it has no such relation." [Italics added]

I find this description of the soul after death to be fascinating; for it seems to me that a soul which remembers previously acquired knowledge and desires to be united with a body is exactly the type of soul which those who believe in reincarnation talk about. But this definition of the soul is not from some New Age journal, it is from a Christian reference which is steeped in orthodox thoughts.

What do these changes mean to today's Christian?

Based on the wide variety of opinions voiced by the early Church Fathers and continued by Christian theologians to this day, it would seem that today's Christian can believe anything he wishes about the soul, for there are no firmly established dogmas, only a variety of beliefs. Today's Christian can consider it immortal, or as existing solely within the physical body. He can consider it to be a separate entity, or to be so intimately incarnated as to be in oneness with the physical body. He can consider it to have no existence outside of the one body to which it has been assigned by God; or he can believe that it is an entity separate from the one body which survives the dissolution of that body and desires to be united with another. He can believe that the soul has enough of a mind that it can remember previously acquired material knowledge even though it is outside of matter, or he can believe that it exists solely in a nether land of nothingness; etc. All that seems to be required in order to be a Christian is to believe that the soul is created by God; for with the possible exception of Arnobius, that seems to be the only unanimous belief on the part of all.

In conclusion, it seems that if a follower of Christ wishes to believe that the eternal soul created by God unites with matter more than once, nothing biblical or dogmatic keeps him from doing so. This thought is explored in greater depth in Section 8.

6. INTOLERANCE[1]

Intolerance is the major factor which is creating two camps within the Christian community today [see Section 1 and Section 2 of this Chapter]. Christ was one of the most tolerant humans ever to walk on Earth. His Church is known as one of the most intolerant organizations in existence. How did this happen?

Concepts at the time of Jesus.

1. At the time of Jesus, the people of Samaria had been hated by the Jewish society for over 700 years. The source of this hatred was deep-rooted. It started with the separation of the combined Kingdom into two Kingdoms after the death of Solomon in about 935 BCE. It was exacerbated by the conquering of the Northern Kingdom by the Assyrians in 721 BCE which caused the dispersal and assimilation of all of the tribes of Israel except for the tribe of Judah and a small portion of the tribe of Benjamin who were in the Southern Kingdom. Those of the Southern Kingdom believed that because of this assimilation, the lost tribes of Israel had turned their back on the true God of Abraham and had worshipped false Gods. The Samarians [or Samaritans] were the hated symbol of this rejection of God. They were truly hated by the Jews during the time of Jesus.

Jesus not only forgave the Samaritans, he loved them and

used them in many examples to show that they lived a life of love and compassion. There is the parable of the Good Samaritan in Luke 10: 29-37; and the story of the Samaritan who was the only one of ten lepers who thanked Jesus for his cure in Luke 17:11-19; and the story of the Samaritan Woman at the Well in John 4:7-26; and the many Samaritans who followed Jesus because he spent two days with them in John 4:39-42. All of these stories were used by Jesus to send a message. His message was that we must *love* those whom we previously hated. It is a message of unconditional love.

2. In the Sermon on the Mount, Jesus said *"You have heard it said, 'You shall love your neighbor and hate your enemy.' But I say to you, Love your enemies and pray for those who persecute you."* [Matt. 5:43-4]. This again is a message of unconditional love; for he did not ask the enemies to change, but for us to love them as they are.

3. In the Lord's Prayer, the words of forgiveness are very explicit. Although there are many versions of the phrase, "Forgive us our debts as we forgive our debtors," the message is clear that in being forgiven, we are to follow in the footsteps of Christ by forgiving others. This is a very important lesson from Jesus Christ. In another lesson, Jesus said that it is necessary to forgive seventy times seven [Matt. 18:21-2]. In Hebraic symbology, the number seven or seventy represents "an excess amount." Therefore, we are asked to forgive a "great excess amount of times."

4. Jesus established no dogma which must be obeyed in order to follow him. He merely presented teachings which contained no fear and no threats about what would happen if you did not follow him. The teachings were offered for acceptance or rejection as the hearer might choose. They taught the people of the world how to live if they would just do it. The teachings contained a great amount of tolerance and compassion for all.

5. Many more examples of the tolerance within the teachings of Jesus could be presented, including the beatitude from the Sermon on the Mount which says, "Blessed are the merciful, for they shall obtain mercy," but these are enough to establish the concept of intolerance as Jesus taught it in his time. That concept was that there is no intolerance; but that enemies, and those whom you hate, and those who have committed sins against you, are all to be forgiven without condition, and are to be given compassionate and unconditional love. It is a powerful lesson. It is the germinative message of Christianity, the religion which converted Law into Love.

Changes in Concepts

Anyone who has studied the history of the Christian Church knows that tolerance for the belief of others has not been one of its strong suits. Three quotes might put this into perspective. They are:

"We are required by faith to believe and hold that there is one holy, catholic and apostolic Church; we firmly believe it and unreservedly profess it; outside it there is neither salvation nor remission of sins.... Further, we declare, say, define and proclaim that to submit to the Roman Pontiff is, for every human creature, an utter necessity of salvation." [Pope Boniface VIII in 1302]

"No one remaining outside the Catholic Church, not just pagans, but also Jews or heretics or schismatics, can become partakers of eternal life; but they will go to the everlasting fire which was prepared for the devil and his angels, unless before the end of life they are joined to the Church." [The Seventeenth Ecumenical Council at Florence in 1438-45]

"In the years since the war, more than one billion souls have passed into eternity and more than half of these went to the torment of hell fire without even hearing of Jesus Christ, who He was, or why He died on the cross of Calvary." [Protestant speech at the Congress on World Mission at Chicago in 1960].[28]

These viewpoints demonstrate an intolerance for those who resist the organized Churches, a view which does not coincide with that of Jesus in any way. But the intolerance done in the name of Christ is not restricted to merely feeling sorry for those who do not understand the "blessings" of Church membership. Intolerance flows over to the rejection of beliefs which are not orthodox [i.e. are heretical] with "orthodox" meaning "truth as decided by the vote of the majority"; and intolerance is also used in the rejection of those who simply prefer their own beliefs to those of the sectarian Church.

Although these changes in the concept of toleration presented by Jesus started immediately after the Church was established, I believe that this early history has been adequately covered in the controversies presented in Appendix A. Instead, this section will present only a few of those intolerances which developed after the Church really got mean. The starting point for that meanness is the Crusade against the Cathars, the Waldenses and the Witches. This subject was adequately covered on pages 101-105 and will not be repeated here. However, the following examples should present an adequate indication of the "meanness" practiced by the Church rather than the Love taught by Jesus the Christ.

1. In the twelfth century, Gratian, a Benedictine monk wrote *Decretium,* or Code of Canon Law, probably the most influential book ever written by a Catholic. It quotes 324 passages from the popes of the first 400 years, one of which was that excommunicated persons were to be treated as heretics, which meant that they were to be tortured and killed as ordained by Pope Urban II.[29] Some have claimed that many of the quotes used by Gratian were forgeries. However, this makes no difference, for the major point is that the Church accepted them and followed them as canon law for about 800 years, intolerant though they may be.

2. In 1520, Pope Leo X condemned Luther for daring to question whether burning heretics was truly the will of God. In 1572, Pope Gregory XIII commemorated with joy the Massacre of St. Bartholomew in which thousands of Huguenot Protestants were killed by the troops of the papacy. Pope Clement VIII attacked the Edict of Nantes in 1598 because it gave equality of citizenship to all, regardless of their religion. In the seventeenth century, Pope Innocent X condemned the Peace of Westphalia for daring to grant toleration to all citizens regardless of their religion or lack of it. In every instance and over centuries, the Catholic Church proudly proclaimed its dogma of religious intolerance, and its desire to alter the politics of State.[30]

3. In 1832, Pope Gregory XVI declared that liberty of conscious was a mad opinion. He condemned freedoms of worship, the press, assembly and education as a filthy sewer full of "heretical vomit." In 1864, Pius IX attacked freedom of religion by saying "In the present day...the Catholic religion should be the only religion of the state, to the exclusion of all other forms of worship." In the late nineteenth century, Pope Leo XIII said that the Church has the right of a monopoly of religion in any Catholic state; and further declared that since freedom and truth are incompatible, then truth must be enforced by the state at the church's command wherever possible, even at the expense of freedom.[31]

4. As one Roman Catholic writer put it when describing some 1600 years of the church's history, "The Church began with the principle of absolute toleration; it ended with the stake. Is this true 'development'?"[32]

5. But this intolerance of others because of religious belief was not the sole province of the Roman Catholic Church. The Protestants participated as well. In 1543, long after he had left the Catholic Church, Martin Luther said:

"What shall we Christians do with ...the Jews?...I shall give you my sincere advice:

First, set fire to their synagogues or schools and to bury and cover with dirt whatever will not burn, so that no man ever again will see a stone or cinder of them. This is to be done in honor of our Lord and our Christendom...

Second, I advise that their houses also be razed and destroyed. For they pursue in them the same aims as in their synagogues...

Third, I advise that all their prayer books and Talmudic writings, in which such idolatry, lies, cursing and blasphemy are taught, be taken from them.

Fourth, I advise that their rabbis be forbidden to teach henceforth on pain of loss of life and limb.

Fifth, I advise that safe-conduct on the highways be abolished completely for the Jews." [33]

6. Although John Calvin was somewhat quieter than Martin Luther in his published announcements, in 1551 he had Jerome Bolsec, a former Catholic priest who had become a Protestant physician in Geneva, exiled by the Swiss government for questioning the concept of predestination; and in 1553, Calvin caused Michael Servetus to be burned at the stake for questioning the truth of the Trinity. All of this was done in an attempt to make Calvinism the politically accepted form of religion in the Swiss State and to have that State reject any other form of religion.[34]

7. To show that intolerance can also be practiced within the Church, in 1907, Pope Pius X wrote his *Lamentabili* which attacked any new interpretation of dogmas or Scripture. This was done in an attempt to stop scholarly research on the origin and meanings of Scripture, since all Truth had already been Revealed to the Church. This twentieth-century decision was similar to the Church's rejection of Galileo in the sixteenth century because the Church had already been given the "Revealed Truth" that the Sun orbited around the Earth. It smacks of "No facts, please. My mind is made up!"

As a result of *Lamentabili*, most of the intellectuals and scholars within the Church were purged via excommunication, which fortunately no longer meant a trip to a fiery stake. It merely meant that they were no longer welcome in their own church.[35] It is still happening in the Catholic and in the Protestant Churches of today. There is intolerance expressed to the presentation of new ideas; and new thoughts continue to be rejected as thoroughly as they ever have been. One need only think about how the Revised Standard Version of the Bible was so thoroughly rejected by the fundamental wing of the church to understand how new thinking is being fought. In addition, the rejection of the efforts of the Jesus Seminar [See footnote 12 on page 81 for particulars] is a sad commentary on our willingness to accept anything new. Furthermore, if any reader wants to see the methodology of closed minds in action, I would recommend that he read the "Readers Reply" page of any issue of *BR* [*Bible Review*] published bimonthly by the Biblical Archaeology Society in Washington DC. It is a truly fascinating experience in understanding how scholarly research on the meaning of Scripture falls upon deaf ears.

8. Finally, to bring religious intolerance up to date, the present-day problems in Northern Ireland, in the Balkans and in the Holy Land all have their origin firmly based on religious intolerance, as do the activities of the KKK and the Neo-Nazis. As the old folk song "Where Have All the Flowers Gone" so aptly asked, "Oh when will they ever learn, When will they ever learn?"

Present-day Status

The present-day sectarian churches remain as intolerant of the belief of others as they ever have been. Jesus was rejected by the religious leaders of the Jewish society of his day because he dined with prostitutes and sinners; but a well-known television preacher who claims to speak in the name of Jesus calls certain people in Washington, "those perverts" and tells his audience to "wait until 1996 when we will throw all of them out."[36]

If there is any hope for toleration within the Church originally based on Love, it is because a recognition is slowly dawning that some of the early conclusions made by the Church are simply not correct. It is slowly being recognized that Christianity has never been a universal religion; and as the world continues to accept itself as itself and not in the mold of the Western civilization, Christianity in its present form will have less and less potential to become a universal religion. What this means is that despite all the force used by the Western colonial powers to make it so, or perhaps because of all of that force, Christianity will never be a religion universally accepted by all. And the more Christianity tries to present itself as the *only* way, the more it will be rejected. This is true for all religions which seek exclusivity by calling themselves "the *only* true religion" and demonstrate that belief by practicing intolerance against others.

Jesus said "In my Father's house are many rooms" [John 14: 2]. Mohandas K. Ghandi said, "All religions are true religions." If God truly loves all made in his image, then He means for all those to be with Him. And so again I must ask how can anyone reconcile the notion of there being one, and *only* one, true religion if they believe in God's universal saving Love? How can the Church continue to be so intolerant of the beliefs of others?

What do these changes mean to today's Christian?

I am a Christian. I believe in Jesus Christ and I follow his teachings to the best of my human capability. I choose to follow Jesus Christ even though I believe that the Bible, in the language in which it was originally written, does not call him the "*only* Son of God." I feel that my belief that he was not necessarily the only Son of God, coupled with my action that I still choose him, has strengthened my belief in him. And yet, the Church to which I once belonged does not accept this approach, and asks that I confess him as the *only* Son.

With this type of intolerance still prevalent within the sectarian churches, then the question that today's Christian must ask himself is this: How can I be faithful to Christ while being as tolerant as Jesus was rather than as intolerant as his Church has become? To me, the answer to this question on Intolerance is the same as the answer which was given to the question on Salvation. It is found in Mark 9: 40-41 which says, *"For he that is not against us is for us. For truly I say to you, whoever gives you a cup of water to drink because you bear the name of Christ, will by no means lose his reward."* In that spirit, then those who are not against Jesus are with him; and many other religious paths which are not against Christianity, are therefore with it. Each may be very different and each very unique—but each can be with each other as long as they are not against each other!

In that spirit, today's Christian can return to the tolerant concept of Jesus Christ and turn away from the intolerant concept of the Church which bears his name.

7. WORLD AFFAIRS

If there is any one subject in which it should be completely obvious that the men of the Church have altered the teachings of Christ, it is in the area of World Affairs.

Concepts at the time of Jesus.

1. If Jesus Christ had believed that the affairs of the world were his, he would have succumbed to the third temptation offered by Satan, for the third Temptation was that of becoming a political Messiah [Matt 4:8-10]. This had to be the strongest of all Temptations, for God had promised His people their own land; but for almost 600 years that had not happened. The down-trodden Jews fully expected their Messiah to be a political Messiah who would lead them in their rule over other nations and give them world leadership. They fully expected that their Messiah would demand that Rome pay taxes to them!

Jesus resisted this Temptation for two reasons: [1] he would have had to accept Satan as his Lord whereas he had just been baptized as accepting God; and [2] ruling an empire such as Rome was not his job, because God's rule in men's lives could never be imposed from the outside like all governments do. Instead of rules and regulations such as those promulgated by governments and even by well-meaning churches, men needed to create God's society by their own free will and moral choice. Instead of an earthly kingdom of tyranny and cruelty by Jews to replace the similar authoritarianism of Rome, God's new society would be based on the inner nature of those who served and worshipped God alone. And so, this most tempting of temptations was rejected by Jesus in the strongest of terms, "BEGONE SATAN!"

2. When Jesus Christ was asked if it were proper to pay taxes to the Roman government [Matt. 22:15-22], he replied that taxes were to be paid by rendering "to Caesar the things that are Caesar's and to God the things that are God's." By doing so, he alienated the Zealots who were against doing anything for Rome; but by doing so he also made the very strong point that his kingdom was not of the present world.

3. When asked when the kingdom of God was coming [Luke 17:20-1], Jesus replied that the kingdom was not coming with signs to be observed, "for behold, the kingdom of God is in the midst of you [or within you]." It is possible that the word which Jesus used in this statement was an Aramaic word which is more correctly translated as "kingship" rather than "kingdom," but whether this is a true concept or not, it is almost universally accepted that Jesus did not mean a piece of territory when he used the word "kingdom"; for his was never a message of territorial conquest. This is substantiated in the many parables when Jesus said that the kingdom of heaven is "like a man who sowed good seed in his field"; or "like a mustard seed"; or "like a treasure hidden in the field"; or "like a merchant in search of a fine pearl"; or "like a net thrown in the sea"; but never like a great nation of the Earth.

4. When Jesus was asked what a man must do in order to inherit eternal life [Mark 10:17-22], he replied, "go, sell what you have, and give to the poor, and you will have treasure in heaven; and come, follow me."

The evidence is just too substantial to think that in the time of Jesus, his kingdom was one of worldly affairs or of riches. His was a kingdom of compassionate love and unrewarded service for all. In fact, he chose to be crucified rather than to impose his views on anyone. And those who followed him, both by example and deed, were those to whom worldly affairs were not as important as eternal life.

Changes in Concepts

It is difficult to determine when these concepts about the kingdom of God or the kingdom of heaven were changed. Certainly the Apostles seemed to follow his teachings about property and the world affairs; but by the time of Constantine's conversion, the innocent dream of the kingdom of God gave way to a desire for pomp, for riches and for the right to make decisions about nations. With only a few exceptions such as the Franciscans and the Poor Clares, the Church often fought against those who tried to follow the example of poverty and service presented by Jesus. The following paragraphs present a few examples to substantiate the desire of the Church for participation in world affairs.

1. Although Jesus used titles rarely, and when he did the most often used one was "son of man," the titles of the pope include: Bishop of Rome, Vicar of Christ, Successor of the Apostles, Pontifex Maximus of the Universal Church, Patriarch of the West, Primate of Italy, Archbishop and Metropolitan of the Province of Rome, State Sovereign of Vatican City, and Servant of the Servants of God. Originally the title Pontifex Maximus referred to the head of the pagan cult in Rome. Constantine kept the title as an Imperial title, but since then it has been usurped by the pope.[37]

2. Although Jesus had no place to lay his head and wanted to give what he had to the poor, today the pope lives in a palace of 11,000 rooms and has a beautiful summer villa, each of which contains some of the world's greatest art treasures.[38]

3. Although Jesus wanted no part of the world of power and politics, by the time Stephen III became pope in 752, the church had replaced the Roman Empire in the extravagance and extent of its operations and in effect had become a mirror of what the Roman Empire once had been. By this time, the pope had become obsessed with power and possession, and acted like an emperor who lorded it over church and state.[39]

4. Innocent II condemned Arnold of Brescia at the Second Lateran Council in 1139 [Tenth Ecumenical Council] because this

Augustinian canon and abbot taught that the clergy, in order to be Christ's true disciples, should abandon all property and worldly power and live only on the voluntary contributions of the faithful. Arnold was not only excommunicated from the Church, he was banished from Italy solely because he spoke out against the "Revealed Truth" that the clerics were to live in luxury.[40]

5. Pope Innocent III [1198-1216], arguably the most worldly pope, declared the Magna Carta null and void![41]

6. About 100 years later, in 1292, Celestine V was elected pope in a very unusual election. He was a simple man who traveled on a donkey like Jesus had, not in the manner to which the popes had become accustomed. He started to give away the church's posses-sions to the poor and to the impoverished monks with whom he had always associated, just as Jesus had recommended. He even stayed away from banquets, eating only a crust of bread and some water at times, in a manner reminiscent of the Apostles. He slept in a poor monk's cell rather than in papal splendor, again reminiscent of the early Christianity. All of this was of great concern to the Cardinals. They decided that he had to go, and so they installed a speaking tube into his monk's cell which made him think he was hearing the Holy Ghost in his dreams. This ploy got him to resign. When Boniface VIII succeeded him, he locked up the poor monk in an isolated cell reserved for those who were thought to be insane. He starved to death in this cell. The Church later made him a Saint.[42]

7. Less than ten years later, Boniface VIII published *Unam Sanctam* in 1302. It ended with "We declare, announce and define that it is altogether necessary for salvation for every creature to be subject to the Roman Pontiff." Although there are those in the Church who have said that they wish such a document had never been written, it was written; and it was the established belief of the Church. Three hundred years after writing this, Boniface was honored as a martyr of the Church.[43]

8. Shortly after that, in 1323 John XXII in his bull *Cum inter nonnullos* said that to maintain that Christ and the apostles had no property is a perversion of Scripture. This, of course, contradicted Scripture and many prior popes who had declared that Christ and the Apostles had lived in poverty. By this statement, John XXII made heretics out of the Franciscans who had taken vows of poverty. When John XXII also said that the emperor had to take an oath of loyalty to him as administrative head of the empire, the political forces tried to declare him a heretic and have him deposed; but John was too good a politician for that. By 1330, it was the official teaching of the Catholic Church that Christ and the apostles did not live a life of poverty.[44] A major part of the need for the Church to do this was brought on by the Crusade against the Cathars and the Waldenses who were gentle people and believed strongly in their vow of poverty.

9. It is a very unusual story, but the Church can rightfully claim to have changed the meaning of the word "usury." In a classical sense, usury means *all* gains from money-lending. For over eighteen hundred years, the Roman Catholic Church had dogmatically stated that the charging of any interest on a loan was absolutely forbidden as being contrary to divine law. The prohibition was restated in various church councils, among which were Arles [314]; First Ecumenical at Niceae [325]; Carthage [345]; Aix [789]; and Tenth Ecumenical at Lateran [1139] at which usurers were to be excommunicated. Although the laws of many states made the practice of charging interest legal, it was still heresy within the Church until 1830 when the Church changed its position. Thus, by courtesy of the Roman Catholic Church, usury now means lending money at *exorbitant* rates of interest; whereas lending money at acceptable rates is perfectly all right, even for the Church.[45]

10. After it became acceptable for the Church to generate money from capital by charging interest, the financial affairs of the Church started to become as important as its spiritual affairs. In recent times, Bernardino Nogara has been the man who handled the financial affairs of the Catholic Church. He did this for many years during the twentieth century. He successfully invested the church's funds and got the church involved in many of the world's financial practices. He was the man who demonstrated that, whatever Christ's kingdom might be, that of the Catholic Church was most assuredly of this world; for upon his death, he was given a memorable epitaph by Cardinal Spellman of New York who said, "Next to Jesus Christ, the greatest thing that has happened to the Catholic Church is Bernardino Nogara."[46]

11. In 1929, the Roman Catholic Church concluded a deal with Mussolini which not only recognized the Vatican as a sovereign state and exempted it from paying taxes to Italy, it gave the Holy See an amount of money which today would be in excess of one billion dollars. This was the basis of the investment nest-egg which Nogara grew very successfully. In 1933, the Church cut another deal, this time with Adolph Hitler which confirmed the *Kirchensteuer*, a tax collected by the state and given to the Church for its use. It represented about 10% of all the income taxes collected in Germany. Although it was given to all churches [including Protestant], the Catholic Church received the lion's share. It should be emphasized that this was not a tithe given freely by a Christian to his church; it was an income tax placed on the individual by the State, out of which the church got its cut.[47]

12. What would the one who declared "Blessed are the poor" feel about the sale of Vatican stamps [at over $1 million per year profit]; or the annual collection of Peter's Pence, a fund which goes directly to the pope for his use and which in many years has exceeded $20 Million[48]; or the way funds collected in His name have been used by the Jimmy Swaggarts or the Jim and Tammy Faye Bakkers of the world?

Present-day Status

The present-day status of the Church is that of being intimately tied into the affairs of the world. This activity is commendable when it is concerned with charitable acts of compassionate love. Many churches are actively involved with beneficial activities such as Habitat for Humanity, the Salvation Army, homeless shelters and many, many others of the like. The Church of Jesus Christ would hardly be following him if they did not show a compassionate love in this type of participation in World Affairs, for Jesus did recommend giving what you have to the poor. It is not an intent of this sub-section to say that none of that type of participation exists, for it does. Many churches pride themselves in donating over half of all that they receive to such kinds of work. This is indeed to be commended. That is World Affairs of the proper kind.

But it is not a proper mission of the Church to take over and use the public sphere to promulgate an agenda of its own whatever that agenda might be. This happens in both the Catholic and the Protestant Churches. Jerry Falwell, a very prominent minister of the Protestant Religious Right, is reported to have said, "It is time that Christians take back the power to run their own country....The constitution in the hands of Christians is a holy document; in the hands of non-Christians it can be used by the devil to defeat us."[49]

The implications of that statement are indeed frightening; for it is not within the meaning of religion, and certainly not within the meaning of a religion whose members follow Christ, to use that religion to undermine the rights of those who do not agree with it. The ability for dissent is a basic foundation of the United States. When religion attempts to stifle such dissent, it can hardly be called the religion of Christ; for after all, Christ was one who spoke out in dissent against all the major elements of the society of his day.

What do these changes mean to today's Christian?

It must be obvious to anyone who has read the last two sections that the concepts of tolerance and "the kingdom which is not of this world" which Christ taught have been significantly changed by man. Jesus Christ refused to accept the world when Satan offered it to him; but when Constantine offered the Empire, the Church accepted. If the Church had been able to keep itself aligned with the principles of the Christ, then this acceptance could conceivably have been of benefit to the concepts of Christ. But unfortunately, the Altar and the Throne became so intertwined, that the goals of the Church became those of the State; and the goals of the State became those of the Church. The result is a Church which believes that the world should bow down to it while it negotiates its agendas and cuts its deals with the Mussolinis, the Hitlers and political platform committees of the West, all in the name of the Christ who taught compassionate, tolerant Love for all.

8. REINCARNATION AND KARMA[1]

Of all of the ideas or theories ever proposed by any religion, few have as universal an appeal as does the concept of the soul returning to a physical body, the concept presently called reincarnation. It seems that any time a religion is changed, many proponents of the

change want to have reincarnation included. However, any understanding of the concept of reincarnation is incomplete without some
understanding of the concept of its companion, karma. When used
together, these two concepts generate a self-induced impetus to live
a God-centered, moral life. Almost no other religious practice has
been as effective in generating this desired effect.

The term "reincarnation" is simply defined as the rebirth of
the soul into another physical body. The definition of "karma" is a
more complex. It generally means the sum and consequences of an
entity's actions during successive phases of its existence, regarded as
determining its destiny. The following description of karma is
presented on page 133 in Vol. 8 of the *New Catholic Encyclopedia*:

"Karma, a term literally meaning 'action', came to be used in
Hindu doctrine to signify a chain of cause and effect by which every
action necessarily produces a given effect, not only in the physical,
but also in moral order. Karma is believed to extend beyond a normal
lifetime and can refer to the actions of a previous life. The goal of
every soul is ultimately, by good works which are mainly of a religious nature, to be set free from karma and to attain liberation."

But as complex as karma may seem, the interaction of
reincarnation with karma becomes even more complex; for it is karma
which determines what the new incarnation will be like. As presented
in detail in *Christianity and the New Age Religion*, karma is instrumental in determining what experiences Spirit will ask Soul to accept and resolve in each incarnation [see also page 119]. Consequently,
reincarnation and karma walk hand-in-hand to guide the entity on its
pathway back to God.

In the following paragraphs, reincarnation will be emphasized more than karma, not because of importance, but because the
concept of karma is almost meaningless until one has accepted the
probability of reincarnation; and after the concept of reincarnation
has been accepted, then karma falls into place almost automatically.

Concepts at the time of Jesus.

The concepts of reincarnation and karma were very prevalent
during the time of Jesus. The documented information which established this fact, and the biblical citations which justified a scriptural

background for belief in these concepts were presented in *Christianity and the New Age Religion.* That information will not be repeated here in that same depth. Instead, the conclusions will merely be presented in outline form.

1. Both the Pharisees and the Essenes at the time of Jesus believed in reincarnation as documented by Josephus. Although the Sadducees did not have this belief, this is understandable; for the Sadducees did not believe in an afterlife of any kind, even the kind that sectarian Christians believe in.

2. There are five major pieces of Scripture which are difficult to interpret in any way other than that there was a belief in reincarnation at that time. These verses are Matt. 11:13-15; Matt. 14:1-3; Matt. 17:9-12; Mark 8:27-8; and John 1:6. These verses present substantial support for belief in reincarnation at the time of Jesus.

3. In addition to these five verses, an author who has a Doctor of Divinity degree from an accredited theological seminary has proposed that there are over 200 verses of scripture which indicate a belief in reincarnation, though on a somewhat less substantial basis than the ones mentioned above [see *Reincarnation, a Biblical Doctrine* by Marilynn McDermit, DD].

4. Furthermore, there is much evidence in the Bible which indicates that the pre-existence of the soul was accepted at the time of Jesus. John 1:6 makes absolutely no sense without there having been an existence of the soul of John the Baptist before he was born; for in what other way could the Bible have said, "There was a man sent from God, whose name was John."? In addition, John 9:2 strongly suggests the pre-existence of the soul; for how else could the man who was born blind have sinned before his birth? Finally in Romans 9:10-13, it is strongly suggested by Paul that Jacob was loved but Esau was hated before they were born. One wonders how this could be without the pre-existence of the soul. The pre-existence of the soul is a requirement of the reincarnation of a soul, although not a requirement of the initial incarnation of the soul. It is only by accepting this understanding that the concept of reincarnation and the orthodox concept of the soul presented in Vol. 13, page 471 of the *New Catholic Encyclopedia* [see page 167] start to come together to make sense.

5. Finally, when Paul wrote, "Do not be deceived; God is not mocked, for whatever a man sows, that he will also reap" in Gal. 6:7, he was making one of the strongest statements on karma which has ever been recorded.

Although some may try to counter this presentation by stating that the words "reincarnation" or "karma" are not used in the Bible, that does not mean that the concepts are not presented; for although the word "trinity" is not used in the Bible, this hardly kept it from being promulgated as a Christian dogma.

However, it is not the purpose of this review to state that either reincarnation or karma is taught in the Bible; only that neither is denied. Since these concepts were prevalent at the time, they would have been denied if Jesus considered them to be wrong. John 9:2 would have been a perfect time for Jesus to have done this, but he did not. One need only look at Matt. 5:38 for a striking example of how Jesus denied prevalent concepts which he deemed to be unacceptable. The fact that Jesus did not deny the reincarnation/karma concept does not make it an acceptable Christian doctrine; but it does mean that any denial by the Church is built on a shaky foundation.

This then leads to the question of why Jesus did not *teach* the reincarnation/karma concept since he did not deny it. Jesus did not teach these concepts in his time because he did not have to. He taught only those things which needed to be changed, and he taught them strongly. But he did not teach either reincarnation, or the pre-existence of the soul, or karma when he had the opportunity to do so because he did not feel that there was any need to change the prevailing attitude about these concepts. Consequently, in order to leave those concepts alone, he neither denied not taught the concepts of karma, of reincarnation or of the pre-existence of the soul.

Changes in Concepts

In the very first days after the resurrection [i.e. in the times of the Apostles], there is little if any mention of reincarnation, although karma may have entered into a few minds. This is understandable, for in those days the immediate Second Coming of Christ was thought to be imminent. This would introduce the new age with its new and better order under Christ's kingship. When this was coming so soon, why would anyone be concerned with rebirth in another body? In essence, when the world as they knew it would end possibly tomorrow, but certainly within the lifetime of the young members of the Christian community, why worry about where the soul had been or where it would go?

When the end of the world did not happen immediately, people started to look at the longer term, which meant establishing and organizing the church. In the primitive Christian Church, the notion of rebirth was widespread. Thoughts on that subject were entertained by many responsible thinkers committed to the ancient catholic faith. There still exist many quotations made by those presently considered to be Church Fathers which can hardly be interpreted as anything other than a strong belief in reincarnation, the pre-existence of the soul and karma. Following that period, these concepts, particularly reincarnation started to be ignored based on a few rather spurious references from Scripture. That is still the case today. While neither reincarnation nor the pre-existence of the soul has been officially rejected by the teachings of the Church, these concepts have not been officially accepted by the teachings of the Church. In other words, they have been ignored.

The following outline will develop this picture by presenting quotations or thoughts in a roughly chronological order. Some of these thoughts are related to reincarnation, others to the pre-existence of the soul, others to karma, and still others to an interaction of all of these concepts.

1. Within about a century of the death of Christ, Justin Martyr in his *Dialogue with Trypho* taught that human souls inhabit more than one body in the course of their earthly pilgrimage. He even suggested the possibility that those who live such carnal lives that they deprive themselves of the capacity to see God may be reincarnated as beasts.[50] This, of course, is both reincarnation and karma as taught by one of the earliest Church Fathers.

2. At the end of the second century CE, Clement of Alexandria in his *Exhortations to the Pagans* wrote that man was **"in being long before the foundation of the world...and God showed pity on us in our wanderings, He pitied us from the very beginning."**[52] This is a stirring presentation of the pre-existence of the soul by an outstanding Eastern theologian of the early Church.

3. About 30 years later, Origen, who was possibly the greatest theologian and teacher of the early Church, said, **"the soul at one time puts off one body, which was necessary before but which is no longer adequate in its changed state, and it exchanges it for another."** In slightly later writing he said, **"Every soul comes into this world strengthened by the victories or weakened by the defeats of its previous life."** Origen thus teaches both reincarnation and karma.

4. In about 370 CE, Gregory of Nyssa, who with Athanasius was the early Church's greatest defender of the divinity of Jesus Christ, said, **"It is absolutely necessary that the soul should be healed and purified, and if this does not take place during its life on earth, it must be accomplished in future lives."**[53]

5. At about the same time, Arnobius in his *Adversus Gentes* said, **"We die many times, and often do we rise from the dead."**[54] Some might suggest that Arnobius was merely referring to the small deaths which occur often in life and which ultimately lead to the final physical death of the body. In response, the reincarnationist would state an acceptance of that belief, then continue to the larger picture in which there are many physical deaths and rebirths, all of which ultimately lead to the final exit of the physical life followed by a rebirth in spirit.

6. In the early fourth century, Lactantius, a Christian writer whom Jerome called "the Christian Cicero" said that the soul was capable of immortality and of bodily survival only on the hypothesis that it existed before the body.[54] He thus proposes the pre-existence of the soul.

7. Augustine defined purgatory in the same manner as his teacher, Ambrose, who said that all departed souls await the end of the world in various "habitations" which vary according to their works on earth. This is quite a Karmic statement. Augustine expanded on this in *De Civitate Dei* to say that the souls of men are judged immediately on death and then go at once to a place of purification. The reincarnationist sees these "habitations" as the Monad where the soul and the spirit come together to evaluate the life just experienced and to program the next set of experiences. This possibility was explored in detail in *Christianity and the New Age Religion* [see also page 119].

8. In *The Confessions of St. Augustine*, Augustine writes, **"...did my infancy succeed another age of mine that died before it?...and what before that life, O God, was I in any body? For this I have none to tell me, neither father nor mother, nor experience of others, nor mine own memory."**[55]

9. In the late fourth century, Synesius, Bishop of Ptolemais, in his *Treatise on Dreams* wrote, **"The soul which did not quickly return to the heavenly region from which it was sent down to Earth, had to go through many lives of wandering."**[56]

10. Among those whom the Church rejected, the Manichaens, the Priscillians, the Marcionists, the Paulicians, the Bogomils, the Cathars and many others openly taught the doctrine of reincarnation. As has been previously noted in Appendix A and in the section on the Cathars, most of these were rejected by the Church for reasons other then their doctrine of reincarnation. The Cathars represent an interesting case. They taught that our reason for being on Earth is that we all are fallen spirits forced to be incarcerated in bodies and to work out our liberation through transmigration from one body to another. However, they saw in Christ the instrument of divine redemption from the wheel of rebirth. They were excommunicated and presented with genocide for having these beliefs.

11. In the nineteenth century, John Henry Newman, after he left the Anglican Church and became a Catholic Cardinal, proposed that after death, the soul goes to an undesignated place of state in which it has opportunities for further growth and development.[57] This is very similar to the description presented by Augustine and Ambrose in paragraph 7 above and fits into the same interpretation by the reincarnationist [see also page 119].

Present-day Status

In order to understand the present-day status, it will be necessary to outline some positive thoughts and then follow these with the arguments which the Church has used to justify its ignoring the concept of reincarnation. In presenting these thoughts and arguments, karma will be ignored on the basis that until reincarnation is accepted, karma has little meaning; and after i. .carnation is accepted, the acceptance of karma is almost automatic. These thoughts and arguments will be presented in outline form.

1. It should be understood that there is absolutely no historical basis on which the Church would reject reincarnation and therefore no reason why reincarnation could not be accepted by the Christian Church. In other words, there has been no historically developed Church dogma which has opposed reincarnation. The Church has never been overly keen to formulate dogmas which must be believed until it has been forced into doing so. So far, it has not been forced into such action by the concept of reincarnation.

2. There is nothing in biblical thought, and nothing in Christian tradition which excludes reincarnation. The concept does not conflict with Scripture or other historical teachings, and the theological reasons for rejecting reincarnation often seem so flimsy as to be virtually spurious. On the positive side, reincarnation would tend to support the central Christian concept of unconditional love, would tend to enhance the Christian concept of Grace, would tend to ameliorate the spirituality of the West, and has the ability to present a strong moral force which would keep one from participating in violent or warlike activities.

3. In some Christian literature, and even in some New Age literature, it is proposed that a general council of the Church condemned Origen's thoughts on the pre-existence of the soul and therefore condemned reincarnation. Reports have appeared in New Age literature that this happened at the Council of Nicaea [First Ecumenical Council]. Reports have appeared in Christian literature that this happened at the second Council of Constantinople [Fifth Ecumenical Council]. By all the historical records that I can find, including both the *Encyclopaedia Britannica* and the *New Catholic Encyclopedia* each of which gives a quite balanced viewpoint of the activities of all Ecumenical Councils, neither report is historically correct. In no general Council has the Western Church ever condemned reincarnation. The First Ecumenical Council has been adequately covered in Chapter Two of *Book One*. Because the Fifth Ecumenical Council is the one most often thought by the Christian to have refuted reincarnation, its minute details are presented in

Appendix C. The final sentence of Appendix C says "A Christian would therefore not be going against the teachings of the ecumenical Church if he were to accept either belief." The two beliefs mentioned are reincarnation and the pre-existence of the soul.

4. From a Christian viewpoint, one major problem with reincarnation is that those who accept it believe that man is a part of God, or a spark of the divine, much as Meister Eckhart and most of the other Christian mystics did [see page 160]. This conflicts with Christian teaching which proposes that although man is made in the image of God, he is no more than an image; for he is a creation of God and not an emanation. The doctrines of the Church had to take this stand to support the uniqueness of Jesus Christ as the *only* emanation of God.

5. In order to justify the teaching that "it is appointed to men to die once and after this comes the judgment," Christian theologians often refer to four verses of scripture: *viz.* Heb. 9:27; Luke 16:19-31; Luke 23:43; and 2 Cor 5:10. Based on this scripture, the Christian teaching is that man has but one life on Earth in which to earn his eternal destiny. Each portion of Scripture is discussed in the following paragraphs.

6. Hebrews 9:27-8 says *"And just as it is appointed for men to die once, and after that comes judgment, so Christ, having been offered once to bear the sins of many, will appear a second time, not to deal with sin but to save those who are eagerly waiting for him."*

The author has read many commentaries on Heb 9:27 including those of Barclay, the *Anchor Bible*, etc. In these, the commentators state that the purpose of this verse of Scripture is to declare that Christ made the perfect sacrifice for us, and that in so doing, he only had to do it once. The presentation that man lives only once is used purely as an example of the once-for-allness of Christ's act. It does not address the issue of another birth for a human soul. Instead, it merely uses the death of the physical body as something which happens only once; and even though the physical body tends to die a little bit each day, it is true that it dies only once. In the same manner, Jesus had to die only once to overcome sin. That is the message of Heb. 9:27. It was never intended to be a denial of reincarnation, although some have chosen to use it for that purpose.

In addition to these conventional commentaries, there is a highly regarded work entitled the *Theological Dictionary of New Testament* which is aimed at defining the Greek words used in the New Testament by using their full essence. In Vol. V on page 917, the following statement appears: "The author of Hebrews uses a Greek word in 9:27 which is normally translated as 'passion' rather than as 'death'. Had he truly meant a dying kind of death, he could have used a more explicit word which was available to him." In Vol. III page 14, it says: "In Hebrews 9:27 we all are enslaved to death [or passion] with the only exceptions being Enoch [Heb. 11:5] and Melchizedek [Heb. 7:3]"; and on page 17, it states: "that physical death is not the final end but is followed by the judgment... and is either reversed by the resurrection or ...is followed by a period of torment in hell."

In summary, the purpose of Heb. 9:27 is not to speak against reincarnation, but is to express the doctrine that Christ only had to die once in order to grant salvation and the remission of sins. And since most who believe in reincarnation believe that it is a resurrection, then a physical death which is followed by a judgment, and which then is followed by a resurrection, is all completely compatible with the reincarnation concept. Consequently, looking solely at Heb. 9:27-8, it is entirely possible that one who follows Christ can believe in reincarnation without losing his belief in either the Scriptures or in the message and person of Jesus Christ.

7. Luke 16:19-31 is a long parable which will not be repeated here. It is the story of Dives, a rich man who died rich but without faith, and Lazarus, a poor man who died with faith. The parable tells what happened to each in the afterlife. It also makes the point that even if the rich man were to return from the dead, he could not save his rich brothers unless they obeyed Moses and the prophets [i.e. followed the Law]. The point which is being made is that those who do not have faith have a crisis in their lives whether they realize it or not; and that even a messenger from the dead would not change them if they did not heed God's word. This parable hardly represents justification against the concept of reincarnation; and those who use it as such are stretching a point.

8. Luke 23:43 says, "Jesus replied to him, 'Believe me, today you shall be with me in Paradise.' " This was said by Jesus to one of the criminals who was being crucified with him. The commentaries in the *Anchor Bible* state that although the word "paradise" originally meant "enclosed park or garden" and as such was used to represent the Garden of Eden in Genesis, by the time of Jesus, it had come to mean "the mystical place or abode of the righteous after death." Those who quote this scripture as an argument against reincarnation place strong emphasis on the word "today" in justifying that man only lives once. It hardly seems to be germane.

9. 2 Cor. 5:10 says "For we must all appear before the judgment seat of Christ, so that each one may receive good or evil, according to what he has done in the body." Those who believe in reincarnation, and even those who believe in karma, would certainly agree with this piece of Scripture. But what does it have to do with whether or not reincarnation is a viable concept?

10. It seems to this author that almost anyone with an open mind would have to say that if this is the only Scripture which can be cited against reincarnation, then it is a pretty weak case; and that to the thinking Christian, reincarnation is not rejected by any of the Scripture which is normally cited against it.

11. However, there is the fact that some Christian theologians have applied great importance to the concept that we must be resurrected in the "same body," though in a glorified form. This was emphasized at the Twelfth Ecumenical Council held at the Lateran against the Albigenses [Cathars] in 1215 which asserted that all shall rise again in their own bodies, *the bodies they now have: omnes cum suis propriis resurgent corporibus, quae nunc gestant.* Thomas Aquinas affirmed this when he stated that if it were not the same body, then the term "resurrection" would have to be replaced with the term "assumption of a new body."[58]

All of this was, of course, conceived in a climate of now antiquated scientific concepts. With the new belief of Quantum Physics that all matter, even the human cell, is no more than energy in a special arrangement, and with the understanding that all cells of one's body are totally changed within about a seven year period, the former necessity that "soul" and "body" are intimately connected and thus would have to be reunited, no longer seems appropriate. In addition,

1 Cor. 15:35-58 can readily be interpreted as speaking directly against the concept of needing the physical body for resurrection.

Reincarnation was not rejected either by the Fifth Ecumenical Council [see Appendix C] or the resurrection language of the Twelfth Council, a Council which was never approved by the Eastern Church. Consequently, it would seem that only the conscience of the individual Christian is left to govern whether he will accept or he will reject the concept of reincarnation.

What do these thoughts mean to today's Christian?

When the concept of reincarnation is accepted by a Christian, then many things are presented in a new light. This is not the first time that a Christian has had to apply a new light to the old way that he looked at things. As one example, the biological theory of evolution introduced by Darwin presented the Christian with a new way of looking at the Creation Story in Genesis. Once the thinking Christian accepted that in God's universe the word "day" does not necessarily mean "our 24 hours," then the Creation Story became very acceptable to many Christians and enabled them to make more sense out of a traditional doctrine.

If reincarnation and its companion karma were to become as accepted as the biological theory of evolution, then many new lights would turn on for the Christian. He might even be able to understand the presence of Evil, a presence which has baffled many who believe in a loving God. In addition, the traditional doctrines of Salvation, Providence, the Presence of God, and Grace would be viewed with a new light of expansion. Grace, God's divine love and protection, is particularly susceptible to this new light; for with reincarnation, Grace and free will become more completely intertwined. Without the additional opportunities to use free will to accept Grace as an act of love, then the acceptance of Grace tends to be generated by fear. When that happens, Grace loses its meaning. It becomes something which is forced upon one rather than being chosen by one.

The Christian believes that Grace is fundamental to all the good we can hope to do and to all the moral and spiritual growth we can hope to attain. If this is accepted, then what keeps reincarnation from being a companion of Grace as a part of God's plan? As a part of the entire scheme of God, He would provide His Grace and His plan of salvation through Christ to those who would so choose; and the choice could be made in this life, or in the multitude of lives available throughout the eternity of the immortal soul. Granted, the sooner the choice is made to accept God's Grace, the better things would be for the immortal soul; but "sooner" is one of the messages of reincarnation anyway.

On the basis of free will, the choice to investigate and to further understand reincarnation and karma is the Christian's to make; for it has not been prohibited by Scripture or by the teachings of the ecumenical Church. The thoughts about what the acceptance of the reincarnation concept could lead to are truly mind-expanding. The absence of the concept of reincarnation plus the presence of the concept of intolerance constitute the two major reasons I chose to leave Christianity for Christianess.

9. ANGELS

The term "angel" is derived from a Greek word meaning "messenger" and thus angels are described more by what they do than by what they are. They have generally been described as being the ones who bring messages from the transcendent God to the immanent man. In this activity, they have been intermediaries between God and man; and man is thought to come to his highest knowledge of who he is, of what his origin is, and of what his destiny is through the celestial messenger, the angel.

There is a strong belief in angels within the Judeo-Christian heritage. In Judaism, the concept of angels was seriously developed during the periods of the Babylonian exile [6th-5th centuries BCE] under the influence of Zoroasterianism. In the canonical Old Testament, Yahweh is called the Lord of hosts [Sabaoth] which is an angelic army capable of fighting evil and performing numerous duties. Two archangels are mentioned in the Old Testament: *Michael*, the warrior leader of the heavenly hosts and *Gabriel*, the heavenly messenger. Two others are mentioned in the apocryphal Old Testament: *Raphael*, God's helper, and *Uriel*, the watcher over the world. These four archangels symbolically imply perfection. They are related to the four cardinal points of the compass and to the four basic elements of Earth, Air Fire and Water. As mentioned earlier [see page 38], some noncanonical Hebrew manuscripts mention seven archangels. In addition to the archangels, there are other orders of angels in the Hebrew literature: the cherubim and the seraphim.

In the New Testament, celestial beings are grouped into seven ranks: angels, archangels, principalities, powers, virtues, dominions and thrones. To these, the Old Testament cherubim and seraphim are often added to comprise the nine choirs of angels presented in later Christian mystical theology such as Dante's *The Divine Comedy*. In the *Shepherd of Hermas*, six orders of angels are presented; whereas Clement of Alexandria and most other early Christian writers mention seven orders of angels.

By any analysis, angels are an important part of our Judeo-Christian heritage.

Concepts at the time of Jesus.

1. In the gospels of Matthew and Luke, angels play an important part in the birth of Jesus including announcements to Mary by Gabriel, announcements by angels to the shepherds who were in the field and were afraid, and choirs of angels which sang of the glorious birth. Angels were very involved with the birth of Jesus Christ.

2. Jesus spoke often of angels and their duties including how he will use their services. As one example, Jesus says, "The Son of man will send his angels and they will gather out of his kingdom all causes of sin and all evildoers" [Matt. 13:41]. Another example has Jesus saying, "For whoever is ashamed of me and of my words, of him will the Son of man be ashamed when he comes in his glory and the glory of the Father and of the holy angels" [Luke 9:26]. Jesus therefore places angels at the side of God. All-in-all, there are about thirty references to angels in the gospels.

3. It can therefore be readily stated that at the time of Jesus, angels were a very active part of God's work on Earth.

Changes in Concepts

1. Throughout much of the history of the Church, there have been very few changes in the concepts of angels. Some of the quotations or statements which support this conclusion are presented in this sub-section in approximately their chronological order.

However, as described in the following sub-section, the present status is not as it once was and today's Church has tended to ignore the concept of angels given us by Jesus.

2. Hebrews 13:2 "Be not forgetful to entertain strangers: for thereby some have entertained angels unawares."

3. Tertullian: "Beauty is not necessary to God's Angels."

4. Origen: "Angels may become men or demons, and again from the latter they may rise to be men or angels."

5. Ambrose: "We should pray to the angels, for they were given to us as guardians."

6. Augustine stated that angels, who have ethereal bodies, may be able to assume material bodies. He also said: "The Devil often transforms himself into an angel to tempt men, some for their instruction and some for their ruin."

7. Pope Gregory I the Great: "There are nine orders of angels, to wit, angels, archangels, virtues, powers, principalities, dominations, thrones, cherubim, and seraphim."

8. Martin Luther [ca. 1530]: "An angel is a spiritual creature created by God, without a body, for the service of Christendom and of the Church."

9. John Calvin [ca. 1550]: "The angels are the dispensers and administrators of the Divine beneficence toward us; they regard our safety, undertake our defense, direct our ways, and exercise a constant solicitude that no evil befall us."

10. St. Francis de Sales [ca. 1600]: "Make yourself familiar with angels, and behold them frequently in spirit; for without being seen, they are present with you."

11. John Milton [ca. 1650]: "Millions of spiritual creatures walk the earth unseen, both when we sleep and when we awake."

12. Henry Ward Beecher [ca. 1870]: "We not only live among men, but there are airy hosts, blessed spectators, sympathetic lookers-on, that see and know and appreciate our thoughts and feelings and acts."

13. Billy Graham [ca. 1975]: "Angels are created spirit beings who can become visible when necessary. They can appear and disappear. They think, feel, will and display emotions." and "God uses angels to work out the destinies of men and nations."

Present-day Status

The following quote is from Billy Graham's 1975 book entitled, <u>Angels: God's Secret Agents</u>: *"When I decided to preach a sermon on angels, I found practically nothing in my library. Upon investigation I soon discovered that little had been written on the subject in this century. This seemed a strange and ominous omission. Bookstores and libraries have shelves of books on demons, the occult and the devil. Why was the devil getting so much more attention from writers than angels? Some people seem to put the devil on a par with God. Actually, Satan is a fallen angel."* [59]

The purpose of including this quotation in this work is not to defend the last sentence of Billy Graham's statement, for that is up to the reader to believe or not. Instead, this quotation from him is included in this work to emphasize what this author has also found: *viz.* that the writers of theology and the ministers of the Christian Church of today have either forgotten about the existence of angels, or have chosen to ignore the importance of the work they do on this physical plane. I would like every reader to answer the following question: When was the last time you heard a representative of the present Christian Church attribute any great work on this Earth to the activity of an angel? If you can answer that question with a recent date, then you are in an extraordinary branch of the Church, for the work done by the angels and their presence in our lives is generally neglected by today's Church.

And that is quite a change from the concept which Jesus Christ presented!

What do these changes mean to today's Christian?

There may be some who will wonder if this subject has the impact or the importance of the other subjects addressed in this Chapter. This may arise even though the issue of *Time* magazine dated December 27, 1993 stated that 69% of the American people believe in angels, an attitude "which many clerics view with alarm." In response to those who might question the importance of this subject, I would suggest the following:

As will be described in the next section, the Church has

changed the original concept of sex and in so doing has removed free will as a possibility for many Christians. The Church did this to establish that it has authority and control over all who wish to profess Jesus Christ. In a similar attempt at control, the Church also has removed the help of the angelic host in favor of the one Holy Spirit. That is quite a change in belief from the concept which was available to the early Christian and which was presented in the statements of Jesus Christ. By saying this, I do not in any way belittle the work done by the Holy Spirit, for I feel that its work is of vital importance. But I also believe that the work done by the angelic kingdom is extremely important to those of us who exist on this physical plane.

When the work of the angels was so important to Jesus Christ and to the Apostles [in addition to the Gospels, see Acts 7:53], then why does the Christian Church of today tend to ignore them so completely, or to view an interest in them with "so much alarm"?

10. SEX or SEXUALITY[1]

Sex is considered to be one of the strongest of all possible urges in humankind; for there are times when the desire for sexual activity can cause the postponement of other significant urges such as the desire to work, to eat, to drink or to sleep. It is also one of humankind's greatest enigmas; for no one has been able to explain this puzzling activity in a way which might be accepted and understood by all. Religions have almost always felt the need to comment on sex. In doing so, religious attitudes about sex or sexuality have ranged all the way from temple prostitutes and fertility rites, to the belief that total abstinence [i.e. celibacy] would allow man to walk closer to God.

Even within the Judeo-Christian heritage, attitudes about sex have varied widely and perplexed many. The subject has been the theme of intense debates, an example of which was the twelve year running feud between Augustine and Julian [see pages 203-204]. As an example of how this subject perplexes many, I find it rather remarkable that the *New Catholic Encyclopedia,* a work of more than 15,000 pages, has less than three pages on the subject of sex or sexuality. This absence of comment is either in spite of, or possibly because of, all the problems which the Catholic Church has had with this very human drive.

Concepts at the time of Jesus.

To understand the sexual mores and attitudes of an individual, it is almost always necessary to understand something of the mores and attitudes of the society of his time. Jesus is no exception. In general, his viewpoints and teachings echoed those of the Jewish society of his time, although in three instances, he took them at least one step further.

The Jewish society had very definite attitudes about sex which are expressed throughout the Old Testament. In general, it was believed that sex was essentially a good thing. God created man and woman and blessed them as He asked them to be fruitful, to multiply and to fill the Earth. As this attitude progressed through the Jewish society, sex was seen as an activity which fit into a societal context of family and tribe, and not as a personal one. Therefore, whatever man did in his sexual activities, he did it as a member of a society fulfilling God's desires. The rite of circumcision, so important to the Jewish male within the Jewish society, was seen as an initiation to marriage and the family life. It was an initiation which set the stage for sexual activities.

The 18th Chapter of Leviticus is the major scriptural reference which presents a list of sexual liaisons that are forbidden. In this chapter, there are some 12 verses which define and forbid incest; one verse which forbids sexual relations during the time of the menstrual cycle; one verse which forbids fornication [i.e. non-marital sex between a man and a woman]; one verse which forbids the sacrifice of children by burning; one verse which forbids homosexuality of the male-male type; and one verse which forbids bestiality of both the male-beast and the female-beast types. Homosexuality is defined as an "abomination"; whereas bestiality is defined as a "perversion." The 20th Chapter of Leviticus gives the punishment for the sexual practices forbidden in the 18th chapter. In most cases, the punishment is exile or death. Among sexual activities which were accepted at that time but frowned upon today are those of polygamy and concubinage as attested to, among others, by the activities of Abraham with Hagar. Since neither of these activities went against God's desires to "be fruitful and multiply," they were not forbidden. However, since male homosexuality wasted semen, a resource which is needed for procreation, it was forbidden.

Jacob Milgrom is a rabbi and on the Editorial Advisory Board of *Bible Review* [*BR*]. In the December, 1993 issue of *BR*, Milgrom presents an interesting article entitled "Does the Bible Prohibit Homosexuality?" Through a very reasoned argument and discussion, he comes to the conclusion that Lesbians are not mentioned in the Bible and neither are non-Jewish gay men unless they happen to live in the Holy Land. He further suggests that all the sexual prohibitions are based on the "spilling of seed" with its symbolic loss of life, or at least with the loss of the potential to produce "children of Israel"; for God had admonished His chosen people to be "fruitful and multiply" in Gen. 1:28. In this manner, male masturbation, though not mentioned, would be as prohibited as male homosexuality. In neither case would such female activities be prohibited for they did not waste a potential source of offspring. In the <u>Letters</u> section of subsequent issues of *BR*, Milgrom was strongly criticized for taking this stance. However, he continued to defend his case and was given support by many scholars. In all of this effort, Milgrom is careful to state that although he uses the term "Bible," as a Rabbi he is examining only what the Christian would call the Old Testament.

One more point should be made about the context of Jesus' background on sexual matters before examining what he did. That is the Jewish attitude about divorce. As in any patriarchal society, the divorce laws were written almost totally for the benefit of men. It was virtually impossible for a woman to obtain a divorce; whereas a man could obtain a divorce on almost any pretext. In fact, the law stated that if a man were in a childless marriage for ten years, he was either required to get a divorce and marry another, or else keep his barren wife and take a second wife to produce his children.[60] If a woman were divorced, she was deemed to have few sexual opportunities; for all such activities by an unmarried woman, whether for hire or not, were termed "prostitution." In fact, the same Hebrew word *zana* could be translated as "to fornicate" or "to be a harlot or a whore," thus indicating that any female fornication was an act of prostitution. In all of the Old Testament, only the Song of Solomon with its obviously erotic imagery deviates from the major sexual theme of the Jewish society which was that sex was preserved for the family situation, and that the purpose of sex is procreation.

Jesus continued the teachings that sex is good in itself and that marriage and birth were occasions for great joy [John 2:1-10; 16:21; Matt. 9:15]. However, Jesus deviated from the Jewish teachings in three instances, each of which surprised those who were with him. First, whereas the Jews were harsh on those who committed sexual transgressions, including stoning an adulteress, Jesus was merciful to sexual sinners [Luke 7:36-50; John 4:7-45; 8:1-11] even though he did condemn adultery both in thought and deed [Matt. 5:27-32]. Secondly, and even more surprising for those of his society, Jesus completely changed the ground-rules on divorce. In one case [Mark 10:2-10] he said that there was no possible reason for divorce; and in another case [Matt. 19:3-9], he said that the only possible reason for divorce was "unchastity," which is translated as "fornication" in the King James Version of the Bible. Consequently, the days of easy divorce for the men were over. In this, and in other examples such as demonstrating the fact that society considered adultery to be different for men than for women when there was no difference [John 8:1-12], Jesus tried to break the stranglehold which the strongly patriarchal society had on women's rights. Even today, society has not completely accepted these teachings. Thirdly, and most interesting, Jesus praised those who were celibate [Matt. 19:11-12] and even stated that the women who were barren would be considered the lucky ones [Luke 23:27-29]. These two statements were against many centuries of Jewish belief, but possibly were made because of the immediacy of the Second Coming and the belief that children would be bothered by the accompanying tribulation.

Because of these mixed signals which Jesus is giving, the attitude of Jesus and his immediate disciples toward marriage and sex is a rather tortuous path to follow and interpret. Although Jesus reemphasized the Judaic belief in the evil of adultery, he also made several remarks which downgraded the concept of marriage and family life by recommending the kingdom over marriage. Some of these remarks were made in Matt. 8:21-2; 10:34-37; 19:10-12; Luke 8:19-21; and 11:27-28. Although there are several books which report that Jesus was married and had a family,[61] neither the Scriptures nor the early writings of the Apostles or the Church Fathers report such an occurrence.

In respect to the disciples, Peter was definitely married when Jesus first approached him, but since his wife is not mentioned again in the Scriptures, it is presumed that he must have left her to join the disciples. Paul never married, practiced celibacy and counseled that marriage represented a compromise with the spiritual life. This statement by Paul later gave credence to the Western Church's desire to ban marriage in the priesthood, a major change from the Judaic attitude of requiring that their religious teachers be married and know about married life before they could be a Rabbi. In Paul's pastoral letters [which many modern scholars think were not written by Paul], he returns to the Hebrew concept of devotion to family, the only change being the recommendation that males restrain from pre-marital sex, an act which Judaism had never criticized. Neither the marriage status nor the celibacy status of the other disciples is mentioned in the Scriptures.

The tension between sexual renunciation and full participation in married life was not decisively resolved in early Christianity as represented by the apocryphal writings of Paul and Thecle, and by the writings of Tertullian, Jerome, and the tremendous guilt over sex which is a repetitive theme in many of the writings of Augustine. Some of these are described below.

In general, Jesus supported the centuries of Jewish thought which believed that sex was good, generally belonged within the family context, and represented man and woman doing God's will. However, he also taught that changes should be instituted among which were the rights of women, forgiveness of sexual offenses, and the praise for being celibate. The latter thought is believed to relate to the conviction that the end of the world as they knew it was going to happen soon, and that Jesus was advising people against bringing children into the tribulation which would result.

Changes in Concepts[62]

1. The first change in the concept held by Judaism for so long, was proposed by Paul who acknowledged that marriage was not a sin, but still encouraged those who could avoid marriage to do so [1 Cor. 7:1-9]; whereas within Judaism, marriage was the goal of all. Later, in one of the pastoral letters, Paul did concede that women would be saved by the bearing of children [1 Ti. 1:15].

2. Although these are not necessarily changes from the Jewish concept, it should be mentioned that in the New Testament, there are also references to unnatural sexual acts. These are presented in Romans 1:26-7 and in 1 Tim. 1:10 in which "sodomites" are equated with "liars, kidnappers, perjurers and whatever else is contrary to sound doctrine." In addition, in 1 Cor. 6:9 it is stated that among others, adulterers and sexual perverts will not inherit the kingdom of God. There are other writings of Paul which are often used as sexual prohibitions; but in most cases, the offense is quite often in the interpretation of the reader rather than in the message of the writer.

3. As Christianity continued to spread during the first and second centuries, many people changed their sexual attitude to that of Judeo-Christianity. Many had been brought up to believe that marriage was a social and economic arrangement, homosexuality was an element of male education, male and female prostitution was acceptable, and abortion or even infanticide was practical normalcy; but as they converted, they started to accept that marriage was the place for sex while continuing to believe that sex was good.

4. By the early third century, Christian Ascetics were emphasizing the differences which Jesus and Paul had with the Judaic sexual heritage more than they were accepting the similarities. As a consequence, the thought that the only good Christian was a celibate Christian was starting to spread, caused primarily by the proposition that the sin of Adam and Eve was carnal knowledge and not disobedience to God as all before had taught. These thoughts were advocated by the Ascetics, but were partially countered, at least for the time being, by Clement of Alexandria and Irenaeus who taught that the primary reason for the fall of Adam was disobedience of God's commands, even though the disobedience might have had a sexual nature to it. Judaism had always taught that the reason for Adam's being kicked out of Paradise was his disobedience to God's command.

5. By the fourth century, things really started to change, led by Gregory of Nyssa, Jerome and finally Augustine. By the time

Augustine was through, Christian concepts about sex were irreversibly different from the Judeo-heritage, and even from the most extreme teachings of Jesus and Paul.

Gregory, a married man, wrote longingly for the life of an ascetic where he could live for himself and God alone. In doing so, he stated that there was no need to encourage people to marry since that was the natural human instinct; whereas virginity thwarts natural instincts and thus is more like God.

Jerome, a confirmed ascetic, believed that all women should strive for virginity, a belief which he emphasized in his treatise *The Perpetual Virginity of the Blessed Mary*. This treatise was later used by medieval monks to substantiate their belief that Jesus was born out of the side of Mary, just as Eve had been pulled out of the side of Adam. Jerome further taught that Adam and Eve were meant to be virgins and were joined in marriage only after they were expelled in disgrace from "the Paradise of virginity." In this and other writings, Jerome expressed a loathing for the flesh. Much of this writing was done in opposition to Jovian, a Christian monk who, though celibate, stated that celibacy was no more holy than marriage.

Augustine then took up the fight. His fight was first against the followers of John Chrysostom and later against Pelagius, both of whom proposed that man had free will in making moral decisions. The arguments between the partisans of Augustine and Pelagius became so active that riots actually broke out in the streets over whether man had free will in making moral decisions. Two popes and three councils declared the teachings of Pelagius to be orthodox, all of which were subsequently overturned by the efforts of Augustine. Finally, Pope Zosimus, after initially declaring Pelagius orthodox, reversed himself because of Augustine's protests and excommunicated Pelagius.

This decision against free will seemed so unfair to Julian, Bishop of Eclanum, that he started into an acrimonious debate with Augustine which lasted until Augustine's death, twelve years later. In this debate, Augustine's definitions of "original sin" were a major difference of opinion. To many Christians of that time, the theory of "original sin" repudiated the twin foundations of Christian faith: [1] the goodness of God's creation [including sex]; and [2] the freedom of the human will. To Augustine, a man tortured by his earlier sexual transgressions, the original sin of Adam was totally sexual in nature; and man had no free will to fight it because man is helpless in his fight against sexual desire. Therefore, since everyone after Adam had been born as the result of sexual activity, everyone has been born in sin; and no one has the ability to fight sin except solely through the unmerited gift of God's grace.

Partially to honor Augustine in his death, and partially to validate the Church's authority over the will of its members, the Church accepted Augustine's views and declared Julian a heretic.

6. And so, about 400 years after the crucifixion of Jesus Christ, the entire concept of why Christ had to incarnate was changed from its Judaic base. Instead of needing a savior to raise up man who had fallen because he disobeyed God, we needed a savior to raise up man because he had participated in sex! In addition, no longer were men and women doing God's will when having marital sex. The guilt which has resulted from those changes is incalculable; and so is the concurrent loss of free will.

7. Although it is not nearly as important, one other aspect of how sex got changed from the time of Jesus is worth mentioning. Almost all the early Church Fathers took it for granted that divorce was permitted on the grounds of infidelity. St. Basil particularly wrote on this.[63] How did this get so changed by the Church in the intervening years? Was the change yet another attempt to establish the Church's control over all aspects of life?

Present-day Status

There is probably no one issue on which sectarian Christianity is so schizophrenic as it is on the issue of sexuality.

In respect to teachings about the sex aspects of marriage, there are churches who teach that sex is a positive force for strengthening the bonds of love and companionship between man and woman and even for teaching a woman's feelings to a man and vice versa; whereas others teach that the only purpose of sex is procreation and that those who have sexual relations at times which are not the most positive times for procreation are going against their teachings. And there are all degrees in between.

In respect to homosexuality, there are some who advocate ostracism and "throwing those perverts out"; others who love them in every way except as ordained ministers; and still others who accept them totally with unconditional love. There are some who accept female homosexuality but reject male homosexuality. And there are all degrees in between.

In respect to divorce, there are churches who recommend divorce when incompatibility causes the slightest discord and who encourage remarriage on the part of either partner; others who condone divorce on certain grounds, but do not permit remarriage; and still others who prohibit divorce within the church on any grounds and will not perform a marriage ceremony for any who have been previously married until the original partner has died. And there are all degrees in between.

Finally, there are those who consider sex of any sort to be a sin for which a type of penance must be made. This is an Augustinian heritage which has shortchanged a major part of Christianity for almost 1500 years. If the reader wants to dig deeper into how Augustine, and others of the Church, have sponsored the sexual mutilation and manipulation of its members, the book entitled *Eunuchs for the Kingdom of Heaven* by Uta Ranke-Heinemann is highly recommended. Dr. Ranke-Heinemann has a doctorate in Catholic Theology. If the reader wants to understand how sexuality is a God-given mechanism for strengthening spirituality, the book *Sexuality and Spiritual Growth* by Joan Timmerman is also highly recommended. Professor Timmerman is a Professor of Theology at the College of St. Catherine in St. Paul, Minnesota. Each author is highly qualified to address the designated issue.

What do these changes mean to today's Christian?

In respect to sexuality, by far the most important change in concept from the time of Jesus was the change in the definition of why man fell from the presence of God: from the Judaic concept of disobedience to the Augustinian carnal concept of "original sin." Basic to all of Augustine's thoughts is his famous statement, "I wish to know God and the soul. Nothing else. Nothing else at all, but God and the soul!" In Augustinian tradition, the source of all religious philosophy is the presence of God in the soul. Augustine said that "The soul died when it was left alone by God, as the body will die when it is left by the soul." According to Augustine, the soul which is religiously dead has lost control over the body thus introducing sin. This sin, possible only when man turned away from God, was concupiscence, or the strong sexual desire. In other words, according to Augustine, Adam introduced libido, desire, into the process of sexual generation; and this element was passed on by heredity to all prosperity. That is the meaning of Augustine's "original sin," and it is a long way from the Judaic concept of why man left God or the Judaic concept that sex is good. In fact, the belief that sex is not good broaches upon the "material evil" of Gnosticism, a belief which Christianity felt was heresy [see Appendix A].

This is by no means a complete explanation of Augustine's thoughts on "original sin" much of which was not accepted by the Catholic Church at the Council of Orange in 529 CE where they accepted his thoughts on grace, predestination and free will [see Appendix B]. However, many Protestant sects have vigorously revived his thoughts, not only on sin, but also on the absence of free will.

It seems to many that if there is a need in religion for an original sin, it most certainly must be a spiritual sin of the soul. However, Augustine had great difficulty in uniting the spiritual sin in everybody with the easily defined bodily sin which he so feared. As a consequence of his personal fears and problems, all Christianity has been designated as having sinned through the sexual activities of Adam. Since that original sin could be changed only by a special act of God, then during the fourth to the sixth centuries, the Church experimented with theological theories which not only changed the concept of why man fell, it changed the concept of the one who came to save mankind after that fall. The present Church is the result of those theological theories and definitions.

11. SUMMARY

In this chapter, a number of subject areas have been addressed in an attempt to show how the teachings of Christ, or the concepts which were prevalent during the time of Christ, have been changed or altered by some of the men who came after him.

The first subject examined was that of Christology or the definition of Jesus Christ. It took the early Church Fathers six Ecumenical Councils or about 650 years after the Resurrection to decide on a complete definition of Christ. Today, most devout Christians seem to believe that the definition was immediately given to humankind by God; but that belief is not consistent with the facts of history. The subject of Christology has made more Saints and more Sinners than any other subject in the history of the Christian Church; and there was truly very little difference between the people who were thus characterized. Each was devout in his beliefs, and each was an ardent follower of the Christ in whom he believed.

The next subject was that of the Christian or the follower of Jesus Christ. The definition of a Christian changed greatly during the first 500 years of the Church's existence; and so did the Christian's attitude about his life and religion. So many restrictions were placed upon him, that he was a changed person, as we will see in the next chapter.

The next section took a deeper look at the Apostolic Tradition and Succession, a tradition which is venerated by the Church, but which has little if any historical justification.

This subject was followed by Soul and Salvation, two interacting subjects. However, although these subjects do interact, the ecumenical Church has said very little about the former and a whole lot about the latter, especially by developing the belief that the Church has a required role in Salvation.

The next two subjects, Intolerance and World Affairs, are two of the failures of the Christian Church in their role of being the spiritual foundation upon which the beliefs of their adherents are to be based. The Christian Church has practiced an Intolerance never taught by Jesus Christ; and has entered strongly into World Affairs despite his teachings to stay away from them. In truth there can be little argument that the men of the Church have altered the teachings of Christ in both of these subject areas.

The next subject, Reincarnation/Karma, represents concepts which were prevalent in society during the time of Jesus; and yet, he did not teach against these concepts or try to change them in any way. It thus seems logical to believe that he accepted them. Consequently, it is somewhat unusual not to find these concepts present in the teachings of today's Church, especially since those teachings are supposed to represent the beliefs or teachings of Jesus Christ.

The final two subjects, Angels and Sexuality, are ones which have been significantly altered by the men of the Church. Belief in the active participation of Angels was prevalent in the society of Jesus and in the early Church. Today, the active participation of Angels seems to be feared by the men of the Church. One wonders why this is so. In regard to sexuality, many elements of today's Church seem to want to cast guilt feelings on all sexual acts, even those which occur within the marital context. This is a significant change form the attitude displayed by Jesus Christ.

In every case examined, the changes in concepts or alterations in the teachings of Jesus Christ have been substantial. Because of this, the Christian has changed his belief system substantially from that which was offered to him by Christ.

The effect of these changes in the Christian's belief system, and the change in the Christian's attitude which resulted from these alterations, will be addressed in the next chapter, Chapter Two.

CHAPTER TWO
THE RESULTS OF THE CHANGES

This chapter will use the analysis presented in Chapter One in an attempt to present the results of the changes which man has made on the concepts of Christ. To do this, the following five issues will be addressed:

1. What was it like to be a Christian in 55 CE?
2. What was it like to be a Christian in 555 CE?
3. How did these changes happen?
4. Are the preceding thoughts a fair treatment of the subject matter?
5. Where do we go from here?

What was it like to be a Christian in 55 CE?

During the first generation of Christianity, before the men of the following five centuries changed the concepts of Christ, Christianity was not a uniform religion. Beliefs at that time were very diverse; for one who was "on the Way" could believe in many things without being ostracized by others who followed the faith, or without being excommunicated by the establishment who ran the faith.

A follower of Christ might believe that the one he followed was divine, or was merely a leader whom the follower would choose to believe in. He might be caught up in the complex hierarchy of a well-defined heaven with its multiplicity of angels, or simply believe that by following Jesus, he would have no fears about the present life and would walk with God just as his leader did. He could believe that this was not the only time he had walked on this planet; and since his leader had not denied the concept of reincarnation, then he could believe that by his continued progress on the Way over many life-times, he would eventually arrive in a place of fellowship with those who had gone before him.

If he were Jewish, it is probable that he acknowledged the existence of other Gods around him and expressed a tolerance for them, even though he, himself, would believe that he was right in following the Father or Yahweh. It is possible that he had not considered whether or not the soul was immortal; but if he were Greek, then he almost certainly felt that a part of him did exist throughout eternity. He certainly believed that all he had to do was confess his belief in Jesus Christ and he would be "saved," even though he might have been somewhat confused about what he was to be "saved" from. He believed that since his leader had accepted all people unconditionally, then he should work hard to tolerate the idiosyncrasies of everyone else. Since his chosen leader had no interest in world affairs and did not teach that the world was his home, then he probably had little interest in worldly goods or in the affairs of state.

He certainly believed in peace among all of his brothers, and the thought of entering the army or of killing another who might offend him was one of the farthest things from his mind. He believed in the family, believed in having a good time when he was with loved ones, and believed that sex was good so long as it was used in a loving, family manner for the continued generation of the nation.

He believed that if he were to die, then he would immediately be taken upward to be with Jesus, for his Lord and Master had told him that, "I go and prepare a place for you...that where I am you may be also." He believed that in the immediate future, his leader would establish his kingdom on Earth, and that all who followed him would live at peace in that kingdom for at least 1,000 years.

His was a life of Love and of Hope.

What was it like to be a Christian in 555 CE?

During the following 500 years, considerable changes had occurred. By 555 CE, Christianity had become a religion which was relatively uniform in its beliefs; and it would stay that way for about another 1,000 years until the Reformation reintroduced elements of diversity.

In order to follow Christ in 555 CE, an orthodox Christian on the "true way" had to believe that his leader was completely divine and completely human, with two natures and two wills, even though the belief in the "two wills" would not be officially confirmed for another 130 years. He had to believe that his Lord was divine in a way that no one else could ever be divine, for he had been born of a Virgin. He had to believe that his Lord was the only Son of God, and as such was the *only* one he could follow.

He believed that there was a simple heaven above, and a simple hell below. In the simple heaven, there were three persons in one being; but with the exception of the angels, heaven would contain very few others until after the Second Coming of Christ. He was told that after death, he would have to wait until his body would be resurrected at the Second Coming before he could be with his Lord.

He was confused about the soul and did not know whether it was something which was separate from his physical body or something which required his physical body for its existence. He believed it was necessary to be "saved" and in order for this saving to occur, he had to be baptized by the Church; for he believed that the Church was his Mother, just as God was his Father. He knew that he had to be "saved" from the "original sin" which he had inherited from Adam; and that even though sex felt good, it shouldn't, because it kept him from walking with God. He believed that the Jews had killed his savior, and so he should hate them wherever they were. He was taught that all who did not accept Christ would be eternally damned; and that if they did not accept all which the Church taught, they would be kicked out of the Church and thereafter could never be "saved."

He was told that the Church and the State were inseparable, and that if he wanted to be a citizen of the State, or if he wished to join the army and kill the foes of the State, then first he would have to accept Christ as his savior and be baptized by the Church.

He believed that all the world should be forced to follow his leader, for he was extremely intolerant of the beliefs of others. He was asked to be on the alert for those who did not agree with his Mother, the Church; and he was asked to let the leaders of the Church know who was practicing such heresy.

His was a life of Conflict and of Fear.

How did these changes happen?

Anyone who has plowed through the history of the Church during its first 500 years will probably agree that these changes did happen, and that they probably happened for five major reasons:

1. Sincere men of the Church felt that they had to defend the Christian faith against intrusions of belief which they felt did not agree with what the majority of the Church leaders believed. However, they had been given very little in the way of solid statements of belief which told them what should be believed and what should be rejected. Consequently, they had to define a belief system and make certain that there were as few deviations from this belief system as possible. Otherwise, they were afraid that the faith introduced by Jesus Christ would degenerate into many belief systems instead of one, and that such a happenstance would confuse the people. In an attempt to minimize confusion, they decided to state in definite terms what was to be believed and what was to be rejected. They not only rejected certain beliefs, they rejected the people who held those beliefs.

2. Of utmost importance was the fact that the Emperor needed uniformity within the Religion in order to have uniformity within the Empire. Consequently, any time the Emperor would see that a religious debate was causing dissension within the Empire, he would insist that the Church come up with an answer to quiet the disturbance. The Church responded by developing answers and making decisions; and by promising excommunication and eternal damnation to those who did not agree with the answers or conform with the decisions they made.

3. Of additional importance was the belief on the part of the Church that all needed to be "saved," that only a God could save, and that God, as represented by the Holy Spirit, was found only within the Church. Since Jesus Christ was the savior, and since humans had touched him, then he had to be not only a God, but also a human. Because there was only one God, then Jesus Christ had to be defined in an unusual way, possibly one with which he would not agree. He had to be defined as being equal with God in all ways, not merely in qualitative terms, but also in quantitative terms.

4. Because these sincere men of the Church were involved in acrimonious debates in an attempt to establish the beliefs of the Church which were to be accepted, then the leaders were those who were good writers and debaters. Because of their talents, they carried the day and won their debates. In other words, Church doctrines and Church history were written by the winners. The losers were kicked out of the Church.

5. Because Jerome had many talents as an excellent writer and translator, this aggressive debater was vitally needed by the Church. Therefore, his views on sex were given credence. Because Augustine also was an excellent debater, his views on sex and free will were also supported. As a result, one of the most humane religions ever introduced on Earth was placed in direct conflict with two of humankind's greatest drives—that of having the ability to make a freewill choice on matters of importance, and that of satisfying the sexual urge without a feeling of guilt.

As a result of all of this, mankind started to accept his religion on the basis of guilt and fear rather than compassion and love.

Are the preceding five paragraphs a fair treatment?

This book was written by one person, and even though he asked many friends about their opinions on certain points, the conclusions are his alone. I accept full responsibility for them.

Although I felt that the concepts of Christ had been significantly changed by the actions of man, I ended up reading over 60 books plus doing extensive research in encyclopedias to find historical justification for that viewpoint. Based on this research, I feel certain that the men who defined the present Christian belief system felt that they were guided by the Holy Spirit as they were taking their actions; but I also have to believe that the Church has felt that all of its "Revealed Truths" were the result of an interaction with the Holy Spirit. The "Revealed Truth" cabinet has had some strange occupants. At various times in the history of the Church, it has been revealed to the Church that the Sun orbits the Earth; that the priests were to live in luxury; that the entire world was to pay homage to the pope; that abortion was not murder until after the period of 40 days if a male or 80 days if a female fetus; that all abortion is murder; that Mary was conceived in sin; that Mary was immaculately conceived; etc. etc. etc. Is the "Revealed Truth" that Jesus was the "*only* son of God" and that he is "*equal* to God in all ways" still a "Revealed Truth" even though neither statement is in the Scriptures and even though the Earth is but a tiny part of God's universe? Is it possible that at times man can think he is hearing the Holy Spirit when he is merely reacting to his own ego?

But the question asked was whether the five paragraphs presented above were fair. Any author who puts words down on a piece of paper does so in an expression of his own bias; and the words of the five paragraphs presented above are biased as I am biased. As one example of how others might see bias in me, many people may feel that I am biased when I state that many of the doctrines which came out of the first six Ecumenical Councils were generated more by the political necessities of the worldly Empire than by the need to have an expression of Jesus Christ. As another example of how others might see bias in me, many people may feel that I am biased when I state the belief that the Church has no place in the political life of the State and that in general, spiritual matters and governmental matters should not be mixed. There are certainly many in today's Christian Church who will take exception to that bias even though Jesus Christ, himself, seems to teach this lesson when he says, "Render therefore to Caesar the things that are Caesar's and to God the things that are God's." [Matt. 22:21].

And so, as one shortcoming of this or any other book, the writings are not fair because they express the bias of the writer. In addition to this shortcoming, many authors try to create some sort of conflict between the adversaries in their book. I have chosen to create a conflict between the teachings of Christ and the teachings of the men who believed they were speaking for Christ. If those teachings were identical, then there would be no conflict. I feel that those teachings are far apart, and that consequently there is a conflict between them. Almost any author will exaggerate the elements of his conflict in order to inform the reader that indeed a conflict does exist. In conflict writing such as a spy novel, the villain is often over-played or exaggerated so that we hate him; and the hero is so clever that we admire him. But conflict writing is not restricted to the novel. Conflict writing is also important to the historian. In the accepted writing of American history, those historians who defend Manifest Destiny present the Native Americans as the villains and the imported white men as the heroes; whereas the historian who defends the contrasting viewpoint loves Sitting Bull and hates Custer. In all cases of conflict writing, the real truth is probably someplace between the extremes painted by the author.

Are the paragraphs fair? From my viewpoint, they are historically correct and the conflict is presented with only a slight amount of exaggeration. From the viewpoint of my former minister, they are probably historically biased and greatly exaggerated. The real truth, if it were to be known, is probably someplace between these contrasting viewpoints.

Are the five preceding paragraphs fair? What do you, the reader, think?

Where do we go from here?

In my opinion, the doctrines and dogmas generated by the Christian Church in the fourth and fifth centuries are theological theories which can be accepted or rejected by the individual who chooses to follow Christ without changing in any way the progress which that individual makes on his pathway back to God. But that is only my opinion, and it would probably be actively debated by any person presently employed by any of the sectarian churches of the world.

However, I do have to say this. I almost abandoned this book several times, for I felt that I was completely alone as a follower of Christ who no longer accepted what the Church taught as a belief system. Then I came across periodicals such as *Christian * New Age Quarterly*. In this journal, many contributors who are both active and former ministers or priests address many subjects which are somewhat "unorthodox." Furthermore, I came across periodicals such as *Bible Review* [or *BR*] in which many respected theologians challenge the frontiers of religious belief in an attempt to generate understanding. Finally, I came across authors such as John Hick and others, and I came to understand the excellent biblical research work which is being done at the Claremont Graduate School and the School of Theology at Claremont [California]. This biblical research work expands the horizon for the thinking Christian; and does so without destroying the follower's belief in Jesus the Christ unless the follower wants that belief to be destroyed. From all of these sources, I found that I was not alone. Consequently, I wrote this book in an attempt to communicate some complex thoughts in a manner which would be as simple as possible.

In answer to the question, "Where do we go from here?" I would suggest that the answer to that question is one whose personal development is the responsibility of every individual human. I would further say that Jesus taught a personal approach to God, and also taught the belief that he could help with that personal approach. The fact that I choose to trod the pathway back to God with the help of Jesus the Christ is a personal decision on my part. It is a decision which I have no fear talking about; but which I would force on no other, for the only way to be on the pathway is to choose to do so, and not to be forced thereon.

Book Three which follows is a short book which may give some additional insight on where we might go from here.

BOOK THREE
SUMMARY AND CONCLUSIONS

*B*ook One gave a detailed presentation of the history of the Christian Church during the first 500 years of its existence. The conclusions were that a lot happened, that man caused most of this to happen, and that the beliefs of Christianity were quite different at the end of that 500 year history than they had been at the beginning. Because of the details which must be included in such a presentation, readability of the narrative became seriously hampered. Consequently, much of the detail was removed to three Appendixes. Those three Appendixes are: Appendix A which is an Expanded Glossary of People and Controversies; Appendix B which is a presentation of the Early Creeds of the Church; and Appendix C which is a presentation of the Details of the Fifth Ecumenical Council in 553 CE. These Appendixes could be read or skipped, based on the desires of the reader.

Book Two gave an analysis of the changes which occurred and tracked the effect of those changes on a follower of Christ. In *Book Two*, in-depth presentations were made on ten subjects ranging from Christology to Sexuality. These presentations included commentaries on the changes which occurred during the first 500 years of the Church's existence; stated that the Christian at the end of that 500 year history was quite different from the Christian at the beginning of the period; and further suggested that the Christian beliefs taught in the sectarian churches of today are more like the Christian beliefs of Augustine and the other Church Fathers than the beliefs of the earlier Christians who followed Christ. As a result, the concepts or teachings which Christ gave us have been significantly changed or altered by the men of the sectarian Church.

Book Three is a presentation to try to help the Christian who wants to follow the teachings of Christ rather than the teachings of the sectarian churches. The thoughts expressed here are a synthesis of ideas generated while interacting with the writings of three men, all originally of the Church. They are John Hick, Albert Nolan and John Groff, Jr. A short biography of each is presented in a footnote.[1]

In an attempt to help break from old teaching and to help build a "much needed bridge between traditional belief systems and the new paradigm of thinking and perceiving in our world" [see page 12], three issues should be considered. These issues are:

1. There have been several reports about the Divine which have been presented by different religious traditions, each of which tended to present its God as the *only true* God. These reports include the Adonai of Judaism, the Father of Jesus Christ, the Allah of Islam, the Krishna and the Shiva of theistic Hinduism, and the Brahman of advaitic Hinduism among others. Each Divine Being has had Saints to support it.

2. The attitude of adherents to each of these religious traditions was the same: *viz.* that theirs is the *only true* God. The attitude of Christians to these other religions was initially generated in the complete ignorance of the beliefs held by the others. Initially, the Christian completely rejected all others and condemned them all to Hell. Later, there was a growing awareness that an experience of a Christian nature may occur within other religions by people who are really Christian whether they realize it or not. This period of the "anonymous Christian" was then followed by a recent attempt to define the possibility that an outsider might accept Christ in some sort of an "afterlife." But all of these have been done in the belief that Jesus was not the *chosen* way to God, he was the *only* way.

3. Again, however, this attitude is not unique to the Christian. The Christian might sing, "there is no other name given among men whereby we might be saved, than the name of Jesus"; but at the same time the Jew says, "Moses tells us that we are God's only chosen people"; and the Muslim chants, "Mohammed is the seal of the prophets, bringing God's final revelation"; and the Buddhist or the Hindu tones, "we have been given the highest truths while others are only partial truths," etc. In *Jewish Quarterly Review* of 1895, Claude Goldsmid Montefiore said, *"Many pathways may all lead Godward, and the world is richer for that the paths are not new."* It is a statement worth examining, for it may be that the ineffable God is the same to all, and only the way of finding Him is different as God tries His many approaches to lead us back to Him.[2]

These three issues should be considered if the Christian wants to consider whether there is the possibility of following Christ even if one is outside of the sectarian churches; for it is true that all religions have a divinity which has been shown to them, all religions ignore one another, and all religions tout themselves as being the only religion.

What is really basic is that an individual will define God based on what represents the highest value to that person. On the mundane level, if the highest value which an individual can perceive is represented by material things, then possibly a Mercedes has become God to that person. If the highest value which an individual can perceive is represented by a position, then possibly the presidency of General Motors or the United States has become God. If the highest value which an individual can perceive is represented by the love of family, then possibly the husband, or the wife, or the child or the family unit has become God. In no way am I saying that these are not important and often interrelated values; but I am suggesting that an individual will accept that which has the highest value to him or her as their God, whether they call it by that name or not.

In the same manner, but on a higher level, if the contemplative life which leads to Nirvana represents the highest value which an individual can perceive, then that individual will become a Buddhist and will follow that pathway back to his God. If the final revelation presented by Mohammed is the highest value which an individual can perceive, then that individual will become a Muslim and will follow that pathway back to his God. If the principles and teachings of Jesus Christ represent the highest value which an individual can perceive, then that individual will become a Christian and will follow that pathway back to his God. In no way am I intending to state that one pathway is superior to another, for the pathway is the individual's choice to make based on *his* or *her* perception of values. But I am suggesting that each individual should respect and tolerate the choice of others as he or she makes the personal choice.

The reason for there being multiple ways back to God is because God can not be seen and can not be defined. He is ineffable. Therefore, our concept of God comes only from that which shows Him to us. To believe that Jesus stands for your God is to accept him as the definition of your pathway. To say that he does not represent your God is to make someone or something else represent your God. What we choose to represent God to us will represent God to us, even if we choose to have our God represented by a Mercedes. Paul referred to this in Romans 1:20 which says, *"Ever since the creation of the world his invisible nature, namely, his eternal power and deity, has been clearly perceived in the things that have been made."* Paul was saying that God, who cannot be understood, is shown to us and is therefore understood by us in things which we can understand. But in the examples used above, a Mercedes, though easily understood, is not eternal; and so the values seen in that particular God may not be eternal either.

The major understanding which I am trying to transmit is that God is represented to us by something else, by the reflection of God which is made in the activities and the stance of another. In the case of the Christ, if you accept the beliefs of Jesus and what he stands for, then you are a Christian and have the Father as your God. If another appeals, then another pathway is open to you.

In his magnificent book, *Jesus Before Christianity*, Albert Nolan described the God who would be reflected by Jesus Christ. The following words are not his, for they have been changed to fit the context of this work. However, the sense of the words is similar.

If you see God in Jesus Christ, then the God that you see is a God:

1. *who is tolerant of others rather than being intolerant of their beliefs;*
2. *who serves the needs of others rather than being served by them;*
3. *who is without rank in the world rather than ruling the world;*

4. *who proposes love rather than fear or blind obedience;*
5. *who chooses to be associated with people of compassion rather than of power;*
6. *who liberates humankind rather than enslaving it to dogmas;*
7. *who practices unconditional love for all rather than accepting only those who think as he does.*

If that is the picture of God to you, then your God is more human and more thoroughly humane than any human being. He is the God who has been pictured by what Jesus Christ stood for, and not necessarily by what the Church has stood for. If that is the picture of God to you, then you are blessed, whatever the Church may say. You are with the Most Radiant One.

But whatever has been chosen as the model for the ineffable God to you, merely choosing the model is not the end. Although I would be the last to try to define a system which must be followed or a belief which must be obeyed, I would still like to present some thoughts. These thoughts will be presented as a paraphrased version of an article by Father Groff which was entitled "The Channels of Christmas."[1] The paraphrased version is expressed in these five stages of development:

1. **Stage 1** is represented by belief in things created by man. The key phrase for this stage is *active achievement.*
2. **Stage 2** is represented by belief in Gods created by man. The key phrase for this stage is *worshipping adoration.*
3. **Stage 3** is represented by belief in Gods created by spirit. The key phrase for this stage is *peaceful flowing.*
4. **Stage 4** is represented by belief in nothing but unconditional Love. The key phrase for this stage is *lovingly being.*
5. **Stage 5** is represented by belief in nothing which is everything. The key phrase for this stage is *absolute awareness.*

Some may choose to criticize these stages for a variety of reasons, some of which could be: Stage 1 represents <u>doing</u> which therefore eliminates the contemplative life; or Stage 2 represents active <u>participation</u> in the Church which turns off those who emphasize spirituality; or Stage 3 represents <u>leaving</u> the Church which is discomforting to many; or Stages 4 and 5 are <u>unorthodox</u> and are therefore heresy. Whether the criticisms are valid or not is for you to decide; for these stages are merely offered for contemplation.

The third book of this series will address itself to a fuller understanding of these stages and how they might fit together with reincarnation and karma for a pathway back to God. This fuller understanding would include two additional stages of service, thus generating the seven gateways which an individual goes through on his individual path. Each of these gateways is closed by a personal seal which is to be opened by the individual. It is this relationship between the gates and the personal seal to be opened by the individual which constitutes the Seven Seals mentioned in Revelations 5:1-5.

When written, the third book will be presented as a contemplation for individual choice, and not as dogma.

<u>SO BE IT !</u>

REFERENCE

MATERIAL

APPENDIX A:
AN EXPANDED GLOSSARY OF PEOPLE
AND CONTROVERSIES

Introduction to Appendix A

Appendix A is presented in the following format:

1. It is alphabetical;

2. If there is a specific person connected with a controversy, both the name of the person and the name of the controversy will be presented in **CAPITAL LETTERS** with the name of the person being presented first. The name of the person will be immediately followed by a short, glossary-type description, followed by a full **Biography**. The associated controversy will follow the biography, again with a short, glossary-type presentation followed by a longer **Description**.

3. If a person is presented without an associated controversy, then the short, glossary-type presentation again will be first, followed by the longer **Biography**.

4. If no particular person is associated with a controversy, then the controversy will be presented by itself, again with a short, glossary-type presentation followed by a longer **Description**.

5. Any capitalized item will be set apart from its neighbors with spacing and will include the approximate dates associated with them.

6. It is hoped that this type of Expanded Glossary will permit easy access to as much information as the reader wants at any particular time.

References

The people in Appendix A are presented using a synthesis of the biographies found in the following books: *Saint Watching* by Phyllis McGinley; *Saints in Folklore* by Christina Hole; *A Gallery of the Saints* by Randall Garrett; *Dictionary of Saints* by John I. Delaney; *The Chair of Peter, A History of the Papacy* by Friedrich Gontard; and *The Avenel*

Dictionary of Saints by Donald Attwater. This synthesis was then checked out and adjusted when necessary by use of the following reference material: *The History of Christianity, A Lion Handbook*, edited by Dr. Tim Dowley; *A History of the Christian Church,* by Williston Walker; the *Encyclodaedia Britannica*; and the *New Catholic Encyclopedia.*

The controversies in Appendix A were used the following major reference material: *The History of Christianity, A Lion Handbook*, edited by Dr. Tim Dowley; *A History of the Christian Church,* by Williston Walker; the *Encyclodaedia Britannica*; and the *New Catholic Encyclopedia.*

Saints and Sinners

Many of the people in Appendix A are either Saints or Sinners. Out of a possible list of hundreds who could have been chosen, only the following twenty-nine people, listed here in the approximate chronological order of their lives, will be examined in any depth: Clement I; Ignatius of Antioch; Polycarp; Justin Martyr; Irenaeus of Lyons; Clement of Alexandria; Tertullian; Hippolytus of Rome; Origen; Cyprian of Carthage; Arius; Eusebius of Vercelli; Eusebius of Caesarea; Athanasius; Basil of Caesarea; Gregory of Nazianzus; Gregory of Nyssa; Ambrose of Milan; Paula; John Chrysostom; Jerome; Augustine; Cyril of Alexandria; Eutyches; Leo I the Great; Benedict of Nursia; Justinian; Gregory I the Great; and Thomas Aquinas. There are certainly others who contributed strongly to the history of the early Church, and a few of them may be mentioned in passing in the descriptions of the Controversies. However their biographies will not be presented in depth; and the twenty-nine whose biographies are presented should give enough of the flavor of the period to understand why the Church developed and defined itself as it did.

This list does not include any of the major figures in the Bible such as Paul, Peter, or the other Apostles such as Stephen, Philip and John. These are omitted because their life and important activities are presented in the Bible and thus are readily available for review. In addition, many of their activities were covered in the text.

Before going into the historical lives and activities of these people, since many of them have been declared Saints of the Church, it might be worthwhile to understand why the Christian Church felt the need to establish who were her Saints. This understanding is given in the *Dogmatic Constitution on the Church, No. 50*, which states the following:

" *The Church has always believed that the apostles and Christ's martyrs, who gave the supreme witness of faith and charity by the shedding of their blood, are closely united with us in Christ; she has always venerated them with the Blessed Virgin Mary and the holy angels, with special love, and has asked piously for the help of their intercession. Soon there were added to these others who had chosen to imitate more closely the virginity and poverty of Christ, and still others whom the outstanding practices of the Christian virtues and the wonderful graces of God recommended to the pious devotion and imitation of the faithful.*

"Exactly as Christian communion between men on their earthly pilgrimage brings us closer to Christ, so our community with the saints joins us to Christ, from whom as from its fountain and head issues all graces and the life of the People of God itself. It is most fitting, therefore, that we love those friends and co-heirs of Jesus Christ who are also our brothers and outstanding benefactors, and that we give due thanks to God for them, humbly invoking them, and having recourse to their prayers, their aid and help in obtaining from God through his son, Jesus Christ, Our Lord, our only Redeemer and Savior, the benefits we need. Every authentic witness of love, indeed, offered by us to those who are in heaven tends to and terminates in Christ, 'the crown of all the saints,' and through him in God who is wonderful in his saints, and is glorified in them."

It also might be worthwhile to understand what is a heretic or Sinner. The Church seems to feel a need to defend itself against that which it feels is false or which it otherwise refuses to accept. It often does this by designating certain people as heretics or Sinners, or by declaring that the thoughts or actions of certain people are heretical or sinful acts.

And so, with a little understanding as to why the Church declares Saints and Sinners, Appendix A will present some of the activities of those who contributed greatly to the definition of the Church during its early existence. They did this by presenting two kinds of activities: either what the Church chose to accept or what the Church chose to reject.

The Controversies

Some of what the Church chose to reject is covered in Appendix A.

In the first two centuries after the Crucifixion, the early Church found itself involved in fighting several sects, condemning many heresies, rejecting numerous movements and debating a number of controversies. During this period, there was no accepted Christian Bible; for the New Testament canon was not generally accepted until 367 CE and not officially accepted for almost 1600 years. Consequently, there was no accepted reference work against which beliefs could be tested; nor was there an officially accepted code of conduct for Christians. Nevertheless, the early Church did not like several activities, and so they rejected them.

The Edict of Milan in 313 CE caused a considerable increase in the rejection rate. When Church started to have rules of conduct and methods of operation which were accepted by the majority, and when the State started to have a great impact on who could be called a Christian, then the many who did not wish to comply with those rules were left out in the cold.

This created a quite a problem, for Christianity had been started with the guiding principle that no one was to be excluded from the love of God. In demonstrating this principle with love and compassion, Jesus Christ made enemies of the Pharisees of his day by dining with sinners, talking with prostitutes and even accepting the Samarians. But despite the conflicts which Jesus created with the society of his day [see *Christianity and the New Age Religion* for a full description of these conflicts], Jesus did them anyway; for he had the full knowledge that by doing so, he was demonstrating that he accepted all with compassion and unconditional love.

During the 240 years following the Edict of Milan, the Christian Church had a very difficult time following the guiding principle of unconditional love. In this time, the Church had the greatest rejection rate in its history; for it actively rejected those who did not accept the rules of conduct, operation and belief which had been decided by a selected majority of bishops. In instituting this policy of rejection, the Church fought many movements, heresies and controversies. Several of them will be described .

These movements were named "heretical movements"; and all of the people associated with them were named "heretics." These declarations were generally made during the general or "Ecumenical" Councils of the Church. The definition of the word "Ecumenical" is "universal or worldwide." In respect to the Christian Church, the word means "the worldwide Church, particularly in regard to its unity." At these Councils, some of which were not as "worldwide" or "conducted in the spirit of unity" as one might suppose, movements were debated, people were excommunicated and doctrines were defined and accepted. The actual voting record during the Councils has never been presented in any reliable historical literature which the author has been able to find; and is suspiciously absent in the otherwise very complete *New Catholic Encyclopedia* which merely states that historical information from the early Councils is lacking. Nevertheless, Church tradition states that the decisions were always the result of a unanimous vote. Based on the subsequent activities of some of those who were present at each Ecumenical Council, the accepted traditions do not seem to hold water; and a unanimous vote seems highly unlikely. But it was this "spirit of Unity" which allowed the Church to declare that many movements were heretical and that many people who participated in those movements were heretics. The heretics or "sinners" [at least as defined by the Church of the period] will generally be described alongside the description of the movement with which they were associated.

-A-

ADOPTIONISM [Ca. 180 and Ca. 780] A belief which stated that Jesus Christ was an adopted Son of God. Declared a Christian heresy.

Description Adoptionism is a term applied to one of two heresies, each of which implied that Christ was an adopted Son of God. The first heresy was developed in about 180 CE and continued as an active movement for about 100 years. It is also known as Dynamic Monarchianism and is described more fully under "Monarchianism."

The second heresy was developed in the eighth century in Spain. Although it does not describe the early years of the Church's development, it is presented because its principles are so similar to Dynamic Monarchianism. The later Adoptionism is concerned with the teaching of Elipandus, archbishop of Toledo in Spain. Elipandus wished to distinguish Christ in the operations of each of his natures, human and divine; and so he referred to Christ in the human form as the adopted Son of God, whereas Christ in His divinity was the Son of God by nature. Because of this, the son of God through Mary was the Son of God by adoption and not by nature. This view was supported by Felix, bishop of Urgel. In 798, Pope Leo III held a council in Rome and condemned the Adoptionism of Felix who was forced to recant. Elipandus remained unrepentant and was archbishop until his death after which Adoptionism was virtually abandoned. In the twelfth century it was revived by the teachings of Peter Abelard.

The importance of these two Adoptionist beliefs, each of which was declared heretical by the Church, is that one was proposed before the holding of the Ecumenical Councils which defined the nature of Jesus Christ [a point which was discussed in the first six councils, 325 to 680], and the other was proposed after these Councils had been held. They thus indicate that debates about the nature of Jesus Christ was a constantly revived matter of debate and contention for more than 600 years. It remains a matter of debate and contention among many believers in Christ today, some of whom believe that the sectarian Churches make a mistake in holding their members to definitions arrived at in such a contentious manner.

Albigenses See Cathars.

AMBROSE [340-397] Bishop of Milan who fought Arianism in the West during the fourth century.

Biography Ambrose of Milan, a Roman, was born in Trier Germany in 340, the son of Ambrose the praetorian prefect of Gaul. His father died early, and Ambrose was taken back to Rome for his education. He became a lawyer who was noted for his oratory and learning. In 372, Emperor Valentinian appointed him governor of Liguria and Aemilia with his capital at Milan, a position he filled with great ability and justice.

In 374, the death of Auxentius, bishop of Milan who was an Arian, threw the city into turmoil as Arians and Catholics fought to have their candidate made bishop. When Ambrose, nominally a Christian but not yet baptized, went to the cathedral in an attempt to quiet the passions of the mob, he was unanimously elected bishop by all parties. Despite his refusal to accept the office, he was forced to do so when the Emperor confirmed the election. This is merely one of the many examples which could be cited to show how the leadership of the Church had become so intermingled with the political needs of the State that it was difficult to see where one stopped and the other started. Despite this start, Ambrose later became noted for his opposition to secular authority over the Church.

After accepting the position, Ambrose was baptized; and on December 12, 374, he was consecrated bishop. He gave away his possessions, began to study Scripture, and began to live a life of great austerity. He became the most eloquent preacher of his day and the most formidable opponent of Arianism in the West. He became an adviser to Emperor Gratian, and in 379 persuaded him to outlaw Arianism. Later, Ambrose defeated an attempt to restore the cult of the goddess of victory in Rome; and in 385, he successfully resisted Emperor Valentinian's order to turn over several churches in Milan to his mother, a secret Arian. Still later, when Emperor Theodosius I gained control over both the Eastern and Western empires, Arianism was outlawed within the Empire, primarily because of Ambrose.

Later, Theodosius and Ambrose came into conflict when Ambrose denounced an order given by Theodosius to rebuild a Jewish synagogue destroyed by the Christians in Kallinikum, Mesopotamia, an order which Theodosius then rescinded. But in 390 CE, the two clashed again when the troops of Theodosius massacred some 7,000 people in Thessalonica in reprisal for the murder of the governor, Butheric. Ambrose denounced the Emperor for his action and refused him the sacraments until he performed a severe public penance, which Theodosius did. In 393, Ambrose denounced the murder of Valentius II which was done in an attempt to restore paganism. This act was supported by Theodosius, and thus paganism was ended in the Empire. Theodosius died a few months later in the arms of Ambrose who preached his funeral oration. Ambrose died in 397 in Milan.

Ambrose was one of the great figures of early Christianity. More than any other man, he was responsible for the rise of Christianity in the West as the Roman Empire was dying. He was a fierce defender of the independence of the Church against the secular authority. He wrote profusely on the Bible, theology and asceticism. He brought Augustine, who revered him, back to his Catholic faith, baptizing him in 387. He was considered by his contemporaries as the perfect bishop—holy, learned, courageous, patient, and immovable when necessary for the faith. He is considered a worthy Doctor of the Church. His best known works are *De officiis ministrorum* [a treatise on Christian ethics especially directed to the clergy], *De virginibus* [written for his sister, St. Marcellina], and *De fide* [written against the Arians for Gratian].

Ambrose is included in this short list of people not only because he fought Arianism and the return of paganism, but more particularly because he made the words "Christian" and "Roman" almost synonyms. Although he enforced upon Theodosius the need to be a son rather than a master of the Church, he did force him to make Christianity the preferred religion of Rome and to recommend it to all Roman citizens whether they believed in Christ or not. In this action, Ambrose started a tradition of State-Church relationship which tended to corrupt the Church over the next 1,000 years. In fact, it was such an activity which later gave Emperor Justinian the idea of forcing all of his followers to become Christian as a matter of citizenship. Indeed, Ambrose had quite an effect on Christianity.

APOLLINARIS [Ca. 310-390] Fourth century Bishop who first proposed a systematic study of the person and qualities of Jesus Christ

Biography Apollinaris was born in about 310 CE. Little is known of him before he became bishop of Laodicea in Syria. He was one of the first Christian thinkers to try to develop a systematic Christology, i.e. a systemic study of Christ's person and qualities. In this activity he was to spawn many followers, not all of whom agreed with him. But at least, he did start the early thinkers of the Church in the direction of systemic thinking and in doing so, became one of the thinkers of the Church to which the Church has not been particularly kind.

Apollinaris was a strong supporter of the Creed of Nicaea. He was also a friend of Athanasius, and he was the one who converted Basil of Caesarea to the orthodox thinking about the substance of Christ. He was greatly admired by his contemporaries for his analytical skills and his ascetic life; and he was greatly loved by the populace of his See who adored the Creed of Nicaea. In other words, if anyone of this period could be called "orthodox," it would be Apollinaris. Nevertheless, he was excommunicated twice by the Church and forgiven only once. In spite of this, he continued to be loved by the faithful with whom he worked.

Apollinaris died in about 390, but not before making a lot of other people start to think in a systematic way about the nature of Jesus Christ. In this way, Apollinaris was among the major definers of the doctrines and the dogmas of the Christian Church today; for although his thoughts were not the ones which were finally accepted, without his pioneering effort in starting the process, possibly no one would have addressed the issue.

APOLLINARIANISM [Ca. 360-381] A fourth century belief system in which Jesus Christ had a human body and soul but a divine intellect. Declared a heresy at the Second Ecumenical Council.

Description Apollinarianism is one of the strangest and yet most appealing controversies of the early Christian Church. It represents the movement which had been founded on the position developed by Apollinaris, one of the strangest yet most appealing men of the early church. It represents a movement which was fought by Gregory of Nazianzus, and by other accepted Church Fathers.

The major desire of Apollinaris, like that of Athanasius, was to affirm the divinity of Jesus Christ in opposition to the position of Arius. To do this, he took the thought expressed in the Scriptures [1 Thess. 5:23] that man is made of body, spirit and soul. He then substituted God for spirit in the composition of Christ. In this way, Jesus Christ became a human being from heaven who had a human body and a human soul; but instead of a human spirit or intellect, had a divine one. In this way, he was different than any other human. However, by doing this Apollinaris inadvertently and unfortunately represented the humanity of Christ as being incomplete. This view was attacked by Gregory of Nyssa in his treatise *Against Apollinaris* in which he attacks Apollinaris for confusing Christ's divinity and his humanity and for failing to observe any distinction between the created and the uncreated. Gregory of Nazianzus also attacked Apollinaris by insisting that Jesus Christ had to have a completely human nature and not something which was a mixture of God and man.

The teachings of Apollinaris [i.e. Apollinarianism] were condemned at a Roman synod in 377, forgiven in the next year, and then once again condemned by a synod in Antioch which supported the Roman view that Christ had to be born as a complete human being. His teachings were finally condemned at the Second Ecumenical Council in 381.

APOSTOLIC FATHERS [Ca. 60-120] Church fathers, including Clement of Rome, Ignatius of Antioch and Polycarp of Smyrna who were thought to have received instruction directly from the Apostles themselves, or possibly from direct disciples of the Apostles.

ARIUS [Ca. 250-336] Christian priest of Alexandria who believed so strongly in the uniqueness of God that he denied full divinity to the Christ and was therefore declared a heretic. Followers of his belief are called Arians and they practice Arianism.

Biography Arius was born in Libya and died in Constantinople. He was a Christian priest of Alexandria whose teachings led to Arianism, a doctrine which affirmed the finite nature of Christ. Arianism was denounced by the early church as a major heresy. However, Arianism continued to have an extensive following for almost 300 years.

Arius was a leader who lived an ascetical, moral life. His self-sacrifice and moral code were above reproach. It is, in fact, this stringent morality which caused him to be declared a heretic by the Church. His moral belief in God was so great that he felt guided to declare the absolute oneness of the divinity as the highest perfection; and he further declared that this absolute oneness should be used in the context of a literal, rationalistic approach to the texts of both the Old and the New Testaments. As an example, he felt that Proverbs 8:22 stated that the Christ was created by God; and since he had been created, then he could not *be* God. This and other examples led Arius to the strong belief that God had never been divided in any way, but remained entire and whole in oneness. This approach to religion incorporated many elements of Neo-Platonism and attracted a large following of people to Arius. These people all believed in the supremacy of God. His point of view was publicized in 323 through the poetic verse of his major work *Thalia* ["Banquet"] and was widely spread by popular songs written for laborers and travelers.

The major quotation of Arius which expresses his belief is presented on page 132 of John Leith's book, *Basic Christian Doctrine*. It says: *"We acknowledge one God, alone ingenerate, alone everlasting, alone without beginning, alone true, alone having immortality, alone good, alone sovereign; Judge, Governor, Provider of all, unalterable, unchangeable, just and good, God of the law and prophets and the New Testaments."*

Those who are familiar with Mark 10:18 and its corresponding verses in Matthew 19:17 and Luke 18:19 will recognize that Arius was presenting one of the great teachings of Jesus in this statement. Those who are familiar with the modern Church affairs will recognize that Aries is proposing a basic belief of the modern Ecumenical movement in this statement. Those who are familiar with the history of the Christian Church will recognize that because of this statement, this gentle man of God was hounded out of the Church and branded a heretic.

Because of his strong belief in the oneness of God, Arius simply could not accept Jesus as *God*. He felt that if he did this, then he would diminish God, and Arius was faithful to his God. So were his followers. The Council of Nicaea in May, 325 declared Arius a heretic after he refused to sign the formula of faith stating that Christ was of the same divine nature as God. He later was willing to sign a compromise; but before he could be reconciled with the Church, he collapsed on the streets on Constantinople and died.

Although Arius had been willing to become reconciled to the Church, the followers of Arianism continued to be a major threat to Christian orthodoxy throughout the fourth-sixth centuries. The movement far out-shadowed the relatively obscure life of its instigator. He is included in this short list of the people of the early church because of the importance of the movement which bears his name.

ARIANISM A form of Christianity during the third through the seventh centuries. It believed that God was so unique that He could not be divided or diminished in any way and as a consequence, Jesus Christ was less than God. It became orthodox Christianity's greatest challenge.

Description Arianism [or the Arian Controversy] was arguably the most raging controversy ever faced by the Church. Only Gnosticism, Origenism or possibly Nestorianism could present any competition to Arianism as a Church controversy, unless Protestantism is considered as a controversy rather than as a separate branch of the Church.

To show the importance of Arianism, it is conceivable that without it, the concept of the Trinity [which is *not* in the Scriptures] might never have been developed. In addition, Arianism had the direct responsibility for the calling of the first two Ecumenical Councils and had an indirect responsibility for the calling of the next three. It is therefore the key controversy around which all of the first five Ecumenical Councils were oriented. Finally, Arianism brought the Emperor into Church matters in a big way.

The man, Arius, was a charismatic and handsome presbyter, or elder, in the Church of Alexandria and a devout, moral man whose belief in God was so strong that he could not see God divided in any way. Because of the strength of this belief, Arianism affirmed that Christ is not truly divine but is instead a created being, a belief which Arius felt was confirmed by Scripture. The fundamental premise of Arius, and thus of Arianism, was that God alone is unique; and that in this uniqueness, He alone is self-existent and immutable [i.e. not created and not changing]. Because the Son is not self-existent, he cannot *be* God. In addition, because the Gospels represent that the Son is mutable and subject to growth and change [see Luke 2:40 for an example of how Jesus "grew"], then again he cannot *be* God. And finally, because the Godhead is unique, it cannot be shared or communicated thus again stating that the Son cannot *be* God. Because of all of this, the Son must therefore be a creature who has been called into existence out of nothing. He therefore had a beginning and thus again cannot *be* God. Moreover, the Son can have no knowledge of the Father since the Son is finite and is of a different order of existence.

According to its opponents, especially Athanasius, Arianism reduced Christ to a demigod [i.e. a semi-divine being such as would come from the mating of a God with a human]. In addition, it reintroduced polytheism since the worship of the Son was not abandoned, but continued to be worshipped even in Arianism. Finally, Arianism undermined the Christian concept of redemption since only He who is *truly* God could have the power to reconcile man to the Godhead. In other words, the Church said that Arianism prevented redemption through Jesus Christ.

Arianism raced through the land as the first major challenge to orthodox Christianity. According to Gregory of Nyssa, sailors and travelers were singing versions of popular ditties which proclaimed that the Father alone was true God; bath attendants would harangue their bathers with the insistence that the Son came from nothingness; money changers gave long dissertations on the difference between the created order and the uncreated God; and bakers would inform their customers that the Father was greater than the Son. People would discuss these and other ambiguous questions with the same enthusiasm used to describe football games or political candidates today. [See Childress, p. 93].

The First Ecumenical Council [325 CE] condemned the teachings of Arius and promulgated the Creed of Nicaea [see Appendix B] which established that Jesus was God. The Second Ecumenical Council [381] condemned Arius and Arianism and reaffirmed the Creed of Nicaea which in a shortened and slightly modified form became known as the Nicene Creed [also in Appendix B]. Despite these condemnations, Arianism continued to grow in its following and remained as a powerful force until well into the seventh century.

The major opponents of Arianism were Gregory of Nyssa, Ambrose, Anthony of Egypt, Athanasius, Basil of Ancyra, Basil the Great, Gregory of Nazianzus, Pope John I, Pope Julius I, Justinian, Liberius, and all the adherents to the Creed of Nicaea. One of the major followers of Arianism was Auxentius who was bishop of Milan until Ambrose replaced him.

Although the condemnations at the Ecumenical Councils were thought to have stopped Arianism, the movement continued as a powerful force for over 300 years. In fact, it continues within Christianity today; for some Unitarians are virtually Arians in that they are unwilling either to reduce Christ to a mere human being or to attribute to him a divine nature identical with that of the Father. In addition, the Christology of Jehovah's Witnesses is a form of Arianism in that they regard Arius a forerunner of Charles Taze Russell, the founder of the movement.

The most important contribution of Arianism to the Christian Church of today is that the movement forced the Church to define the nature of Jesus Christ. That nature was defined in several of the Ecumenical Councils. The "final" definition was the "Definition of Chalcedon" which was formulated at the Fourth Ecumenical Council in 451. The nature of Jesus Christ which was defined at these Councils through much deliberation, caused several other movements to be established, most of which were subsequently declared heretical, and several of which are covered in this Appendix. Despite all of this effort, most Christians do not know the results of these debates and do not know how the Church defined the nature of Jesus Christ. It sometimes makes one wonder if Jesus himself would accept the definition of his nature and that if he did, would that change his message of unconditional love and compassion in any way? In other words, would Jesus Christ demand, as the Church demands, that his followers accept the definitions of his nature in order to be called Christian? And would Jesus Christ who loved even the Samarians approve of all the acrimony caused by those who debated this issue in his name?

ATHANASIUS [297-373] Fourth century Bishop of Alexandria who fought Arianism.

Biography Athanasius was a Greek, born of Christian parents in Alexandria in about 297 CE. He was well educated, especially in Scripture and theology. In early years of the fourth century, the Christians in Egypt were greatly persecuted. Any one actively practicing Christianity would have one eye put out and their Achilles' tendon would be cut thus crippling them. They then would be sent to the mines as slaves. In 312, Athanasius was almost caught, but he escaped to a Christian desert community founded by Anthony whose biography Athanasius later wrote. During this period, it is said that Athanasius completely committed to memory all of the known

Scripture of his day. In about 318, Athanasius returned to Alexandria where he was ordained a deacon. He was elected Bishop of Alexandria in 327. After a very active life, Athanasius died in Alexandria in 373 CE.

In 323, Arius began preaching that Jesus was more than man, but not divine. Although he was excommunicated, he went on preaching. Athanasius wrote pamphlets against Arius and attended the Council called by Constantine at Nicaea [i.e. the First Ecumenical Council] to resolve the Arian controversy. Athanasius spoke against Arius at the Council, helped to sway many votes against Arius at the Council, and then helped to design the Creed of Nicaea. Because the Arians later threw many accusations at Athanasius when Constantine was seeking unity, Constantine expelled Athanasius from the Church and sent into exile. Eventually, the anti-Arian movement won out, and Athanasius was returned to his See.

As a short synopsis of his life, Athanasius held the faith against Arianism, as did Basil of Caesarea and Ambrose of Milan. He was also a friend of the monks, aided the ascetic movement in Egypt, was among the first to introduce monasticism to the West and wrote many treatises such as *Contra gentes* [or "Against the Gentiles" which was a reasoned argument against the pagan objections to Christianity]; and *De incarnatione verbi Dei* [which was a defense of the Incarnation and redemption]. He also wrote four major treatises while exile: *Apologia to Constantius, Defense of Flight, Letter to the Monks,* and *History of the Arians.* His name has come down to us through the Athanasian Creed, a wordy, early Church creed which is thoroughly Augustinian in nature. Athanasius did not write this Creed, but it was drawn from his writings. He is considered by the Church to be one of the great figures of Christianity. He was made a Doctor of the Church and has been called "the champion of orthodoxy."

AUGUSTINE [354-430] Fourth century African theologian who is considered one of the towering intellects of the early Church.

Biography A younger contemporary of Jerome, Augustine was born at Tagaste, northern Africa. He was the son of Patricius, a pagan Roman official and Monica, a Christian of the somewhat superstitious North African style. He received a Christian upbringing and at age sixteen went to the university at Carthage to study rhetoric with a view to becoming a lawyer. He gave up law to devote himself to literary pursuits and gradually abandoned his Christian faith, taking a mistress with whom he lived for 15 years and who bore him a son. He became interested in philosophy and about 373, he embraced Manichaeism. After teaching at Tagaste and Carthage for the next decade, he went to Rome in 383 and opened a school of rhetoric, but became discouraged with the attitudes of his students. In 384 he accepted the chair of rhetoric at Milan. He was so impressed by the sermons of Ambrose that he returned to his Christian faith and was baptized in 387. With his mother, brother and several others, he lived a community life of prayer and meditation.

Later that year, the community started on a journey back to Africa. His mother died along the way, and two years later, his son also died. In 391, Augustine was ordained at Hippo in North Africa [present-day Algeria] where he established a religious community. Although he continued to live a monastic life, he also began to preach. He met with great success. In 396 he was made Bishop of Hippo. He became the dominant figure in African Church affairs and was the leader in the bitter fights against Manichaeism, Donatism, and Pelagianism. He died at Hippo on August 28, 430 during a siege of the city by Gaiseric, a Vandal chieftain who conquered most of North Africa.

Augustine's intellect molded the thought of Western Christianity for a thousand years after his death. As one of his most profound philosophies, Augustine stated that he had tried to find a faith by himself, but he could not. He felt that only by the sheer grace of God was he finally converted. This established the first principle of Augustine. Later, when others argued that man could find his own salvation, he replied that man was helpless without God's free and unmerited grace. Augustine wrote profusely. Even today, many of his 200 treatises, over 300 letters and nearly 400 sermons are important theological and philosophical contributions. Among his best known works are his *Confessions* [one of the great spiritual classics of all time] and *The City of God* [a magnificent exposition of a Christian philosophy of history]. In his work *On the Trinity*, Augustine proposed the "double procession" which means that the Holy Spirit proceeds from both the Father and the Son rather than only from the Father as the Eastern Churches taught. This difference in belief caused a permanent rift between the Eastern and the Western Churches. He also wrote highly regarded treatises against Manichaeism and the Pelagians.

Called "Doctor of Grace," Augustine is a Father and Doctor of the Church; and with the possible exception of Thomas Aquinas, he is the greatest single intellect the Catholic Church has ever produced. Whether you agree with his thoughts or not, he would be on a short list of important Christian persons whatever period of time was being considered.

-B-

BASIL [329-379] Fourth century Bishop of Caesarea who fought Arianism. One of the "Cappadocian Fathers."

Biography Basil of Caesarea was born in 329 CE in Caesarea, Cappadocia, Asia Minor as one of the ten children of St. Basil the Elder and St. Emmelia. He was educated by his father and his grandmother, St. Macrina the Elder. If you are counting, this makes three generations of Saints in the same family.

Basil took advanced studies at Constantinople and Athens where Gregory Nazianzus and the future Emperor Julian the Apostate were classmates. On the completion of his studies, Basil taught rhetoric at Caesarea and then decided to pursue the religious life. He was baptized and proceeded to visit monasteries in Palestine, Syria and Egypt. In 358, he settled as a hermit by the Iris River in Pontus. He attracted numerous disciples whom he organized into the first monastery in Asia Minor.

He was ordained in 363 CE at Caesarea, but returned to the hermit's life in Pontus because of a disagreement with archbishop Eusebius of Caesarea. In 365, Gregory requested his assistance in combating Arianism in Nazianzus. He returned to Caesarea, was reconciled to Eusebius, and became his successor as Archbishop of Caesarea in 370. Later he became metropolitan of some fifty-nine bishops despite the opposition of the Arian Emperor, Valens. When Valens launched his persecution of the orthodox, he demanded that Basil submit to his demands. Basil refused, and in the confrontation of wills that followed, Valens capitulated and left Caesarea. Basil became the leader of the orthodox in the continuing struggle against Arianism in the East sponsored by Emperor Valens. Basil died at Caesarea in 379 CE, a few months after Valens died on the battlefield and the accession of Gratian as Emperor halted the spread of Arianism.

Basil is considered to be one of the giants of the early Church. He was responsible for the triumph of Nicene orthodoxy over Arianism in the Byzantine East. The denunciation of Arianism at the Second Ecumenical Council in 381 was in large measure due to his efforts. The organization and rule he devised at Pontus became the basis of monastic life in the East in a manner similar to that of Benedict in the West. Basil fought simony, aided the victims of drought and famine, insisted on rigid clerical discipline, and excommunicated those involved in the widespread prostitution traffic in Cappadocia. He was one of the great orators of Christianity. His doctrinal writings and his 400 letters [many still extant] had tremendous influence. Among his outstanding treatises are *On the Holy Spirit* and *Philocalia* [with Gregory Nazianzus]. The latter is a selection of passages from Origen's writings. He is a Doctor of the Church and patriarch of Eastern monks. He, like Athanasius and Ambrose, is included in this short list of people because of his activity against Arianism.

BENEDICT [Ca. 480-547] Sixth century monk who established Western Monasticism.

Biography Benedict of Nursia [or Norcia] was the founder of the Benedictine monastery of Monte Cassino and father of Western monasticism. The order that he founded became the norm for monastic living throughout Europe.

The only record of Benedict's life is that presented by St. Gregory the Great [see Gregory I] who said that he obtained his information from four of Benedict's disciples. In this report, it was stated that Benedict was born in Nursia Italy, was educated in Rome, was repelled by the vices of the city and in about 500 CE fled to Enfide, 30 miles away. He decided to live the life of a hermit and settled at mountainous Subiaco, where he lived in a cave for three years fed by a monk named Romanus. Despite Benedict's desire for solitude, his holiness became known and he was asked to be the abbot by a community of monks at Vicovaro. He accepted, but when the monks resisted his strict rule and tried to poison him, he returned to Subiaco where he soon attracted a great number of disciples. He organized them into twelve monasteries under individual priors of his appointment, and he made manual work a part of their program. Soon Subiaco became a center of spirituality and learning.

He left suddenly, reportedly because of the efforts of a local priest to undermine his work; and in about 525 settled at Monte Cassino. He destroyed a temple to Apollo on its crest, brought the people of the neighboring area back to Christianity, and in about 530 began to build the monastery that was to be the birthplace of Western monasticism. Soon disciples again flocked to him as his reputation for holiness, wisdom, and miracles spread far and wide. He organized the monks into a single monastic community and wrote his famous Rule which prescribed a life of moderate asceticism, prayer, study and manual work. It also prescribed that the community life be directed by one superior. It stressed obedience, stability and zeal, and had the Divine Order as the center of monastic life.

The Rule is now believed not to be original with Benedict, but it was he who made it into a force which would affect spiritual and monastic life in the West for centuries to come. Although neither Benedict nor most of his monks were ordained, they counseled rulers and Popes, ministered to the poor and destitute, and tried to repair the ravages of the Lombard

Totila's invasion. Gregory described Benedict's Rule as being "clear in language and outstanding in its discretion." Benedict died at Monte Cassino on March 21, 547. He is included in this short list of people primarily because he made a significant contribution to the activities of the Church while remaining entirely apart from the debates about heresies, about the nature of the Christ, about who should be excommunicated, about who was truly "Christian" and the like. Such a contribution was unique, and was certainly different than any other Church Father reported on in this Appendix. In a manner later echoed by St. Francis of Assisi, Benedict showed that salvation was possible while remaining outside of the contentious part of the Church.

-C-

CATHARS [Twelth -Thirteenth Centuries] A group of very pious and morally dedicated Christians in the twelfth and thirteenth centuries. The Pope mounted a Crusade against them. They were exterminated. Their presence was the major reason for the establishment of the Inquisition. The word "Cathar" means "pure ones." They were also known as the Albigenses from one of their major locations near the town of Albi in southern France. A major section on the Cathers is presented on pages 101-105.

CLARE [1194-1253] Thirteenth century Saint who established the Poor Clares. A close friend of Francis of Assisi. [For biography, see pages 112-115].

CLEMENT I [Ca. 30-100] Early, possibly second, Bishop of Rome, a position later entitled "pope." Wrote two letters which were considered Scripture for almost 300 years and which were almost included in the Bible. Died a martyr in about 100 CE.

Biography Pope Clement I is one of the most obscure men of the early Church. All that is known with certainty is that he was a Roman and suffered martyrdom away from Rome. According to tradition, he was a freed man in the Imperial household who was baptized by St. Peter. Irenaeus states that Clement was a witness to the preaching of the Apostles. Clement succeeded Cletus as Bishop of Rome in 91 or 92 CE, thus becoming the second to hold that title, a title which later became "pope." Cletus was the first to hold that title because none of the early Church Fathers such as Cyprian, Origen, Cyril, Jerome, Ambrose or Augustine ever felt that the Bishop of Rome succeeded to any title based on the biblical admonition of "you are Peter, and on this rock I shall build my church" [Matt. 16:18].

They all analyzed it and came to the conclusion that only Peter had been given that title. Only in the much later periods of the Church's history was the thought advanced that the pope was the successor to Peter as the "Rock." As a consequence, the early Church never had Peter as the first Bishop of Rome, although the present Church does.

Church tradition states that Clement was exiled to the Crimea by Emperor Trajan. In the Crimea, Clement labored so zealously preaching the faith among the prisoners who worked in the mines that he was condemned to death. Tradition states that he was thrown into the sea with an anchor around his neck.

Scholars know something about him from his writings. As a few examples, in one letter Clement states that "Christ comes with a message from God, and the Apostles with a message from Christ." In this manner, Clement laid the groundwork for the Apostolic Tradition. In another letter, in talking about the example set by Christ he says, "You see, beloved, what the example is that has been given us. Through him our unintelligent and darkened mind shoots up into the light. Through him the Master was pleased to let us taste the knowledge that never fades." In this manner, Clement laid additional groundwork for the thought that in Christ we have seen God.

It is also generally accepted by scholars that Clement was the first to make a distinction between laymen and the clergy [which he calls "priests" and "high priests" of the Church], and that he was the author of a letter to the church at Corinth in which he rebuked them for a schism which had broken out. This letter was important in that it showed that Rome intervened authoritatively in local church matters even during the first century. It was such an important letter that many Christians regarded it as Scripture during the third and fourth centuries. It almost became canon. It is thought that Clement died about 99 CE. He was among the very first to be made a Saint when the Church started its canonization proceedings.

Clement is on our short list of the important people in Christianity's early period for two major reasons: [1] by writing that the message is carried from God by Christ to the Apostles and then from the Apostles to us, he started the "Apostolic Succession" philosophy which became so important for the Church during the controversies which sprang up in the fourth-seventh centuries; and [2] by rebuking the Church at Corinth, he presents evidence that the central Church in Rome was trying to establish itself as the one which determined policy for the outlying churches, an activity which was emphasized in the Photian schism of the ninth century [see page 77].

CLEMENT OF ALEXANDRIA [Ca. 150-215] Early Bishop of Alexandria and director of the first catechetical school in the world. Known as the missionary to the Greek world. Proposed Christian *Gnosis*. This, among other things, got him delisted as a Saint 1350 years after his death.

Biography. Clement of Alexandria was born of pagan parents in Athens. Little is known of his early life. He was converted to Christianity by his teacher, Pantaenus, who had been a Stoic philosopher and was possibly the first teacher of the catechetical school at Alexandria. This school was the first catechetical school in the world.

Clement is probably best known as being a missionary to the Greek world by presenting the history of Judaism to the Greeks. In his writings he claimed that "Moses and the Jewish race went back further in their origins than the Greeks," and that "many of the thoughts of Plato had their origin with the Hebrews." He became director of the catechetical school in about 180 CE. For the following twenty years, he was the intellectual leader of the Christians in Alexandria, a city which was the intellectual center of the world at that time. He steered for a middle ground in the balance of intellectualism and belief in religion. He battled the Gnostics who tended to feel that knowledge was everything in religion; but he also battled Christians who did not accept any intellectualism in Christianity. He trained many later leaders, one of whom was Bishop Alexander of Palestine.

In his approach to the Greek world, Clement presented a program of witnessing in thought and in action. He believed that intellectual philosophy was to the Greeks as the Law of Moses was to the Jews; and he hoped that a blend of the two would make Christian beliefs acceptable to each and thus bring both worlds into Christianity. However, the uneducated Christians of Alexandria looked askance at anything having to do with intellectualism because this smacked of Gnosticism. Led by Demetrius, who later was made Bishop of Alexandria, they taught a legalistic doctrine of salvation which preached that the Christian was saved solely by faith and that knowledge had no place in salvation. Clement attempted to mediate between the heretical Gnostics and the legalistic orthodox Christians by defining *Gnosis* for the Christian as the knowledge of faith which teaches the ignorant to love and honor God the Almighty. In this manner, Clement's *Gnosis* would preach to all by creating new insights causing them to live a highly moral life. He proposed that faith was the basis of salvation, but also the basis of *Gnosis*, the spiritual and mystical knowledge.

Though much of Clement's attention was focused upon the reorientation of men's personal lives in accordance with the Christian gospels, he also got involved in the economic and political forces of his time. Like

Augustine of some 200 years later, he saw two cities, the City of Heaven and the City of Earth; but unlike Augustine, he never equated the City of Heaven with the institutional Church. Instead, he equated it with a high moral life which opposed the normal life on Earth. In response to the desire on the part of the Christian poor of Alexandria that the Christian rich sell what they had and give it to the poor, Clement wrote that wealth was a neutral factor in the problem and that it could be used either to generate good or evil. He said, "The Word does not command us to renounce property but to manage property without inordinate affection." In this manner, he was directing all activities toward a high moral tone.

Because of the persecution of Christians in Alexandria under the Roman Emperor Severus in 201-202, Clement had to leave the school to seek sanctuary. He was replaced by his young, gifted student, Origen, who became one of the great theologians of the Christian Church. Clement found safety and work in Palestine under his former student, Alexander, who was then Bishop of Palestine. He died there, sometime in the period 211-215.

In his various roles, particularly as missionary, theologian and Apologist, Clement presented ideas which influenced Christian thought in the areas of Monasticism, politics, economics and theology. He made the Greeks accept the belief that Christ was God's final answer to their questions. Despite this missionary effort, the Greek Church later felt that his theology was too close to Origen's, some of which was considered heretical. In spite of this, in the Latin Church Clement was considered a Saint. However, because some of his views were questioned in regard to orthodoxy, in 1586, some 1350 years after his death, Pope Sixtus V deleted his name from the list of Roman Saints.

Clement is included in this list of influential people because his actions broadened Christianity in its intellectual appeal and thus extended Christianity to the prosperous and well-educated Greek community; and because as an early Church leader, he proposed a common meeting ground for those who had slightly differing points of view. This, of course, was following in the footsteps of Christ; but this is also one of the reasons that this great theologian and educator was later blacklisted by the Church.

CYPRIAN [Ca. 200-258] Bishop of Carthage who was martyred in 258 CE. He fought with the pope over whether those who had lapsed in their faith were to be forgiven.

Biography Cyprian of Carthage was probably born in Carthage. His full name was Thascius Caecilius Cyprianus and in his early life, he was a pagan rhetorician, lawyer and teacher. He was converted to Christianity by Caecilius, an old priest, in about 246. Following this, he became a profound scholar of the Bible and an avid reader of the great religious authors, especially Tertullian. In 248, he was elected Bishop of Carthage. Cyprian was forced to flee Decius' persecution of Christians in 249, but continued to rule his See by correspondence from his hiding place. He was greatly criticized by his fellow Carthaginians for fleeing. Consequently, when he returned in 251, he found that many of the faithful had apostatized during the persecution and that a priest named Novatus was in schism because he was receiving back into the Church with no penance those who had lapsed from the faith [the *lapsi*]. Cyprian denounced Novatus for his leniency and convened a council at Carthage in 251 which set forth the terms under which the *lapsi* could be received back into the Church. He further had the council excommunicate the schismatic leaders and assert the supremacy of the pope. It was at this council that Cyprian read his *De unitate ecclesia* [i.e. the united clergy].

Novatus left for Rome, where he joined forces with Novatian who believed that apostasy was an unforgivable sin. Consequently, the Church could not bring back the *lapsi* under any conditions. Novatian created another schism and had himself elected Bishop of Rome as antipope to Pope Cornelius who had reinstated the *lapsi* under certain defined conditions. Cyprian actively supported Pope Cornelius and rallied the African bishops behind him. Thus, Cyprian supported the stand that the Church could decide under what conditions certain things could be accomplished, even though part of the clergy would feel so strongly about it that they would create a schism over the issue.

In 252-4, Carthage was stricken with a terrible plague. Although Cyprian was a leader in helping alleviate its effects, the Christians were blamed for the plague. Hatred for Cyprian and the Christians intensified. It was at this time that he wrote *De mortalite* to give comfort to his flock.

Soon after, he and other African bishops came into conflict with Pope Stephen I when they refused to recognize the validity of baptisms performed by schismatics, although Stephen had approved them. Three African councils [255-256] demanded re-baptism for those who had been baptized by schismatics. Cyprian engaged in acrimonious correspondence with Stephen which was cut short when an Imperial decree was issued which forbid assembly by Christians. It also required all bishops, priests and deacons to forgo Christianity in order to participate in the official state religion. This decree ushered in Valerian's persecution of the Christians. Cyprian was arrested and exiled to Curubis, a small town 50 miles from Carthage. The following year, another Imperial decree ordered that all

bishops, priest and deacons were to be put to death. When Cyprian continued to ignore the pagan Gods, he was beheaded.

Cyprian wrote numerous theological treatises on the Church, the
ministry, the Bible, virginity and the *lapsi* and is considered to be a pioneer
of Latin Christian literature. He is included in our short list for the simple
reason that he supported the pope on certain issues which others fought,
and he fought the pope [even one who was later sainted] on other issues
which others supported. In each issue, he refused to forgive those who did
not agree with him. Despite this unforgiving attitude, Cyprian is remembered today. It would seem that this is a case of history having been written
by the ones which the Church viewed as winners, even though the winners
were not following the teachings of the Christ whom they were dedicated
to follow.

CYRIL [375-444] Fifth century Bishop of Alexandria who fought
Nestorianism by accepting the Definition of Chalcedon.

Biography Cyril of Alexandria was a Christian theologian and
bishop who was active in many of the great and complex doctrinal struggles
of the fifth century, particularly Nestorianism. Cyril was named a Doctor
of the Church in 1882.

Cyril became Bishop of Alexandria in 412 and immediately came
in conflict with the governmental authorities over his defense of orthodoxy. He closed the churches of the Novatians who had denied the authority of
the Church to pardon those who had lapsed into idolatry during persecution. He
also expelled the Jews from Alexandria because they did not become Christian.

Cyril's defense against Nestorianism was based on two fears: [1]
that their belief was heretical; and [2] that if they won out in the debate,
then Constantinople would win out over Alexandria as the religious center
of Christianity in the East. In the doctrinal debate, Cyril taught that Christ
had two natures within the same person; whereas Nestorius so emphasized
the distinctness of these divine and human natures as to split Christ into
two persons acting in concert. The final dispute between these two men
came when Cyril insisted that the Virgin Mary be called *Theotokos* [or
"God-bearer"] to describe the intimate union of the two natures in the
incarnation. Nestorius refused to accept such terminology and the dispute
was referred to the Third Ecumenical Council at Ephesus in 431 CE at
which Cyril condemned Nestorius prior to the arrival of the Eastern bishops.
However, when the Eastern bishops arrived, the council was reconvened
and condemned Cyril [see pages 66-68]. Pope Celestine I sided with the
first council, and Nestorius was banished as a heretic.

Cyril is included in this short list of people because of his teachings. Although earlier he had emphasized the divine nature of Christ, in the latter years he presented a compromise which emphasized the distinctness of the two natures within the one Person of the Christ. This compromise became the foundation for much of the debate against Nestorianism. In addition, his teachings ultimately led to the reaffirmation of the Nicene Creed at the Fourth Ecumenical Council in 451 CE. His honors show what a fine line of distinction was drawn between thoughts which were declared heretical [i.e. his early teachings] and those which were declared orthodox [i.e. his later compromise]. Each was done by the same man. If the Church were to wish to do so, it could call Cyril both a Saint and a Sinner. The Church decided to name him a Saint, and Nestorius a Sinner. It was a very close decision.

-D-

DOCETISM [Second Century] A special form of Gnosticism which believed that since all material things are evil, then Jesus Christ did not have a material body but only seemed to have one. [For additional information, see Gnosticism].

DONATUS [Ca. 290-355] Charismatic Bishop of Carthage, known primarily because of the Donatism schism or controversy. He is called Donatus the Great because he headed the "church of the martyrs." Other than this, little is known of him.

DONATISM A form of North African Christianity which opposed State influence in Church affairs and which strongly believed in martyrdom for its members. Declared a heresy by the Church in 411.

Description Donatism was fought by several of the Church Fathers, particularly Augustine. Donatism denotes the movement established by a Christian group which broke away from the Catholics over the election of Caecilian as bishop of Carthage.

Donatism belonged to the tradition of early Christianity which also produced the Montanist and Novatianist movements in Asia Minor and the Meletian controversy in Egypt. [For the early history, see "Cyprian."] The Donatists opposed state influence in Church affairs, promoted a series of social changes which were led by eschatological thoughts, and glorified martyrdom. In addition, Donatists believed that it was a sin to be rich and that worldly gain was to be shunned. Their goal was to live a life of poverty and penance which would be ended with martyrdom. Despite continuous pressure from successive Roman, Vandal and Byzantine rulers, the Donatist church survived until the extinction of Christianity in North Africa by Islamic conquest in the early Middle Ages.

The final break between the Donatists and the Christians was caused by the Donatist belief that since the validity of the sacraments was based on the presence of the Holy Spirit in the minister, then a minister who was not in a state of grace could not administer a valid sacrament. In 311, Caecilian was elected bishop of the church in Carthage which was called "catholic" because it was in communion with the other churches in the Roman Empire. However, he was opposed by many, not only because Donatus was bishop of a rival church devoted to North African beliefs, but also because during the persecutions by Emperor Diocletian in 303, Caecilian had discouraged martyrdom. In addition, one of the bishops who consecrated Caecilian had apostatized himself by turning the church's sacred books over to the authorities. He was therefore considered to be a minister who was not in grace and thus unable to perform a valid sacrament.

The primate of Numidia arrived in Carthage and declared the election of Caecilian to be invalid. The new emperor, Constantine, ordered the controversy between Caecilian and Donatus to be arbitrated. In 313, a council of Gaulic and Italian bishops found Caecilian to be innocent of all charges. This was appealed by Donatus. Another council ruled likewise and despite further appeals, Caecilian was made bishop in 316. This did not solve the schism; and persecution of the "martyrdom" church by the "catholic" church persisted for another five years. In 321, Constantine grudgingly granted toleration to the Donatists as a political necessity.

For several years Donatism grew, but in 347, Emperor Constans I exiled Donatus and the other leaders to Gaul where Donatus died in about 355. When Julian the Apostate became emperor in 361, the Donatists returned to Africa and were the major Christian party there for the next thirty years. During all this time, they defended their thoughts on martyrdom and their opposition to the Church in Rome which they thought of as a worldly church. However, their orthodox opponents, led by Augustine of Hippo, continued to gain strength. In 411, a conference decided against the Donatists and for the Catholics. This conference was headed by a friend of Augustine.

In 412 and 414, severe laws denied the Donatists their ecclesiastical rights. However, the Donatists expected hostility from the outside world as a part of the natural order of things. As a consequence of their belief system, they survived into the seventh century when, like many Christian sects of Asia Minor and Africa, they were overcome by the Islamic movement.

Today, Donatism is not thought by Church historians to have been much of a controversy or to have had much impact on the development of the Church. However, it is worthy of study for two reasons. In the first place, an examination of the history of Donatism readily shows that the Church in Rome neglected local beliefs and directions despite the fact that these local beliefs were consistent with the life of Christ and the Apostles, all of whom admonished the faithful to neglect the riches of this world and not to avoid martyrdom in defense of the Faith. And secondly, after reviewing the history of Donatism is it any wonder that North Africa, once one of the strongest locales of Christian activity, was lost to Islam? It is a matter of unbiased historical fact that the Islamic conquests were as much spiritual conquests as they were conquests of the sword; for the North African desire for the rewards of martyrdom so prevalent in Donatism, continues today within the Islamic framework to a greater extent than within any part of Christianity.

-E-

EUSEBIUS OF CAESAREA [Ca. 260-340] Early fourth century Bishop of Constantinople who has generated a continuing puzzle for Church historians.

Biography Eusebius of Caesarea was baptized and ordained at Caesarea, a city in Asia Minor which had become a great center of Christian learning because of the long residence of Origen there. During this time of learning, Eusebius had a prodigious literary output including *Martyrs of Palestine, Defense of Origen,* [written with others] and most importantly, *Ecclesiastical History*, a Christian history for which he is best remembered. He also became noted as a masterly Christian scholar based on *Praeparatio* ["Preparation"] and *Demonstratio evangelica* ["Demonstration of the Gospel"]. He became Bishop of the See at Palestine in 313.

Eusebius of Caesarea defended Arius as having been misunderstood, an act for which he was provisionally excommunicated by a synod at Antioch in early 325. At the Council at Nicaea later that year, he successfully defended himself and was exonerated with the explicit approval of Emperor Constantine, a man with whom he was always in great favor. Although Eusebius did not agree with the term *homoousios* ["of one substance"] which was chosen at the First Ecumenical Council to describe the relation of the Father and the Son, his recent experience with provisional excommunication and the Emperor's desire to have the term accepted caused him to accept it.

After the Council at Nicaea, Emperor Constantine was so desirous of unity within the Church that he made compromises with the Arians. As a result, the supporters of Nicaea found themselves in the position of being dissidents. Some were even expelled from the Church. Eusebius took part in the expulsion of Eustathius of Antioch and Athanasius of Alexandria, both anti-Arians. Despite his support of these expulsions and the disunity which they created, Eusebius constantly remained in the good graces of Emperor Constantine. He declared that the Empire and the Church belonged together since the Emperor ruled solely by God's grace; but later he had to retract from this declaration when the Empire and the Church came into conflict under the Emperor Constantius II.

This Eusebius has always been a puzzle to the orthodox historians of the Church. Although his scholarship on basic Christian principles can hardly be questioned, his leanings toward Arianism bothered them. He was wholeheartedly supported by the church historian Socrates [380-445]; but at the Seventh Ecumenical Council at Nicaea in 787, he was condemned as being double-minded and unstable in his ways. This condemnation occurred about 400 years after his death.

EUSEBIUS OF VERCELLI [283-371] Early fourth century Bishop of Vercelli who fought Arianism and defended Athanasius.

Biography Eusebius of Vercelli was born in Sardinia, the son of a Christian martyr. He died in Vercelli. He was brought to Rome as an infant, and was raised there. He was ordained a lector and then went to Vercelli where in 345 he was elected first bishop of the city. He reformed his clergy, was the first Western bishop to unite the clerical and the monastic life, and lived in community with his clergy. He was a defender of Athanasius and restorer of the Creed of Nicaea, the orthodox doctrine adopted by the First Ecumenical Council which declared the equality of the Son and the Father.

In 354 CE, Eusebius was sent by Pope Liberius to ask Emperor Constantius II, the son of Constantine, to call a council to settle the differences between Catholics and Arians. At the Council of Milan called by Constantius the following year, Eusebius vehemently refused to sign the condemnation of Athanasius and demanded that all the bishops present sign the Creed of Nicaea before considering the case of Athanasius. Because of this, Eusebius was threatened with death by the Emperor who then banished him to Palestine in the custody of an Arian, Bishop Patrophilus.

At Scythopolis in Palestine, Eusebius was humiliated and persecuted by the Arians. He was moved first to Cappadocia and then to Upper Thebaid, Egypt where he continued his uncompromising opposition to Arianism. He returned from exile to attend a council at Alexandria in 362 when Emperor Julian the Apostate, a supporter of the Creed of Nicaea, permitted the exiled bishops to return to their Sees.

Following the council in Alexandria, Eusebius was delegated to go to Antioch to heal the breach between the Eustathians and the Meletians [see Meletian Controversy]. The Eustathians were the followers of Eustathius, whom the Arians had exiled in 331. The Meletians were the followers of Meletius whom the Arians had elected bishop of Antioch in 361. Eusebius settled the dispute by recognizing Meletius . However, Lucifer of Carthage complicated the situation by consecrating Paulinus, leader of the Eustathians, bishop of Carthage. This action began the Luciferian schism.

After Antioch, Eusebius traveled through the East visiting various churches to bolster their orthodoxy. He returned to Vercelli in 363 and spent the rest of his life fighting Arianism in the Western Church. He was one of the authors of the Athanasian Creed; and a manuscript copy of the Latin gospels he is reputed to have copied, the *Codex Vercellensis*, is the oldest such manuscript in existence. In addition, he is presently considered to be the author of the first seven books of *de Trinitate*, an early work which defended the equality of the persons of the Trinity. Originally this work had been attributed to Athanasius.

Eusebius of Vercelli is a Saint of the Church. He is included in this short list not only because of his strong defense against Arianism, but also because his life shows some of the dictatorial attitudes which the State [i.e. the Emperor] took towards the Church during this formative period of the Church's history. He is also included as a contrast to Eusebius of Caesarea.

There are other men with the name Eusebius who were connected with the early Church. In particular, there is the well-known Eusebius, Bishop of Nicomedia, a key proponent of Arianism who became leader of an Arian group called "the Eusebians." He is the one who baptized Constantine on his deathbed. However, the two men just presented, Eusebius of Caesarea and Eusebius of Vercelli, were chosen for this list because they represent the extremes of Church schizophrenia during the years of definition. One Eusebius fought Arianism while the other defended it; one defended Athanasius while the other condemned him; one fought the Emperor while the other supported him; one was made a Saint of the Church while the other, possibly a more able man at least in his scholarship, was condemned by it. This is merely one of the many stories which could be developed about "the winners and the losers" in the early Church debates. But which of these men more nearly represents the Christ of the Scriptures? That is the point which needs to be addressed; and it can hardly be argued by those who accept the Scriptures that when Jesus said, "Only God is good" [Mark 10:18], he was stating that he was *not divine in the sense that God is divine*, a point which Arius and the other Arians such as Eusebius of Caesarea were trying to make.

EUTYCHES [375-454] Fifth century monastic superior at Constantinople whose teachings emphasized the divine nature of the Christ. Founded Eutychianism, an extreme form of Monophysitism which emphasized the <u>exclusiveness</u> of the divinity in Christ. Was declared a heretic at the Fourth Ecumenical Council.

Biography Little is known about the early life of Eutyches, but in his adulthood, he became the revered monastic superior in the Eastern Church at Constantinople. Eutyches came to the viewpoint which founded Eutychianism because of his early education in the Alexandrian school of Christology, possibly under the influence of Cyril prior to "the Compromise" [see" Cyril"]. In professing the one nature of Christ, Eutyches opposed the Antioch belief propounded by Nestorius which maintained that Christ had two separate natures: a divine nature as the son of God; and a human nature as the son of Mary. In this manner, Nestorius did not believe that the Virgin was the mother of God, but instead was merely the mother of the human nature of Jesus [see "Nestorianism"].

Because of his belief solely in the divinity of Christ, Eutyches was declared a heretic by Bishop Eusebius of Dorylaeum in Asia Minor and was summoned to a synod by Flavian, Patriarch in Constantinople. Flavian was a strong opponent of Monophysitism. At the synod, Eutyches refused to discuss the nature of Christ but defended himself by saying that he was in complete agreement with the Council at Nicaea [325] which had addressed primarily the divinity of Christ and his equality in the Trinity rather than his nature. Eutyches repeatedly stated the affirmation "two natures before, one after the incarnation." This affirmation was one of the strong arguments of the Monophysites who believed that during incarnation, Christ's human nature was deified and subsumed into a single divine essence; and that his humanity differed from that of other humans. For stating this position, Eutyches was excommunicated by the synod. The excommunication was supported by Pope Leo I in his *Tome* in which he called Eutyches "an extremely foolish and altogether ignorant man"; but was opposed by the Patriarch Dioscorus who asked Emperor Theodosius II to call a council at Ephesus in 449 CE. This council, later called the Robber Synod and generally not recognized by the powers of either the Eastern or the Western Churches, reinstated Eutyches and excommunicated Flavian and the other defenders of the two-nature Christ. In doing this, they felt that Leo's *Tome* was an expression of sheer Nestorianism.

In 450 CE, Theodosius II suffered an accidental death, and was succeeded by his sister, Pulcheria and her undistinguished soldier-husband, Marcian, who convened the Council of Chalcedon in 451 [see pages 68-9 and also see "Leo"]. At this council, later called the Fourth Ecumenical Council, Eutyches was declared a heretic; and a compromise doctrine was accepted which declared that Christ had two perfect and indivisible but distinct natures: one human and one divine. In other words, Christ was "one *prosopon* and one *hypostasis*" which exists "in two natures" which are at once "unconfused and unaltered." With this decision, often called the "Definition of Chalcedon," Eutyches faded from history. He died in 454.

Eutyches is included in this list of people because his teachings became the prod which forced the calling of the Fourth Ecumenical Council at which the nature of Christ became "fully and permanently" defined.

EUTYCHIANISM A fifth century movement which emphasized the divine nature of Jesus Christ at the expense of his human nature. Declared a heretical movement at the Fourth Ecumenical Council.

Description Eutychianism is regarded as an extreme form of Monophysite heresy that emphasized the exclusive prevalence of the divinity of Christ. In emphasizing Christ's divinity, Eutyches opposed the Nestorians. Eutychianism was in favor with all of the Fathers of Nicaea who had de-emphasized the human nature of Christ by emphasizing his divinity and his equality in the Trinity.

The "home synod" of Constantinople under the presidency of Flavian declared Eutychianism a heretical movement and excommunicated Eutyches. Flavian reported on this to Pope Leo I who on June 13, 449 issued his celebrated *Tome* further condemning Eutychianism. The Council of Chaldecon in 451 confirmed both decisions and established a centrist doctrine which was accepted as a cornerstone by both the Eastern and the Western Churches. The Council held that Christ had two perfect and indivisible, but distinct natures: one human and one divine. Eutyches disappeared, but his influence grew as Monophysitism spread throughout the East; for despite the decision at the Fourth Ecumenical Council, the Monophysite doctrine continued to be believed by many people. It is still believed in today. However, it does so generally outside the sectarian Christian Church, often in regional, national or independent churches which have always been opposed to the gathering power and dominance of mainstream, centralized, sectarian Christianity. One such Church which opposed both Rome and Constantinople while remaining Christian was the Nestorian Church within the Persian Empire. This Church remained a vital force even under Islamic rule. Although it was destroyed in Persia by the Mongol invasion of the later Middle Ages, it continues to exist today in many parts of the world. The Nestorian Church is further described in "Nestorianism." The Monophysitic movement is further described in "Monophysitism."

-F-

FRANCIS [1181-1253] A thirteenth century monk who founded the Franciscans. [For **Biography**, see pages 112-115].

-G-

GNOSTICISM [Ca. 150-Present] A very early challenge to the Christian Church. It believed that all material things are evil and all spiritual things are good. Had a very structured universe populated with a hierarchy of Gods which jointly produced Jesus Christ.

Description One of the most potent forces operating in the Church's environment during the second and third centuries [i.e. 100-200 CE], was Gnosticism, a name applied to a group of sects or schools having a wide variety of beliefs. Theologians such as Irenaeus, Tertullian and Hippolytus treated this non-uniform system as a Christian heresy; for they considered it to be an adulteration of Apostolic doctrine with pagan philosophy, Greek mystery beliefs and astrology. They also charged that Simon the Magician who had become a Christian and traveled with Philip [see Acts of the Apostles, Chapter 8], originated it. Many modern scholars have described Gnosticism as the "extreme Hellenization of Christianity," for it added a great deal of Wisdom or Knowledge [Greek *gnosis*] to the simple system of faith taught by Jesus. Most of the Gnostic systems were Christian in intention; although some went so far into a knowledge-based system as to make the need for Christ almost non-essential.

Gnosticism was not spawned by Christianity, for it had been practiced by a large number of Jews prior to the appearance of Jesus. In other words, Gnosticism was a movement which had been practiced for years as it attempted to solve the problems of evil and human destiny. By the second century, many Gnostic schools flourished, both in Alexandria and in Rome; and by the end of the second century, most of these Gnostic schools included significant elements of Christianity in their teachings.

To help understand some of the appeal of Gnosticism, it might be useful to examine the rather complex teachings of one such school. This school had a Christian bent, but also believed that beyond the Earth, there was a very structured and well-defined universe. Beyond this universe was the dwelling place of the supreme pair of Aeons [or "eternal ones"]. These supreme beings were the Father [Bythos] with Silence [Sige] who is His Thought [Ennoia] by his side. From these two supreme beings, three pairs of Aeons were generated. These are: [1] Nous [or Monogenes] with Aletheia [Truth]; [2] Logos with Zoe [Life]; and [3] Anthropos [Man] with Ecclesia [Church]. These four pairs of Aeons complete the Ogdoad, or the "upper hierarchy."

Logos and Zoe produced five pairs of Aeons [the Decad]. Anthropos and Ecclesia produced six pairs [the Dodecad]. These thirty entities form the fullness *[Pleroma]* of the Godhead. However, since only Nous [Monogenes] possesses the possibility of knowing and revealing the Father, then Nous and Aletheia, at the Father's behest, produce a new pair of Aeons, *Christ* and the *Holy Spirit*. These new Aeons were needed in order to instruct the other Aeons on their true relationship with the Father. When all the Aeons realized their true relationship with the Father, they got together and produced *Jesus* as the perfect fruit of the *Pleroma* [Godhead]. Through the knowledge and imitation of Jesus, the people would also become "perfect fruits" and therefore could overcome all the problems associated with the material world.

Gnosticism was really not an organized church. Instead it was a collection of teachers such as Basilides and Valentinus, each with his own following. But although there was no single Gnostic church, there was a common stock of four ideas which could allow any organization to come up with its own answers to the problems of existence, evil and salvation. The first idea was that all Gnostics were dualistic, meaning that they believed in a spiritual world and a material world. These worlds were far apart, with the spiritual world being good and the material world being evil. Secondly, they believed that the material world did not originate with the ultimate God of Light and Goodness, but was the result of some primeval disorder which happened in the higher realm and which was caused by some being who was less than the ultimate God. Thirdly, they believed that there was a spiritual element in the elite of mankind which is a stranger to this world and which yearns to be freed from matter in order to ascend to its true home. Because of this, they further believed that mankind would be freed as each individual would discover the Kingdom of God within his elect soul and learn how to pass the hostile powers barring the soul's ascent to bliss. Fourth, and finally, they believed that there are many mediators who constantly descend to Earth to help make this happen. By use of these four ideas they could explain why man would feel alien to this world. As far as redemption goes, it is generated by knowledge or *"gnosis"* rather than by any of the *Pleroma* [Godhead].

Many people were attracted to this set of beliefs, including Christians; for in the early days, the Christian Church offered men saving knowledge and set Christ before them as the revelation of the Father in a manner similar to the Gnostic use of *Nous* who was their "Monogenes" just as Christ is the "Monogenes" to the Christian. [Note: For a description of the meaning of "Monogenes" and how it was mistranslated from Greek into Latin and from there into English, see *Christianity and the New Age Religion.*]

Many early Christians used the Gospel of John to support their relationship with the Gnostics, for in that Gospel, eternal life consists of knowledge of God and of Christ. Many of the greatest of the Gnostic teachers regarded themselves as Christians and were merely attempting to relate the truths of Christianity in a way which the intelligentsia of the day would find more satisfying. The principle reason for the incompatibility between Christianity and Gnosticism really lay, as the second-century fathers such as Irenaeus quickly perceived, in their different attitudes to the material order and the historical process. Because of their disregard for history and their hostility to matter, the Gnostics did not give full value to the fundamental Christian doctrine of the incarnation of the Word. This incarnation had Jesus, an historical figure, appearing in the flesh, a material substance. Since Gnosticism rejected both history and material things, then they simply could not accept the orthodox beliefs of the incarnation.

Docetism presents a perfect example to illustrate this latter point. The word "Docetism" comes from the Greek word *dokein* which in addition to meaning "to think" as a precursor to "dogma" can also mean "to seem." This movement was a Christian-oriented form of Gnosticism which believed that Christ had no real material body, but only <u>seemed</u> to have one. In this manner, they could deny the material [i.e. "evil"] nature of Jesus and accept only the spiritual [i.e. "good"] nature of the Christ. However, since the Christ had no material body, then he only <u>seemed</u> [or appeared] to have been crucified, resurrected and ascended. This could not be accepted by the Church. Consequently, Docetism was attacked as a heresy by all opponents of Gnosticism, particularly by Ignatius of Antioch who believed that Docetism was refuted by the first Letter of John.

As a consequence of all of this, the Church fought Gnosticism in its various forms, not only because it denied the historical importance of a Jesus who "came in the flesh" to redeem the Christians, but also because it taught its beliefs in secret and only to the intelligentsia who were capable of absorbing its *gnosis* or meaning. In addition, Christians felt that evil was a "thing" which was to be fought; whereas the Gnostics felt that evil was not a "thing" but was a way of choosing. Since orthodox Christians defined

Gnosticism as an evil, then the Church fought it with all the talent it could bring to bear. This fight is considered by most Church historians to be the first great crisis faced by the Church. Despite this fight, elements of Gnosticism continue today in the Coptic Church and in some of the other churches of the Monophysitic or Jacobite Conventions.

GREGORY I [540-604] Sixth century Pope who significantly increased the power of the papacy. Known as "the Great."

Biography Pope Gregory I the Great was born in Rome, the son of a wealthy patrician, Gordianus. He was educated in Rome, and was prefect of Rome when the Lombard invasion of Italy threatened in 571. Since he had been attracted to the religious life for a long time, in about 574 he converted his house in Rome into St. Andrew's Monastery. Gregory became a monk there, and founded six monasteries on his estates in Sicily. After several years of seclusion at St. Andrews, he was ordained by Pope Pelagius II and was made one of the seven papal deacons in 578. A year later he was named as papal emissary to the Byzantine court, a post he served for six years. When he was recalled, he returned to the monastic life and became abbot at St. Andrews. He set out to evangelize England but was brought back to Rome by Pope Pelagius when the plague struck Rome in 589-90. Pelagius was stricken and died. Gregory was elected pope and was consecrated on September 3, 590.

Pope Gregory is known as a reformer. After becoming pope, he suppressed the practice of simony, forced the clergy to rid themselves of their mistresses, abolished cleric fees for burials and ordinations, and restored discipline to the monastic orders. He also ransomed captives from the Lombards, protected Jews from unjust coercion and fed victims of the famine. In 593, he persuaded the invading Lombards under Agilulf to spare Rome and negotiated peace with the Lombard King. This was an unprecedented move which usurped the authority of the Byzantine Emperor, and was the beginning of a series of actions by which Gregory resisted the Byzantine authorities. He appointed governors to many Italian cities and provided them with war materials which permitted them to denounce the heavy taxes levied by the Byzantine officials. He thus started the acquisition and exercise of temporal and political power by the papacy.

In addition, he was responsible for the conversion of England to Christianity. He did this by his interest in that country, and by sending St. Augustine of Canterbury and forty monks from St. Andrew's to England. He denounced John, Patriarch of Constantinople, for his use of the title "Ecumenical Patriarch." By doing this, Gregory suggested that the authority of the papacy was the supreme authority in the Church. Gregory himself preferred his own title, *Servus Servorum Dei,* or "Servant of the Servants of God," a title used by the popes today, some 1400 years later.

Gregory was responsible for the restoration of Rome which had been devastated by the invasions, pillages and earthquakes of the century before his pontificate. He was an eloquent preacher who wrote treatises, notably his *Dialogues* [a collection of visions, prophecies, miracles and lives of Italian saints] and *Liber regullae pastoralis* [on the duties of bishops]. He also wrote hundreds of sermons and letters. Whether he was compiler of the Antiphony on which the Roman *schola cantorum* was based and several hymns is uncertain, but he did greatly influence the Roman liturgy including the use of the Gregorian Chants. The custom of saying 30 successive Masses for a dead person goes back to him and bears his name. He actively encouraged Benedictine monasticism, and his grants of privileges to monks was the beginning of bringing the religious orders directly under papal control. He is the last of the traditional Latin Doctors of the Church, is justly called "the Great" and is considered to be the founder of the medieval papacy. He died in Rome on March 12, 604 and was canonized by acclimation immediately after his death.

He is included on this short list of people because his necessary reforms indicate the state of the Church and its activities during the time in which the Church was defining itself. The reformations of Gregory were so extensive that his activities could well be called the First Reformation of the Church.

GREGORY OF NAZIANZUS [329-389] Fourth century Bishop of Constantinople who fought Arianism. One of "the Cappadocian Fathers."

Biography Gregory of Nazianzus was born at Nazianzus, Cappadocia, Asia Minor, the son of Gregory of Nazianzus the Elder, bishop of Nazianzus for 45 years, and St. Nonna. He studied at Caesarea, Cappadocia where he met Basil. He then attended the rhetorical school at Caesarea, Palestine and for ten years, studied at Athens where both Basil and the future Emperor Julian were studying. When about 30, Gregory returned to Nazianzus but soon joined Basil at the Iris River to live the life of a hermit. After two years there, Gregory returned home to assist his father who was now over eighty years of age. He was ordained, most unwillingly, in 362 by his father, and was made bishop of Sasima in 372. The See was in Arian territory, was rent with civil strife and had been created by Basil. Gregory was consecrated as Bishop, but never went to Sasima, much to the Basil's dismay. When Gregory's father died in 374,

Gregory continued with the See until a new bishop was named. He suffered a breakdown in 375 and spent the next five years in recovery.

On the death of Valens and the subsequent drop in persecutions against the orthodox clergy, a group of bishops invited Gregory to Constantinople to help revitalize the Church in the East by restoring orthodoxy to this Arian-dominated city. There his eloquent preaching at the Church of Anastasia [a house he had converted to a church] brought floods of converts and torrents of abuse from the Arians and the Apollinarists. In 380, the newly-baptized Emperor, Theodosius, decreed that his subjects must be orthodox and that the Arians must submit or leave. They left. Theodosius named Gregory archbishop of Constantinople. A few months later controversy started anew, and the validity of his election was questioned at the Second Ecumenical Council in 381 at which he presided. He resigned in hopes of getting peace since orthodoxy had been restored in Constantinople. He retired to Nazianzus and lived a quiet life of austerity until his death.

He is a Doctor of the Church and is often called "the Theologian" for his eloquent defense of orthodoxy against Arianism and his celebrated sermons on the Trinity. This series was entitled *Five Theological Orations,* and was delivered at the Church of Anastasia in Constantinople.

GREGORY OF NYSSA [330-395] Another of the "Cappadocian Fathers" and compatriot of Gregory of Nazianzus.

Biography Gregory of Nyssa was born at Caesarea, Cappadocia, another of the sons of St. Basil and St. Emmelia. He was raised by his brother, St. Basil, and his sister Macrina who unfortunately, never became a Saint. That must have disappointed the family greatly.

Gregory was well educated, became a rhetorician, and married Theosebeia. He became a professor of rhetoric and, depressed by his students, was turned to the religious life by Gregory of Nazianzus. He was ordained a priest, and may have lived a hermit's life in Pontus for the first years of his priesthood. At the suggestion of his brother Basil, Bishop of Caesarea, Gregory was named bishop of Nyssa, Lower Armenia in 372.

When Gregory became bishop, he found his See infested with Arianism. He was attacked by the Arian governor of Pontus, Demosthenes, who accused him of stealing church property. He was imprisoned. He escaped, but was deposed by a synod of Galatian and Pontic bishops in 376. He remained in exile for two years when Emperor Gratian restored him to his See. In 379 he attended the Council of Antioch which denounced the Meletian heresy. He was sent from that council to Palestine and Arabia to combat heresy there. He was active at the Second Ecumenical Council in 381, which attacked Arianism and reaffirmed the decrees of the Council of Nicaea. By this time he was venerated as a great opponent of Arianism.

Gregory was influenced by the writings of Origen and Plato. As a consequence, he wrote numerous theological treatises, many of which were considered to be the true exposition of the Catholic faith. Among these treatises were his *Catechetical Discourse, Against Eunimius* and *Against Apollinaris*, a book on virginity, and numerous commentaries on Scripture. Like many others, he is included on this list of people because of his defense of the orthodox beliefs against Arianism. It is interesting to note that in the history of the Church, Gregory is always considered to be highly orthodox despite his constant defense of and belief in Origen.

-H-

HIPPOLYTUS [Died Ca. 235] Third century Roman theologian who, in writing *The Apostolic Tradition,* presented the Church with a powerful argument that in addition to Scripture, the traditions of the Church could be the basis for Christian doctrines and dogmas.

Biography Neither the date nor the place of his birth is recorded, but it is believed that Hippolytus died in about 235 CE. If this date is about correct, then it can be said that Hippolytus was born at least 100 years after the last Apostle was in Rome. There were, therefore, several generations which separated Hippolytus from direct contact with any Apostle.

Hippolytus was a priest in Rome who was noted for his learning as well as for his theological writings. He was also somewhat of a maverick in that: [1] he denounced Pope Zephrinus for being too lenient in his activities against Modalism and Sabellianism; and [2] when Pope Callistus II was elected in 217, Hippolytus allowed himself to be elected antipope by his small band of followers. He did this because he felt that the Church was the society of the redeemed in which serious sins could not be tolerated; whereas Callistus believed that the aim of the Church was to bring sinners to salvation and to do this, you could not forbid them to enter the Church. Later, Hippolytus also opposed Pope Urban and Pontian, who were the successors to Callistus. As a final note, Hippolytus publicly stated that Rome was the Antichrist.

Hippolytus was banished to Sardinia during the persecution of the Christians by Emperor Maximinus in 235 CE. Pope Pontian also was banished. During this banishment, Pope Pontian brought Hippolytus back to the Church. Hippolytus died on Sardinia as a martyr from the sufferings he endured. His most important work was probably *The Apostolic Tradition,* although he also wrote commentaries on Daniel and the

Song of Songs and *A Refutation of all Heresies.*

Hippolytus is included on our short list for three major reasons. First, he is considered to be one of the early major theologians produced by the Church. As a consequence, his writings show what the early Church was thinking. Secondly, his disagreements with the policies of three popes show that all was not harmonious at the topmost levels of the Roman Church during his time. However, at this early period dissension seems to have been accepted without excommunication, a policy which was reversed in later periods. Finally, Hippolytus firmly established the possibility that Church tradition could augment Scripture in defining Church doctrines and dogma. He did this in his book *The Apostolic Tradition* which established that certain traditions such as the liturgy of the sacraments were truly from Christ because they had been handed down to the Church through the Apostolic line, even though they had not been written in the Scriptures. Partially because of this argument, the Apostolic Church could take the stand that it preceded the published Scriptures; and that it therefore not only could decide what constituted Scripture, it also had a significant role in deciding what the non-Scriptural doctrines of the Church would be, either by "accepted tradition" or by "revealed truth." This latter role was countered 1400 years later by the Reformationists who shouted *sola Scriptura,* or "Scripture only" in deciding Church doctrines. However, in the meantime a lot of Church teachings became based on "accepted tradition" rather than Scripture; and few of these were ever overturned by the Protestants. It was the men of the Church who decided what "acceptable tradition" or "revealed truth" was.

-I-

IGNATIUS [Died Ca. 110] Early Bishop of Antioch in Asia Minor who died a martyr in Rome. Wrote seven highly regarded letters which were later used as a basis for much of the dogma of the Christian Church.

Biography Ignatius of Antioch was also known as Ignatius Theophoros which in Greek means "God Bearer." Little is known of his life except that he was Bishop of Antioch at the time of his arrest and extradition to Rome where he was condemned to the wild beasts. This was during the reign of Trajan [98-117 CE]. It is not known whether he was a native of Antioch, but his writings have a certain oriental influence characteristic of that region. Church tradition states that Ignatius had known the Apostle John; and it is documented by several sources that he was a personal friend of Polycarp. The death of Ignatius in the Roman arena was recorded by Polycarp's disciple Irenaeus, almost 100 years after the fact.

Ignatius is known from his writings, particularly from the seven highly regarded letters he wrote during his journey to Rome. These letters establish several important points for the early Church. First, they abound in warnings against false doctrines and false teachers. In particular, Ignatius wrote against the teachings of the Judaizers who did not accept the authority of the New Testament and who kept the Jewish observance of the Sabbath; and against the teachings of the Docetists [see "Gnosticism"] who held that Christ's sufferings and death did not really happen, but were illusions which only seemed to happen. To Ignatius, Christ was truly human and he truly suffered. Further, Ignatius felt that the historical fact of the Resurrection was important as a guarantee of our "life everlasting" within the Risen Christ.

Because of his strong stand that Jesus was a man as well as a God, Ignatius established the basis for many doctrines and dogma which were accepted by the Church during the 500 years after his death. As an additional point from his letters, Ignatius supports the authority of the bishops as the unique focus of unity without which there would be no sacraments and no Church. By so doing, he helped to establish the vital position of the college of bishops. Finally, his Letter to the Ephesians lends support to Paul's short and very personal Letter to Philemon by indicating that the former slave of Philemon, Onesimus, became not only a successful Christian, but possibly Bishop of Ephesus. Thus, the Letter of Ignatius may have influenced the selection of Paul's Letter to the canon of the New Testament.

The original letters written by Ignatius during his trip to Rome were collected by Polycarp and sent to the Church at Philippi. From there, they became available to the men of the Church during the formative debates on Church dogma. During the fourth to the sixth century, many letters were forged in the name of Ignatius in order to make debate points; and some of the original Letters of Ignatius had several paragraphs added to them for the same purpose. During the thirteenth century, attempts were made to restore the letters to their original content [i.e. unadulterated by additions made during the fourth-sixth centuries]. During the Protestant Reformation, much was made of the belief that the Church at Rome had adulterated Ignatius' Letters in order to bolster the authority of the Church.

Ignatius is included in the short list of people of this period for four reasons: [1] his strong statements that the faith must be defended against false teachings gave credence to those who later did just that; [2] his strong belief in the humanity of Jesus the Christ established the basis for many doctrines and dogmas which were debated during the first five Ecumenical Councils; [3] his writings on the importance of the bishops later generated the thought of establishing the college of bishops as a successor to the college of the Apostles; and [4] his strong desire for martyrdom was based on his belief that such an example would link him into a union with the Christ, and this belief was used by many who followed him into their martyrdom. Because of all of this, Ignatius was a pioneer not only in developing the government of the Church, but also in developing many of the attitudes displayed by the Church Fathers and leaders who came after him.

IRENAEUS [Ca. 125-203] Early Bishop of Lyons in southern France. Pushed hard for uniformity in scriptural interpretation and in central Church policies. Fought many heresies.

Biography Irenaeus of Lyons was born in Asia Minor, probably at Smyrna. He was raised in a prosperous environment which allowed him to be well-educated. He was influenced by men who were thought to know the Apostles, especially Polycarp, who was said to have been a pupil of John the Evangelist. According to Gregory of Tours, Polycarp sent Irenaeus as a missionary to Gaul where he was a priest under Pothinus at Lyons. At this time, Lyons was a major city of at least 200,000 people and second only to Rome among the cities of Europe. Because of this "transfer," Irenaeus is identified with a parish in Europe rather than one in Asia Minor.

In 177 CE, Irenaeus went from Lyons to Rome with a letter pleading for the pope to grant leniency to the Montanists in Phrygia, a district of ancient Turkey. Because of acts such as this, Irenaeus became known as a peacemaker among the Churches of Asia Minor. This peacemaking activity was needed because Asia Minor had been torn apart by accusations of heresy and by people leaving the Church to join other sects.

When Irenaeus was absent from Lyons, a violent persecution of Christians broke out claiming Pothinus as one of its martyrs. Consequently, when Irenaeus returned to Lyons in 178, he returned as bishop. He was active in evangelizing the area around Lyons and was the fierce opponent of Gnosticism in Gaul which he refuted in a five-book treatise, *Adversus omnes haereses.* In this book he refuted all heretics. This refutation was to continue as the active policy of the Church for many years. In this book, he also stated that the only way to prevent Christianity from disintegrating into a thousand sects was for all Christians to accept humbly one doctrinal authority which was the Episcopal councils of the Church. This admonition also became the policy for the Church and prevented sectarianism until the time of the Reformation, almost 1400 years later.

Because of this stand against having the Church splinter into many differing sects, Irenaeus worked to bring repentant sects back into the fold.

In 190 CE, he was successful in reconciling the Quartodecimans who had been excommunicated by Pope Victor III for refusing to celebrate Easter on the date of Western usage adopted by Rome. In many other instances, he worked to reconcile sects, some of which had been branded as heretics. He was sometimes successful; but when he was not, he would condemn the unbelievers with his full capabilities.

Irenaeus was the first great Catholic theologian. He led an unusual life which bridged the early years and the early geography of the Church. Tradition says that the Apostle John lived in Ephesus as an old man. There he trained St. Polycarp who subsequently trained Irenaeus. As a consequence, Irenaeus is only three generations removed from Jesus of Nazareth; and yet he fought against many heretics. It is interesting to realize that so many sects which differed from orthodoxy were being established this short a time after the birth of the Church. In addition, because of the location of his birth, Irenaeus was instrumental in establishing close ties between the Christians of Asia Minor and the Christians of Southern France.

Finally, his writings had great impact on the early Church. His treatise against the Gnostics is witness to the validity of the Old Testament and to the sacredness of the Apostolic Tradition. In addition, this treatise is a testimony to the primacy of the pope, even though it was written at a very early date in the history of the papacy. Finally, the writings of Irenaeus are also known for presenting a strong centrist policy, despite his early training by Polycarp who believed in the decentralization of the Church. Irenaeus came to this change of direction because of the variety of Scriptural interpretations which had become widespread during the time he lived. Irenaeus was made a Saint in the very early canonization proceedings of the Church.

-J-

JEROME [342-420] Fourth century theologian whose greatest achievement [among many] was the development of the Vulgate Bible.

Biography Jerome was born at Strido, near Aquileia, Dalmatia [presently southern France]. His full name was Eusebius Hieronymus Sophronius. He studied at Rome under Danatus, the famous grammarian where he acquired great skill and knowledge of Latin and Greek. It has been said that he almost became addicted to grammar, rhetoric and the great classical authors and became such a master of these skills that he is considered to be the greatest scholar which the early Western Church produced.

In 360, he was baptized by Pope Liberius at Rome. After further study at Treves and travel in Gaul, Jerome became an ascetic at Aquileia in 370, joining a group of scholars under Bishop Valerian, among whom was

Rufinus. When a quarrel broke up the group, Jerome traveled in the East. He settled in Antioch where he had a vision of Christ which caused him to go to Chalcis in the Syrian desert. There he lived as a hermit for four years, praying, fasting, learning Hebrew, and writing the life of St. Paul of Thebes. On Jerome's return to Antioch, he was ordained by Paulinus and entered into the Meletian controversy, supporting Paulinus and denouncing the schism in his treatise, *Altercatio luciferiani et orthodoxi.*

Jerome went to Constantinople to study Scripture under Gregory of Nazianzus, and in 382 went to Rome where he remained as secretary to Pope Damasus. While there, at the suggestion of Damasus, he revised the Latin version of the four gospels, St. Paul's Epistles and the Psalms. He also wrote *Adversum Helvidium,* denouncing a book by Helvidius declaring that Mary had several children besides Jesus. In Rome, Jerome encouraged a group of noble ladies to study Scripture. He also lectured to them on the virtue of celibacy, a belief which he emphasized in his treatise *The Perpetual Virginity of the Blessed Mary.* This belief, plus his fierce attacks on the life-styles of influential Romans, made him a number of enemies.

In 384, Damasus, his protector and patron, died. Jerome's enemies and the vicious rumors that were circulating about him [including a scandalous rumor concerning his relations with Paula] made him decide to return to the East. He visited Antioch where Paula, Eustochium and others of the Roman group joined him. They visited Egypt and Palestine. In 386 they all settled at Bethlehem where Paula built three convents for women and a monastery for men which Jerome headed. Most of his time was devoted to his translation of the Bible into Latin from the original languages. This chore had been suggested to him by Pope Damasus. However, he also found time to become involved in numerous controversies. In 393 he wrote *Adversus Jovianianum* to refute another belief that Mary had children besides Jesus. Further, Jerome's *Contra Vigilantium* denounced Vigilantius' condemnation of celibacy. But Jerome's most bitter controversy was with Rufinus, his old friend from Aquileia who supported Origen and translated many of Origen's works into Latin. This occurred when Jerome attacked Origenism in *Apologetici adversus Rufinum* in 395 CE. Soon after, he even attacked Augustine who had questioned Jerome's analysis of the second chapter of Paul's Epistle to the Romans.

Jerome's greatest achievement was his translation of the Old Testament from Hebrew and his revision of the Latin version of the New Testament in 390-405, a feat of scholarship unequaled in the early Church. This version, called the Vulgate Bible [see page 33], was declared the official Latin text of the Bible for Catholics by the Council of Trent [1545-

1563]; and it was from it that almost all English Catholic translations were made until the middle of the 20th century, when scholars began to use original sources. It remained the official Latin text of the Bible for the Catholic Church until Pope John Paul II replaced it with the New Vulgate in 1979, almost 1600 years after Jerome's original work.

From 405 until his death in 420, he produced a series of notable biblical commentaries. In 415 his denunciation of Pelagianism in *Dialogi contra Pelagianos* caused a new furor; and a year later, groups of armed Pelagian monks burned the monasteries at Bethlehem. Although Jerome escaped unharmed, he was left poverty-stricken. He died in Bethlehem after a lingering illness on September 30.

In addition to the works mentioned above, Jerome corresponded widely. Some 120 of his letters of historical importance are still in existence. He also compiled a bibliography of ecclesiastical writers, *De viris illustribus*, and he translated and continued Eusebius' *Chronicle*. Jerome is venerated as a Doctor of the Church. It is obvious that if he had done nothing but create the universally used Vulgate Bible, he would be on any short list of great persons. He is included here not only because of these great feats, but also because his schizophrenia about Origen mirrors the schizophrenia of a Church which supposedly made only unanimous decisions.

JOHN CHRYSOSTOM [347-407] Fourth century preacher of Antioch who was so gifted he was designated "Chrysostom" which means "Golden-mouthed." Was known to hate Jews.

Biography John Chrysostom was born at Antioch, Syria. He was the son of an imperial military officer. He studied rhetoric under the famous rhetorician Diodorus of Tarsus, leader of the Antiochene School. John was baptized by bishop Meletius in about 369. Five years later, he became a hermit under Basil, but later came home to Antioch when that life undermined his health. He became a deacon in 381, and was ordained in 386 by bishop Flavian of Antioch whom he served for twelve years.

John became famed for his preaching which had a tremendous effect on the spiritual life of Antioch. Beginning in 390, he preached a series of sermons on the New Testament, including eighty eight sermons on John, ninety on Matthew and thirty two on Romans. This voluminous work made him one of the great expositors of the Christian faith. However, in his preaching John Chrysostom is also reported to have said, "I hate the Jews. God hates the Jews and always did" [see De Rosa, page 157]. This was a politically motivated statement in its day. Although Jesus the Christ might not have presented such a thought in his teachings, thoughts such as this are somewhat typical of the Christian attitude four centuries later.

In 398, John was named Patriarch of Constantinople against his personal wishes. He began to reform the church there. He made large donations to the poor, abolished ecclesiastical pomp and luxury, opposed idolatry and immoral entertainment and in general created a conflict with all who had been in power before him. Among his enemies thus created were; [1] Empress Eudoxia who resented his criticism of her vanity, lack of charity and enticing dress; [2] Gainas who was commander-in-chief of the military, leader of the Arians and who had a profitable business going on within the churches; [3] the churchmen whose extravagant life-style he restricted; and [4] Theophilus of Alexandria who wanted to be patriarch of Constantinople in place of John.

In 403, Theophilus and some 36 hostile bishops condemned John at the Synod of the Oak. The condemnation included twenty nine charges, among which were a belief in Origenism and an attack on the Empress in a sermon in which he criticized the luxury of women. These bishops wanted him deposed and exiled. The Empress agreed. Civil war was about to break out when an earthquake hit the city. The Empress rescinded the banishment order. Later, when John denounced the excesses of some games which celebrated the erection of a silver statue to her, she renewed her enmity.

In 404, Emperor Arcadius ordered John into exile at Cuscusus, Armenia. This happened despite the support which John had from the people of Constantinople, from Pope Innocent I and from the whole Western Church. From Cuscusus, John wrote some 238 letters that are still extant. When the Western Church tried to have John reestablished in his See, the followers of Theophilus imprisoned the bishops who were sent, and then sent John even further away to Pityus at the far end of the Black Sea. In late 407, John died from the long forced marches on foot in the stifling heat.

John Chrysostom was declared a Doctor of the Universal Church at the Fourth Ecumenical Council in 451 CE and was named patron of preachers by Pope Pius X. He is included in this list of people because his conflicts give an indication of the attitudes prevalent within the Eastern Church at that time, tell us something about the State-Church relationship in the East and also give an early indication of Christianity's attitude toward the Jews. Later, this attitude was strongly echoed by Martin Luther.

JUSTIN MARTYR [Died Ca. 165] Early preacher and writer who was martyred in Rome. Was instrumental in tying Christian thought into Greek philosophy.

Biography Justin Martyr had neither his birth date nor death date recorded by history, but he is known as one of the more important of the Greek philosopher-Apologists of the early Church. His writings tie together Christian revelation with Greek philosophy in a very positive way. By doing this, he laid the basis for the historical development of Christian theology.

Justin was reared in a Jewish environment. He was converted to Christianity, possibly at Ephesus. Afterwards, he went to Rome and preached the new religion there. He was denounced to the Roman authorities and was condemned to death. He was made a Saint by the Church's very early canonization proceedings. Other than this, almost nothing is known of his life.

Instead, as with many others of this period, most of what is known about Justin is based on his writings. He was among the first writers to paraphrase from the Acts of the Apostles; and in his writings he refers to each of the first three gospels and to the letters of Paul and Peter. In addition, his writings defend the liturgical sacraments of Baptism and the Eucharist as having extremely deep and profound meanings and therefore not being mere rituals such as the pagans previously had used. Finally, he writes strongly on the need for the Roman state to become Christian and to abandon its various mystical cults. An example of this is found in his *First Apology* in which he asks the emperor to punish those who do not follow Christian teachings. Such writing would obviously anger pagan Roman emperors. Based on the trouble he had with all the Roman authorities, he not only angered them with his writing, he also angered them when he spoke out.

Justin is included on this short list because he is one of the earliest Christians whose identified writings have survived in great amounts. He thus gives us a very early look at the primitive church, even before it could logically be called a Church. In addition, his writings are the first to propose a divine historical plan in which the Old Testament meets with Greek philosophy to form the single stream of Christianity. Furthermore, because so much of his writings have survived, he is often credited with starting the theological tradition of the Church. And finally, he is the first whose writings on Apologetics [i.e. the defense of Christianity] have survived. They show that Apologetics was actively practiced during the early second century. When his writings are taken in context with others such as those of Origen and Tertullian, it shows that Apologetics was being practiced not only in the East, but also in the West.

JUSTINIAN [Ca. 482-565] Sixth century Byzantine Emperor who single-handedly conducted the Fifth Ecumenical Council.

Biography Justinian was born of lowly Illyrian, possibly Slavic, parents near the city now called Sofia in present-day Bulgaria. His uncle, a military commander in Constantinople named Justin, adopted him and brought him to Constantinople where he got a good education and became a distinguished officer in the Byzantine army. When Justin usurped the throne in 518, he left the running of the Empire mainly to his brilliant nephew who then succeeded him as Emperor in 527. When Justinian died at the age of 83 years, he had been Emperor for 38 years.

Justinian found the Empire of the East in great shape, even though the Roman Empire in the West was falling into chaos. During the 130 years preceding Justinian, a series of obscure but effective Emperors had kept the Eastern Empire safe and had built many public works while still building a significant treasury. The only discord in the Empire was the theological problem of the nature of Christ; for many in the East, including many Emperors, were confirmed Monophysites who accepted only the divine nature of the Christ. There were also many Monophysites who were close to Justinian. Chief among these was his wife, Theodora, who was reputed to be one of the most beautiful women in the world. She was also reputed to have had a very unsavory life prior to marriage, but that did not seem to bother Justinian who greatly trusted her judgment and relied on her thoughts.

Justinian is one of the most controversial rulers of recorded history. Because of his lowly birth and the insecure method in which he acquired the throne, he was both demanding of his people but accessible to them; willing to make big and bold decisions but often swayed by his friends and especially by his wife; considered his person to be *sacred* as did most of the Eastern Emperors who were considered to be the "living image of Christ," but almost left this sacredness by abdicating the throne during his early troubles; wanted to be known as a poet, musician, author, lawyer and theologian but often practiced the Byzantine traits of assassination and robbery; loved and honored his favorite general, Belisarius, but feared and resented him as well; etc. Finally, Justinian fought many wars which included the re-conquest of Italy and the conquest of Carthaginian Africa. However, these wars bankrupted the nation while gaining nothing of permanence. He is not noted by history for these wars, but he is noted for the two major "accomplishments" achieved by his administration. These accomplishments are legal and theological.

The legal part refers to the Code of Justinian through which some major tenets of Roman law were retained during the Dark Ages and were made available for later use. The Code of Justinian had many detractions, especially in its intolerance; however, it was a Code which presented a unifying thread of law throughout a major part of the civilized world during a time when the "law" of many nations was determined by the whim of its leader. In other words, the Code of Justinian promoted uniformity.

This unifying thread was also applied to the theological "accomplishments" of Justinian. Justinian very much wanted a uniform Church; for in having such a uniform thread of faith throughout the Empire, Justinian felt that the Empire itself would be unified. In order to accomplish this, Justinian not only built the Great Church [as Hagia Sophia was called], he constantly tried to live a pious and fasting life within the palace, often acting more like a monk than a king. In his many attempts at establishing theological unity, Justinian supported the viewpoint of the papacy in conflicts with the patriarch while supporting the patriarch in his conflicts with Monophystism, a "heresy" which had so divided the East that many parts were lost to orthodox Christianity almost a century before the Moslems came. But after all these efforts to create unity, Justinian actually created disunity by acts such as forcing Pope Vigilius to subscribe to Justinian's theological viewpoint about the Three Chapters Controversy, and by insisting that Pelagius be elected Pope to replace Pope Vigilius. Never before had an Emperor made such an attempt to dominate the papacy.

Justinian's ultimate insult to the Church was the Fifth Ecumenical Council which he completely controlled [see pages 69-72 and Appendix C]. This Council so acceded to Justinian's formulas that the West did not immediately accept many of the decisions. Later, Pope Pelagius I attempted to force the Western Church to accept the decisions made at the Council. He did this in an attempt to reconcile a Church which had been once more separated by the decisions of Justinian and by the controversies generated in an Ecumenical Council. However, a report in the *Catholic Encyclopedia* states that the Roman Pope accepted only the "Three Chapters" decision of the fifth Council and never officially accepted any of the others such as the condemnation of Origen and the establishment of the numerous anathemas. A later report in the *New Catholic Encyclopedia* states that along with the "Three Chapters" decision, the Fifth Ecumenical Council did condemn the Christology theories of Origen's followers and in so doing condemned the same thoughts of Origen. Today, it is reported that many priests of the Roman Catholic Church teach that none of the decisions of the confusing Fifth Ecumenical Council represent a statement of faith to the modern Catholic.

Justinian is included in the short list of people in this Chapter solely because of his ecclesiastical activities, some of which were later branded heretical by the Church, particularly his belief in the incorruptibility of the physical body of Jesus the Christ [see pages 320-1]. But it is his impact on the Fifth Ecumenical Council which in itself would require his being included. An general examination of this Council is presented on pages 69-72, and a detailed examination is presented in Appendix C.

-L-

LEO I [Died in 461] Fifth century Pope whose activities strengthened the papacy and set the stage for the activities of Pope Gregory. Also called "the Great."

Biography Pope Leo I the Great is thought to have been born in Rome, possibly of Tuscan parents. He served as deacon under Popes Celestine I and Sixtus III, acted as peacemaker between Aetius and Albinus, the imperial generals whose quarrels were leaving Gaul open to attacks by barbarians, and was elected Pope to succeed Sixtus III. He was consecrated on September 29, 440 and at once began his pastoral duties with a series of ninety six sermons on faith and charity, most of which are still in existence. In addition, he supported strenuous opposition to Manichaeism, Pelagianism, Priscillianism, and Nestorianism.

In 448, Leo I was faced with the Eutychian problem [see "Eutychianism"]. Eutyches had been deposed as abbot by Patriarch Flavian of Constantinople for denying the two natures of Christ. Supported by Emperor Theodosius II, Eutyches appealed to Leo for reinstatement. The Emperor summoned a packed council at Ephesus in 449 [the notorious Robber Synod], which acquitted Eutyches and at which Flavian was physically attacked and mortally wounded. This Synod also refused to allow papal legates to read a letter from Leo; and further declared Flavian deposed.

In 451, Leo requested that a general council be called at Chalcedon. At this council, later designated the Fourth Ecumenical Council, Leo's letter of two years earlier was read. This letter clarified the doctrine of the Incarnation and vindicated Flavian. It excommunicated and deposed Dioscorus, Eutyches' friend, who had been designated patriarch of Constantinople in place of Flavian by Theodosius. This letter was Leo's famous *Tome*. It was received with great acclamation.

In 452, Attila and his Huns invaded Italy and were about to attack defenseless Rome when Attila was dissuaded by Leo at Peschiera. Three years later, Leo was not so successful with the Vandal Gaiseric, who plundered Rome. Leo ministered to the stricken populace and worked to rebuild the city and the churches. He sent missionaries to Africa to minister to the captives Gaiseric took there with him. Leo died in Rome in 461.

Leo is included in this short list of people because he advanced the influence of the papacy to what was then an unprecedented height. He did this not only by his authoritative approach to events, but also by his firm belief that the Holy See in Rome was the supreme authority in human affairs. He believed this not only because of divine and scriptural mandate, but also because he insisted that the pope was the heir of Peter who was the prime Apostle. In a time of great disorder, he was a strong man who promised stability, authority, action and wisdom. As a consequence, his pontificate was to affect the concept of the papacy for centuries to come. He was declared a Doctor of the Church in 1754.

-M-

MANI [Died Ca. 275] Third century Persian prophet known as the "Apostle of the Light," or the "Supreme Illuminator." Founded the new religion of Manichaeism.

Biography Mani was born in southern Babylon [presently Iraq] in about 216 CE. He had his "annunciation" at age twenty-four when he was told to manifest himself publicly and to create a new religion. From then on he preached throughout the Persian Empire.

Mani viewed himself as the last in a line of prophets beginning with Adam and including Zoroaster, Buddha and Jesus. He felt that earlier revelations by prophets had been limited because they were local and were taught only in one language and to one people. In addition, he felt that the followers of these earlier revelations had lost sight of the original truth which the revelations had presented. Mani felt that his was a universal religion to replace all others. He wrote all his teachings and canonized them within his lifetime to overcome the problems of having the followers distort his teachings, an event which has seemed to happen to all religions, particularly Christianity and Islam.

Mani was initially unopposed, but later the king, Bahram I, opposed him. He was imprisoned. After twenty-six days of trials which his followers called the "Passion of the Illuminator" or "Mani's Crucifixion," he delivered his final message and died as a martyr sometime about 275.

MANICHAEISM A third century religion which followed Mani, the "Illuminated One." Was a universal Gnostic religion which tied together elements of many religions.

Description Manichaeism was a dualistic religion which had a special impact on Christian thought. It was established in Persia in the 3rd century by the prophet, Mani. Although often classified as a Christian heresy, it was really a completely independent religion in its own right. It embodied Judeo-Christian thoughts, but it also involved Buddhist and Zoroaster elements. It claimed to be the only universal religion, and it claimed to express the complete revelation which prophets prior to Mani had only communicated in fragments.

Manichaeism was very missionary in its attempt to convert the world. It rapidly spread into and through the Roman Empire, including North Africa where a young Augustine became a convert. It reached its missionary peak during the fourth century when it had churches in Gaul and Spain. Both the state and the Church, led by an older Augustine and an active Leo I, attacked it vigorously. It disappeared from the Roman Empire by the end of the sixth century, but continued in Persia until the tenth century when Muslim persecutions forced the transfer of the Manichaeism leadership to Samarkand. Manichaeism reached China in 694 and was given freedom of religion by imperial edict in 732. In 843 it was abolished in China, but continued underground until the fourteenth century. In East Turkistan it continued until the Mongol invasion in the thirteenth century. Teachings similar to Manichaeism showed up in Europe in the Middle Ages. Teachings such as that generated by Mani were presented by groups such as the Paulicians in Armenia in the seventh century, the Bogomilists in Bulgaria in the tenth century, and the Cathars [see pages 101-105] in southern France in the twelfth century.

Mani sought to found a truly ecumenical and universal religion which would integrate into itself all of the partial truths of previous religions, particularly those of Zoroaster, Buddha and Jesus. It also tried to develop truths which would fit into all the cultures it might meet wherever it went in the world. Because of this, Manichaeism could resemble Persian religions, or Indian religions, or Christianity, Buddhism or Taoism, depending on where it was presented. At its core, Manichaeism was a type of Gnosticism in that it offered salvation through special knowledge of spiritual truth. Like all forms of Gnosticism, Manichaeism taught that life in this world is unbearably painful and radically evil. It taught that as he exists, man is tragically involved in the material order and is, therefore, fallen and lost. However, it taught that man is actually an article of Light, belonging to the transcendent world, although he has been exiled from it. It taught that man is of the same essence as God, and human souls are fragments of the divine substance. Because of this, man's salvation lies in grasping this truth by an interior illumination which may be spontaneous, but usually comes by means of the spirit of intelligence [*Nous*] or knowledge. This knowledge is the only way to salvation; and in the process of salvation, paradoxically, God is at once redeemer and redeemed. This is a deep, but profoundly intriguing, philosophical thought.

The story of the religion as visualized by Mani was that there were three stages: [1] the past period during which Spirit and Matter, Good and Evil, Light and Darkness have split apart; [2] the present period in which these two radically opposite substances mix together with each other; and [3] the future period in which the original duality will be reestablished. At death, the soul of the righteous person [the *Elect*] proceeds to Paradise. The soul of the person who has persisted in the way of the flesh with fornication, procreation, possessions, eating of meat, and the drinking of wine is condemned to rebirth in a series of bodies. Consequently, the all-important thing was to withdraw oneself from the contamination of the material flesh which was fundamentally evil.

As is readily apparent from the above, Manichaeism believed in reincarnation. The *Elect*, or Liberators of Light, went directly to join the Paradise of Light after death; whereas the Auditors [or Catechumens], the more numerous and less highly evolved people, entered into transmigration as a means of liberation and purification. These entities would return in the luminous bodies of fruits, especially melons, and would thus enter into the body of an *Elect* and become liberated. The *Elect* always ate a ritual meal every day during which they would bless the food and chant over it. This meal consisted solely of luminous foods [i.e. those which had light particles within them which needed to be liberated] such as fruits and especially melons. The *Elect* completely avoided dark foods such as wine and meat, did not destroy plants or animals, and were celibate.

With the possible exception of the daily ritual for the *Elect*, the Manichaens appear to have had no sacraments since salvation came through knowledge and virtue alone. The basics of their worship consisted of praying, singing hymns and confession. Fasting and alms-giving were also important elements of their communal life. The canon generated by Manichaeism includes seven works, all written by Mani and all originally written in Syriac. These were lost in the Middle Ages, but partially rediscovered in the twentieth century, mainly in Chinese Turkistan and in Egypt.

The above presents the teachings of Manichaeism. Add to these teachings a highly organized church with its graded hierarchy of adherents ["auditors," "elect," "priests," "bishops," "apostles" and "masters"] and its corresponding degrees of asceticism, and you will have a picture of the religion which swept over Europe, Africa and Asia and won such notable adherents as the young Augustine. In this missionary effort, Manichaeism was stern competition for Christianity, for it fought for men's souls with comparable vigor. However, it fought only for souls and in this way neglected to cooperate with the government. By the time Manichaeism had become successful, Christianity and the Empire were working together. When Church and State decided to go after Manichaeism together, it was only a matter of time before the souls of men were won to Christianity rather than to Manichaeism; for Christianity promised not only a paradise after death, it promised a lack of conflict with the State in the meantime.

MARCION [Ca. 120-170] A wealthy Christian of the second century who believed so strongly in the love and compassion preached by Jesus Christ that he could not accept the harsh, judgmental God of Judaism. He therefore taught that the Old Testament had no relevance to a Christian. The Church declared him a heretic. In establishing a canon for Marcionism, he spurred the Christian Church to start developing a canon of its own. Further information on Marcion is presented on pages 53-4.

MELETIAN CONTROVERSY [Ca. 380-400] A controversy which originated over which individual should become Bishop of Antioch. It split the Church until decided by Pope Siricius, one of the pope's first decisions over local matters in the Eastern Church.

Description The Meletian controversy was a complex schism presently considered to be a rather minor event in the history of the Church. It is presented in this Appendix because it represents the first major attempt to have the Bishop of Rome exercise direct authority over the Eastern Church in order to solve a dispute between the Eastern and Western branches.

At the Second Ecumenical Council in 381 CE, it was declared that the Bishop of Constantinople was second only to the Bishop of Rome. The real reason for this declaration was that Constantinople wanted to outrank Alexandria in the East, and to do this, the Eastern Church needed support from the Western Church even though no Western bishops attended the Council. The declaration was made, but it presented a rather unforeseen result in that the Western Church then started to make decisions on matters of a purely Eastern interest such as those of local organization and local elections. Because of this, the Fourth Ecumenical Council in 451, which again was primarily attended by Eastern bishops, reversed this declaration and declared that Rome and Constantinople had equal rights.

The pope who first started to decide things in the East based on the declaration at the Second Ecumenical Council was Pope Siricius who was pope from 384-399 and was later made a Saint of the Church. After much prodding, he sent instructions to the Council of Caesarea [393] that Flavian I was to be accepted as the legitimate bishop of Antioch instead of Evagius.

In this manner, the pope settled the Meletian Controversy which had persisted through two generations of bishops in Antioch; but he also extended his authority to discipline clerics into the East as well as Spain, Gaul and Italy. In this spirit, he sent out the first letter dictating that priests in the East should be celibate and dictating how the sacraments were to be done. He not only felt he had the right to intercede in the affairs of the Eastern church, he also felt he had the authority to include sanctions against those who did not obey him.

Although history has tended to let his great contemporary, Ambrose of Milan, overshadow Siricius, there is no question that Siricius was the one who greatly advanced the authority of the pope to legislate the day-to-day activities of all within the Church and to discipline those who did not obey him. In this manner, the power of the Church over all Christendom was greatly enhanced. Also, in this manner Pope Siricius pioneered the path later followed with great success by both Pope Leo I the Great, and by Pope Gregory I the Great, each of whom exercised great papal power. The Meletian Controversy in of interest because its settlement represents one of the earliest examples of papal power. It is also of interest because in generating this papal power, this Controversy contributed to the great schism between the Eastern and the Western branches of the Church [see pages 73-78].

MITHRAISM and SOL INVICTUS [Ca. 300] Mithraism was an ancient religion of Persia, established in about 800 BCE, which was popular in Rome in the fourth century CE. Roman Christianity borrowed many traditions from Mithraism. Sol Invictus ["Unconquered Sun"] was a similar religion, but established much later in Rome.

Description Although Mithraism was established much earlier than the time period covered in this work, it is included here because it had become very popular in Rome by about 300 CE. Mithraism was the worship of the Iranian God of the Sun in pre-Zoroastrian Iran. Another cult which was popular at this time in Rome was Sol Invictus, a religion also based on the Iranian God of the Sun. These distinct, but similar, religions represented an impediment to the growing power of Christianity in the time period shortly after the Edict of Milan.

When Christianity was recommended to Rome by Constantine, the Sun God represented the God of loyalty to the Emperor. After the declaration of Christianity as the preferred religion for a good Roman citizen by Theodosius I in about 380, worship of the Sun God rapidly declined as people accepted Christianity for their demonstration of loyalty to the Emperor. This decline was helped along by the early Roman Christians who accepted several Sun God practices into Christianity.

Some of the Sun God activities which continued within Christianity are:

1. Unlike Judaism but like Christianity, Mithraism and Sol Invictus had Sunday [the "Sun's day"] as their day of rest, i.e. their Sabbath. The change of the Sabbath from that practiced by the early Judeo-Christians was emphasized when Constantine passed legislation making Sunday the day of rest in the Roman Empire in an attempt to win over the followers of Mithraism or Sol Invictus to Christianity. As an added inducement, mosaics were created which showed Jesus as the Sun God, riding in his solar chariot. This made many Romans more comfortable with their new God. This is also a direct transference of pagan practices into Christianity, a possibility which would have been unthinkable to any original Jewish follower of Jesus.

2. By all historical accounts, Jesus Christ was *not* born on December 25, but was born sometime in the early spring [based on "lambing" concepts] or sometime in the fall [based on astronomical concepts]. However, December 25 was a Mithraic and a Sol Invictus holiday which celebrated the Sun's birth or rebirth as evidenced by four consecutive days of seeing the Sun for a longer time each day [i.e. four days after the Winter Solstice]. It therefore became very easy for a Christian celebration of the "Son's birth" to replace the previous celebration of the "Sun's birth."

3. Another thought about why December 25 was chose to celebrate the birth date of Jesus Christ is related to the Roman festival of Saturnalia, a festival which celebrated the coming harvest by rejoicing at the return of the Sun. The festival feast of Saturnalia was held on December 17 and lasted for seven days to end on what is now Christmas Eve. Whatever festival was actually replaced by the Church's desire to celebrate the birth of Jesus, it is a probability of history that it was instituted by Roman officials to entice Roman pagans into Christianity, and that it was a festival which previously had celebrated the Sun's birth, return or impending return.

4. Another Mithraic tradition adapted by the Christians was that of fasting and being penitent for a period of time prior to a major religious event, an activity which the Christians of Rome accepted as their Lent.

5. An additional Mithraic tradition which was adopted by Christians relates to the European custom of depicting the Nativity scene in a cave-like structure. This started with early statements that Christ had been born in a cave. Since early Mithraism had always worshipped in a cave, then the cave had become a very important symbol of the Mithraic belief system; and bringing that symbology into Christianity was very comforting to the early Christian converts in Rome.

6. Finally, there is a point which was given to me by a friend who has done a great deal of study on Sol Invictus. I had missed this point, but have since confirmed it. The point is that the followers of Sol Invictus believed that he was a literal "Son of God who had been born of a Virgin on December 25." I will leave the conclusions to the reader.

And so, although neither Mithraism nor Sol Invictus, nor even the Saturnalia celebration was much of a controversy within the Christian Church, each of them helped to lead to the definition of several Christian activities. They therefore helped to define what the Christian Church of today has become.

MODALISM [Ca. 210] A movement declared heretical by Hippolytus because it stated that if something could not be proved, then it could not be true. Hippolytus believed in the truth of eternal life in Christ even though it could not be proven.

Description Modalism, which appeared in about 210 CE, was another variation of Monarchianism. Although not a major heresy, it was fought by Hippolytus, a major player in establishing that the Church's traditions were as important as Scripture. Hippolytus fought Modalism because it was based on the modal logic of Aristotle. In this logic, propositions such as *possibility* or *necessity* are considered to be opposed to concepts such as *truth* or *falsity*. Thus, in Modalism, possibilities could never be accepted as the truth. An example of Modalistic thought might be "Some humans have immortality." Since this can never be known as absolutely true or absolutely false, it is a possibility and thus must be the opposite of truth in the thinking of the Modalist. Modalism was fought by Hippolytus on the basis that Christianity presents the certainty of an eternal life, even though such a life cannot be proven as either true or false. Reputations were made on such fine points in the early Church.

The major point to be made here is that early Christianity fought against the possibility that doubts of any sort could exist. They did this although several Apostles [e.g. Philip, Peter and Thomas] had expressed doubts even when Jesus walked amongst them. Some Christian Churches still carry this thinking to an extreme today by stating that "to doubt is to deny."

MONARCHIANISM [Ca. 190] A movement which declared that there is only one monarch, God. It spawned many other movements, all of which were declared heretical.

Description Monarchianism is a movement which implies that God is the sole monarch, undiluted by any separate part or "Person." It was deemed to be a Christian heresy. It developed in the second and third centuries and fathered Adoptionism, Modalism and Sabellianism, all Christian heresies. It was an early precursor to Arianism.

Monarchianism opposed the doctrine of an independent, personal substance of the *Logos* [i.e. the "Word" which Christians believe is Jesus Christ]. By affirming the sole deity of God the Father, it represented the extreme monotheistic viewpoint, an activity taken over by Arius in the following century. Though it regarded Christ as the Redeemer, it clung to the numerical unity of the Deity. Two types of Monarchianism developed: the Dynamic [or Adoptionist] and the Modalistic [or Sabellian] type.

Dynamic Monarchianism held that Christ was a mere man who had been miraculously conceived, but who had become the Son of God simply by the infinitely high degree in which he had been filled with divine wisdom and power. He was thus an adopted Son of God. This was taught in Rome at the end of the 2nd century by Theodotus who was excommunicated by Pope Victor. It was later taught by Artemon who was executed by Pope Zephyrinus. In about 260 CE, it was taught by Paul of Samosata. It later became the principle belief of Arianism. It is the present belief of many modern Unitarians.

Modalistic Monarchianism took exception to having two "persons" such as "the Father" and "the Son." They maintained that the terms "Father" and "Son" were merely different names of the same subject, the one God who "with reference to the relations in which He had previously stood to the world is called the Father, but in reference to His appearance in humanity is called the Son." It was taught by Praxeas, a priest from Asia Minor, in Rome about 206 CE and was opposed by Tertullian in *Adversus Praxean*, a tract which is an important contribution by Tertullian to the doctrine of the Trinity.

MONOPHYSITISM [Ca. 450] A movement which taught that Christ had only a divine nature.

Description In Christianity, a Monophysite [or follower of Monophysitism] was one who was accused of teaching that there was only one nature in the person of Jesus Christ. In order to understand why this was declared a heresy by the Church, it might be useful to present an overview on where the debate about the nature and person of Jesus Christ had taken the Church during the 400 years after Paul's first Letters were written.

During these four centuries, the doctrines of the person of Jesus Christ had gone through several divergent traditions. In addition, many different attempts at a systematic definition had been rejected or declared heretical. By the time of the Fourth Ecumenical Council at Chalcedon in 451, it had been decided that Jesus was: [1] divine in the sense that he was equal in all ways to the divinity of God; [2] human in his incarnation in the sense that he was not unlike us in any way; [3] different than God by more than just name; [4] in possession of two natures, not just one and not with one nature merely being an extension of the other; [5] in possession of only one person, not two even though that one person had two natures; [6] and on and on.

With this to work on, and with the insistence on the part of the Imperial court that the Council define Christ once and for all, the Council at Chalcedon adopted a formula usually referred to as the "Definition" of the Council of Chalcedon [see Appendix B]. To satisfy Cyril's desires on the unity of the Christ, this Definition affirmed that Christ was "one and the same Son...complete in his deity and complete...in his humanity"; but to satisfy those who had been winning the recent debates, he was also said to exist in two natures which are at once unconfused and unaltered [against Eutyches] and on the other hand are undivided and inseparable [against Nestorius]. As another way of saying some of this, the decree said that "Christ was acknowledged in two natures without being mixed, transmitted, divided or separated."

The Council proposed this definition only after having been forced to develop something by the Imperial court. The Council really did not want to draft such a definition, and what they drafted shows their reluctance; for the Definition is one which tended to be directed against the definitions of others rather than being a definition which would stand on its own. On the one hand, it was against the Nestorian doctrine that the two natures in Jesus Christ had remained separate and thus were really two Persons; and on the other hand it was against the position of Eutyches who taught that after Incarnation, Jesus Christ had only one nature and that therefore the humanity of the incarnate Christ was not the same as the substance of other men. It is a definition which could not really hold water on its own. If there were nothing to be against, it would constitute an almost meaningless definition. However, it has not been replaced as official Church dogma for over 1500 years.

In addition to this type of work, the Fourth Ecumenical Council addressed numerous political problems within the Church. Political and other reasons led to the Council to excommunicate the patriarch of Alexandria, Dioscorus, and to label the church which had supported him as a Monophysite Church. The label of Monophysite was also placed on several other theologians and groups, some of whom were so labeled because they merely felt that the language of the Definition of Chalcedon was self-contradictory. Most modern theologians tend to think that most of these accused groups diverged from orthodoxy more in their emphasis on the intimacy of the union between God and man as shown in Jesus Christ than in any denial of Christ's humanity; but there were probably groups whose beliefs spread all over the spectrum in regard to the Definition.

In modern times, those churches previously labeled Monophysite such as the Coptic, the Syrian, and the Armenian have been accepted by the Roman Catholic, the Eastern Orthodox and the Protestant Churches as being essentially orthodox in their doctrine of the Person of Jesus Christ. This not only shows that the Definition is a difficult one to accept in modern times, it also shows that the Church can admit to the fact that some of the decrees which came out of the Ecumenical Councils were politically motivated for their day rather than being a universal and eternal "Revealed Truth" from God as was originally proposed. As another example of this "more modern" thinking, most Roman Catholic scholars express doubts that the anathemas issued at the Fifth Ecumenical Council are presently binding on the conscience of their Church members.

But one does not have to come forward to modern times in order to get some sort of feeling about the ambivalence which subjects such as Monophysitism created. In the early days, the principle of Monophysitism was opposed by Honorius I, John of Scythopolis, Justin II, Mellchite, Anastasius Sinaita, Simplicius and other highly regarded people of that day. However, it was supported by Anastasius, Anthimus, Basiliscus, Eutyches, Jacob of Serugh, and other highly regarded people of that day. Because of such a diversity of opinion, it continues to boggle the mind when history records that the votes at the Ecumenical Councils were unanimous.

MONOTHELITISM [622-681] A movement which taught that although Christ had two natures, he had only one will. It was condemned at the Sixth Ecumenical Council in 680-681.

Description Following the death of Justinian in 565, the Empire was ruled by Emperors who kept losing any territorial gains which Justinian had made for the Empire. In 610, Heraclius ascended to the throne. Two years later, the Persians conquered Syria. By 618, they had added Palestine and Egypt. Heraclius conducted brilliant campaigns in 622-628 which took back all this territory.

In an attempt to overcome the Monophysitic problem which had caused religious friction between the See at Constantinople and these outlying areas, Heraclius followed the lead previously suggested by Sergius [the Patriarch in Constantinople] in which Christ was to have two natures as presented by the Fourth Ecumenical Council, but was to have only one *energeia* or *hypostasis*. After some initial success, this suggestion stumbled, first because it was not accepted by the Chalcedonian monks of Palestine and secondly, because Pope Honorius judged that only an Ecumenical Council could introduce new dogma. However, Honorius went on to say that he was willing to consider one "will" in Christ.

In 638, Heraclius published *Ekthesis* which supported Pope Honorius by forbidding talk of one or two "energies," but went on to make dogma of the pope's thought that Christ had only one "will." In this activity, an Emperor had created Church dogma rather than having an Ecumenical Council do it for him as others had previously done. This "one will" proposal satisfied neither the Monophysites nor the Chalcedons. In 642, Heraclius died; but his *Ekthesis* continued as Imperial orthodoxy until Emperor Constantine IV called the Sixth Ecumenical Council in 680-81. At this Council, it was declared that Christ has "two natural wills or willings...not contrary one to the other...but his human will follows, not as resisting nor reluctant, but rather as subject to his divine and omnipotent will." In arriving at this decision, the Council condemned Pope Honorius who had died over 40 years previously.

The Sixth Ecumenical Council ended any thought of Monothelitism, a movement which had gained little support anyway.

MONTANUS [Died 179] A charismatic prophet in Asia Minor who established Montanism [or "New Prophecy"] in about 160.

Biography Little is known about the life of Montanus except that he was a prophet who converted to Christianity. One day in the Christian Church in Phrygia, Asia Minor, he fell into a trance and began to prophesy under the influence of the Spirit. This activity gave him a following. Montanus believed that he had a later word than that presented by Christ. He believed himself to be the final prophet, for he said, "After me shall be no prophetess any more, but the consummation."

MONTANISM A movement established by Montanus in the mid-second century CE. He generated a large following including Tertullian. Montanism was declared to be a heresy.

Description Montanism, also known as the Cataphrygian Heresy or New Prophecy, taught that there were three ages of the world: [1] the age of the Father [Old Testament]; [2] the age of the Son [New Testament]; and [3] the age of the Spirit [heralded by Montanus]. The guiding principle of Montanism was that the *Paraclete*, the Spirit of Truth promised by Jesus Christ, was manifesting itself to the world through Montanus.

At first, this did not seem to be against any church doctrine because the charismatic gift of prophecy had been honored by the Church. In addition, this did not seem to attack the authority of the bishops. However, Montanus implied that he had the final revelation of the Holy Spirit. Because of this, the Church would have to add something to the teaching of Jesus and the Apostles. The Church objected to doing this. Also, Montanus said that the second coming of the Christ was imminent. His followers believed that the heavenly Jerusalem would soon descend on the Earth in a plain between the two villages of Pepuza and Tymion in Phrygia [present Turkey]. Many Christian communities were abandoned in the haste to get to that site. The Church objected to losing this membership.

In addition to prophesy, Montanus taught a rigid system of morality based on legal-sounding statutes. As a few examples, the time of fasting was lengthened, all followers were forbidden to flee from martyrdom, marriage was discouraged and a second marriage was forbidden. When it was decided that these doctrines conflicted with the teachings of the Catholic Faith, a synod was called in about 177 which excommunicated the Montanists. Montanism survived as a separate, albeit excommunicated sect of Christianity until Justinian presented severe legislation against them in the middle sixth century. This essentially destroyed them, although some small remnants stayed until the ninth century.

This movement had many backers among those whom the present Church considers to be its founding fathers. As two examples, in the latter years of his life, Tertullian joined the movement; and Irenaeus of Lyons supported leniency for them. The highest point of Montanism was in Carthage where Tertullian joined them in 212 because he supported the rigorous discipline and moral life which they led in contrast to the moral laxity of the Catholic bishops. When Tertullian converted, he said that the Christian Pope was the "shepherd of adulterers," and that such leadership would not be permitted under the rigorous moralism of the Montanists.

The Church had two principle arguments with the Montanists. The first was the Montanist belief that there was a message which had come after the message brought by Jesus Christ; and the second was that they did not accept the life of luxury which the hierarchy of the Church were becoming accustomed to enjoy. As a consequence, those who were "of the Church" destroyed those who were not, even though the destroyed ones believed strongly in Jesus Christ and followed many of his messages, including the one on poverty.

-N-

NESTORIUS [Ca. 390-451] Founder of Nestorianism which was condemned at the Fourth Ecumenical Council.

Biography Nestorius was born of Persian parents. He was trained at Antioch where he was ordained presbyter. Following this he entered the nearby monastery of St. Euprepius where he became an acclaimed preacher. In 428 when Emperor Theodosius II invited him to become bishop of Constantinople, the situation in the capitol was disturbed. There was a question of who was the duly elected bishop, and there were a number of heretical groups whose presence was disturbing orthodoxy. Preaching at his consecration, Nestorius said, "Give me, O Emperor, the earth purged from heretics and I will repay you with heaven." As a direct result of this request, Theodosius issued an edict against heretics. No one was more zealous in the suppression and persecution of heretics than was Nestorius.

Nestorius had brought with him to Constantinople a chaplain named Anastasius who preached a sermon which objected to the title *"Theotokos"* or " God-Bearer" for Mary. The congregation was scandalized because the title had been used for years. Nestorius supported Anastasius and on Christmas Day began a series of sermons arguing that Mary was not *Theotokos* since he believed that if she were given that title, it would represent a return to Arianism. But to most people, it seemed as if Nestorius were denying the divinity of Jesus Christ and regarding him as a mere man who had been adopted by God as His Son. Nestorius was charged with reviving the heresy of Paul of Samosata, bishop of Antioch [260-270] who had taught a type of Adoptionist Monarchianism.

At this point Cyril, Bishop of Alexandria [421-444], chose to step in and to set in motion a series of events which finally resulted in the downfall of Nestorius as an orthodox Christian. Cyril issued a circular letter which attacked the Nestorian views as undermining the purity of the faith and denying the unity of God-man in Jesus Christ. In addition to the debate on orthodoxy, Cyril, as bishop of Alexandria, wanted to belittle his rival, Nestorius, the bishop of Constantinople, just as his predecessor, Theophilus, had belittled John Chrysostom. In this way, the theological and the political desires of Cyril were combined. When Cyril called upon Nestorius to admit the errors, he got a curt reply from Nestorius. In another letter, Cyril hurled twelve anathemas [things for which one would be cursed] at Nestorius who then replied with twelve of his own against Cyril. Cyril then involved the Bishop of Rome, Celestine I [422-432]. Celestine did not like Nestorius, because Nestorius had pardoned some of the followers of Pelagius who had previously been condemned in Rome. Celestine sent the Nestorian writings to John Cassian, the leading theologian of the time [see page 289]. Based on the report from Cassian, Celestine held council in 430 which condemned Nestorius. Cyril then wrote to Nestorius requiring him to anathematize [i.e. to denounce or to curse] twelve proclamations and stated that if he did not do so, then he would be excommunicated.

When the Pope's envoys reached Constantinople, they found that the Emperor had summoned a council to meet at Ephesus by Pentecost, 431 CE. This is the council which has been recorded in history as the Third Ecumenical Council. It was the hope of Nestorius that the Council would condemn Cyril on charges made against him by Egyptian refugees. At one session of the Council headed by those who were for Cyril, Nestorius was condemned. At another session headed by John, bishop of Antioch [428-441] who supported Nestorius, Cyril was deposed. A month later, three Roman legates representing Celestine arrived and Nestorius was again condemned. Finally the emperor, Theodosius, influenced by his sister Pulcheria whom Nestorius had offended, stepped in and exiled Nestorius to his former monastery near Antioch.

As a result of the decisions made at the Third Ecumenical Council, particularly the final decision made by the Emperor, Nestorius lost influence, but was not totally isolated. He followed the Eutychian Controversy [see "Eutychianism"] which was a reaction to his own teaching. Nestorius died in 451 at about the time of the calling of the Fourth Ecumenical Council.

NESTORIANISM A very powerful movement which was first condemned, and then approved, and finally condemned again by the Third Ecumenical Council in 381 CE. It taught that Christ's human nature was an extension of his divine nature. It sponsored many churches which broke away from orthodoxy.

Description Nestorianism is arguably one of the three or four greatest controversies faced by the orthodoxy [i.e. "true doctrine"] of the Christian Church, ranking on a par with Gnosticism, Arianism and the like. It was fought by Cyril of Alexandria, by Pope Leo I and by others.

Nestorianism was a movement based on the teachings of Nestorius whose views on the person and the nature of Jesus Christ were the specific purpose for the calling of the Third Ecumenical Council. The condemnation of these teachings led to the creation of a separate Nestorian Church which still exists today. In opposing Nestorianism, Cyril took the position that it so insisted on the full humanity of Christ's human nature that it seemed to divide him into two Persons, one human and the other divine. Nestorius insisted that Cyril's interpretation was based on a misunderstanding. What Nestorius actually taught was a union in which the self-manifestation of a person can be extended in much the same way that the self-manifestation of a painter is extended by his brush. In this way, Nestorius taught that the Son of God used manhood for his self-manifestation and manhood was therefore an extension of his person. He therefore was a single object of presentation with his human nature being an extension of his divine nature.

This proposal made a lot of sense to a number of devout people; and while Nestorianism was crushed in the Roman Empire by the Third Ecumenical Council, it survived outside the frontiers of the Empire. The Persians accepted Nestorianism to show their rulers that while they were Christians, they were not following the dictates of the Roman Emperor who was an enemy of the Persians. In 1551, some 1100 years after the death of Nestorius, a number of Nestorians reunited with the Roman Church and were called "Chaldeans." The Nestorian Church in India rejoined with the Roman Church in 1599, and then part split off to give allegiance to the Syrian Jacobite [Monophysite] patriarch of Antioch. In 1898, in Iran a group of Nestorians were welcomed into the communion of the Russian orthodox Church. Today there are Nestorians in Russia, Iraq, Iran, Syria and North and South America. The total of Nestorians today is about 170,000.

There have been reports in the literature which state that Nestorianism believed in reincarnation, karma and that Jesus Christ was the Archangel Melchizedek. I can find no corroborating evidence, and requests to the author of those reports for his reference source have not been answered. In more accepted reference works such as the *Encyclopaedia Britannica,* the *New Catholic Encyclopedia,* or Walker's book, the only stated reason for Nestorianism to be declared a heretical movement was the difference of opinion about the nature of Jesus Christ as described above.

Nestorianism is worthy for study because the history of the feud between Cyril and Nestorius demonstrates the extreme political bias of many of the decisions which were made at the early Ecumenical Councils; and also because Nestorianism is an unorthodox sect of Christianity which split away from the main Church, but which survived with enough following that it continues to exist despite opposition to it on the part of the Church.

-O-

ORIGEN [Ca. 185-254] Third century theologian in Alexandria. Considered by some to be one of the Church's greatest theologians, and by others to be a heretic. Certainly, a great mind whose achievements would satisfy several great men. Condemned for his Christology at the Fifth Ecumenical Council.

Biography Origen will be the most difficult of the early Christian teachers or writers to describe concisely, for he was at the same time one of the most respected and one of the most despised men of the early Church. There were even instances when the great respect and great hatred was generated by the same man, depending on the whims of the Church at the time of the reaction. An example is Jerome who once called Origen, "the greatest Christian teacher of all time with the possible exception of the Apostles"; but later fought the teachings of Origen with all the skill and cunning that he could muster. Whether generating an aura of holiness and belief or an aura of contempt and rejection, it can certainly be stated that the writings of Origen greatly influenced the early direction of the Church in a way that would never be changed; and it also can be said that they influenced many subsequent leaders of the Church, not the least of whom was Gregory of Nyssa.

Origen, whose full Latin name was Oregenes Asamantius, was born of Christian parents in Alexandria. His father, Leonides, was martyred in the persecution of Christians in 202, leaving Origen with the responsibility of taking care of his mother and numerous siblings.

Origen was a pupil of Clement of Alexandria. He lived the life of a strenuous ascetic until Demetrius, the bishop of Alexandria, chose him to replace Clement as head of the catechetical school. It is stated by some historians that Origen castrated himself so that he would have no distractions from the female students at the school; but whether he went through emasculation or not, almost all historians agree that he was totally celibate. It is a fact of history that in many Christian periods, a lot of castration occurred, primarily justified by Matthew 19:12 and 5:28-30. The story on Origen's emasculation was reported by Eusebius of Caesarea who tends to embellish everything Origen did as if he were a suffering saint. Eusebius strongly supported Origen in all the debate about him which occurred some 300 years following his death .

Origen was a deep student of Neo-Platonism. He shared this learning with Heraclas who was first his fellow teacher and friend, later his rival, and finally his enemy when Heraclas was Bishop of Alexandria. In the early days when Heraclas was assisting Origen in the school, Origen had time to think and write. In this period he: [1] started *Hexapla*; [2] converted a wealthy Christian, Ambrose, from the heretical teachings of Valentinus; and [3] established a curriculum which was the forerunner of all the subsequent Western liberal arts curricula. Any one of these achievements would have been a lifetime's accomplishment for most individuals, but Origen did not stop there. Instead, he generated prolific writings, including commentaries on the writings of St. John to refute the Gnostic followers of Valentinus. In addition, he visited Rome and met Hippolytus;

and also traveled to Arabia, Antioch and Jerusalem.

His reputation as an astute theologian gave him many invitations as a preacher. Bishop Demetrius disapproved because Origen was not, at that time, ordained as a priest and Demetrius wanted to prohibit lay preaching. It is said that Demetrius refused to ordain Origen because his emasculation made him unfit as a priest, but this view has weak historical substantiation. Nevertheless, following his refusal of ordination by Demetrius, Origen traveled to Greece to debate another follower of Valentinus and was ordained as presbyter [i.e. Elder] at Caesarea. In the debates, Origen made the point that Satan was not beyond repentance, for if he made the decision to fall by his own will, then he could also repent on his own. Demetrius was angry at the ordination of Origen and furious at the doctrinal view which Origen had expressed in the debate; for the orthodox viewpoint at that time was that repentance was meaningless without the salvation offered by Jesus Christ. Consequently, he called a synod to condemn Origen. This condemnation was honored in Alexandria, but was not accepted in Greece or Palestine. As a result, Origen moved to Caesarea in Palestine where he attracted many pupils, one of whom was Gregory Thaumaturgus, later bishop of Neocaesarea.

From Caesarea, Origen traveled to Cappadocia during the persecution of Maximinus. He wrote on this to Ambrose and later wrote of a debate at a church council in Arabia where a local bishop was accused of denying the pre-existence of the divine Word and where various debates on such subjects as to whether or not the soul contained blood were in furious activity. During the persecution under Emperor Decius in 250, Origen was imprisoned and tortured, but survived. He died several years later. His tomb at Tyre was still in existence and cared for during the time of the Crusades, almost 1,000 years after his death.

If orthodoxy were defined as intention, no one would be more orthodox than Origen and none more devoted to the Christian faith. His natural temper denied the world; his life was saintly in its living; his commentaries on the Bible and faith were later plagiarized by many; and his thoughts were basic to the beginning of monasticism. Greek asceticism was based on his work, and his teachings were the basis of all which was done by John Cassian [360-435] who was considered to be the leading theologian of his day [see page 285]. Yet, he was charged with many heresies. In his life, some said that he adulterated the Gospel with pagan philosophy. Shortly after his death, there was some mild but respectful criticism of his spiritualizing doctrine of the resurrection. Some 125 years later, after the Church had become much more set in her ways, there was harsh criticism against

Origen expressed by Epiphanius. At this time many, including Jerome, came to the defense of Origen. However, some 25 years later, Jerome violently criticized Origen during his quarrel with Rufinus.

Throughout the 300 years after his death, Origen was supported by many great men of the Church such as Eusebius of Caesarea, Didymus the Blind, Athanasius, Basil the Great, Gregory of Nazianzus, Gregory of Nyssa, Rufinus, and Theodorek Ascidas II; however, at various times he was opposed by Epiphanius, Anastasius, Jerome, Justinian, and Pontan. In the sixth century, the "New Laura" monastery in Palestine became a center of the Origenistic movement, hospitable to thoughts about the pre-existence of souls and universal salvation. This infuriated the Byzantine Emperor, Justinian, who denounced Origen in 543.

Origen had vast influence on all who came after him, and because of him, Christianity ceased to be merely faith; it became full-fledged philosophy, buttressed with Scripture but proudly resting on reason. It is reported that he wrote over 6,000 books and that Jerome once said "Which of us can read all that he has written?" There is much in Origen's teaching to justify Jerome's first judgment that Origen was the greatest teacher in the early church; but there is also much which later became controversial. It is just this schizophrenia of the early Christian Church which demands that Origen be examined very carefully. It truly addresses an important issue. That issue is: How can a Church which today states that it presents only the truth as generated by the Apostolic Tradition, have been so torn apart by the thoughts of a man who was so devoted to the Christian faith and teachings, and who was so admired during the time that the Apostolic Tradition was becoming the generator of doctrine? The opinions of Origen which caused such a stir have to be examined. One of these opinions is an opinion which some have called his most significant gift. It was the also the principle by which he himself lived and upon which the Reformation was established. It was *sola Scriptura*, or "only the Scriptures."

ORIGENISM An informal movement established by those who followed the teachings of Origen. Declared a heresy by the Church.

Description Origenism refers to those who followed the writings or teachings of Origen, some of which was condemned at the Fifth Ecumenical Council under Justinian, a Byzantine Emperor who was himself later placed under notice of formal condemnation by the Church.

Origen's teachings were voluminous and with no accepted Bible to guide him, it is only natural to expect that some of his teachings are presently considered to be orthodox Christianity, whereas others are considered to be heresy. One truth which is often repeated in modern Church teaching is Origen's thought that it was a part of the divine plan for Jesus to be born under the Emperor Augustus because for the first time, the whole Mediterranean world had an excellent system of roads which could be used for extensive missionary efforts. In addition, Origen was the earliest Christian philosopher who proposed that the soul was immortal, was created by God, and was infused into the body at the time of conception. This contrasted with the prevailing Hindu belief which taught that the soul was created at the beginning of time and is imprisoned into the body at the time of birth. In later Christian theology, Augustine built on the idea proposed by Origen when he talked of the soul as being a "rider on the body " and thus declared a clear split between the material body and the immaterial soul. Others have disagreed with both Origen and Augustine. The indecision within the Church as to how the soul and the body interrelate continues in today's abortion controversy

Origen strongly defended Christianity and claimed that one could be both a philosopher and a Christian. He felt that Christianity was a ladder of divine ascent, and that the beginner must learn to mount it at the bottom, and then join with the saints in a never-ceasing advance up the ladder. All of his works emphasize the goodness of God and the freedom of the creatures which He created with His overflowing love. Origen taught that God created the material world as a discipline for his creatures and not as their prison or as their final destination. He speculated that souls fell to varying degrees, some becoming angels, others becoming humans and still others falling all the way to becoming devils. Although Origen strongly believed in the pre-existence of souls and their continuing and repeated incarnation into human bodies, he did not believe in the incarnation of rational souls into animal bodies.

Origen felt that Redemption was a grand education by Providence, restoring all souls to their original blessedness; for he felt that no one, even Satan, was beyond Redemption. He felt that God never coerces, but that He might punish in a remedial fashion. He felt that the climax of Redemption was the Incarnation of the pre-existent Son who was one soul which had not fallen but had remained with God. Origen taught that Christ had free will just as all souls do, for he said, "If you remove free will from virtue, you destroy its essence."; but Origen thought that the union of the Son with the Father was so intense as to preclude any inclination for change via free will and therefore Jesus was "never changing." Origen thought that after the transfiguration, the body of Jesus appeared in a different form to different observers depending on their spiritual capacities since some saw nothing remarkable, whereas others saw him as their Lord and Savior. In his commentary on St. John, Origen collected the many titles of the Son [Lamb, Redeemer, Wisdom, Light, Life] and said that although the Father is one, the Son is many grades like the rungs on a ladder of mystical ascent, or like the steps up to the Holy of Holies, or like the beatific vision which appears in different forms to different people depending on their development in the faith.

Jerome felt that Origen's commentary on the Song of Solomon was his masterpiece. In this ground-breaking epistle, Origen said that the Song of Solomon portrayed the mystery of how the individual soul would be the bride of the *Logos* and thus form a union just as the Christ formed a union with the God. In this way, redemption would restore fallen souls from matter to spirit and from image to reality. Origen saw the spiritual life of the believer as a progressive process. He felt that the Church could help in this process for he believed that it was a great "school of souls" in which errant souls could be disciplined and taught. Origen also taught that Hell cannot be absolute and eternal since God would not abandon any creature. Because of God's respect for individual freedom and free will, it might take a considerable amount of time for every creature to find its way back to God; but ultimately, it would happen and all would be with Him. Origen thought that because of freedom, there would be no finality; and that once all free souls had been redeemed and had once again become one with God, then the whole thing would start all over again because freedom pre-empts finality. This is a deep, but intriguing philosophical thought.

As Origenism developed, the person of Origen tended to get lost in what his followers taught. Origen himself was defined as a Stoic, a Neo-Pythagorean, a Platonist and a Gnostic; but he also was defined as one who was resolved, nevertheless, to be a Christian. One famous statement which was made about Origen was that he spent his lifetime teaching Plato while thinking he was preaching Christ. Possibly because of this, in Origenism, God is not Yahweh, but is the First Principle of all things; and Christ is not the human figure described in the New Testament, but is the *Logos* or Reason who organized the world. As such he was created by the Father and was subordinate to him. Christianity, of course, argues against this by stating that Jesus was not created, even by the Father at the beginning of time. Instead, he was always there with the Father. In addition, in Origenism the soul passes through a succession of stages before reaching the body and after death it will pass through a like succession before reaching God. In addition, the world will continue to improve and if ever destroyed will revive to be better and this will happen again and again until finally all will be with God as worked out slowly to God's will. Christianity, on the other hand, believes that the soul rested before birth and will rest after death until resurrected with the Second Coming at which time all will be eternally right between the believer and God.

But despite these differences, they are not the ones which the Church used in declaring Origenism to be heretical. Instead, there were five major accusations which the Church made against Origen as follows: [1] making the Son inferior to the Father thus presenting a thought which became followed by Arianism; [2] denying Hell which thus destroyed one of the Church's greatest inducements to the discipline of its members; [3] speculating about the pre-existence of souls and the resulting world cycles throughout eternity [i.e. nothing is ever finalized]; [4] dissolving redemptive history by treating the historical scriptures as if they were allegories rather than fact as Origen did with the Garden of Eden and the Jonah-whale stories; and [5] using allegorical interpretation to demonstrate that all Christian dogmas were derived from the writings of the philosophers.

As a further case against him, the Church stated that Origen believed that the literal meaning of Scripture overlay two deeper layers of meaning, the moral and the spiritual; and that only the esoteric and educated few would be able to understand the spiritual part. He thus placed Christians into categories or classes depending on their spiritual development. In this case, it would seem that Origen was following the teaching of the Christ who stated that only a few would be able to understand the Parables [see Matthew 13:10-17]; but the Church seems to reject this kind of thinking and the people who develop such thoughts.

In the final analysis, it is probable that the major reason the Church condemned Origen was because he proposed that individual judgment be used instead of blindly following the dictates of the Church. Because of Origen, Celsus stated that Christians were "split up in every such way, each individual desiring to have his own party." In 187, Irenaeus listed 20 varieties of Christians. By 384, a mere two hundred years later, Ephiphanius reported that there were 80 varieties of Christians. It seemed to the orthodox leaders of the Church that because of the teachings of individual freedom by Origen, foreign ideas were creeping into the Church and people were leaving to join weird sects. Consequently, in an attempt to make unity within the Church and to make all Christians believe exactly the same, Origenism was declared heresy by the Church. Even today there are major parts of the Christian Church which deny an individual his freedom to follow Christ in a manner which his free will dictates.

-P-

PAULA [347-404] Close friend of Jerome's who established a number of monasteries and convents, mostly in Palestine.

Biography Paula was born in Rome to a noble family. She married Toxotius and had five children. Theirs was regarded as an ideal marriage. When he died in 379, she renounced the world, lived in great austerity and devoted herself to helping the poor. She met Jerome in 382 and became closely associated with him in his work. In 384, the death of her daughter left her heartbroken. A year later she left Rome with her son, Eustochium. They traveled through the Holy Land with Jerome. In 386, they settled in Bethlehem under Jerome's spiritual direction.

In Bethlehem, she and Eustochium built a hospice, a monastery, and a convent which she governed. She became Jerome's closest confidant, taking care of him and helping him in his biblical work. She built numerous churches which were to cause her financial problems in her old age, and died in Bethlehem in 404 CE. She is the patroness of widows.

It has often been said by the Saint-watchers of the Church that Jerome had his needs just as everyone does. Although the Saints seemed to try to do their best to discipline their love so that it did not interfere with their holiness, there are numerous examples which show that they did feel that love. Jerome had his Saint Paula trailing after him wherever he went. When he left Rome for the desert, she also went, not only to establish her own community, but also to remain in contact with him and to help submit her soothing influence while he translated the Bible or did other such monastic work. As another example, although the Rule of Benedict paid great attention to the vow of chastity, Benedict called his sister, St. Scholastica, his "twin soul" and left his monastic community to meet with her once a year. And finally there is the friendship of Clare with Francis of Assisi [see pages 112-115]. They were companions not only in the Faith but also in the establishment of orders: hers as dedicated to the vow of poverty as was his. Francis believed that he loved her with a perfect love.

While the writing in this Appendix is not meant to imply that anything untoward occurred between any of these individuals, Paula is included among the short list of people to show that the argument proposed by Jerome that the celibate state is superior to that of marriage, could be maintained even though the presence of Paula would certainly create a conflict. On the other hand, it is to be understood that the pope did not order automatic excommunication of married priests until 1074; and in view of Tertullian's description of the pope as a "shepherd of adulterers," it could be thought that the Church of the early days was composed of humans who were men as well as Saints. This is acceptable, for after all, the Saints are not angels. They came to this Earth just like the rest of us.

PELAGIUS [Ca. 354-418] A non-ordained British ascetic who believed strongly in free will and in strict obedience to all of the commandments.

Biography Pelagius is thought to have been born in Britain and to have died in Palestine. Very little is known of his life except that he came to Rome in 380 and immediately came to abhor the spiritual sloth and moral laxity of the Roman Christians. He blamed the moral decay on the doctrine of divine grace presented in the *Confessions* of Augustine. In this doctrine, Augustine beseeched God to grant whatever grace His will would allow. Pelagius felt that such a entreaty would lead people to believe that any moral transgression could be forgiven. In this way, such an entreaty would imperil the entire structure of moral law. He soon had a large following of devout people who believed likewise. They believed in strict adherence to *all* of the commandments.

When Rome fell to the Visgoth Chieftain Alaric in 410, Pelagius went to Africa. While there, Pelagius was highly criticized by Augustine who wrote many letters denouncing the doctrine that man has a basically good moral nature and thus has the responsibility for voluntarily choosing Christian asceticism for his spiritual advancement. Because of this criticism, Pelagius went to Palestine where he was condemned by the synod of Jerusalem. Based on further attacks from Augustine and Jerome, Pelagius wrote *De libero arbitrio* ["On Free Will"] in 416 which got him further condemned by two African councils. In 417, Pope Innocent I excommunicated Pelagius. Later Pope Zosimus pronounced him innocent on the basis of Pelagius's *Libellus fidei* ["Brief Statement of Faith"]; but after further investigation at the Council of Carthage in 418, Pope Zosimus confirmed the council's nine canons condemning Pelagius. Nothing more is known of Pelagius after this date.

PELAGIANISM A fifth century movement which was declared heretical because it believed that man has the free will to voluntarily choose Christianity and a moral life. Those who opposed Pelagius believed that man gave up his free will when he fell into original sin. Origen had also been condemned earlier for some of the same thoughts.

Description Pelagianism was opposed by a rather impressive crew among whom were Augustine, Boniface I, Celestine I, Gregory of Rimini, Innocent I, Jansen, Jerome, Leo I and Zosimus, primarily because they believed that Pelagius had denied original sin in his search for man's free will.

The rejection of man's "free will" has had a rather interesting history within the Church, for several Christian sects have used this rejection as justification for accepting the concept of predestination and the philosophy of Determinism [see *Christianity and the New Age Religion*]. Determinism is a concept which proposes that there is no free will and that everything has already been determined. It is supported by the writings of Augustine and Martin Luther, both of whom believed that man gave up his free will when he fell into the original sin. Determinism is also inherent in the Christian doctrine of "double predestination" which was presented by the Synod of Dort [Reformed church movement]. It was basic to the thinking of the Jansenists in the seventeenth century.

At the time of the Reformation, free will was a major issue because of the belief in predestination sponsored by Calvinism. John Calvin had the state exile those who advocated free will in place of predestination; and James I of England and Scotland who had very strong Calvinistic beliefs, not only had John Legate and Edward Wightman burned for Unitarianism, he also burned the books of Konrad van den Vorst and had him exiled for preaching the Arminian belief in free will in place of Calvinistc predestination. Later, James I calmed down and became a king who had a great deal of religious toleration; but for a while he was very intolerant of those who believed in free will.

A philosophy which proposes that man has absolutely nothing to do his destiny or with the destination of his life would greatly disturb Pelagius. It would greatly disturb Julian, Bishop of Eclanum, who spent twelve years in debate with Augustine about it. It would disturb many thinking people today. For this reason alone, Pelagianism is worthy of study.

PHILO [30 BCE-45 CE] Jewish/Greek philosopher of the first century CE whose ideas strongly influenced the early Christians in Alexandria [see pages 38-40].

POLYCARP [Died 155] Early bishop of Smyrna who was martyred in 155 CE. Fought Marcion. Was the teacher of Irenaeus

Biography Polycarp was a Greek bishop of Smyrna, a port city in Asia Minor [Turkey] southeast of Constantinople. Smyrna is presently known as Izmi. His long lifetime was important for two major reasons. First, he is a bridge between the Apostolic Father period and the Church Father [patristic] period of the Church's development. The Apostles were those who had known Christ. The Apostolic Fathers were those who had known an Apostle. Polycarp was said to have traveled with John the Evangelist and others who had seen the Lord; and later he became a teacher of Irenaeus who was one of the early Church Fathers. He thus bridged the gap between those who knew the Lord, and those who decided what the Lord's message would be. Secondly, he is an early martyred Eastern Christian, possibly more noted than any except Stephen the Apostle. After his martyrdom, his church at Smyrna wrote a long account of his death to the church of Philimelium in Pisidia [present central Turkey]. The text of this letter, entitled *Martyrdom of Polycarp*, is one of the earliest preserved Christian documents of this nature.

During his lifetime, Polycarp fought the Marcionites and kept them from establishing major churches in Asia Minor. He did this by writing his *Letter to the Philippians*, and by his moral authority. By this activity, he kept the Hebraic Old Testament deity from being replaced by a totally new God. He also fought the Gnostics in many ways, one of which was by defending the Resurrection as a fact of history. He did this by referring to the Letters of Paul. He often referred to the writing of others. In his *Letter to the Philippians*, Polycarp quotes various documents which later were included in the Bible among which were material from the Gospels of Matthew and Luke, from the Acts of the Apostles, and from the first letters of St. Peter and St. John. This is the first known instance of their having been quoted. His writing thus gives a clue as to the date of the writing of these works.

His teaching proposed the continued decentralization of the Church, and his visit to Rome toward the end of his life concerning the "Quartodeciman" controversy [see Irenaeus] was based on his belief that if a particular Church had the desire to celebrate Easter at a time different than another Church, they should be allowed to do so. This, of course, was not accepted by the central Church.

After his return from Rome to Smyrna, Polycarp was betrayed and led before a proconsul in the stadium where a crowd was assembled for the games. The proconsul urged him to forswear his religion and to curse Christ. Polycarp refused. The people yelled for the blood of the man "who destroys our gods." As a result, Polycarp was ordered to be burned alive. This fulfilled a prophecy which Polycarp had already made about his death.

Polycarp is included on the short list of the people of this period primarily because of his effect on Irenaeus. Through him, the tradition got established that there was a stream of people leading from the Lord to the Church Fathers. This connection thus helped to establish the Apostolic Tradition, a tradition which was very important in justifying certain dogmas and doctrines of the Christian Church.

PRISCILLIAN [Ca. 340-385] Early Spanish bishop who was the first heretic to receive capital punishment under the orders of the Church.

Biography In about 375, Priscillian started to teach a doctrine that was similar to both Gnosticism and Manichaeism in its dualistic belief that matter was evil and spirit was good. Priscillian taught that angels and human souls emanated from the Godhead, that bodies were created by the Devil, and that human souls were joined to bodies as a punishment for sins. Unfortunately, the Church felt that these beliefs led to a denial of the true humanity of Christ. Priscillian led his followers in a secret society that aimed for higher perfection through ascetic practices and outlawed all sensual pleasure, marriage, and the consumption of meat or wine.

Because the movement grew at the expense of the southern Spanish Churches, the local bishops started to oppose the movement. In 380, the council at Saragossa in Spain condemned Priscillian, who nevertheless was elected bishop of Avila, Spain. The Roman Emperor, Gratian, was persuaded by Priscillian's enemies to exile him to Italy. Later, he was tried under an order issued by the Roman Emperor, Magnus Maximus. In 384, he was condemned by a synod at Bordeaux. Priscillian appealed to Maximus who ordered him to Trier where he was judged guilty of sorcery and immorality and was executed.

PRISCILLIANISM A movement of the late fourth century founded by Priscillian which taught a doctrine similar to Gnosticism in that the material world was evil.

Description After the execution of Priscillian, Priscillianism went into hiding. The fall of Maximus in 388 led to a regeneration of the movement; but later councils in Spain condemned some of Priscillian's doctrines. In 563, the council of Braga renewed the condemnation of Priscillianism which soon disappeared as an organized movement.

In 1889, eleven treatises ascribed to Priscillian were discovered and published. This work revealed that the doctrines proposed by Priscillian were unorthodox in an unusual way in that Priscillian proposed that in the Trinity, the Son differs from the Father in <u>name</u> only. In this manner, Priscillian was defending the basic biblical verse which was possibly the most important part of Scripture in the early Church debate about the definition of the Christ. That verse was John 10:30 which says, "I and the Father are one." But although his doctrine on the Trinity was the key doctrine used against Priscillian in showing his unorthodoxy, there were other aspects which made Priscillian unpopular with his contemporaries. This unpopularity was so great that he was condemned to death. Among these unpopular aspects were his insistence on complete abstinence in regard to sex, meat and wine. In addition, the judgment of sorcery was probably based on Priscillian's belief in one aspect of astronomy: *viz.* that the positions of the stars could show God's will to those who could understand what those positions were trying to tell us.

Priscillianism is included in this Appendix for two reasons. First, a study of its history shows the interaction between Church and State in this period and the power which the Church was developing in that the Church could force the Roman Emperor to exile and to try one whom the leaders of the Church did not like. And secondly, a study of the reasons for the execution of Priscillian shows how the Church, and particularly the Church in Spain, was beginning to worry about such things as sorcery and witchcraft within its membership, a concern which helped to establish the Spanish Inquisition several centuries later.

-Q-

QUARTODECIMAN [Late second century] A controversy caused by certain Eastern Christian sects who wanted to celebrate Easter at a different time than that dictated by Rome. As a consequence, Pope Victor III excommunicated them. Irenaeus sponsored their reconciliation in 190.

-S-

SABELLIANISM [Early third century] A form of Monarchianism established by Sabellius.

Description Sabellianism was fought by Hippolytus who declared it to be a Christian heresy. It was a more developed and less naive form of Monarchianism than any which had previously been proposed. It was articulated by Sabellius in about 220 CE. Sabellius was a presbyter [elder of the congregation] in Rome, but little detail is known about him because the only reports come from the obviously prejudiced Hippolytus who was very anti-Monarchian.

In the early third century, there was a terrific debate in Rome between the Monarchists and those who affirmed permanent distinctions or "Persons" within the Godhead. The Monarchists had a concern for the absolute unity and indivisibility of God. They denied that any distinctions or "Persons" were permanent within the Godhead. Sabellius taught that God is a monad expressing itself as three operations: as Father in Creation; as Son in Redemption; and as holy Spirit in Sanctification. Pope Calixtus at first accepted the teachings of Sabellius, but later condemned them and excommunicated him.

Thirty years later the heresy broke out again in Libya; and in the fourth century, Arius accused the bishop of Alexandria of practicing Sabellianism. Throughout the entire Arian controversy, the Arians accused the orthodox supporters of the Creed of Nicaea of believing that there was no Personal distinction within the Godhead. About 375, the heresy was brought up again at Neocaesarea; and in Spain, Priscillian seems to have taught divine unity in Sabellian terms. At the time of the Reformation, Sabellianism was reformulated by Michael Servetus, a Spanish theologian and physician, to the effect that Christ and the Holy Spirit are merely representative forms of the one Godhead, the Father. John Calvin fought against Servetus with a singular intolerance which could almost be described as non-Christian, in that there was no forgiveness as Servetus was burned at the stake. In the eighteenth century, Emanuel Swedenborg, a Swedish mystical philosopher and scientist also taught a doctrine similar to Sabellianism as did his disciples who founded the New Church.

As can be seen in the examination of Arianism, the nature of Jesus the Christ and his relationship to the Father and the Holy Spirit was one which separated and confused many sincere Christians for hundreds of years. It still does. It all started with the declaration that Monarchianism and its descendants [e.g. Sabellianism] are Christian heresies because they do not accept the absolute definition of the Trinity, a definition first proposed by Tertullian in the early third century and not officially accepted by the Church until almost 500 years later.

SOL INVICTUS See Mithraism

-T-

TATIAN [Ca. 160] Syrian disciple of Justin Martyr who is most famous for having harmonized the four Gospels in his *Diatessaron*. Also wrote an early apology entitled, *Discourse to the Greeks*.

TERTULLIAN [Ca.155-220] Early [third century] African theologian who created ecclesiastical Latin and developed the formula for the Trinity which the Church accepted some 400 years after his death. Left the Church to become a Montanist.

Biography Tertullian was born in Carthage, a city in North Africa near the present-day city of Tunis. He was an important early Christian theologian and moralist who, as the initiator of ecclesiastical Latin, was instrumental in shaping the vocabulary and thought of Western civilization for over 1000 years. Knowledge of his life is based on the writings of men who lived fully 100 years after him. Because of this, Tertullian's life continues to generate scholarly dispute.

At the time of Tertullian's birth, Carthage was second only to Rome as a cultural and educational center of the West. His father may have been with an African-based Roman legion, which would explain why Tertullian was well educated. After finishing his education in Carthage, he traveled to Rome for further education and became interested in the Christian movement there. He converted to Christianity in Carthage toward the end of the second century. He accepted Christianity because of his interest in certain Christian beliefs, particularly the courage and determination of the martyrs, moral rigorism and an uncompromising belief in one God.

At the time of his conversion, the Church in Carthage was a firmly established, powerful force in North Africa. Although it is not known if Tertullian ever became a priest, he was a church leader based on his teaching and his defense of the faith. Tertullian spent the next 25 years [age 40 to 65] writing in an original Latin style which he developed and which became known as ecclesiastical Latin. He was a tremendous propagandist for the faith with his light and witty writings.

Sometime before 210 CE, Tertullian left the orthodox church to join a new prophetic sectarian movement known as Montanism. He did this because he was dissatisfied with the laxity of contemporary Christians in moral matters and felt that Christianity was too interested in the present world. He later became dissatisfied with Montanism and left it to establish his own order in the desert which lasted well into the fifth century. He is said to have died an old man, but nothing is historically known of him after about 220 CE.

In antiquity, most Christians never forgave him for his leaving the Church. Later, most Christian writers and theologians neglected him completely. Interest in him was revived in the 19th and 20th centuries and based on these new studies, he is now considered to be one of the formative figures in the development of Christian life and thought in the West. He is considered to be the outstanding proponent of the view that Christianity must stand against its surrounding culture. As an educated man, he appreciated the values of the Greco-Roman culture; but he accepted only those values which fit within his extreme moral rigors. He rejected the rest. One famous quote from Tertullian is "God's Son died. It is believable precisely because it is absurd. He was buried and rose again: it is certain because it is impossible." Another rather famous quote was given when he left Catholic Christianity. At that time he called the pope a "shepherd of adulterers."

Tertullian is included on our short list of Christian figures of the early Church for two reasons: [1] because he loved the Christian Way so much that he became one of its major spokespersons during his time; and [2] because he came to despise the Church so much that he left it while still a vigorous man. This dichotomy between early Christian love and the early Church is one of the major themes being explored in this book. Tertullian is one of the major players in the early history of the Church. Because of his being blacklisted by the Church, no honors such as Sainthood or being named a Father or Doctor of the Church were ever bestowed upon him, despite the fact that his contributions were critical during the early development of the Church. In fact, his concept of the Trinity was accepted by the Church almost 500 years after his death.

THOMAS AQUINAS [1225-1274] Thirteenth century theologian who is often called the "greatest intellect the Church has produced."

Biography Thomas was born at the family castle of Roccasecca near Aquino, Italy. He was the son of Count Landulf of Aquino, a relative of nobility. He was sent for his education to a nearby Benedictine Monastery as an oblate when he was five years old. In about 1239, he went to the university of Naples to finish his education. In 1244, he joined the Dominicans, a move so strongly opposed by his family that they kidnapped him and held him captive at Roccasecca Castle for fifteen months in an attempt to deter his decision. He persisted, joined the Order in 1245, and studied at Paris, 1245-48. He was ordained at Cologne in 1250. He became a master of theology at Paris in 1256 and taught at Naples, Anagni, Orvieto, Rome, and Viterbo, 1259-68, finishing his *Summa contra Gentiles* and beginning his *Summa theologiae* during those years. He returned to Paris in 1269.

When dissension racked the university in 1272, he was sent as regent to head a new Dominican house of studies at Naples. In 1274, he was appointed to attend the General Council of Lyons which was called by Pope Gregory X to discuss the reunion of the Greek and the Latin Churches. However, he died on the way to Lyons at the Cistercian abbey of Fossa Nuova near Terracina Italy on March 7, 1274. He was canonized by Pope John XXII in 1323, was declared a Doctor of the Church by Pope Pius V in 1567, and was named patron of all universities, colleges and schools in 1880 by Pope Leo XIII whose bull *Aeterni Patris* required all theological students to study the thoughts of Thomas Aquinas.

Thomas was probably the greatest theological master of Christianity. His thoughts replaced many of those proposed by Augustine in the theology of the Roman Catholic Church. However, during the Reformation, the Protestants returned to the Augustinian base. As a consequence, many present

Protestant teachings are more involved with the concepts of sin, God's grace, the necessity of faith and the denial of free will than are those of Roman Catholicism.

The thoughts of Thomas are often characterized by his sharp distinction between faith and reason. He emphasized that the great fundamental Christian doctrines are not contrary to reason even though they reach us by revelation. He believed that many truths such as the existence of God, his eternity, his creative power and his providence could all be discovered by natural reason. His magnum opus, the unfinished *Summa theologiae*, is probably the greatest exposition of theological thought ever written. It is the accepted basis for modern Catholic theology, especially as a textbook for beginners. Among his other writings are *Summa contra Gentiles* [used by Dominican missionaries for preaching to Muslims, Jews and heretical Christians in Spain], *De unitate intellectus contra Averroistas,* and his commentaries on the *Sentences* of Peter Lombard, on Boethius, and on Aristotle.

In addition to his towering intellect, Thomas was a man of great humility and holiness. He experienced visions, ecstasies, and revelations. As one example, he left *Summa theologiae* unfinished because of a revelation he experienced while saying Mass in 1273. That revelation was related to the fact that God's work would <u>never</u> be finished. He composed the office for the feast of Corpus Christi, and wrote hymns still used in church services. He wrote commentaries on the Lord's Prayer, the Apostles' Creed, and parts of the Bible. In him, the Middle Ages reached its full flowering and Christianity received its most towering and influential intellect.

THREE CHAPTERS [Ca. 550] A controversy which helped justify the calling of the Fifth Ecumenical Council.

Description The "Three Chapters" Controversy [originally called the three heads controversy] was settled at the Fifth Ecumenical Council. This Controversy refers to some of the writings of Theodore of Mopsuestia, Theodoret of Cyrrhus and Ibas of Edessa, each of whom was a Christian teacher in the patriarch of Antioch. Their writings had been condemned as Nestorianism by Emperor Justinian in his edict of 544 CE. Actually these teachings were Monophysitic in nature, but Justinian did not want to call them that because his wife, Theodora, was a strong champion of the Monophysite beliefs and Justinian wanted to keep peace with her and with her Monophysitic friends. In addition, the tone of these particular writings was objected to by the Monophysites. However, Justinian had to do something because Pope Agapetus I insisted that he stop giving the Monophysites so much freedom and Imperial consideration. Since Nestorianism had previously been declared heresy, this was Justinian's political way out; but it pleased no one in the East and angered almost everyone in the West.

This relatively minor Controversy is included in this Appendix for one purpose only; and that is to give an example of how strongly Justinian paid attention to the political situation and the desires of the Imperial court even when he addressed ecclesiastical matters. This is important background information to have when thinking about the activities of the Fifth Ecumenical Council which was completely under the political control of Justinian [see Appendix C].

-U-

UNITARIANISM [1571-Present] A movement which is monotheistic and which rejects the doctrine of the Trinity.

Description Unitarianism is not a heretical movement which was condemned during the first 500 years of the existence of the Church. Instead, it is a relatively modern movement based on old principals. There are those who see it as a reincarnation of Arianism [see pages 236 and 279].

The starting date for Unitarianism is presented as 1571, for that is the date when King John II Sigismund of Hungary granted a decree which gave it legal standing. This is considered by many to be a milestone of religious toleration in Europe. Unitarianism really got its start with the religious freedom of the Reformation movement. Because of this freedom, many of the concerns about the person and work of Jesus Christ boiled to the surface. These had remained hidden for years because of the intolerance of the Church. The first and most noted case is that of Michael Servetus, an acknowledged genius who, emboldened by the freedom of the Reformation movement, published *De Trinitatis Erroribus* [On the Errors of the Trinity] in 1531. His subsequent writings which continued to criticize the Nicene doctrine of the Trinity caused him to be condemned to death by the Catholic Church. He escaped to Geneva where he was captured by Calvin. He was burned at the stake as a heretic on October 27, 1553. Although this caused much of the questioning of the Trinity again to go below the surface, the movement was revived by Francis David [1510-1579] who was successively the superintendent of the Lutheran, the Calvinist and then the Unitarian Churches of Transylvania. In 1565, David began to preach actively against the doctrine of the Trinity. This message was picked up by some Anabaptists and was augmented by the birth of Socinianism. By the dawn of the eighteenth century, this "Arian trend" gave birth to Unitarianism in England which then spawned a similar movement in New England.

In the latter part of the eighteenth century, the United States entered into a short reversion to orthodoxy. However, in the early nineteenth century, Arian Christology had a rebirth, primarily in the Boston area. This led to the establishment of the American Unitarian Association in 1825. In 1961, the Unitarian and the Universalist Churches came together. Today, there are over 1,000 Unitarian Universalist Churches in the US with membership of about 150,000. These are people who believe that the decisions of the early Ecumenical Council have no hold on them; and yet they love Jesus Christ and follow his teachings.

-W-

WALDENSES   [Twelfth Century CE]. A group similar to the Cathars. It was established by Valdes in about 1175 and became a very popular Christian movement in southern France. The Waldenses were a very pious group who believed in poverty and in preaching the Bible. In becoming popular, they drew people out of the established churches. The Church established a Crusade against this movement in which the Waldenses were almost wiped out. A few survived until the Reformation when they became Protestants. A fuller description of this sect is presented on pages 101-195.

APPENDIX B:
EARLY CREEDS OF THE CHURCH

References

The major reference works for this Appendix were *Early Christian Creeds*, and *Early Christian Doctrines*, each by J. N. D. Kelly; and *Creeds of the Churches*, Edited by John H. Leith. These references were then checked against the *Encyclopaedia Britannica* and the *New Catholic Encyclopedia*.

Introduction

Christianity is a creedal religion based on the tradition of Judaism with its declamatory affirmations of faith. Creeds are a formal declaration of faith which use intelligible words to clarify the faith, and to affirm a deep commitment on the part of the one saying the creed.

While creeds are an attempt to give intelligible expression to faith, the Christian creeds were not fashioned in the isolation of a scholar's study, but in the historical events in which God is believed to have disclosed himself. As a result, they have never been written in the quiet times of the religion's history, but in the turbulent times when the Church felt the need to express what it believed.

In certain situations, the only creed needed has been the simple, "Jesus is Lord" or "Jesus is the Christ." Other situations have demanded that the creed be more definitive. Many creeds that have been universal in their intent have not been universal in fact, for many have been written for the express purpose of excluding people who consider themselves to be Christian, but whom the writer of the creed chose to reject. In the very beginning, creedal statements were associated with Baptism. In addition, early creedal statements often served as the basis for the catechetical instruction given to the pre-baptized.

In very simple terms, the creed is the Church's understanding and interpretation of Scripture. It is also a rallying point for those who need to coordinate their activities against the world. Although there have been attempts to dispense with dogma and minimize creeds, these attempts have never been successful because there has never been consistent or universal agreement on what the Scripture says. Consequently, the creeds give a uniformity to the belief system promulgated by the Church.

The awareness that every creed is a human achievement means that a creed will become authoritative only when it becomes the consensus of the Christian community; for no one individual can create a creed of the Church. Instead, the creed must be accepted by democratic consensus or by an official Church council. The democratic consensus tends to give the creeds a better long-term basis for authority than the mere action of a Church council, although acceptance by a Church council prior to consensus acceptance is considered to be the optimum.

Very Early Creeds

Although there are no true creeds presented in the Bible, C. H. Dodd has compiled one from the Pauline epistles. The resulting *Pauline Kerygma* is as follows:

The prophecies are fulfilled and the New Age is inaugurated by the coming of Christ. He was born of the seed of David. He died according to the Scriptures, to deliver us out of the present evil age. He was buried. He rose on the third day according to the Scriptures. He is exalted at the right hand of God, as Son of God and lord of the quick and dead. He will come again as Judge and Savior of men.

The earliest creed is possibly that presented in *Epistula Apostolotum* [Dialogues of Jesus with His Disciples after the Resurrection]. It is dated about 150 CE and came from Asia Minor or Egypt. It is:

In the Father, the Ruler of the Universe,
And in Jesus Christ, our Redeemer,
In the Holy Spirit, the Paraclete,
In the Holy Church,
And in the Forgiveness of Sins.

The word *Paraclete* means Holy Ghost. It comes form the Greek word *Parakletos* which means "the Comforter" or the "one called to help" from *para* meaning "to the side of" and *kalein* meaning "to call."

Although they were not truly creeds, there were several "**Rules of Faith**" which served a similar purpose in that they gave the theologians of the ancient Church some guidelines for their thinking and served as the basis for the teaching ministry of the early Church.

In about 165, Justin Martyr presented his Rule of Faith as follows:

We worship the God of the Christians, whom we consider One from the beginning, the creator and the maker of all creation, visible and invisible.

And the Lord Jesus Christ, the Servant of God, who had also been acclaimed beforehand by the prophets as about to be present with the race of men, the herald of salvation and teacher of good instruction.

I think that it is interesting to note that in this early Rule of Faith, nothing is mentioned about the divinity of Jesus Christ, just that he was Lord [i.e. one to whom homage is paid], and was the "Servant of God."

In about 180, the Presbyters who condemned Noetus at Smyrna professed their faith in a form that has been preserved as a Rule of Faith by Hippolytus. It is:

We also know in truth one God, we know Christ, we know the Son, suffering as he suffered, dying as he died, and risen on the third day, and abiding at the right hand of the Father, and coming to judge the living and the dead. And in saying this we say what has been handed down to us.

Again, it is interesting to note the absence of statements about the divinity of Christ. In addition, having "Christ" and "Son" as separate parts of the statement, could infer that these Presbyters were considering these as two distinct and different entities.

The Rules of Faith presented by Irenaeus in about 190 are:

The Church, though dispersed throughout the whole world, even to the ends of the earth, has received from the Apostles and their disciples this faith: She believes in one God, the Father Almighty, Maker of heaven, and earth, and the sea, and all things that are in them; and in one Christ Jesus, the Son of God, who became incarnate for our salvation; and in the Holy Spirit, who proclaimed through the prophets the dispensations of God, and the advents, and the birth from a virgin, and the passion, and the resurrections from the dead, and the ascension into heaven in the flesh of the beloved Christ Jesus, our Lord, and His [future] manifestation from heaven in the glory of the Father "to gather all things in one," and to raise up anew all flesh of the whole human race, in order that to Christ Jesus, our Lord, and God, and Savior, and King, according to the will of the invisible Father, "every knee should bow, of things in heaven, and things in earth, and things under the earth, and that every tongue should confess" to Him, and that He should execute just judgment towards all; that He may send "spiritual wickedness," and the angels who transgressed and became apostates, together with the ungodly, and unrighteous, and wicked, and profane among men, into everlasting fire; but may, in the exercise of His grace, confer immortality on the righteous, and holy, and those who have kept His commandments, and have persevered in His love, some from the beginning [of their Christian course], and others from [the date of] their repentance, and may surround them with everlasting glory.

I think that from reading this, it is easy to see why the Church has proclaimed that Irenaeus was its first great theologian. The principles set forth and the language used could almost be that which was written after the Christological debates instead of before.

The Rules of Faith presented Tertullian in about 200 are:

We however as always, the more so now as better equipped through the Paraclete, that leader into all truth, believe [as these do] in one only God, yet subject to this dispensation [which is our word for "economy"] that the one only God has also a Son, his Word who has proceeded from himself, by whom all things were made without whom nothing has been made: that this Son was sent by the Father into the virgin and was born of her both man and God, and was named Jesus Christ: that he suffered, died, and was buried, according to the scriptures, and, having been raised up by the Father and taken back into heaven, sits at the right hand of the Father and will come to judge the quick and the dead: and that thereafter he, according to his promise, sent from the Father the Holy Spirit the Paraclete, the sanctifier of the faith of those who believe in the Father and the Son and the Holy Spirit. That this Rule has come down from the beginning of the Gospel, even before all former heretics, not to speak of Praxeas of yesterday, will be proved as well by the comparative lateness of all heretics as by the very novelty of Praxeas of yesterday.

As with Irenaeus, these words seem to be those of a highly developed Church.

Creeds associated with the Definition of Jesus Christ

Most creeds of the Church have been established in order to define Christ. The most commonly used Creed of this type which is used in the present-day Church is the **Apostle's Creed** which, incidentally, was certainly neither written by nor spoken by any Apostle. As Kelly said in *Early Christian Creeds*, "Once the question is squarely faced, the extreme unlikelihood of the Apostles having drafted an official summary of faith scarcely merits discussion. Since the Reformation, the theory that they did has been completely set aside."; and later, "Everything goes to show that the infant communities looked upon themselves as the bearers of a unique story of redemption. It was their faith in the gospel which had called them into being, and which they felt obliged to communicate to newcomers." In other words, the infant communities had no creed which they recited, and they certainly did not have anything as definitive as the Apostles Creed. They merely had the gospel.

The date and place of the origin of the present form of the Apostles'

Creed cannot be fixed with precision. It owes its ancestry to the Roman Symbol [i.e. saying] which developed in Rome during the second century. There is considerable evidence for an actual date in the late sixth or seventh century, somewhere in southwest France. The earliest appearance of the Apostle's Creed is in about 710-24 CE. The creed became the common creed of the Western Church some time during the reign of Pope Innocent III [about 1200 CE]. At the Council of Florence in 1439, the Eastern representatives declared that they knew nothing of an Apostles' Creed, and scholars will state that the Apostles knew nothing about it either. The Apostles' Creed presently used in the Church is:

I BELIEVE in God the Father Almighty, Maker of heaven and earth; And in Jesus Christ His only Son our Lord; who was conceived by the Holy Ghost, born of the Virgin Mary, suffered under Pontius Pilate, was crucified, dead and buried; He descended into hell*; the third day He rose again from the dead; He ascended into heaven, and sitteth on the right hand of God the Father Almighty; from thence He shall come to judge the quick and the dead.

I believe in the Holy Ghost; the holy Catholic Church; the communion of saints; the forgiveness of sins; the resurrection of the body; and the life everlasting. AMEN.

* Some churches omit this.

The earliest legitimate Eastern Creed is probably that of the **Creed of Caesarea** presented by Eusebius of Caesarea in about 325 AD. It is:

We believe in one God, the Father All Governing, Creator of everything visible and invisible.

And in one Lord Jesus Christ, the Word of God, God from God, Light from Light, Life from Life, the only-begotten Son, the first born of all creation, begotten of the Father before all time, by whom also everything came into being, who for our salvation became incarnate and lived among men. He suffered, and arose the third day, and ascended to the Father, and will come again in glory to judge the living and the dead.

We believe in one Holy Spirit.

It is interesting to note that this is the first recorded incident I could find in which the word "only" is used in a creedal reference to Jesus Christ.

The development of creeds entered a new stage at the First Ecumenical Council at Nicaea in 325 CE when the council adopted a creed that was to be a test for orthodoxy and was to be authoritative for the whole Church. It was a creed that if not accepted by an individual, allowed the Church to curse that individual. Although there had been some similar attempts to develop a definitive creed at the Councils of Antioch [268 and 325], the Council of Nicaea took a major step forward in defining what was required in order to be an orthodox follower of Christ.

The reason for calling the Council of Nicaea was the theology of Arius. In order to refute Arianism, the orthodox Church had to define the meaning and the significance of Jesus Christ. The Christian community had regarded Jesus as both God and man, but Arius forced the Church to define in what sense he was a God. Arius insisted that the Word or Son was a creature created by God, that he had a beginning and that he was subject to change [see Appendix A]. This would mean, as Athanasius pointed out, that in Jesus Christ, man is not really confronted by God. **The Creed of Nicaea** insisted that God has fully come into human history in Jesus Christ. It sought to make this clear through certain key phrases in the creed, such as: "That is, of the essence of the Father"; "True God from true God"; "Begotten, not created"; " Of one essence [reality] with the Father." This last phrase was decisive in condemning Arianism, but it also was the cause of considerable controversy. It was not a phrase which was used in the Bible, and it had previously been used in other theological contexts that placed it under suspicion.

The Creed of Nicaea is:

We believe in one God, the Father All Governing, creator of all things visible and invisible.

And in one Lord Jesus Christ, the Son of God, begotten of the Father as only begotten, that is, from the essence [reality] of the Father, God from God, Light from Light, true God from true God, begotten, not created, of the same essence as the Father, through whom all things came into being, both in heaven and in earth; Who for us men and for our salvation came down and was incarnate, becoming human. He suffered and the third day he rose and ascended into the heavens. And he will come to judge both the living and the dead.

And we believe in the Holy Spirit.

But those who say, Once he was not, or he was not before his generation, or he came to be out of nothing, or who assert that he, the Son of God, is of a different hypostasis or ousia, or that he is a creature, or changeable, or mutable, the Catholic and Apostolic Church anathematizes them.

For 50 years after Nicaea, the Church debated the affirmation, "Of one essence with the Father." In other creeds, various alternatives were tried, such as: "Exact image with the Godhead"; or "Like the Father who begot Him according to the Scriptures" or "Like the Father in all things";

or "Of like essence with the Father"; or "Unlike the Father" [Second Creed of Sirium, 357]. In the end, the Church accepted the Nicaea affirmation of "Of one essence [reality] with the Father" as the only way to express that it had been confronted with nothing less than God himself in Jesus Christ. In a theological sense, the assertion that Christ was only like God undermined the Christian community's conviction that he might not be completely like God and that someone more nearly like God might later appear. Christianity would therefore be only one of many religions. But if God himself were incarnate in Jesus Christ, then this is the *final* Word and there could be no new religion because there is nothing further to be said.

The Constantinopolitan Creed of 381 is popularly known as the **Nicene Creed**. It has been associated with the Council of Constantinople [381] although the records of the Council do not contain the Creed and it was not accepted before the Council of Chalcedon in 451. The creed is Nicene in that it affirms the theology of Nicaea; but it goes beyond Nicaea in that it confers full deity on the Holy Spirit. It is liturgical in form and was probably used as liturgy. It is:

We believe in one God, The Father All Governing, creator of heaven and earth, of all things visible and invisible;

And in one Lord Jesus Christ, the only-begotten Son of God, begotten from the Father before all time, Light from Light, true God from true God, begotten not created, of the same essence as the Father, through whom all things came into being, Who for us men and because of our salvation came down from heaven, and was incarnate by the Holy Spirit and the Virgin Mary and became human. He was crucified for us under Pontius Pilate, and suffered and was buried, and rose on the third day, according to the Scriptures, and ascended to heaven, and sits on the right hand of the Father, and will come again with glory to judge the living and the dead. His Kingdom shall have no end.

And in the Holy Spirit, the Lord and life-giver, Who proceeds from the Father, Who is worshipped and glorified together with the Father and Son, Who spoke through the prophets; and one holy, catholic, and apostolic Church. We confess one baptism for the remission of sins. We look forward to the resurrection of the dead and the life of the world to come. Amen.

It is interesting to note that this creed, developed in the East and accepted at a Council attended primarily [if not totally] by Eastern bishops, has the Holy Spirit proceeding from the Father, and not from the Father and the Son as the Western Church later insisted.

Although the Council at Nicaea settled the question of whether the

Son was truly God, the question of the person of Jesus Christ remained. How was he both God and man? Various answers were tried. Apollinarianism truncated the manhood, but the Church wanted him to be truly man. Nestorianism proposed two persons, but the Church wanted only one person who was both God and man. Eutychianism absorbed the human into the divine, but the Church wanted him to be both human and divine. The Christological settlement at Chalcedon in 451 involved theology form Alexandria, Antioch and the Western Church. It could not have been developed by any one of the three. It was shared theology. While the **Definition of Chalcedon** did not fully satisfy the Church of that day, and probably does not satisfy the Church of today, no one has proposed anything better. It was considered to be the best that man could come up with in trying to define that which cannot be defined.

The Definition of Chalcedon is:

Following, then the holy fathers, we unite in teaching all men to confess the one and only Son, our Lord Jesus Christ. The selfsame one is perfect both in deity and also in human-ness; this selfsame one is also actually God and actually man, with rational soul and a body. He is of the same reality as God as far as his deity is concerned and of the same reality as we are ourselves as far as his human-ness is concerned; thus like us in all respects, sin only excepted. Before time began he was begotten of the Father, in respect of his deity, and now in these "last days" for us and on behalf of our salvation, this selfsame one was born of Mary the virgin, who is God-bearer in respect of his human-ness.

[We also teach] that we apprehend this one and only Christ-Son, Lord, only-be-gotten-in two natures; [and we do this] without confusing the two natures, without transmuting one nature into the other, without dividing them into two separate categories, without contrasting them according to area or function. The distinctiveness of each nature is not nullified by the union. Instead, the "properties" of each nature are conserved and both natures concur in one "person" and in one hypostasis. They are not divided or cut into two prosopa, but are together the one and only and only-begotten Logos of God, the Lord Jesus Christ. Thus have the prophets of old testified; thus the Lord Jesus Christ himself taught us; thus the Symbol of the Father has been handed down to us.

Later Canons or Beliefs

In addition to the creeds of the Church, there are numerous other canons [i.e. law] or confessions [i.e. a statement of belief in Church doctrines] which are worth examining to see how the Church developed. Only a few of these will be presented here.

Although the **Council of Orange** in 529 is not considered today to be an Ecumenical Council, it did attempt to fight heresy and define orthodoxy by presenting a declaration of 25 Canons plus a conclusion. A typical Canon is over 100 words in length and will not be reproduced here in its totality. Besides, many of the Canons verge on being incomprehensible because of their wordiness. However, the conclusion will be presented in its totality. Prior to that, the main points of the Canons are summarized as:

1. If anyone thinks that it is only the physical body which is impacted by Adam's sin, he is wrong. The soul is also condemned. And if anyone thinks that the impact of Adam's sin stops with that person's death, he is wrong, for the impact is passed along to his children.

2. If anyone thinks that prayer brings grace, he is wrong, for it is grace that brings prayer. And if anyone thinks that he has the will to be cleansed from sin or even has the desire to be cleansed from sin without the Holy Spirit giving him that will or that desire, then he is wrong.

3. If anyone believes that God has mercy on him or that he can make any right decision or can use his free will to chose the right way without having the Holy Spirit infused in him, then he is wrong.

4. Man's free will was destroyed by Adam and can be returned only by baptism. Furthermore, the courage of Gentiles is produced by greed whereas the courage of Christians is produced by the love of God. In addition, man does not do good, for anything that he might do which is good, God is responsible.

5. If man does anything which displeases God, then it is man's will which did it; but if he does anything which pleases God, it is God's will that caused it. Furthermore, it is entirely a gift of God to love God.

In conclusion, the sin of the first man has so impaired and weakened free will that no one thereafter can either love God or believe in God or do good for God's sake unless the grace of divine mercy has preceded him. Therefore, all the works of the saints of old were not given of natural goodness as they could have been before Adam, but were bestowed solely by the grace of God. And even after Christ, this grace is not to be found in the free will of all who desire to be baptized, but is bestowed solely by the kindness of Christ. Furthermore, if anyone were to believe that anyone is foreordained to evil by the power of God, then he is so wrong that he is to be excommunicated from the Church [i.e., they are anathema]. Finally, man does not take the initiative to do any good work. Instead it is God himself who inspires this and it is presented by the kindness of Christ.

To anyone who has read the theology of the Church Fathers, it is readily obvious that if Augustine had not been a writer, there would have been nothing for the Council of Orange to do. All of these Canons are pure Augustinian, and they certainly do demonstrate how the Church was developing.

As a side issue which will not be pursued here in depth, the Image Controversy is a fascinating one. The use of images or Icons was forbidden with very strong words by the Synod of Constantinople in 753, then permitted with equally strong words by the Council of Nicaea in 787 [a Council which has come down in history as the Seventh Ecumenical Council], then later condemned with equally strong words by the Protestants. It is fascinating history and hardly supports the viewpoint that all decisions made by the major councils of the Church are "Revealed Truths" in which God has played a major role.

At the Council of Florence in 1438-45 [later designated the Seventeenth Ecumenical Council] a significant amount of teaching about the **Sacraments** was developed. A brief paraphrased summary is:

There are seven sacraments of the New Law: baptism, confirmation, the Eucharist, penance, extreme unction, orders and marriage. These are quite different from the sacraments of the Old Law, which did not cause grace, but foreshadowed the grace which was to be given solely through the passion of Christ. Our sacraments not only contain grace, but also confer it on those who receive them worthily. The first five of these Sacraments have been ordained for the spiritual perfection of every individual in himself; the last two for the government and increase of the whole Church. Through baptism we are spiritually reborn; through confirmation we grow in grace and are strengthened in faith. Having been regenerated and strengthened, we are sustained by the divine food of the Eucharist. But if we become sick in soul through sin, we are healed spiritually, through penance, and healed spiritually as well as physically, in proportion as it benefits the soul, through extreme unction. Through orders the Church is governed and grows spiritually, while through marriage it grows physically.

Three elements are involved in the full administration of all of these sacraments: things as the matter, words as the form, and the person of the minister performing the sacrament with the intention of doing what the Church does. If any one of these is lacking, the sacrament is not effected. There are three of the sacraments, baptism, confirmation and orders which imprint on the soul in indelible character, i.e. a kind of spiritual seal distinct from the others. They are not, therefore to be received more than once by the same individual. The rest, however, do not imprint a character and may be performed more than once.

As a consequence of these definitions, the Church demonstrated how it was to bestow Grace upon its members, a province previously restricted to God.

With the coming of Reformation, many, many creeds got established, particularly by the Lutherans [e.g. the Angsburg Confession of 1530] and by the people of the Reformed Movement [i.e. Zwingli and Calvin] who wrote a lot of creeds in order not to worship any one creed, for worshipping anything other than God was an anathema to them. The people of the Reformed Movement debated with the Catholics all the time. One prime example is the **Ten Conclusions of Berne**, 1528. They are [somewhat paraphrased]:

1. The holy Christian Church, whose only Head is Christ, is born of the Word of God, and abides in the same and listens not to the voice of a stranger.

2. The Church of Christ makes no laws or commandments apart from the Word of God; hence all human traditions are not binding unless they are grounded upon the Word of God.

3. Christ is the only source of salvation.

4. The Eucharist is not defined in Scripture as being the actual body and blood of Christ.

5. The mass, in which Christ is offered to God as our sacrifice, is contrary to Scripture and is therefore an abomination to God.

6. Since Christ alone died for us, then there is no other mediator between us and God.

7. Scripture does not say there is a place where souls are purged, and therefore any services for the dead are vain.

8. Images are against the Word of God and are therefore to be abolished.

9. Marriage is not forbidden by Scripture to any class of man, but is commanded to avoid fornication.

10. Since Scripture forbids fornication, any priest who commits it is really in trouble.

It is rather obvious to anyone who has looked at the development of the Church over its first 1500 years of existence, that every one of these conclusions is a direct slap at the Roman Catholic Church.

In the Second Helvetic Confession [1566] of the Reformed Movement, the following appears as **True Interpretation of Scripture**:

The Apostle Peter has said that "no prophecy of Scripture is a matter of one's own interpretation" [2 Peter 1:20]. Therefore, we do not allow all kinds of exposition. Whereupon we do not acknowledge that which they call the instinct of the Church of Rome for the true and natural inter-pretation of the Scriptures; which, forsooth, the defenders of the Romish Church do strive to force all men simply to receive; but we acknowledge only that the interpretation of Scriptures for orthodox and genuine which, being taken from the Scriptures themselves [that is, from the spirit of the tongue in which they were written, they being also weighed according to the circumstances and expounded according to the proportion of places, either of like or of unlike, also more and plainer], accords with the rule of faith and charity, and makes notably for God's glory and man's salvation.

Got that friends?

Summary

With the presentation of how the Reformed Church defined the "True Interpretation of Scripture," we will close this Appendix which is intended to present the development of only a few of the beliefs which the Church has asked their members to accept. It should be emphasized for understanding, that no creed of the Church can be developed by a single person, even if that person is a revered preacher. In other words, it is an article of belief within Christianity that no one person speaks for the Church unless he is repeating that which has been given credence by a major council of the Church or by the general acceptance of the entire Christian Community. It is also common practice during the ordination of a minister, that the minister confesses that he will support the declarations made by the major governing body [i.e. the Synod or the Council or whatever] of the Church. This does not keep any minister from voicing his opinion, even from the pulpit; but when those opinions become estranged from the common teaching of his sponsoring Church, that minister is subject to disciplinary actions which often can be quite severe.

In this manner, the Church keeps control of its mavericks, for it not only asks its members to affirm what has been declared a creed of the Church, it asks its ministers to adhere to them also. In the case of the member, only the membership is lost if the creed is not adhered to; but in the case of the minister, his job is at stake.

The Christian Church takes its creeds very seriously. As the Church grew, its creeds became more difficult to understand, and were certainly different than the earliest creed which was probably something like "Jesus is Lord." Consequently, the person who practices the Christianity of the Church is professing to a lot which was not required by the early ones who simply followed Christ.

Appendix C:
Details of the Fifth Ecumenical Council [the Second Council of Constantinople] in 553 CE

References
The major references for this Appendix are: *Early Christian Doctrines* by J. N. D. Kelly: *Reincarnation, an East-West Anthology* by Joseph Head and S. L. Cranston; and the *New Catholic Encyclopedia.*

Introduction
The reason for presenting a special Appendix on the Fifth Ecumenical Council is because there is so much confusion and mis-communication about this particular Council. Many of the Christian community believe that reincarnation was condemned at this Council, but an in-depth look at the activities of this Council do not support that contention. In-depth references to the Fifth Ecumenical Council are not readily available which is one reason why there seems to be so much confusion. The *Encyclopaedia Britannica* has many times the information on other Councils as it has on this one, possibly because the results of this Council were so insignificant. The sparsity of information is one reason why the Britannica is not mentioned in the sources cited above. In addition, *The Encyclopedia of Religion*, in an article entitled "Christian Councils" presents only a short paragraph on the Fifth Council in which it says: "They also condemned the speculative theology of Origen [third century] and his followers, as well as that of the chief opponents of Cyril of Alexandria from the previous century." Again, an in-depth presentation is lacking and so this reference is not cited. Attempts were made to get an in-depth presentation in numerous other sources, but again were not successful. Anyone would think that if the rejection of reincarnation were so important to the Church, and if it occurred at the Fifth Ecumenical Council, then there would be many writers who would have presented in-depth reports

on this particular Council. That is simply not the case.

Of the three references cited above, the *New Catholic Encyclopedia* will be quoted first because if there were any indication that the Fifth Ecumenical Council condemned reincarnation, it should be found there. This will be followed by the Kelly reference in order to present the anathemas which were published in the records of the Fifth Council. This then will be followed by the Head reference which is the most fascinating reading of all, albeit not pertinent in view of the data from the *New Catholic Encyclopedia.*

The *New Catholic Encyclopedia* presents an eight page article on Origen and Origenism in Volume 10. Anyone who is familiar with this Encyclopedia will admit that an eight page article is a lot of information. On pages 773 and 774, the following information [directly quoted] appears;

"The complicated history of the Council of Constantinople II [i.e. the Council which history names the Fifth Ecumenical Council] *in its relation to Origenism has been narrated by F. Diekamp. The council had been retarded by the resistance of Pope Virgilius, and during the interval Justinian had addressed a letter to the bishops [preserved by Georgius Monachus and by Cedrenus; Mansi 9:533-538] to which correspond the 15 anathemas, discovered by P. Lambeck in 1679,* **but which do not appear in the official acts of the council** [bold added]. *They expressly concern the Origenistic monks. A. Guillaumont has shown that they reproduce the* **Christology** *of Evagrius* [bold added].

Justinian opened the council without the agreement of Virgilius; and in its discussions **little attention was paid to Origen, except to put his name in the list of heretics condemned in canon 11** [bold added]. *He was not mentioned in the Emperor's opening discourse, which is the source of the council's anathemas, nor in the letter of Virgilius approving the council after the fact [Mansi 9:413-420]."*

The Encyclopedia then states that Origen was declared a heretic for his views on Christology, that the West continued to appreciate him as a spiritual director until the twelfth century, that he then fell out of favor because of the rise of Aristotelianism, and that he was returned to favor during the Renaissance. In the nineteenth century, he was considered to be

"more of a Greek philosopher than a Christian theologian; he was accused of having preached Plato all during his life thinking he was preaching Christ. But in 1931, W. Volker raised his spiritual doctrine to its proper honor, and in 1950 H. de Lubac rediscovered the technique for understanding his exegesis" [i.e. interpretation of the Scriptures]. *Despite*

variations in appreciation, modern critics can no longer ignore these two aspects of his teaching [his spirituality and his interpretation of Scripture]."

Anyone who reads the above can come to only one conclusion, and that is that in the *official* acts of the Fifth Ecumenical Council, Origen was condemned for his *Christology* [i.e. his definition of Christ] and *not* for his thoughts on the pre-existence of the soul or reincarnation. This point is emphasized in the official anathemas of the Council which are presented in the next paragraph.

In the book, *Early Christian Doctrines* by J. N. D. Kelly, the eleven official anathemas of the Second Council of Constantinople are presented on page 46. They are reproduced here in a slightly paraphrased form.

A person is declared anathema [i.e. excommunicated] if he does any of the following :

1. Does not confess that Father Son and Holy Spirit are one nature, one power, worshipped as a trinity of the same essence, one deity in three hypostates or persons.

2. Does not confess that God the Word [i.e. the Son] was twice begotten, the first before all time by the Father, the second in temporal body by the ever-virgin Mary.

3. Does not say that God the Word and Christ are identical.

4. Says that God the Word is pleased with man [as the raving Theodosius says]; or says God the Word Jesus and Christ [as the Nestorians do thus implying that there are two persons rather than one]; for the holy Church of God recognizes only the union of God the Word with flesh by synthesis or hypostasis which is a union without confusion and without separation.

5. Says that there are two persons but only one person to be worshipped [as Theodosius and Nestorius insanely have written] or does not confess that the Word of God is united with the flesh hypostatically and is therefore only one person.

6. Says that Mary bore a child who became God the Word and does not confess that she was truly a God-bearer.

7. Says that the expression "in two natures" means two persons rather than one person in which neither the nature of the Word has changed into that of the flesh nor that of the flesh has into that of the Word, for the union has destroyed neither.

8. [Repeats #5 and #7 in different words].

9. Says that Christ ought to be worshipped in two natures.

10. Does not confess that our Lord Jesus Christ who was crucified in the flesh is true God and the Lord of Glory and one of the Holy Trinity.

11. Does not anathematize Arius, Eunomius, Macedonius, Apollinaris, Nestorius, Eutyches and Origen, together with their impious, godless writings, and all the other heretics already condemned and anathematized by the holy catholic and apostolic Church, and by the aforementioned four Holy Synods and all those who have held and hold or who in their godlessness persist in holding to the end the same opinion as those heretics just mentioned.

These eleven Canons are the only ones officially presented by the Fifth Ecumenical Council. Canons 10 and 11 are direct quotes. The others have been paraphrased without losing the intent of the meaning. It is rather obvious that all of the men condemned by this Council were condemned for their thoughts on Christology, and that all the official acts of the council are related to issues of Christology and have nothing to do with the pre-existence of the soul or reincarnation.

The book *Reincarnation, an East-West Anthology* by Joseph Head and S. L. Cranston makes fascinating reading. On pages 320-325 the authors present 25 anathemas against Origen as presented by the Fifth Ecumenical Council and an additional 9 anathemas of the Emperor Justinian against Origen. Most of these refer to the pre-existence of the soul, and if they had been enacted by the Council, would have presented a valid argument that the Church did reject reincarnation at the Fifth Ecumenical Council. Again, they make fascinating reading and if anyone has the interest, they most certainly should be perused. I chose not to paraphrase them in this book for three reasons; [1] they would lose some of their intriguing flavor; [2] some of those presented by Justinian were later considered for rejection by the Church [see below]; and [3] as stated above, the *New Catholic Encyclopedia* states that these anathemas were never presented in the official acts of the Council. They therefore could never have been an official act of the Church. As mentioned in Appendix B, individuals can say whatever they want; but it is not a creed or teaching of the Church until it is officially accepted in an recognized Church council.

Anathema II of Justinian is presented in its entirety as an example of the flavor of these anathemas, and as one which was rejected by the Church.

"II. If anyone says or thinks that the soul of the Lord pre-existed and was united with God the Word before the Incarnation and Conception of the Virgin, let him be anathema."

The acceptance of such a creed would have made heretics out of all who said that the Christ had been with the Father from the beginning. It would negate much Scripture. It caused quite a stir in the Church as also did a later statement of Justinian to the effect that the body of Christ was incorruptible and only seemed to suffer. Statements such as this had been condemned as Docetism almost 350 years before they had been uttered by Justinian. Each anathema of Justinian was ready for formal review by the Church and possible rejection at the time of Justinian's death. Because of his death, Justinian's anathemas were merely ignored by the Church.

But again I repeat, these anathemas were never formally accepted by the Church; and the records of the Fifth Ecumenical Council, such as they are, do not state that these anathemas were ever presented for consideration

Summary

There is a belief on the part of many Christians that the concepts of the pre-existence of the soul and reincarnation were rejected by the Church at the Fifth Ecumenical Council in 553 CE. It is such a prevalent belief that even this author reported it in *Christianity and the New Age Religion*, just as Head and Cranston reported it in their book. However, after considerable additional study it is my firm belief that an Ecumenical Council of the Christian Church has never officially rejected the concepts of the pre-existence of the soul or of reincarnation. Although in a section entitled "Metempsychosis" the *New Catholic Encyclopedia* says that there are five references to the teaching of reincarnation being heretical, none of these teachings is considered to be a major one; and none has been officially declared as being heretical by a recognized Ecumenical Council of the Church. Again, individuals, even officials of the Church, may say whatever they want; but it is not a creed or teaching of the Church until it is officially accepted in an recognized Church council. In my opinion, that has never happened either to the concept of the pre-existence of the soul or to the concept of reincarnation.

A Christian would therefore not be going against the teachings of the ecumenical Church if he were to accept either belief.

GLOSSARY OF TERMS

Apologetics The branch of theology that deals with the defense and proof of Christianity

Apostatize To give up or abandon one's faith. To become an apostate.

Apostles Those who had known Jesus Christ personally.

Apostolic Fathers Originally intended to mean only those early Fathers of the Church who had known an Apostle. However, after a while those Fathers of the Church who were a generation removed from the Apostles started to be included on the list whether they had known an Apostle or not.

Ascetic One who denounces comfort as an act of religious devotion.

Asia Minor The western peninsula of Asia. Present-day Turkey.

Canon A code of laws or rules established by a church. The books of the Bible officially acknowledged by the Church.

Catechetical The teaching of basic Christian principles.

Chalcedons Those who support and defend the Definition of Chalcedon established at the Fourth Ecumenical Council.

Diaspora Dispersal of Jewish people to parts of the world outside of Palestine.

Doctor of the Church Possibly the most revered title conferred by the church, particularly the Roman Catholic Church, on its theologians and thinkers.

Doctrine Something which is taught.

Dogma A doctrine or series of doctrines considered to be an absolute truth.

Eschatology The branch of theology which is concerned with the ultimate or the last things, such as death, judgment, heaven, hell and the end of time.

Exegesis Critical exploration or analysis.

Gentile As originally used during the period of history covered by this book, the term "gentile" is considered to mean "non-Jew." Later, the

Christians used the term to mean "pagan" or "non-Christian." Today, the Mormons often use the term to mean "non-Mormon."

Gnosis An esoteric [i.e. "to be understood only by a select few"] form of spiritual truth or knowledge.

Godhead The essential and divine nature of God.

Hagia Sophia The "Great Church" in Constantinople, built by Justinian.

Hellenistic or Hellenized Relating to the ancient Greeks, their language or customs.

Hypostasize To symbolize a concept as a concrete form. A hypostate or hypostasis is that concrete form.

Heretical Characterized as not being of established standards or true beliefs.

Indulgences The remission of temporal punishment due for a sin after the sin has been forgiven. Often the forgiveness involved a payment of some kind either in specie or service.

Logos In Greek philosophy, cosmic reason which is the source of world order. In Christianity, the self-revealing thought and will of God as set forth in the second person of the Trinity [i.e. the Son].

Monad In the 18th century philosophy of Leibniz, the Monad was an infinitesimal, psychophysical entity comprising ultimate reality and ultimate unity. In some parts of New Age philosophy, the Monad is the residing place of Spirit from God, which meets with Soul from personality to design incarnational experiences for progress on the pathway back to God.

Monasticism The act of living in a monastery and therefore isolated from the world. The secluded and contemplative life.

Monotheism The doctrine or belief that there is only one God.

Nag [or Naj] Hammadi A town on the West bank of the Nile in Upper Egypt at which 13 codices of Gnostic scripture and commentaries on 2nd and 3rd century Christianity were discovered in 1945.

Nous In Greek philosophy, the principle of divine reason.

Orthodox or Orthodoxy Adhering to the accepted, traditional or established faith as expressed in the early Christian ecumenical creeds.

Patristic Relating to the Fathers of the early Christian Church or their writings.

Platonism The Greek philosophy of Plato [400 BCE] which asserts the ideal Forms as an absolute and eternal reality of which the world is an imperfect and transitory reflection. Plato's major eternal Forms were virtue, knowledge and absolute goodness.

Polytheism The worship of or belief in more than one God.

Reformation The movement inadvertently instigated by the protests of Martin Luther in the sixteenth century. These protests were against many of the activities of the Roman Church. It generated the Protestant movement

Schism A formal separation into factions within the Christian Church.

See [Often capitalized]. The official seat, jurisdiction or office of a bishop.

Sheol A Hebrew word which appears more than 60 times in the Old Testament to signify the nether world. It is the place of complete inertia that one goes to for reflection when one dies, whether one be wicked or just, rich or poor. It is a precursor to the Christian idea of purgatory.

Simony The buying and/or selling of ecclesiastical pardons or church offices.

Stoicism The Greek philosophy of the Stoics [i.e. those who are free from passion such as joy and pain and accept everything as an unavoidable result of divine will]. Established by Zeno in about 300 BCE.

Transcendent Surpassing all others; pre-eminent; first in everything.

Vatican II Also known as the Twenty-first Ecumenical Council of 1962-5. The Council which caused the Canon Law and the worldwide practices of the Roman Catholic Church to become dramatically altered.

FOOTNOTES

Notes from the Author

1. One major meaning of the word sectarian is "adhering to the dogmatic limits of a sect." This work uses this designation for the described Churches in order to refer to all Christian Churches which follow the dogmatic beliefs generated by the theological debates of the fourth-seventh centuries, and not merely the mainstream Churches. Some religious writers tend to leave some sectarian Churches, such as those of the Religious Right, out of the mainstream category.

2. In this Chapter, and in all subsequent parts of this book, the abbreviations BCE [Before Common Era] and CE [Common Era] and are used in place of BC and AD to designate those years as being before [BCE] or after [CE] the year now commonly accepted throughout most parts of the world as being year 0. I have chosen to use these designations because, like Bishop Spong, I feel that it is pure arrogance to indicate to our non-Christian friends that we do not believe that they can tell time.

3. Quite often in the text of this work, the word "Church" has been capitalized. One reviewer criticized this tendency. However I have decided not to change this practice, because when "Church" is capitalized, I mean to personify it. To personify is to represent an inanimate object as having the personality, thoughts or qualities of a living being. One of the basic points of this work is that the Church did teach, did dictate, did praise individuals or excommunicate [read: eternally damn] them, and did many other activities normally associated with the activities of a living person. In activities in which the "church" did not generate the activities of a personified being, the word has not been capitalized. If this offends anyone, I apologize. I am doing this capitalization in a deliberate attempt to communicate.

4. Panikkar, Raimundo, *The Jordan, the Tiber and the Ganges*, an essay contained in *The Myth of Christian Uniqueness; Toward a Pluralistic Theology of Religions*, John Hick and Paul F. Knitter, Editors [New York, 1987] p. 89-116.

5. Nolan, Albert, *Jesus Before Christianity* . Revised edition published in 1992 by Orbis Books, Maryknoll, NY 10545.

6. This etymology [historical development of a word] was taken from *The Oxford English Dictionary*, prepared by J. A. Simpson and E. S. C. Weiner, Second Edition [Oxford, 1989].

7. Leith, John H., *Basic Christian Doctrine*, [Louisville, 1993], p. 4.

8. Levy, Leonard W., *Blasphemy, Verbal Offense Against the Sacred, from Moses to Salman Rushdie*, quoted by John Hick in his essay, *The Non-Absoluteness of Christianity*, in *The Myth of Christian Uniqueness*, p. 35.

9. Moore, L. David, *Christianity and the New Age Religion*, copyright 1992 by the author. Published by Pendulum Plus Press, 3232 Cobb Parkway, Suite 414, Atlanta, GA 30339, p. 112.

10. De Rosa, Peter, *Vicars of Christ, The Dark Side of the Papacy*, [New York, 1988], p. 79. Since the De Rosa reference is used many times in these footnotes, some justification of his credentials seems warranted. Peter De Rosa, a former Catholic priest, is a graduate of Gregorian University in Rome. He was professor of Metaphysics and Ethics at Westminster Seminary and Dean of Theology at Corpus Christi College in London. He is author of several books on religion. He left the priesthood in 1970. His academic and theological credentials are outstanding.

11. Moore, p. 11.

Preface and Introduction
There is no footnoted material in either of these sections.

BOOK ONE
Chapter One Background Information
There is no footnoted material in this short Chapter.
Chapter Two The Important Events
The general information used in each section of this Chapter was synthesized from a number of sources. The major sources used were the *New Encyclopaedia Britannica*, the *New Catholic Encyclopedia*, Williston Walker's *A History of the Christian Church, The History of Christianity, A Lion Handbook*, The Bible, etc. In the footnotes for which a such synthesizing was done, the footnote will refer to "Misc. Sources." I feel that the *Encyclopaedia Britannica* is so widely respected that no additional credentials need be given it. The *New Catholic Encyclopedia* has the support of the Catholic University of America, and is considered by those of the Roman Catholic faith to be a genuine reflection of their viewpoints. It would seem to be an adequate reference work for establishing orthodox viewpoints on a number of subjects. Williston Walker's book is considered to be a classic in its field by most Protestant ministers and theology professors. It was first published in 1918 and has been frequently updated by recognized authorities in the field. In 1985, the Fourth Edition was published. It is considered to be a very authoritative source of material. *The Lion Handbook* is also a widely accepted reference work.

1. Josephus, *Antiquities of the Jews* [93 AD].

2. Letter by Pliny the Younger [Annals, 15.44] as reported by Green, p. 28-9.

3. Drane, John, *Introducing the New Testament*, [New York, 1986]. Many of these thoughts are presented in Chapter 5.

4. "Misc. Sources" as described above

5. Spong, Bishop John Shelby, *Rescuing the Bible from Fundamentalism,* p. 214.

6. Because this statement about Paul may be an especially sensitive one for those presently of the Christian faith, I will make a special notation about it. The major change which Paul made in the belief system of the Judaic Christians was to accept gentiles as Christians without having them follow the Judaic laws such as being circumcised and the like. Since Jesus had preached love and acceptance rather than the law, this was not a change in the teachings of Jesus. However, Paul went further and made a major change when he identified Jesus as being the Wisdom of the Old Testament [see page 37]. He did this in the first chapter of 1 Corinthians. This is a claim which Jesus never made. Paul then followed this claim with an expanded briefing in Colossians 1:15-20 in which he calls Jesus the "image of the invisible God, the first-born of all creation" and further claims that "all things were created through him and for him." These statements by Paul led to similar identifications in the Gospels of Matthew and of John and in the Letter to the Hebrews, all of which were written after the Letters of Paul. The association which Paul made between Jesus and Wisdom was possibly the earliest written indication that Jesus was divine. It not only led to the statements made in the Gospel of Matthew and the Gospel of John, it also led to many of the Christology theories of the fourth and fifth centuries. Of the many references which cite this change in the message of Christ, possibly the best presentation is made in Chapter 7 [pages 35-40] of Walkers *A History of the Christian Church,* Fourth Edition.

7. Walker, 1984 [fourth] Edition, p. 41.

8. Walker, 1959 [second] Edition, p. 102.

9. Wilson, Ian, *Jesus: The Evidence,* [New York, 1986]. p. 160-3.

10. Walker, 1984 Edition, p. 133-4.

11. *New Catholic Encyclopedia,* Vol. 10, p. 773-4

12. Mack, Burton L., *The Lost Gospel, The Book of Q and Christian Traditions* [New York, 1993], p 181. The sayings of Jesus from the Gospel of Thomas have been highly rated by the Jesus Seminar, a group of New Testament scholars who have undertaken the task of judging whether the sayings of Jesus were really made by Jesus. The work of this Seminar, the methodology they use and the difficulty which they have had in communicating their results to the public is documented in Mack's book, starting on page 193.

13. Hoffman, R. Joseph and Larue, Gerald A., Editors, *Jesus in History and Myth,* [Buffalo, 1986], p. 182.

14. Ibid., p. 143.

Chapter Three Miscellaneous Important Events

1. Unless otherwise noted, the same "Misc. Sources" as described above were the major references used in this Chapter for background information and synthesis.

2. The major reference works used as background for this section were

McDannell and Long for Heaven, and Crockett for Hell.

3. Durant, Will, *The Age of Faith: The Story of Civilization: Part IV* p. 523.

4. The background for this section was obtained from Walker, Fourth Edition, p. 283-90.

5. De Rosa, p. 160-1.

6. Walker, Fourth Edition, p. 308.

7. De Rosa, p. 172-5.

8. Ibid., p. 180.

9. The background for this section was obtained from *The Encyclopedia of Religion* [Macmillen Publishing Co., 1987], Vol. 15, p.415-423. I found this to be a more even-handed treatment on the subject of witchcraft than that found in the encyclopedias normally used as reference material for this work.

10. De Rosa, p. 187-191

11. Hick and Knitter, Editors, p. 35 [Footnote 19]. The author of the article in which this rather astounding information appears as a footnote is John Hick whose credentials are presented later in these footnotes. John Hick is a well-respected professor and writer whose educational background and academic achievements are truly impressive. I have to believe that there is a strong belief on his part that the information is at least directionally factual. However, as mentioned in the text, others have disagreed rather strongly with him.

12. Boorstin, Daniel J., *The Discoverers,* p. 653.

13. Ibid., p. 631

14. Ibid., p. 633.

15. Walker, Fourth Edition, p. 314

16. Hick, John, *The Non-Absoluteness of Christianity,* in *The Myth of Christian Uniqueness,* p. 20-5.

17. De Rosa, p. 22.

BOOK TWO
Chapter One   An Analysis of the Changes

1. In this subject area, and in all subsequent subject areas, the same "Misc. Sources" as described above were used as reference resources. In all these subject areas, specific footnotes will be used only when a statement is made which is not generally recognized or accepted, or which has been found in a source other than those designated "Misc. Sources."

2. Hick, John and Knitter, Paul F., Editors, The *Myth of Christian Uniqueness; Toward a Pluralistic Theology of Religions,* p. 31. This theme is also reported in *Introducing the Old Testament,* by John Drane, p. 88.

3. Hoffman and Larue, p. 146

4. Baigent, Michael; Leigh, Richard; and Lincoln, Henry, *Holy Blood, Holy Grail,* p. 331.

5. De Rosa, p. 208-9

6. Hoffman and Larue, p. 158

7. Ibid., p. 18

8. Hick and Knitter, Editors, p. 121. Professor Seiichi Yagi, the author of the essay *"I" in the Words of Jesus* on pages 117-134 completed his graduate work in Western classics at Tokyo University before continuing his study of the New Testament at the University of Gottingen in Germany. He has taught at several Universities in Japan and in Switzerland and is considered one of the leading figures in Buddhist-Christian dialogue in Japan. He has published several books on Christian and Buddhist subjects. His credentials are outstanding.

9. Dowley, Tim, Editor, *The History of Christianity, A Lion Handbook*, p. 67. One previewer of an early draft of *The Christian Conspiracy* was convinced that this letter had been written by an ardent Christian based on its tone and thus was not written by "those who were not necessarily followers of Christ." I can only state that the reference merely says that the letter was from an anonymous writer, and that the writer consistently uses the word "they" rather than "we" in talking about Christians. Another comment by that previewer was that the statement "they do not kill unwanted babies" sounds as if it is an early Christian statement against abortion. Although this is a possibility, I firmly believe that the statement refers to infanticide. History tells us that infanticide was a common practice during the early centuries CE, and that parents were rarely, if ever, punished for killing their own children.

10. De Rosa, p. 206

11. Ibid., p. 231

12. Ibid., p. 229

13. Ibid., p. 237

14. Ibid., p. 244-7

15. Ibid., p. 250

16. Ibid., p. 303-7

17. Ibid., p. 72

18. *New Catholic Encyclopedia*, Vol. 12, starting with p. 994

19. Hick and Knitter, Editors, p. 16-17

20. Ibid., p. 16

21. Hoffman and Larue, p. 202

22. Hick and Knitter, Editors, p. 138

23. De Rosa, p. 324

24. Hick and Knitter, Editors, p. 25

25. Unless otherwise noted, most of the information on Soul, including many quotations, was found in the *New Catholic Encyclopedia*, Vol. 13 starting with page 447.

26. De Rosa, p. 374

27. Halverson, Marvin and Cohen, Arthur A., Editors, *Handbook of Christian Theology*, article entitled "Soul."

28. All three quotes are presented in John Hick, *God has Many Names*, p. 29-30

29. De Rosa, p. 60

30. Ibid., p. 145

31. Ibid., p. 146

32. Ibid., p. 284.

33. Hoffman and Larue, p. 63.

34. Walker, Fourth Edition, p. 478-9.

35. De Rosa, p. 263.

36. I have decided not to honor the person who said this by presenting his name in this footnote. This quotation was made by a well-known Southern Baptist tele-evangelist who was giving a lecture to his students on "biblical truths" on an educational TV station in October, 1993.

37. De Rosa, p. 11

38. Ibid., p. 26

39. Ibid., p. 45

40. Walker, Fourth Edition, p. 298-9

41. De Rosa, p. 308

42. Ibid., p. 76-7

43. Ibid., p. 78-83

44. Ibid., p. 212-3

45. Yallop, David A., *In God's Name; An Investigation into the Murder of Pope John Paul I,* p. 87

46. Ibid., p. 98

47. Ibid., p. 92

48. Ibid., p. 155

49. Hick and Knitter, Editors, p. 45

50. MacGregor, Geddes, *Reincarnation in Christianity: A New Vision of the Role of Rebirth in Christian Thought,* p. 35-6

51. I sincerely apologize to the reader for having lost the reference to this statement. However, it is in a file which was truthfully copied in all ways except for the registering of the reference.

52. Head, Joseph and Cranston, S. L., *Reincarnation, an East-West Anthology,* p. 35

53. Ibid., p. 36

54. Ibid., p. 37

55. Ibid., p. 38

56. Ibid., p. 39

57. MacGregor, p. 105

58. Ibid., p. 95-6

59. Graham, Billy, *Angels: God's Secret Agents,* p. ix

60. Pagels, Elaine, *Adam, Eve, and the Serpent,* p. 11

61. There are several books which present this thought. Many of them also include the belief that some of the descendents of Jesus were with the Cathars in southern France and thus were slaughtered by the Church. The author will leave the acceptance or rejection of these beliefs to the reader. However, there is quite a lot of thought which states that since it would be so normal for a male of his age to be married in the society of his time, and since it was not mentioned in the Scriptures that he was not married [as it is mentioned for Paul], then he readily

could have been married; especially since he was considered to be a Rabbi and in that society, a Rabbi had to be married in order to teach. Possibly the best book for presenting the thoughts about the marital status and family of Jesus is *Holy Blood, Holy Grail* by Baigent, Leigh, and Lincoln. There are several chapters on this subject in that book, and the book is thoroughly documented with footnotes and bibliography.

62. Most of the references used in this section are from the *Encyclopedia Brittanica* under headings such as Augustine, Julian, Original Sin, Pelagius, Council of Orange, etc. Also, Walker, Chapters 17 and 18 provided significant background.

63. De Rosa, p. 338

Chapter Two   The Results of the Changes

There are no footnotes for this Chapter.

BOOK THREE

1.   **John Hick** is presently Danforth Professor of the Philosophy of Religion, Chair of the Department of Religion, and Director of the Blaisdell Programs in World Religions and Cultures at the Claremont Graduate School, California. He is the author of numerous books. He states that he started his Christian journey as a fundamentalist, but has progressed to the liberal school.

Albert Nolan is a Roman Catholic priest whose book *Jesus Before Christianity,* originally published in 1976, is now in its Third Edition. Fr. Nolan shows extreme compassion for humanity and dedicates the Third Edition of his book "To the people of the Third World."

John W. Groff, Jr. is an Episcopal priest and former monk who runs the Mystic Journey Retreat Center in Alabama. He has been called a "Baptized, Anglicized, Byzantine Buddhist." His essay, "The Channels of Christmas" appeared in the January-March, 1994 issue of *Christian * New Age Quarterly* [Clifton, NJ] for which he often writes.

2. Hick, John, *God Has Many Names,* p. 40

BIBLIOGRAPHY

I. GENERAL REFERENCE RESOURCES

New Catholic Encyclopedia, copyright 1967 by the Catholic University of America, Washington, DC Library of Congress Catalog Card Number 66-22292. Published by the McGraw-Hill Book Company, New York.

The Dictionary used for definitions was *The American Heritage Dictionary of the English Language* published by the American Heritage Publishing Company and Houghton Mifflin Company, New York, copyright 1973.

The New Encyclopaedia Britannica, 15th Edition, copyright 1987.

The Oxford Companion to the Bible, edited by Bruce M. Metzger and Michael D. Coogan, copyright 1993 by Oxford University Press, Inc. Published by Oxford University Press, Inc., 200 Madison Ave., New York, NY 10016.

Unless otherwise noted, all Bible references are from the *Revised Standard Version* published by the American Bible Society, New York and copyrighted 1980 [Old Testament] and 1973 [New Testament] by the Division of Christian Education of the National Council of the Churches of Christ in the USA.

II. PEOPLE

Attwater, Donald, *The Avenel Dictionary of Saints*, Avenel 1981 Edition. Copyright by the estate of Donald Attwater, 1965. Published by Avenel Books, distributed by Crown Publishers, Inc. by arrangement with Penguin Books Ltd.

De Rosa, Peter, *Vicars of Christ, The Dark Side of the Papacy*, copyright 1988 by the author. Published by Crown Publishers, Inc. 225 Park Avenue South, New York, NY 10003

Delaney, John I., *Dictionary of Saints*, copyright by author in 1980. Published in 1980 by Doubleday & Company, Inc. Garden City, New York.

Garrett, Randall, *A Gallery of the Saints*, copyright by author in 1963. Published in 1963 by Monarch Books, Inc., Capital Building, Derby Conn.

Gontard, Friedrich, *The Chair of Peter, A History of the Papacy*. Translated from the German by A. J. and E. F. Peeler, copyright 1964 by Barrie and Rockliff. Published in 1964 [English] by Holt, Reinhart and Winston, New York, Chicago, San Francisco.

Hole, Christina, *Saints in Folklore*, copyright by author in 1965. Published in 1965 by M. Barrows and Company, Inc., an affiliate of William Morrow and Company, Inc.

McGinley, Phyllis, *Saint Watching*, copyright by author in 1969. Published in 1969 by The Viking Press, Inc. 625 Madison Ave. New York, NY 10022.

Woodward, Kenneth, L., *Making Saints: How the Catholic Church Determines Who Becomes a Saint, Who Doesn't, and Why*, copyright 1990 by the author. Published by Simon & Schuster, Rockefeller Center, 1230 Avenue of the Americas, New York, NY 10020.

III. HISTORY

Baigent, Michael, **Leigh,** Richard and **Lincoln** Henry, *Holy Blood, Holy Grail*, copyright 1982, 1983 by the authors. Published by Dell Publishing, a division of Bantam Doubleday Bell Publishing Group, Inc. 666 Fifth Ave. New York, NY 10103.

Boorstin, Daniel J., *The Discoverers,* copyright 1983 by the author. Published by Random House Inc., New York.

Childress, David Hatcher, *Lost Cities and Ancient Mysteries of Africa and Arabia*, copyright 1989, 1993 by the author. Published by Adventures Unlimited Press, Box 22, Stelle, IL 60946.

Dowley, Dr. Tim, *The History of Christianity, A Lion Handbook,*. Revised Edition copyright 1990 by Lion Publishing. Published by Lion Publishing plc, Sandy Lane West, Oxford, England.

Durant, Will, *The Age of Faith, The Story of Civilization: Part IV,* copyright 1950 by the author. Published by Simon and Schuster, A division of Gulf & Western Corp., 1230 Avenue of the Americas, New York, N. Y. 10020 [Note: This Volume covers Christianity from 325 CE to 1300].

Durant, Will, *Caesar and Christ, The Story of Civilization: Part III*, copyright 1944 and 1972 by the author. Published by Simon and Schuster, A division of Gulf & Western Corp., 1230 Avenue of the Americas, New York, N. Y. 10020 [Note: This Volume covers Christianity from its beginning to 325 CE].

Grant, Michael, *Readings in the Classical Historians*, copyright 1992 by the author. Published by Charles Scribner's Sons, Macmillan Publishing Company, 866 Third Ave., New York, NY 10022.

Hoffman, R. Joseph and **Larue,** Gerald A., Editors, *Jesus in History and Myth*, copyright 1986 by the editors. Published by Prometheus Books, 700 East Amherst St., Buffalo, NY 14215.

Kelly, J. N. D., DD, *Early Christian Doctrines*. Second Edition, copyright by the author. Published by Harper & Row, 49 East 33rd Street, New York 16, N. Y.

Kelly, J. N. D., DD, *Early Christian Creeds*. Second Edition, copyright by author, 1960. Published by William Clowes and Sons, Ltd., London and Beccles.

Leith, John H., *Creeds of the Churches*, copyright by the author, 1973. Published by John Knox Press, Atlanta, GA.

Levy, Leonard W., *Blasphemy, Verbal Offense Against the Sacred, from Moses to Salman Rushdie*, copyright 1993 by the author. Published by Alfred A. Knopf, New York.

MacMullen, Ramsay and **Lane**, Eugene N., Editors, *Paganism and Christianity, 100-425 CE: A Sourcebook*, copyright 1992 by Angsburg Fortress, 426 S. Fifth St., Box 1209, Minneapolis, MN 55440.

Moffett, Samuel Hugh, *A History of Christianity in Asia, Volume I: Beginnings to 1500*, copyright 1992 by the author. Published by HarperCollins Publishers, 10 East 53rd Street, New York, NY 10022.

Pelikan, Jaroslav, *The Christian Tradition, A History of the Development of Doctrine*. Volume 1, *The Emergence of the Catholic Tradition [100-600]*, copyright 1971 by the University of Chicago. Published by the University of Chicago Press, Chicago, 60637.

Robinson, Lyle, *Edgar Cayce's Story of the Origin and Destiny of Man*, copyright 1972 by The Edgar Cayce Foundation. Published by Berkeley Medallion Books, Berkeley Publishing Corporation, 200 Madison Avenue, New York, NY 10016.

Walker, Williston, *A History of the Christian Church*. Fourth Edition edited by Richard Norris, David Lotz and Robert Handy, copyright 1985 by Charles Scriber's Sons. Published by Charles Scriber's Sons, Macmillan Publishing Co., 866 Third Ave., New York, N. Y. 10022

Wilson, Ian, *Jesus: The Evidence*, copyright 1984 by the author. Published by Harper & Row, Publishers, Inc., 10 East 53rd St., New Your, NY 10022.

Yallop, David A., *In God's Name; An Investigation into the Murder of Pope John Paul I*, copyright 1984 by Poetic Products Ltd. Published by Bantam Books, Inc., 666 Fifth Ave., New York, NY 10103.

IV. THEOLOGY

Armstrong, Karen, *A History of God*, copyright 1993 by the author. Published in the United States by Alfred A. Knopf, Inc., New York, NY.

Crockett, William V., Editor, *Four Views on Hell*, copyright 1992 by the Editor. Published by Zondervan Publishing House, Grand Rapids, Michigan.

Drane, John, *Introducing the New Testament*, copyright 1986 by the author. Published by Harper & Row, Publishers, Inc., 10 East 53rd Street, New York, NY 10022.

Drane, John, *Introducing the Old Testament*, copyright 1987 by the author. Published in association with Lion Publishing, Ting England by Harper & Row, Publishers, Inc. 10 East 53rd Street, New York NY 10022.

Fox, Matthew, *The Coming of the Cosmic Christ: The Healing of Mother Earth and the Birth of a Global Renaissance*, copyright 1988 by the author. Published by Harper & Row, Publishers, Inc. 10 East 53rd St., New York, NY 10022.

Graham, Billy, *Angels: God's Secret Agents*, copyright 1975 by the author. Published in a Guideposts edition by arrangement with Doubleday & Company, Inc.

Green, Michael, *Was Jesus Who He Said He Was?*, copyright 1989 by the author. Published by Servant Books, P. O. Box 8617, Ann Arbor, MI 48107

Halverson, Marvin and **Cohen**, Arthur A., Editors, *Handbook of Christian Theology*, copyright 1958 by the World Publishing Company. Published by the World Publishing Company, 2231 West 110th Street, Cleveland. Ohio 44102.

Hick, John and **Knitter**, Paul F., Editors, *The Myth of Christian Uniqueness; Toward a Pluralistic Theology of Religions*, copyright 1987 by the editors. Fourth Edition published by Orbis Books, Maryknoll, NY 10545.

Hick, John, Editor, *The Existence of God*, copyright 1964 by Macmillan Publishing Company, 866 Third Ave., New York, NY 10022

Hick, John, *God Has Many Names*, copyright 1982 by the author. Published by Westminster Press, Philadelphia, PA

Leith, John H., *Basic Christian Doctrine*, copyright 1993 by the author. Published by Westminster/John Knox Press, 100 Witherspoon St., Louisville KY 40202-1396

Mack, Burton L., *The Lost Gospel, The Book of Q and Christian Traditions*, copyright 1993 by the author. Published by HarperCollins Publishers, 10 East 53rd Street, New York, NY 10022.

McDannnell, Colleen and **Lang**, Bernhard, *Heaven, A History,* copyright 1988 by the authors. Published by Yale University Press, New Haven and London.

Mitchell, Stephen, *The Gospel According to Jesus*, copyright 1991 by the author. Published by HarperCollins Publishers Inc., 10 East 53rd St., New York, NY 10022.

Morris, Thomas V., *The Logic of God Incarnate*, copyright 1986 by Cornell University. Published by Cornell University Press, 124 Roberts Place, Ithaca, NY 14850

Nolan, Albert, OP, *Jesus Before Christianity* , copyright 1992 by the author. Revised edition published in 1992 by Orbis Books, Maryknoll, NY 10545.

Ramm, Bernard, *After Fundamentalism: The Future of Evangelical Theology*, copyright 1983 by the author. Published by Harper & Row, Publishers, Inc., 10 East 53rd St., New York, NY 10022

Spong, Bishop John Shelby, *Rescuing the Bible from Fundamentalism*, copyright 1991 by the author. Published by HarperCollins Publishers, 10 East 53rd St., New York, NY 10022.

Tillich, Paul, *A History of Christian Thought*. Edited by Carl E. Braaten, copyright 1968 by Hannah Tillich. Published by arrangement with Harper & Row. Touchstone Edition published by Simon & Schuster, Rockefeller Center, 1230 Avenue of the Americas, New York, NY 10020.

V. REINCARNATION

Head, Joseph and **Cranston**, S. L, *Reincarnation, an East-West Anthology*, copyright 1961 by authors. Quest Book Edition published in 1968 by The Theosophical Publishing House, Wheaton, Illinois by special arrangement with The Julian Press, Inc.

MacGregor, Geddes, *Reincarnation in Christianity: A New Vision of the Role of Rebirth in Christian Thought,* copyright 1978 by the author. A Quest Book, published by The Theosophical Publishing House, 306 West Geneva Road, Wheaton, IL 60187.

McDirmit, Marilynn, *Reincarnation: A Biblical Doctrine?,* copyright 1990 by the author. Published by Eagle Publication Co., Maggie Valley, NC.

VI. SEX OR SEXUALITY

Pagels, Elaine, *Adam, Eve, and the Serpent,* copyright 1988 by the author. Published by Random House, Inc., New York, NY.

Ranke-Heinemann, Uta, *Eunuchs for the Kingdom of Heaven,* translated by Peter Heinegg. English translation copyright 1990 by Doubleday, a division of Bantam Doubleday Dell Publishing Group, Inc.

Timmerman, Joan, H., *Sexuality and Spiritual Growth,* copyright 1992 by the author. Published by the Crossroad Publishing Company, 370 Lexington Ave., New York, NY 10017

INDEX

Note: Major Appendix References are **bold**.

The
Christian
Conspiracy

How the Teachings of Christ have been Altered by Christians

by
Dr. L. David Moore

Is also available at all bookstores
through

NEW LEAF DISTRIBUTING COMPANY
5425 TULANE DRIVE SW
ATLANTA, GA 30336-2323
800-326-2665
FAX 800-326-1066

Quality paperback Retail $14.95 360 pages ISBN 0-9635665-2-0
Library of Congress Catalog Number 94-066236

It is also available directly from

PENDULUM PLUS PRESS
141 INDIAN TRAIL
JASPER, GA 30143-2829

Prices [including S&H]: Single book, $16.00
Five book package, $45.00
Twenty book carton, $165.00

About the Author

L. David Moore was born during the early 1930s in West Virginia. In 1953, he received a BS in Chemistry from West Virginia University. After duty in the US Army, he received an MS in Polymer Chemistry from the University of Akron; and in 1959 was awarded a Ph.D. in Organic Chemistry from Purdue University.

During his 30 year business career, some highlights include directing all corporate technology for the world's leading speciality chemical company, one which specialized in creating remedies for environmental problems; being Group Vice President of all chemical operations and a Director of a Fortune 300 company; being Executive Vice President in charge of all operations of a Fortune 50 company where he directed sales of over $3 billion and the activities of some 25,000 employees; and being President of Interchem Corp., a company described in a leading chemical journal as "a company whose sales have galloped forward impressively." After Interchem was sold, Dr. Moore "retired" to writing books and lecturing.

Dave and his wife Jan have been devotedly married since the mid-1950s. They presently live in Atlanta, GA. They have four children and two grandchildren.

As described on page 7 of this book, Dr. Moore has had a lifelong, abiding interest in religious activities. Lately, those interests have included reading many religious works, writing and lecturing on religious subjects, and taking spiritual journeys to the many parts of the world he has read about. Between those trips and his time spent reading, writing and lecturing, his golf game has deteriorated beyond recognition.